A HISTORY OF

Captain John and Sarah Whipple

OF
DORCHESTER, MASSACHUSETTS
AND
PROVIDENCE, RHODE ISLAND
1617-1685

A Multigenerational Study of the First Whipple Family in America

THIRD IN A SERIES OF 21ST CENTURY BOOKS ON
THE WHIPPLE FAMILIES OF AMERICA

COMPILED AND WRITTEN BY

CHARLES M. WHIPPLE JR., PH.D., ED.D., LITT.D.
EMERITUS PROFESSOR OF PSYCHOLOGY AND PHILOSOPHY
UNIVERSITY OF CENTRAL OKLAHOMA

Barbara R. Carroll was the lead researcher on this book. She is a lifelong resident of Rhode Island, and has conducted research in the New England states, and in Canada, England, Ireland and Italy. Barbara is a member of several genealogical societies, and of Th e Association of Professional Genealogists

Order this book online at www.trafford.com
or email orders@trafford.com

Most Trafford titles are also available at major online book retailers.

Print information available on the last page.

ISBN: 978-1-4251-3242-2 (sc)
ISBN: 978-1-4907-7748-1 (e)

Trafford rev. 01/30/2019

www.trafford.com
North America & international
toll-free: 1 888 232 4444 (USA & Canada)
fax: 812 355 4082

Whipple

Sir Bernard Burke, *General Armory of England, Scotland, Ireland And Wales* (London: Harrison and Sons, 1884) 1100

Awarded to a knight in the Middle Ages from Norfolk County in southeastern England.
The cresent is the mark of difference used by the second son and his house.
The swan is a symbol of harmony and peace.

Table of Contents

Chapter One
Captain John Whipple
First known Whipple in America

Chapter Two
The Whipple Children
From 1639 to 1746

Chapter Three
Ensign John Whipple Junior
The Whipples From Constitution Hill

Chapter Four
Samuel Whipple
The Whipples From Providence Neck

Chapter Five
Eleazer Whipple
The Whipples From Louquisett Meadows

Chapter Six
William Whipple
The Whipples From Smithfield

Chapter Seven
Benjamin Whipple
The Whipples From Fruit Hill

Chapter Eight
Ensign David Whipple
The Whipples from Study Hill

Chapter Nine
Colonel Joseph Whipple
The Whipples From Newport

Chapter Ten
Lieutenant Jonathan Whipple
The Whipples From Wanskuck

Chapter Eleven
Sarah, Mary, and Abigail
Daughters of John and Sarah Whipple

ILLUSTRATIONS

Preface and Acknowledgements

A young magazine reporter once asked the late pop singer Bing Crosby about his ancestors. His laconic response: "They were common stock, half male, half female." Crosby's genealogical acumen is seldom noted in historical literature, but his answer is consonant with the lives of most of those first Europeans to settle colonial America.

Common stock is very much an apt description of the young indentured servant who in 1632 was the first Whipple to bring that surname to the new world. As far as has been ascertained, the majority of the estimated ten thousand American families who presently bear this family name are descended from him and two prosperous middle aged Whipple brothers who immigrated to America six years later.

These families lived but a few miles apart for a period of about two decades in what was then called the "Bay Colony." Neither Blaine Whipple, a Whipple researcher for over 50 years and author of the *History and Genealogy of Elder John Whipple of Ipswich, Massachusetts* and *Fifteen Generations of Whipple Descendants of Matthew of Ipswich, Massachusetts, 1590-1647*; nor the accumulated and accumulating information shown on the national Whipple website <www. whipple.org> Weldon Whipple founder and webmaster, have found any evidence of a family relationship. In my opinion, Weldon's website, which is continually updated, is the best single source of information on general issues about Whipple and related families available today.

Blaine Whipple's books and this volume comprise a Whipple trilogy. Each concentrates on one of the three emigrants. Blaine's book on Matthew of Ipswich actually encompasses volume two through five, making this present book volume six. Unlike Blaine's books, this book does not include a genealogical section. However, we are collecting and compiling pedigree data which will be included in a subsequent volume. Work has begun on this, and should any Captain John Whipple descendant wish to be included, please contact me at: 327 Sundance Lane, Edmond, Ok. 73034, or by email to charles@ whipple.net.

This book begins in the early seventeenth century in England where a boy named John, in all likelihood a peasant, was born. Unlike the Ipswich brothers' family and life in England, historical records concerning him are starkly silent. Nothing so far has shown the circumstances of his birth. No one knows of his parentage, only that he was born or adopted into a household whose surname was Whipple. It is presumed that a guardian, perhaps a relative, approved his childhood indenture for a period of five to seven years, to a wealthy individual named Israel Stoughton who promptly took his servant to New England. Thus it seems that, unlike most emigrants who left England for religious reasons, John left for economic betterment.

The few credible facts that antiquarian research has provided is that he was sequestered on a ship the *Lyon* from 22 June until late in the afternoon of 16 September 1632. It is known that he was charged for wasting his master's "powder and shot" shortly thereafter. Historical records again become remarkably absent, revealing only that he fulfilled the terms of his indenture, received land, married a nondescript village girl named Sarah (maiden name unknown), and had several children. It is regrettable that so little is known of him during the first four decades of his life.

Not until his early 40s does John Whipple finally enter the systematic flow of written history in the tiny village of Providence, Rhode Island. That community's copious records reveal him to have been a wealthy landowner, tavern keeper, and craftsman. His skill as a carpenter enabled him to build his own residence, a house that stood for over 250 years. Documents show him to have been a responsible contributor to the public and political life of his community. Indeed, he set in motion a series of events that enabled the Whipple name to become one of the better known and remembered in seventeenth and eighteenth century Rhode Island history.

Four of his sons entered local and colony wide politics, as did his sons-in-law. Most of his children married into socially prominent and politically powerful families. One daughter, Abigail, became the grandmother of a Rhode Island governor and signer of the Declaration of Independence. As an assistant to the governor for many years, John Whipple Junior was the third most powerful politician in the colony. Joseph, Captain John's wealthiest son, was the father and grandfather of two Rhode Island deputy governors. The wealthiest of the grandsons were Samuel Whipple Junior, Joseph Whipple Junior, and Captain John Whipple; the former an iron manufacturer, the second a merchant and sea captain, the latter a physician and land baron. Assuredly, most of Captain John's descendants have been common stock, the "salt of the earth," as labeled in biblical literature. However, a few achieved high political office, or served as scientists, clergymen, judges, professors, military men, and the like. Some of these are discussed in the pages of this book.

While residing in Massachusetts, the religious preference of the Whipple family was undoubtedly that of the state religion, the so-called "New England Way" or Puritanism. The family's preference is not so easily discernable in Rhode Island. There is a strongly inferred suspicion that the Whipples may have been forced to leave Dorchester because of their newly acquired religious heterodoxy. It is known that one son became an Anglican, at least four were Quakers, including two daughters. The others were probably Baptist or were nonreligious. By the fourth generation, Whipples were members of several Protestant denominations. Most of my Whipple lineal ancestors seem to have been at least nominal members of the Congregational or Baptist denominations; thus, appear to have been quite typical of Captain John's descendants.

Of the three Whipple men who settled in Massachusetts in the1630s, only Captain John's gravestone still stands. As his descendants, we are fortunate in that regard in that less than one percent of seventeenth century New England burial markers survive. Remarkably, four of his son's burial sites are also viewable, including my lineal ancestor, William. His and his son William Junior's gravestones were moved to the Moshassuck Cemetery a mile or so up the road from Captain John's burial site, and a monument erected in their place. William Junior's son, Eleazer, is the only one of my lineal Whipple ancestors whose gravestone has not been found and photographed. My lineage is: Charles[10]Whipple (Charles[9], Charles[8], William[7], Jabez[6], Jesse[5], Eleazer[4], William[3], William[2], Captain John[1]). The first four generations are buried in Rhode Island. Jesse moved to Indiana in 1817, where he is buried. William T. Whipple, my great grandfather, moved from Decatur County, Indiana to north Texas in 1882, then homesteaded on the Cheyenne-Arapaho lands of western Oklahoma 14 years later. I had a rather large monument built over his grave at Calumet, Oklahoma. My grandfather and father are also buried there, as will be my son, grandsons, great grandson, and I in our time.

I have been a university professor and writer of books all my adult life. At present, I have written and had published over a dozen academic and trade books in the areas of psychology, education, and theology. Among them are: *The Psychology of Myth, Matching People With People, The Exceptional Individual,* as well as a 900-page tome on the history of psychology. This is only my third excursion into the literary genre of historical genealogy. In 1976, I wrote and had published *The Sons and Daughters of Jesse,* a man whose relatives considered him to be the black sheep of the family because he dared leave the confines of New England to live in the backwoods of frontier America. That book was followed by the publication of *A History of William Whipple of Dorchester, Massachusetts and Providence, Rhode Island.* William was the fourth son of Captain John Whipple and my lineal ancestor. The requirement to become immersed in the subject matter increased my desire to learn more about Captain John and his immediate family. Should you glean a measure of insight, or just simple pleasure, from reading this treatise then our efforts will have been rewarded.

When I say "our efforts," I refer to my research consultant Barbara Carroll, a life long resident of Rhode Island. She is one of those rare genealogists who will not give up until an issue has been resolved and/or an answer to a knotty research problem unraveled. Her unique knowledge of seventeenth century Rhode Island history, genealogy and resources, intuitive insights, and her enumerable hours of meticulous research, were vital to the completion of this book. Careful reading of the endnotes confirms the magnitude of her dedication to this work. I appreciate the enthusiasm and encouragement of Blaine Whipple of Portland, Oregon. The helpful insights and research materials that he unselfishly shared made my task less arduous. The magnitude of his accomplishment in producing the initial volumes on the Whipples in America series set a standard that kept me motivated to do my best. Thousands of Whipple descendants have and will benefit from his 50-year dedication to Whipple family research. Weldon Whipple of Orem, Utah is equally deserving of acknowledgment. His dedication to the cause of Whipple research is second to none. His tireless service in managing the Whipple website over the past 20 years and more is immeasurable. Uncounted thousands have visited the site and been rewarded beyond anticipation. The emails and other correspondence we have shared over the years run into the hundreds. By publishing much of what appears in this volume on the website as it was being developed was helpful in building support for and anticipation about its release.

As a lad growing up in central Oklahoma, my dad often took my brothers and me to the cemetery to pay our respects to his father and grandfather. I vividly recall that he would point his finger at their gravestones and say, "As long as we remember them, they will never die." Many years later, I found a quote from an ancient Egyptian burial marker that I had carved onto their common monument that states, "To speak the name of the dead is to make them live again." Our distant ancestors, and we who are alive today, humbly ask those of you in future generations who read that inscription, or who perchance read this trilogy of books, to please speak our names---especially those of your own lineal ancestors.

Dr. Charles M. Whipple, Jr.
Edmond, Oklahoma
15 June 2007

Foreword

Whipples have been waiting a long time for this publication! In 2004, Blaine Whipple published this series' first title, *History and Genealogy of "Elder" John Whipple of Ipswich, Massachusetts: His English Ancestors and American Descendants*. His second volume in the series, *Fifteen Generations of Whipple Descendants of Matthew of Ipswich, Massachusetts* continues this research. Each elaborates upon respective lines of the great Ipswich Whipple family. Blaine's book on Matthew is volume two through five.

This long over due volume six deals with a distinct second, and only other known, branch of the two great family trees of American Whipples. It traces the antecedents and descendants of another John Whipple, a youthful teenager who arrived in Dorchester Massachusetts in 1632, six years prior to the arrival of the Ipswich brothers. John Whipple served out an apprenticeship as an indentured servant, married and had nine children before moving to Providence, Rhode Island in 1658/59, where he and wife Sarah had two additional children. John enjoyed the honorary title of "Captain" only in the last six years of life. (The abundance of Captains named John Whipple is presently a source of considerable confusion as well as some contention among Whipple genealogists). Hopefully, much of this confusion will be laid to rest with the publication of these volumes.

Most published genealogies consist chiefly of cascading descendancy charts, with an occasional paragraph that explains a significant head of household. By contrast, this volume is an in-depth biography of Captain John and Sarah, and each of their children. It lays to rest a plethora of erroneous information and misguided theories previously published. It is unique in that it touches on relationships---good and bad---between family members, and between them and a matrix of interpersonal, social, and ethical issues with their contemporaries, even as later generations dispersed to other areas of the United States. This is quintessential American history. It mirrors the struggles, uncertainties, and challenges that early New England colonists endured. I am deeply indebted to my 8great grandparents Captain John and Sarah Whipple for the legacy they left behind, as unfolded in the pages of this book.

Kudos to Charles, Barbara, and Blaine, and the numerous Whipple cousins and researchers who have identified and sorted out conflicts and uncovered and illuminated important aspects of the lives our Whipple ancestors. I have enjoyed and was immensely profited by reading this book. I trust you will have the same experience.

Weldon Whipple, Webmaster
http://www.whipple.org
Orem, Utah, USA

Introduction

If you are interested in American history, you are going to like this book. If you are a descendant of Captain John and Sarah Whipple, you will love it. If you are a Whipple who is not sure of his/her ancestry you will probably begin your genealogical search and hope you connect to this family. And your chances of connecting are quite good because John and Sarah bore eight sons, more than the Ipswich Whipple families, from which I descend, combined. Their descendants comprise the largest number of individuals bearing the Whipple name. This book is a treasure trove of American Whipple history. The below examples relate primarily to Captain John. Magnify these by information on his eleven children, as well as ensuing generations of descendants who live in all sections of our land, and you are in for some great reading.

Massachusetts Bay was far more primitive when 15 year old John Whipple arrived in 1632 than when Matthew and John Whipple arrived in Ipswich and were granted land the same month six years later. When John arrived at Dorchester, only about 2000 settlers lived in the Bay Colony, while its population was approaching 20,000 when the other two arrived. John was truly in the vanguard of New England settlers. Not only was he young with little experience to guide him, he had to learn to survive in a society where status was all-important, and where his status as an indentured apprentice carpenter put him at the bottom of the social scale, subject to the whims of his master. By contrast, Matthew, 48, and John, 42, successful clothiers in Bocking, England were awarded one of the larger grants in Ipswich and immediately became part of the hierarchy, assuming leadership roles in church, town, and colony.

To his credit, John overcame all obstacles. He reared a large family whose members achieved notable success. By hard work, he accumulated considerable wealth and because of his innate intelligence and strength of character, earned leadership roles in the society in which he found himself. Who were his parents and where did he come from? Who was his wife? This part of the puzzle is yet to be solved

John married Sarah in about 1638. He would have been 21-22, she 14-15. Sarah's child-bearing spanned 25 years. She was about 15 when she gave birth to John Junior in 1639, 40 when Jonathan was born in about 1664. She died two years later, leaving John with four youngsters to care for: David, 10; Abigail, 8, Joseph, 4; and Jonathan, 2; plus Benjamin, 12, and William, 14. She was mother and grandmother to children of the same approximate age for at least the last year of her life.

After about 20 uneventful, largely unrecorded though financially successful years of married life in the prosperous village of Dorchester, and at about the ages of 41 and 34 respectively, John and Sarah sold their property and moved to Providence, Rhode Island. Why Rhode Island, a place ordinary Puritans regarded as a cesspool of vile heresies and irreligion. Having moved to Massachusetts when it was but a frontier he understood the hard life that lay ahead. Whatever the motivation, the family moved and John soon became a leading citizen and a major contributor to the political life of the town and colony. He was received as a purchaser in July of 1659. By this date, England was ruled by the Protectorate so imagine John's concern when Charles II was crowned King in 1660. After only a year in their new home, the family was confronted with a potentially disruptive change in government. Would Rhode Island's freedom of religion be taken away? Would portions of their territory be given to Massachusetts, Connecticut, or Plymouth? John pledged allegiance to Charles II in 1666 and served the first of seven terms in the general assembly at Newport that year. His last term was in 1679. He served at least three terms as moderator of the Providence town council, as town treasurer and clerk. The paid position of clerk was the most prestigious office in the plantation.

In February of 1676, the central government encouraged main-land residents to move to the island for safety. All but a couple of dozen of Providence's estimated 400 inhabitants responded. The Reverend Roger Williams and John Whipple were among those who remained to defend their town. Imagine the fear that must have been prevalent at the time. The Indian attacks were brutal, carrying off women and children as captives. John's youngest, Joseph and Jonathan, must have been on his mind as were his 25 grandchildren, the oldest about 13, the youngest a baby not yet walking. The decision to stay and fight could not have been easy. However, it was from that war that John received the military title of Captain. It is important to note that two men, both named John Whipple and both with this military title, served in King Philip's War. Many Whipple researchers found it difficult to distinguish one from the other and placed them in the wrong families in their genealogies. John, the Rhode Island Captain (ca1617-1685) served in the February and March 1676 Providence campaign. John, the Massachusetts Captain (1625-1683), son of "Elder" John of Ipswich, and ancestor of General William Whipple, a signatory to the Declaration of Independence, served in Western Massachusetts in February, March, and April of 1676.

John Whipple died in 1685. During his long life he was an inspiration and example to his children and grandchildren, many who followed him into public service. Among those you will be reading about in this book are: John Junior who served in the general assembly, the town council, and as treasurer and town clerk; Samuel and Eleazer who served in the assembly; Joseph who served in the assembly, the town council, and as a colonel in the militia; David who was an Ensign; and grandson Joseph Junior and great grandson Joseph III who both ascended to the office of deputy governor of the colony. Abigail's second husband was William Hopkins, and this union produced John's great-grandsons Stephen and Esek Hopkins. Stephen became governor of Rhode Island, a member of the continental congress, and a signer of the Declaration of Independence. Esek was the first commander-in-chief of the continental navy. Great-great-grandson Commodore Abraham Whipple is remembered in history books as a genuine American hero. These are but a few of the Whipples included in Charles' book. Immerse yourself in it and enjoy some great historical reading.

After enjoying this book, should you still not have found a link to your Whipple ancestors, perhaps such can be found in one my books---volumes one through five of the Whipples in America Series---which chronicles the lives of the Ipswich branch of the family. Good reading and good luck.

Blaine Whipple
Portland, Oregon

Chapter 1

Captain John Whipple
First Known Whipple in America

Arrival at Dorchester Massachusetts

Early seventeenth century Massachusetts Bay Colony was a two-year-old primitive theocratic settlement of approximately 2000 inhabitants when a teenage youth named John Whipple first set foot on its soil.[1] Who was he? Where did he come from? Where and how did he live? Who are his descendants? Several generations of antiquarian researchers have left these questions as yet incompletely addressed.

"September 16, 1632, being the Lord's Day. In the Evening Mr. Pierce, in the ship Lyon arrived and came to an anchor before Boston. He brought 123 passengers including 50 children all in health. He lost not one passenger, save his carpenter, who fell overboard as he was caulking a port. They were 12 weeks abroad. He had five days east wind and thick fog, so as he was forced to come, all that time by the lead, and the first land he made was Cape Ann."[2] This entry in the journal of John Winthrop, Governor of the Massachusetts Bay Colony, attendant to a list of passengers, included 15-year-old John Whipple as one of the 123 *Lyon* emigrants. Thus began the continuing history of the Whipple surname in the new world.[3]

John Whipple of 1632 must not be confused with the two middle-aged Whipple brothers, John and Matthew, who arrived in Massachusetts in 1638. There is no known relationship between the teenager John Whipple and the Whipple brothers, who arrived six years later and settled at Ipswich.[4] The short distance between their settlements meant that the two families would have met very soon after 1638, if they had not already done so in the old country. If so, they likely reminisced and told stories about their families left behind in Old England. Natural curiosity would have led them to seek common kinships, perhaps even writing home to ask if someone there knew if, or how, they were related. Perhaps the brothers knew the circumstances that led to the younger John's apprenticeship at an early age, and how difficult it must have been for his parents to see him leave, knowing that they would probably not see their son again. John was apparently apprenticed as a carpenter to a Mr. Israel Stoughton to pay for his passage to the new world.[5] Records state that on 3 October 1632, "John Wipple and Alex Miller were ordered to pay fines of 3s, 4d to their master Israel Stoughton, for their wasteful expenditure of powder and shot."[6] The Stoughton family lived near the town of Bocking, England, the town from which the Ipswich brothers are known to have immigrated.[7] It is not known if John grew up in that area as well.[8] Neither is it known if he ever returned to Old England for a visit.

The present author engaged the English genealogical firm, Debrett Ancestry Research Limited, to search for a possible relationship between the two Whipple families. Debrett examined the original registers of Bocking for the years 1575-1632. Gaps exist in the registers: marriage registers are missing for 1575-92; baptisms for 1571-72, 1581-82, and 1606-55. The firm next examined the International Genealogical Index of Essex, with negative results. Research was then extended to the nearby parishes of Rayne, Stisted, Shalford, Halstead and Gosfield and to the indexes of the Essex probate courts for the period 1600-1635.

A number of Whipples lived in those areas, including Braintree, whose records, unfortunately, do not begin until 1660. Nineteen marriages of Whipples (and the similarly named) between 1538 and 1837 in Essex were found in Boyd's Marriage Index.[9]

BRIDGE AND GRIST MILL

THE NEPONSET RIVER WAS FIRST BRIDGED AT THIS POINT, AND A GRIST MILL ERECTED IN 1634 BY ISRAEL STOUGHTON, A DEPUTY OF DORCHESTER WHO WAS CENSURED BY GOVERNOR WINTHROP FOR DEFENDING POPULAR RIGHTS

MASSACHUSETTS BAY COLONY TERCENTENARY COMMISSION

Stoughton Mill Marker

(Spelling was until recently not standardized; during the seventeenth century names were spelled inconsistently. Even the educated spelled their names in a variety of ways.) Most Whipples, and those similarly named, lived in a close cluster in the area that surrounded Bocking/Braintree, indicating a possible connection. However, no confirming evidence exists as to whether the 1632 John was related to the Whipples of Bocking. It is assumed that John was born around the year 1617. Only one individual whose christening was close to that date was discovered. His name was John Whaple, baptized 13 December 1618 at Great Waltham, Essex, [about 15 miles south of Bocking] the son of John Whaple and Mary Collett. As yet, "no firm evidence has emerged which proves beyond doubt that the John baptized in 1618 was either the ancestor or related to the Bocking Whipple family."[10]

The Apprenticeship Years

John Whipple would have been put to work immediately upon his arrival in Dorchester. Within less than a year, he could have been on the crew that built New England's first mill, as well as a bridge across the Neponset River. This gristmill, called "Stoughton's Mill", was completed in 1634, and conceivably John was one of a privileged few to witness the very first bushel of grain ground by waterpower in the colonies. He likely participated in building the first fish weir that same year.[11] Consequent to the mill's completion, it was ordered that a road or "cart way" be laid out from the town to the mill, a route of some four miles made necessarily circuitous due to the area's topography. "When Israel Stoughton set up a grist mill on the Neponset River, a road was built across the 'Great Lots' connecting the original settlement with it. This became known as the Lower Road, now Adams Street."[12] At present, the shortest distance between them, by way of Dorchester Avenue, is about three miles.

The below photograph is of the Adams Street Bridge. Some of the surrounding buildings are mill offices, the successors to the original Stoughton Mill. In the picture is seen two bridges one on top of the other. The lower bridge is listed on the National Register of Historical Places. A recent article in a local newspaper stated, "One of the region's oldest surviving bridges has been uncovered this month by workers replacing the Adams Street Bridge over the Neponset River on Milton line in Lower Mills. The granite slabs that make up the doubled-arched bridge have been ferrying people across the Neponset since 1765 and according to workers…it's in better shape than the 1930s-era steel and concreted bridge that was built over its colonial predecessor." The article also alludes to the "needed sandbagging along the raging Neponset to keep the waters from infiltrating their workspace." It likewise mentioned that the sandbagging was needed to, "keep the river's fish from jumping ashore on their upcoming spawning runs upstream…blueback herring, American shad and rainbow smelt are expected to be passing through on their way upstream…[13] Several wooden bridges prior to 1765 had been used, but the annual freezing and thawing of the river necessitated that they be periodically replaced, including the 1634 and the 1651 bridges that John Whipple probably helped build. The water is still raging, although no longer giving power to the mill, and the types of fish that John Whipple could have caught and sold as a boy still populate the same waters almost 400 years later. In addition to catching, selling, and

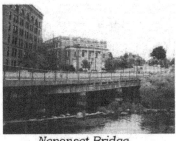

Neponset Bridge

delivering fish for his master, helping to build the mill and bridge, and assisting in laying out the first road from the church to the mill by way of Neponset Village, John could have participated in digging the first canal in the colony. Another profitable skill he could have acquired as a teenager was that of shipbuilding.[14] As an apprentice, he would have been at the bottom of the social class ladder. Undoubtedly life would have been difficult, although he probably ate regularly and had a roof over his head. "The status of a servant may well be shown by the deposition

presented in Court at Salem in 1657 by an apprentice in the town of Newbury, who testified that it was a long while before 'he could eate his master's food, viz, meate and milk, or drink beer saying that he did not know that it was good, because he was not used to eat such victualls, but to eate bread and water porridge and to drink water'."[15] John could have lived on the Stoughton homestead, which was located on the northeast corner of Savin Hill Avenue and Pleasant Street.[16]

3

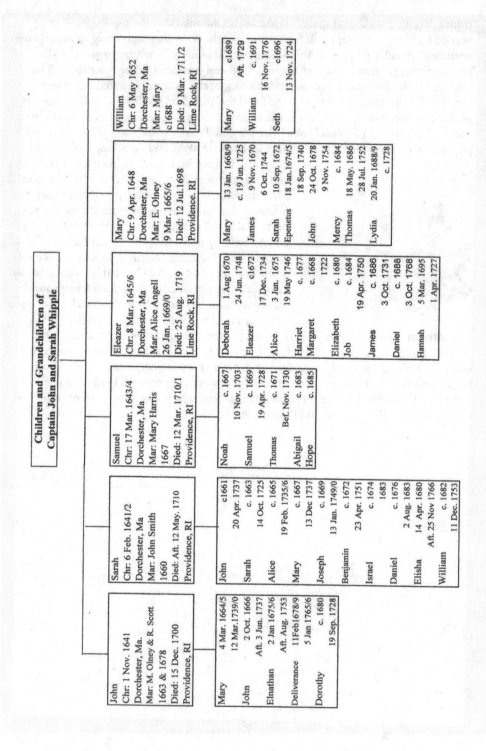

Children and Grandchildren of
Captain John and Sarah Whipple

Children and Grandchildren —cont.

Benjamin
Chr: 4 Jun. 1654
Dorchester, Ma
Mar: R. Mathewson
1 Apr. 1686
Died: 11 Mar. 1703/4
North Providence, RI

Benjamin	11Nov.1688	27 Apr. 1788
Ruth	12 May 1691	
Mary	3 Mar. 1694/5	
Josiah	29 Jul. 1697	
	Bef. 1704	
John	25 Feb. 1699/0	
	13 Nov. 1751	
Abigail	12 Jun. 1703	
	c1787	

David
Chr: 28 Sep. 1656
Dorchester, Ma
Mar: S. Gregory & H. Tower
1775 & 1777
Died: 18 Dec. 1710
Rehoboth, Ma

David	bef. 30 Oct. 1674	
Israel	16 Aug. 1678	13 Jun. 1720
Deborah	12 Sep 1681	c1755
Jeremiah	26 Jun.1683	14 May. 1721
William	27 May. 1685	12 Nov. 1746
Sarah	18 Nov. 1687	27 Sep. 1727
Hannah	9 Jan. 1690/1	16 Oct. 1708
Abigail	20 Oct. 1692	

Abigail
Born: c1658
Dorchester, Ma
Mar: S. Dexter & W.Hopkins
1672 & 1782
Died: 19 Aug. 1725
Providence, RI

John	c. 1673	
Abigail	c. 1675	22 Apr. 1734
William	c. 1683	Aft. Aug. 1725
		Aft. 1739

Joseph
Born: c1662
Providence, RI
Mar: Alice Smith
20 May. 1684
Died: 28 Apr.1746
Providence, RI

John	17 May. 1685	18 May. 1769
Jeremiah	3 Sep. 1686	
Joseph	30 Dec. 1687	Jun. 1750
Amphillis	6 Oct. 1689	Aft. 17 Dec. 1776
Sarah	29 Mar. 1691	c. 1762
Susannah	14 Mar. 1693	15 Dec. 1776
Freelove	18 Mar. 1693/4	Bef. 1781
Alice	6 Feb. 1695/6	
Amy	16 Jun. 1699	23 Dec. 1757
Christopher	14 Sep. 1701	Bef. 1706
Mary	9 Apr.1701	8 Dec. 1733
Christopher	6 Mar. 1706/7	

Jonathan
Born: c1664
Providence, RI
Mar: Margaret Angell
c. 1690
Died: 8 Sep. 1721
North Providence, RI

Jonathan	22 Feb. 1691/2	6 Aug. 1741
Thomas	26 Feb. 1693/4	13 Oct. 1770
Sarah	c. 1696	8 Sep. 1721
Margaret	c. 1697	
Parratine	c. 1698	Aft. 8 Sep.1721
Mary	c. 1699	
Alice	Aft. 1725	c. 1700

Marriage and Family of Captain John Whipple

John's indenture ended when he was 20 or 21 years of age, at which time he became a freeman and landowner. In time, he acquired between 40 and 50 acres of land. After only a few years in the new world, he was a property owner, a circumstance that would have been next to impossible had he stayed in Old England. At the 2 January 1637 Dorchester town meeting, it was ordered that John Whipple be given "eight acres near Stoughton's mill in the area known as Neponset Village, this grant being in regard of a former promise upon record." [17]

Within two years or so of becoming a landed proprietor, John was married to the 15 or 16-year-old Sarah—They, Darling, or Hutchinson.[18] When or where Sarah was born is unknown. Information on her gravestone sets her birth at Dorchester in about 1624, but this is unlikely since only Plymouth Colony was in existence at that time. Sarah Whipple, on 29 October 1641, addressed as "Goodwife Whipple," one of the lowest social class distinctions, was admitted to the Dorchester church.[19] John would have had to be a member by then, as freemen were required to be members of the church.[20] In addition to the qualification of church membership, all males over sixteen years of age were required to take the "Freeman's Oath," as of 14 May 1634, which contained the pledge, "submitting my selfe to the wholesome laws made and established by the same."[21] Children of non-church members were not permitted to be baptized and christened.[22] Uncertainty exists as to the christening date of their first child. The church allowed his mother to join in October of 1641, thus permitting the oldest, John, to be christened three days later, on 1 November 1641. He was at least two years old by then.[23] Sarah, the second child, was christened three months later, 6 February 1641/42. John and Sarah Whipple had 11 children; nine were born in Dorchester, the others in Providence, Rhode Island.[24] The death date of the second child, Sarah, is yet being researched. The 1710 date occurred at the death of her second husband, at which time she was declared to be too aged to handle her own affairs. Nativity and necrology dates of the other children possess a reasonable degree of certitude. With the exception of David all were married and died in the Providence Plantations area.

    i. John Whipple, born about 1639, christened 1 Nov 1641; died 15 Dec 1700; married (1) Mary Olney, (2) Rebecca Scott

   ii. Sarah Whipple, christened 6 Feb 1641/1642; died after 12 May 1710; married John Smith Junior (2) Richard Arnold

  iii. Samuel Whipple, christened 17 Mar 1643/1644; died 12 Mar 1710/11; married Mary Harris.

  iv. Eleazer Whipple, christened 8 Mar 1645/1646; died 25 Aug 1719; married Alice Angell

    v. Mary Whipple, christened 9 Apr 1648; died 12 Jul 1698; married Epenetus Olney.

  vi. William Whipple, christened 16 May 1652; died 9 Mar 1711/12; married Mary (_)

 vii. Benjamin Whipple, christened 4 Jun 1654; died 11 Mar 1703/1704; married Ruth Mathewson.

viii. David Whipple, christened 28 Sep 1656; died 18 Dec 1710 in Rehoboth, Mass.; married (1) Sarah Gregory, (2) Hanna Tower.

ix. *Abigail Whipple, born about 1658; died 19 Aug 1725;*
married (1) Stephen Dexter, (2) William Hopkins

x. *Joseph Whipple, born about 1662; died 28 Apr 1746; married Alice*
Smith.

xi. *Jonathan Whipple, born about 1664; died 8 Sep 1721;*
married (1) Margaret Angell, (2) Anne (_)

If the Whipple household was typical of the time, John was preoccupied with providing for his family, and Sarah was busily engaged in rearing the children. The amount of formal education the Whipple children received can be only conjectured. Whether a child could read and write was usually a consequence of the degree of literacy possessed by the parents, particularly the mother. Sarah's level of education is unknown, but John could read and write.[25] Records of deeds and wills show that most of their children were illiterate to the point that they could not write their names. It is unlikely that any of the older boys would have studied at Cambridge College (Harvard University), which began in 1636, because it was founded for the purpose of training the clergy. They could, however, have attended the town's free public school, founded in 1639, the first such in the colonies.[26] Matters requiring education were usually related to church dogma. Parents, masters, and all others in charge of children were required "to catechize their children, servants, and others...in sound orthodox catechism" so when required, "either in church or privately...shall be judged most conductive to the general good."[27] Failure to comply resulted in a penalty determined by the court, and neighbors were encouraged to spy on each other.

The Whipple children, in all likelihood, had access to but a few books, at least as they are known today. "During the seventeenth century and well into the eighteenth, the books usually found in the average New England family were the Bible, the Psalm Book, an almanac, the New England Primer, a sermon or two and perhaps a copy of Michael Wigglesworth's horrific poem The Day of Doom...This book expressed the quintessence of Calvinism. John Calvin's theology was based on the belief that all men were born sinners and since Adam's fall, by the will of God, predestined from birth to hell and everlasting torment, unless, happily, one of the elect and so foreordained to be saved. Children could actually be put to death for striking their parents. Even for children, frivolous amusements were forbidden; a curfew was established; and all were constrained to save souls and to labor for material development."[28] "It may be stated that few books published prior to the nineteenth century had any educational value for children and youth. Exception should be made in favor of the Shorter Catechism and 'Mother Goose Melodies.' The first was unpopular and of little value...The second has been the popular nursery rhyme book for two hundred years and still lives to bless little children. The opening of the nineteenth century revealed an ability of a few men and women to write attractive and healthful reading for children and youth...Concerning school text-books of the early day, little can be said, for they were very few, even into the nineteenth century. A single book would often serve two or three generations of children of the same family, so carefully were those early text books used and handed down from parents to children."[29] Children often worked six days per week alongside their parents from sunup to sundown, and vacations were practically unknown, thus spending several hours at school each day was simply out of the question. "The New England Puritans only allowed themselves one full holiday in the course of the year and that was

7

Thanksgiving Day, a time for feasting. To be sure, there was Fast Day in the spring which gave freedom from work; but that was a day for a sermon…The celebration of Christmas was not observed by the true New England Puritan until the middle of the nineteenth century."[30]

The Whipple family diet would have been limited to home products, fish, and wild game. Butter and cheese were staples. Fruit was common, including wild berries and other fruits of the forests. Rum brandy, wine, beer, and a little chocolate were in use among their more well to do neighbors. At a commencement dinner at Harvard…four barrels of beer, one of cider and eighteen gallons of wine were served. Because water was not always fresh or pure, the family would likely have consumed mildly alcoholic cider at nearly all their meals. It would have been the unenviable job of the oldest to fill up the cider jug from the cellar every morning. The white potato could not be purchased as yet, but turnips, onions, carrots, and parsnips were readily available. Honey was common. Apple and mince pies were a treat, as were Indian puddings and baked beans with pork, all cooked in their old-style brick oven adjoining the great fireplace, which covered almost one entire wall of the house. If a child had a toothache, tobacco was smoked for relief from the pain.

Community Life

When his indenture was over, John paid a high price to stock and maintain his farm. Livestock was scarce and expensive by the time he acquired his own land. Horses were £27, heifers £13, sheep 50s. Cows were £30 to £40 each, a pair of oxen £40. Commodities were also high, including corn at 5s a bushel. At 3s a day, carpenter's wages were sufficient to purchase about a half-bushel of corn. Surplus produce from his farm not sold in Dorchester he likely took to Boston's Thursday market.[31]

That he was successful is confirmed by the fact that he added substantially to his original allotment of eight acres. A likely extant example of John's craftsmanship is the Barnard Capen house, one of only three surviving seventeenth century houses in Dorchester. It was built around the years 1635/36 on Washington Street opposite Melville Avenue, but "was moved to Milton about the year 1909.[32] John most likely

Bernard Capen House

helped construct the new Dorchester meetinghouse in 1645. Town residents raised £250 for the edifice, which was located on the site of the old church building on Pleasant Street. A few years later it was moved to Meeting House Hill, about one mile closer to John's property. Additional money was raised to make the "walls decent within and without."[33] His skills could have been put to good use in building a new bridge over the Neponset River in 1651. This bridge replaced the long-time ferry that had been operated since the settlement began.

In the year of the Capen house's construction, while still a neophyte apprentice carpenter, John would have witnessed a seminal event in the earliest history of American

8

democracy: the founding of the colony of Connecticut. Approximately half of Dorchester's first colonists, representing a significant part of its wealth and intelligence, left to settle in the Connecticut Valley at Windsor near the junction of the Connecticut and Farmington Rivers. This move was forced upon them by the autocratic, imperialistic policies and restrictions on political and personal freedoms imposed by Governor Winthrop and the majority of the colony's clergy. The governor had little regard for the commoner. He wrote, "The best part of the people is always the least, and of that best part, the wiser is always the lesser." His colleague, The Reverend John Cotton, expressed the position of the majority of the colony's leadership when he stated, "Never did God ordain democracy for the government of the church or the people."[34] Such constraints, repugnant to many Dorcesterites who had left England to escape such repression, caused them to give up five years of hard work to labor in a new wilderness far beyond the jurisdiction of Massachusetts. Israel Stoughton's challenge to the magistrate's power to interpret law as they pleased resulted in his disqualification, and he was barred form public office for three years.[35] It safely can be assumed that John stayed in Dorchester to honor the terms of his indenture to Stoughton, which was to last for two more years. A severely poverty-stricken state of existence would have lent added weight to his decision to stay put.

Colony records are uninformative as to whether John participated in the community life of the town. Due to the fact that he was an integral part of the political and social scene in Providence, it may be assumed that he acquired some social and political skills while in Dorchester. This may, however, not have been possible.[36] He likely was present at the first ever town meeting held in America in 1633, and was undoubtedly aware of the *Dorchester Directory*, which was read at each town meeting. It provided that every person could speak his mind "meekly and without noise, but should not interrupt another speaker, encourage support of town officers in the execution of their offices, and not fault or revile them for doing their duty..."[37] Astonishingly, only twice in almost two decades does John's name appear in public records. As previously noted, "John Whiplle" was the last proprietor to sign a fencing agreement, and he was mentioned in the estate of Edward Bullock probated 29 January 1656, in which it was stated that John was owed 5s for "stockings and a cocke."[38] His name does not appear on a 1637 list of 104 names "of those that were to have land in ye Division of ye Neck, & other Lands." The same was true in a similar 1641 list of 71 names.[39]

"Since John Whipple was a young, unmarried servant when he first arrived in Dorchester, we should not be surprised that he does not appear in the records more in the 1630s, but he generated remarkably few records between 1640 and 1658, during which period he lived as a married man in that town."[40] The factor that eventuated in his abandonment of the colony at the height of his earning power and potential influence may have been the underlying cause of his continued reticence to participate in Dorchester public life. That determinant could have been religious heterodoxy.

Arrival At Providence Rhode Island

Documents are uninformative as to when or why John Whipple of Dorchester, Massachusetts first became interested in the place he was to call home for the remainder of his life. Perhaps he had visited Providence before on business or for pleasure. It was

9

known that Dorchester residents had previously relocated there. He may have had prior knowledge concerning the substantial land grants that were soon to be awarded. Was he asked by friends or relatives while still living in Dorchester to become one of fewer than 50 owners or "proprietors"[41] of the vast expanse of wilderness known as Providence Plantations?[42] Or was he forced, like The Reverend Roger Williams before him, to flee for his life from Bay authorities?[43]

Passable roads between the Bay Colony and Providence were practically non existent; consequently, the 11 member Whipple family, plus household goods, farming and carpentry implements, and livestock, would have embarked by boat around Cape Cod, down the coast to Newport, then 20 miles or so up the Narragansett Bay to their destination. The size of the family itself would have had an immediate impact, increasing Town Street's population by about five percent. The very real possibility of psychological trauma, particularly of the children,[44] caused by interfacing with this unfamiliar environment could have been substantial. They left a well-organized society of life long-friends, and a free public school. The feeling of personal security was summarily disquieted when the new town leaders voted, 27 January 1660, to pay a substantial fee to

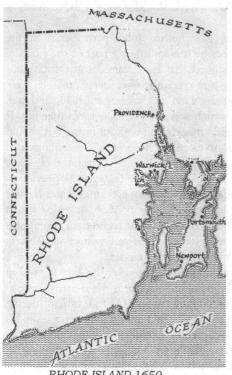

RHODE ISLAND 1659

anyone who killed a wolf. Dorchester had been, by the mid 1650s, a thriving community of approximately 150 dwellings (750 to 800 inhabitants) with 1500 fruit trees, an abundance of livestock, as well as adequate work with sufficient wages for tradesmen like John.[45] Surely, to leave such a commodious situation required a higher purpose: freedom of conscience.

As seen on the map opposite, John had a choice between four "Rhode Island and Providence Plantations" settlements: Newport, Portsmouth, Warwick, or Providence. A fifth choice would have been a small settlement on the Pawtuxet River about five miles south of Providence, which was under the hegemony of Providence. It is generally conceded that Providence was the least desirable of these.[46] In total, the colony's Caucasian population was only about 1000, with Newport being twice the size of the other plantations. Most of the estimated 200 or so residents of Providence lived in "story and one half," dirt-floored[47] houses widely scattered along the east side of a two-mile- long dusty, narrow path, called Towne Streete,[48] which lay between a sea inlet, a shallow salt water cove, a swift running river to the west, and a steeply ascending 200-foot bluff that ran the length of the expanse on the east. Standing on this promontory, looking down on the bucolic scene below for the first time as a middle aged man, John Whipple could not likely have been favorably impressed. He would not have

10

seen a green-lawned courthouse or a parish church[49] with its well-manicured graveyard; not even the presence of a rustic schoolhouse could be detected, or the resemblance of a bridge across the river, or the presence of a ubiquitous wharf-- sights to which he had been accustomed in Dorchester.

"During the seventeenth century there was little need of wharves…They were, in fact dependent upon Massachusetts, or upon occasional Dutch traders for nearly all manufactured articles…In revenge for Rhode Island's refusal to expel the Quakers, they threatened to discontinue all intercourse, and thus to deprive Rhode Island of comfortable existence. 'We have not,' said the Rhode Island legislature, 'English coin, but only that which passeth among these barbarians, only corn, cattle, tobacco, and the like, to make payment in, which they (the Massachusetts people) will have at their own rate, or else not deal with us."[50]   With the exception of the town's gristmill at the north end of the street, business enterprises were nowhere in evidence. Far to the west, across the cove and river, could be detected the plowing and tilling of farmers. Young boys were seen tending herds of livestock. And in that direction, as far as the eye could see, mammoth stands of oak and cedar trees and lush meadows were there to be claimed by the right man. Perhaps John felt that he was that man.

The below panoramic view of the bluff that over looked John's house, located where the lighter colored single row condominium building now stands, was taken from the Smith Street[51] steps of the state capitol building. In his day the capitol area was a lush

meadow where cattle were kept. The hillside above John's house would have been heavily forested, fit for logging and orchards only. The laying out of Benefit Street, the first row of houses above the condominium building, about 65 years after John's death, necessitated the relocation of the Whipple burial plot to the town's cemetery one mile to the north. All of the land seen

Modern Day Whipple Property

in this photograph belonged to Captain John Whipple and/or to his sons, John Junior or Joseph. Shortly after moving his family to this address, John bought an additional 200 acres in adjoining areas. In front of the house was a dirt path named Towne Streete (now Main) that still runs along side a stream called the Moshassuck River---hidden by the trees at the bottom of the ravine.

It would have been readily apparent that his potential neighbors were living at bare subsistence level, particularly if he were viewing this scene in the year 1658, when the little settlement endured a severe drought. Most of those who had congregated around The Reverend Roger Williams over two decades earlier were poor, unskilled, and undereducated. They were the outcasts of Puritan society. "Among the associates of Williams were no men of wealth, or of much mechanical skill. They were nearly all

11

farmers, and expected to draw their subsistence from the soil. Their dreams of prosperity were of meadowlands, corn fields, and flocks in the valley of the Mooshassuc, and not, like those of the men of Boston, of warehouse and anchorage by the shores of the Bay. They had little beside the household effects which they brought with them and their Massachusetts neighbors did their best to prevent their acquiring more."[52]

Population growth had stagnated. Many of the original inhabitants had moved about five miles to the south to establish a sister settlement on the Pawtuxet River. Others had simply become disenchanted and relocated elsewhere in the colony. Several of the original home lots had been abandoned for years, leaving houses, gardens, and orchards in ruin. "It will be sufficient to observe that the old townsmen gave no cordial welcome to emigrants, and offered them no invitation by the establishment of schools, or other means of improvement. They were satisfied to remain a closed corporation. The descendants of the settlers held fast by the home lots of the town street, with the tenacity which in that age characterized the owners of ancestral property. Few new comers could gain a foothold in the town."[53] "The Town Meeting would give no invitation to fugitives from religious intolerance [although Williams did], and set apart no tract or reservation for their benefit. All who came hither came at their own risk, and upon their own responsibility."[54]

"Providence grew very slowly. In 1638 there were only twenty families—about 100 persons; in 1645, about fifty families or 250 persons; in 1675, perhaps 350 to 400 persons. This slow growth resulted in part from fear of the Indians; in part from the instability produced by internal quarrels among the settlers; and in part from the fact that the radical principles upon which Providence was founded appealed only to the ultra-Puritans or more eccentric and bold Englishmen and Englishwomen of that day. Williams said frankly that his purpose in founding the colony was to create a free community of seekers after truth and a haven for those persecuted elsewhere for their conscientious beliefs."[55] He paid scant attention to their educational level or vocational skills. "For the first time in human history State had wholly been dissociated from Church in a commonwealth not utopian but real. For the first time the fundamental idea of modern civilization---that of rights of man as a being responsible primarily to God and not to the community---had been given an impulse powerful and direct.[56]

"Inordinately slow was the town in taking the first step [toward growth]. Down to 1740 or 1742 it was still, as in the seventeenth century, but a long, straggling street by the water front, where on summer evenings the inhabitants sat in their doorways, smoked their clay pipes, and fought the swarms of mosquitoes that rose from the marsh opposite..."[57]

By the late 1650s, about two-dozen settlers had established small houses close together along Providence's one and only unkempt dusty, or alternately mud-drenched straggling dirt path, making friendship easier to establish, particularly between the town's women folk and the newly arrived Mrs. John Whipple. She could immediately welcome them into her rented house, the considerable residence of one of Town Street's leading former citizens. "Women would visit each other with a clean checked apron, a striped loose gown, a handkerchief over the shoulders, and a sun bonnet; then pleasantly sit down and divert themselves over a dish of bohea tea and a piece of bread and butter...On the less attractive side, the physical closeness and small numbers in the community may have undermined privacy, nurtured gossip, and reinforced the

12

patriarchal authority of public institutions. Even so, it had another not-so-obvious advantage. The town's primitive looking, unshaven men [there were no razors for some time] took turns gathering in one of their homes to discuss the days' issues. This gave the wife in whose home they were…the opportunity to join them in their serious and heated discussions of such as the knotty problems of theology, Gortonism or anti-Gortonism, the evils of pedo-baptism, the policy of Williams against that of Massachusetts Bay, the latest news from England then several months old, while the pewter flagon is passed around and the fiery beverage was generously quaffed. Neighbors were few and duly appreciated, communication with the other colonies was neither frequent nor rapid, nor was it regarded as particularly desirable…they were making their own history, and were anxious for non-interference while they laid the foundations of freedom in both church and state."[58]

Sarah Whipple and her older daughters must have been grateful that by the time they had taken up residence in their new home, the first rough-hewn log cabins with dirt floors had given way to frame houses more like their previous house in Dorchester, even though unpainted inside or out. If their temporary rented quarters was typical of the time, there would have been a single large room with a ladder or small stairs leading to a loft where the children made their beds with straw mattresses (certainly not a bed for each), along with a chamber pot and possibly a chest or trunk that Captain John had made to store clothing and bedding. The one lower room held John and Sarah's bed and a chest at one end, perhaps a cradle for their infant daughter Abigail, plus a table and chairs. Chairs were a decided luxury; few families had more than one or two. The Whipple house was likely a bit larger and better equipped. Moreover, the typical residence of their neighbors had only one or two small windows. Window glass was not generally available until about the year 1700. Instead they were covered with paper made translucent (but not transparent) by saturation with linseed oil, protected by wooden shutters that were closed during bad weather. The living-bed space was rarely partitioned off from the kitchen area, the whole heated by a wood-burning fireplace with perhaps small built-in seats at the corners, for the half dozen younger Whipple children, made of stones held together by mud or rude oyster shell mortar. The hearth with its blazing fire, which likely covered one whole side of the house, would have extended several feet into the room.

"Over those great fire-places of colonial times many a wife presented herself as a burnt offering to her lord and master, the good man of the house. The posts and kettles that ornamented the kitchen wall were implements for pre-historic giants rather than for frail women. The brass or copper kettles often holding fifteen gallons, and huge iron pots weighing forty pounds, were lugged hither and thither by women whose every ounce of strength was needed for the too frequent pangs of child-birth. The colonists boasted of the number of generations a kettle would outlast; but perhaps the generations were too short---thanks to the size of the kettle."[59]

As to why the citizens of Providence would relent long enough to allow a middle-aged carpenter his wife and nine children, from the distrusted Bay Colony to join their "closed corporation" is a centuries old conundrum. That information has long since been lost in the mists of time.[60] Not every one who petitioned, even those suffering from severe religious oppression, was admitted into a full share of the town's largess. These were called "quarter-rights men" or simply, freeholders. By means of a lifetime of hard

13

work, John obviously acquired a substantial estate, "much larger than the average purchaser."[61] By some estimates, he could have been one of the wealthiest men in Providence in 1659. It is possible that town leaders realized the wisdom of admitting someone of John's training and years of experience in carpentry and bridge building. There is no indication in town records that anyone from that trade had resided in Providence before John Whipple.[62] One of his first jobs as a new resident was to help build and later repair the town's first bridge over the Moshassuck River.[63]

The Religion of John and Sarah Whipple

The large and growing Whipple family moved to Providence because John wanted more land, and the town needed his skills and money. This is a plausible scenario. But it, by itself, could not likely have provided the decisive impetus to embark on such a drastic life-altering metamorphosis, considering the severity of the consequences that would have ensued. Unless there had been a stronger, more urgent reason, acquisitiveness would probably not have been enough to counter the personal and social stigma that would have attached to such a decision. The divulgence that he was even contemplating such an ill-advised move would have made him suspect. To do so would have resulted in social disgrace for the entire family. Close relatives would have had to disown and vilify them. Their church would have ostracized them. Moreover, it is entirely feasible that the members of the John Whipple family were forced to leave their comfortable home of over 25 years because they had already been ostracized. To become anathema to their life long neighbors and friends could only have been the result of virulent prejudice. The sacrament of baptism/christening would have been denied their children, which may have happened in the case of their youngest daughter born about 1657/58. The Whipples had rejected the religion and/or political leadership of their neighbors, magistrates, and the clergy, so they in turn were rejected. Theirs would have been a desperate flight to find freedom of conscience, even if it meant moving to Rhode Island.[64] And the only place in the New England colonies to find such, in the years 1658/9, was Rhode Island.[65]

This oppression, which possibly drove the family into exile, was deeply rooted in historical circumstances. The religion of the Massachusetts Bay Colony was Puritanism, the only form of Christianity in which John and his family would have been allowed to officially partake. During mandatory Sabbath services, they would have heard that there was but one true church, and that that church was the Congregational, or "New England Way." Sermons told of unbelievers in a hellish place called Providence, led by a man who had been excommunicated from their midst some years before. This Providence, they were told, was a "cesspool of sinners, a vile receptacle of all sorts of riff-raff people that is nothing else but a sewer. It was the asylum for all that are disturbed, a hive of hornets, and the Sinke into which all the Rest of the Coloneys empty their Hereticks."[66] Perhaps John's younger children cringed with fear when hearing from the pulpit that in the dreadful time at the end of the world, their home to be would be none other than hell itself. In summary, no one likely moved to Rhode Island from Massachusetts unless he or she was forced to do so.

It would be instructive to learn the circumstances that surrounded the Whipple's decision to reject their life long religious beliefs and practices.[67] Itinerant Anabaptist preachers from England were not an uncommon sight, even in Dorchester.[68] However, the preponderance of circumstantial evidence suggests that the Whipples at least sympathized with the Society of Friends. However, it is just as conceivable that Captain John could have become disenthralled with religion in general. As it is true in the twenty first century, so then--- freedom of religion was often freedom from religion. "An often-heard criticism of Rhode Island was that much of its citizenry held to no particular religion at all."[69] The motives that urged most of the planters of the Moshassuck seem to have been rather political than religious. They had come to Providence for religious liberty, but only a few of them showed much desire for an active exercise of its rights by setting up any religious assembly. Their chief anxiety was to escape from the despotism of Puritan elders, thus their government functioned only in civil matters. "The records of the town would seem to indicate that the early inhabitants were not of a kind whom church-going was a necessity." [70]

They undoubtedly heard about, or witnessed, the heresy trial and banishment of the proto-Quaker Anne Hutchinson, as well as the later trial of her sister Catherine Scott, a noted Baptist convert to the Society of Friends. "John Winthrop, the political king of Boston, and Rev. John Wilson, its ecclesiastical Bishop, were opposed to Mrs.

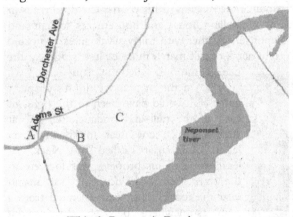

Whipple Property in Dorchester

Hutchinson's doctrine, known by the hard and today meaningless name, 'Antinomian.' The debate...set all of Boston on fire...banishment was the only means of saving the Puritan Church and State..."[71] She and several followers moved to Aquidneck Island, later called Rhode Island, in 1638. Further fear of Boston enticed her to flee, in 1643, to what is now the Bronx, New York, near the Hutchinson River, where she was slain in an Indian uprising.

Most of those who followed her to Rhode Island had become Quakers within less than 10 years. "In the 1650s, the new Quaker doctrines were imported into Newport from Boston. They seemed compatible with much of what Anne Hutchison had taught, and Quakerism quickly became the most important denomination on Aquidneck."[72]

Catherine Marbury Scott lived in Providence, where she had fled to escape Massachusetts. It was Catherine who convinced The Reverend Roger Williams in 1638/39 to establish the first Baptist church in America, although Williams left the church within four months, and Catherine soon converted to Quakerism. She and her husband Richard, who lived next door to Williams, were the grandparents of two of Captain John Whipple's step grandchildren through his eldest son. The Scotts were a constant irritation to Williams, being the first converts to Quakerism in Providence.

"After the arrival of the Quaker ship Woodhouse in Newport in the summer of 1657, missionary evangelists of the new sect fanned out in all directions... It was not long before some of these zealous people decided to invade Massachusetts to preach

15

their views and denounce the laws against Quakers. A widow, Harrod Garner from Newport, was given ten lashes...in May 1658 for that offense. A month later Thomas Harris and another Rhode Islander went to Boston and denounced the sermon after Sabbath service. Both were whipped and imprisoned. In September, Catherine Scott, who had given up the Baptist faith to become a Quaker, received the same treatment. She was told that if she came back again she might be hanged. In 1659 William Robinson and Marmaduke Stephenson were hanged on Boston Commons...Not before 1672 were Quakers allowed to preach in Boston without arrest."[73]

Typical of the religious atmosphere, the heretic Samuel Gorton was arrested in Rhode Island and paraded down the main street of Dorchester in chains, a sight the Whipples could not have missed.[74] Conceivably John was in church on that Sunday morning in the summer of 1658 when Thomas Harris of Providence, the father-in-law to be of his son Samuel, criticized the sermon and was summarily whipped and imprisoned.[75] The final straw might have fallen on 19 October 1658, when Massachusetts enacted a law banishing all Quakers upon pain of death.[76] Within less than one month of that proclamation, 15 November 1658, John sold his property to George Minot, and began preparations to leave, thus making a public declaration, if he had not done so already, of his decision to renounce the religion of his youth. The deed reads in part: "John Whiple...carpenter...his now dwelling house and housements scituate and being in Dorchester near the river Naponset together with thirty-seven acres of upland more or less thereto adjoining, also eight acres of salt marsh more or less lying near the place commonly called the penny ferry."[77]

First Baptist Church

On the map above, John's property letter "C" would have been to the right, or east, of the mill and bridge letter "A" at Adams Street, and near the penny ferry letter "B" in an area called "The Neck." At least some of his property was located on the river itself, eight acres of "salt marsh near the ferry." This ferry operated from a point somewhere between the present Adams Street Bridge and the Granite Avenue Bridge on what is now the north shore of the Neponset River State Reservation.[78] The village of Neponset, not seen on this drawing, was located about one half mile to the northeast at the mouth of the river. The Stoughton Mill area is now called the Lower Mills district.

Having witnessed the unconscionable hanging of two Rhode Island Quakers, which occurred earlier in the same year that he was approved as a Providence purchaser,[79] could only have strengthened his resolve to escape the same fate. Was it mere coincidence that less than one month after the law was enacted that mandated the death sentence for members of the Quaker faith, the Whipples promptly moved to the only safe haven in New England for members of that sect? Massachusetts authorities were totally consumed with the Quaker issue in the 1650s; the few newly arrived Anabaptists from Old England, who differed from them primarily on the doctrine of

16

adult baptism, were largely ignored for the time being. As far as is known, none of the Whipples returned to live in their former hometown.

Consequent to becoming ensconced in his new home, John's religious and/or political preferences became non-issues. Due to laws that mandated separation of church and state, early town records were strictly secular in nature, and parish membership records from that early date are absent or incomplete.[80] It has been assumed that John and Sarah were Baptists based on the observation that "their children married into families that held the same beliefs as Roger Williams."[81] However, as shown herein, their children and grandchildren married into families of Quaker, Baptist, and Anglican communions.[82] The John Whipples are not mentioned in the membership records of the Baptist church in Providence. A proffered document entitled "John Whipple on the Baptist Church" has apparently become lost or misplaced.[83] There is no proof that John Whipple Senior or Junior wrote the document. He may have at one time preached at a Baptist house church some where along Town Street or held some other ecclesial post,[84] in that educational qualifications for the Baptist and Quaker clergy or lay clergy were nonexistent, if not in fact discouraged at the time.[85] The photograph above is that of the sanctuary of the First Baptist Church of Providence, its predecessor being built about 50 years after Captain John's death. Extant records of the church commence about the year 1755; therefore, there is no way to know if seventeenth century Whipples were members. The first listed Whipple communicant dates from 1764. Thomas Olney and The Reverend Roger Williams were implacable enemies.[86] Olney, the father-in-law of John Whipple Junior, withdrew from the church in 1652 and started his own Baptist church. Thomas Olney Junior was its minister until his death in 1722, at which time the church ceased to be. If the Whipples were Baptist they likely were members of the Olney splinter group. In contradistinction to earlier claims, the religious preference of Captain John and Sarah Whipple at Providence cannot at this time be determined with a sufficient degree of certitude.

A Member of the Landed Gentry

In a deed dated 23 November 1663, Captain John Whipple wrote that he owned the former Towne Streete property of Francis Wickes.[87] A deed drawn by Benedict Arnold, governor of the colony, on 10 September 1666 averred that he, Arnold, had sold four home lots, including those of John Greene Junior, Benedict Arnold, Francis Wickes, and William Arnold to John Whipple in 1661. According to his testimony, the "towne granted it to me above Twenty yeares agone. I Benedict Arnold haveing sold the PremiSes to him about five yeares agone."

Due to its historical significance, this deed, which is over 1500 words in length, is discussed in some detail. Several important place names are mentioned.

> "This deed beareing date the Tenth day of September in the Eighteenth yeare of the Reigne of our Soveraine Charles the Second King of England Scotland France & Ireland &c. That I Benedict Arnold of Newport, in ye Collony of Rhode Island & Providence Plantations in New England & (Sen) for good causes hereunto me moveing; And ffor & in ConSideration of NineScore Pounds Current pay of this Collony in hand Received before the Signeing & sealing…ye

17

Whole Right ye said Towne to me Granted ...; The promised Percells hereby Sold, being as followeth; That is to say, ffowre houSelots or homeShares containeing in the whole Six & Twenty Rod be it More or less on ye west party & as Much on ye EaSt party; & one hundred & Twenty Rod in length be it More or less on ye South party, & and as Much on ye North party; Bounded on ye North party by ye Common & partly by ye howSe lot of Edward Manton, & on ye East by the HighWay or Common, & on ye South by land now in the PossesSion of John Throckmorton (Sen) & on the West by the Streete, or Way leadeing into Towne &c; All Which Sd ffowre Lotts together with howSeing, fenceing & other improvements thereupon Wholy Sold unto

Whipple Backyard

John Whipple aforesaid excepting about Two Acres lieing on the South Side toward the East...sold to Thomas Olney. Moreover, the percells of land that are hereafter mentioned are togethere with ye foresaid Howselotts Sold & by these present Made over unto ye above Said John Whipple; That is to Say, one low plot of ground Containeing about Nine Rod of land as it Was by me fenced in many years agone, lieing below the Streete betweene ye Forsd howSelots & ye River below the Mill; Bounded round by ye StreetWay & ye Common..."[88]

It is reasonable to assume that the Whipples lived from 1659 to 1661 in the abandoned house of William Arnold, empty since 1651, the house and land John eventually deeded to John Junior.[89] In addition to the Town Street property, John bought several other parcels of land from Arnold at that same time. He bought five tracts of land of five or six scattered acres in such places as "what cheare bounded on the east by the salt water that goeth up towards Pawtucket falls, etc." Also, "five acres more or less lieing under the hill on the SouthWard side of WeyboySett above ye Bridge... And "one Percell of land to ye north End of Rockey Nooke." Also, "six acres at Solitary Hill near the forementioned River Called WanasSquatucket." Also, "land granted & once laid out to Me on the East Side of the fresh Pond Called MaShapagne" and "Small brooke." John bought an additional two parcels of 60 acres, and two of about 20 acres each. In total, the deed shows that he purchased over 180 acres soon after his arrival in Providence, in addition to the 40 or so acres that the house lots and common encompassed. The deed acknowledged that John had already sold or

18

traded some of the properties. However, a few tracts are mentioned in his last will and testimony. "In 1659, came John Whipple from Massachusetts. He purchased nearly the whole tract eastward of that part of Town street (Constitution Hill)."[90] John bought four lots, about 175 yards of land, along Town Street. Each lot of five acres extended up and over a steep hill[91] to New Hope Street on the east, a distance of about one-half mile. In addition to these lots, he would have been entitled to approximately 25 acres of planting or grazing land north and eastward of Hope Street. The June 2004 photograph

Towne Streete, 1661

above, taken from the rear of a condominium building that now occupies the spot where the Whipple house would have stood [about 75 yards north of Star Street], shows the incline of the hill on the Whipple property. Other areas of the incline rise from an angle of 45 degrees to about 60 degrees. A terraced area immediately to the top of the photograph, on what is now Benefit Street, would have held the family burial plot. The laying out of this street in the mid 1700s

19

caused the Whipples, and about 50 other families, to move their ancestors' graves to the North Burial Ground.

That the Whipple family moved in immediately is evident in a reference to John that appeared in town records in early 1660/61, and his oldest daughter, Sarah, married in 1659 or early 1660. She married into the Smith family, owners of the Smith mill immediately to the northwest (on the map above) of John's property. John's youngest daughter, Abigail, married the oldest son of The Reverend Gregory Dexter, his immediate neighbor to the north. His middle daughter, Mary, married into The Reverend Thomas Olney Senior family (first house south of Gaol Lane), as did John Junior.[92] John Junior's second wife was the widow of Richard Scott's son, the immediate neighbor to the south of the Whipple property. Sons number three and six, Eleazer and Benjamin, married daughters of Thomas Angell (second house south of Gaol Lane). Joseph, Captain John's seventh son, married a granddaughter of the Angells. Samuel, John's second son, married into the Thomas Harris family (fourth house south of Powers Lane) and bought the property of Roger Mowrey, (first house at the top of the map). See individual chapters for further information on the marriages of second generation Whipples.

By virtue of his new status as a part owner of Providence Plantations, within two years of his arrival, John received a grant of land in an area called the "north woods" or Louquisset.[93] This property, located eight to ten miles north of the settlement, was given, by deed and will, to his four oldest sons.[94] In terms of land acquisition, the move to his new home was fortuitous. He became a proprietor two months after the General Assembly gave the town its permission to "buy out and clear out" the

Area of Whipple Property 1661

Indians within plantation territory and purchase adjacent lands. His fellow proprietors, on 27 July 1662, gave him permission to exchange his sixty acres at Mashapauge Pond for additional land at Loquasqussuk.[95] John also participated in the awarding of at least three other land grants. On 19 February 1665/6, he drew lot #45 in the division of lands east of the 7 mile line [an arbitrary line seven miles west of Providence].[96] The surveyor described this property as located "...at the sowth ind by the Wenasketukit [Woonasquatucket] River the sowthermost corner a whit oak the norard Cornar a Small roack ranged with agreet whit oke three or fowar poll from the roack the estar Cornar a whit oke the sowth est Cornar by the river a black oke...be it mor or less laid by me Thomas harris Savaire."[97] John promptly traded some of this grant at the "Tare Breech Plain" on 13 November 1666.[98] John drew lot #43 in the lands on the west side of the seven-mile line on 12 April 1675.[99] In his last land grant of 24 May 1675, he drew lot #91 on the east side of the seven-mile line.[100] He was subsequently given permission to change a 50-acre division of upland later that year.[101] John also petitioned for a small piece of land next to his new orchard on Towne Streete in February of 1661.[102] And on 6 June 1681, he was granted permission to exchange his twenty-five acres at Goatum Valley "which he bought of Mr. Benedict Arnold."[103] The twenty-acre homestead on Town Street, plus twenty-four acres of commoning, that the Whipple family purchased from Benedict Arnold may have been devoid of structures, and its farm fields and orchards overgrown. Early on, the Wickes family had become converts to the religious teachings of a man named Samuel Gorton, who banned by at least two other local settlements, had tried to settle in Providence. "When Gorton applied to the town for admission as a voter and landholder (or freeman) in May 1641, the town denied his request, calling him, 'an insolent, railing and turbulent person.' They also excluded from town fellowship Gorton's followers, John Wickes and Randall Holden."[104] The Wickes family, following Gorton, eventually settled in what is now the town of Warwick, Rhode Island in the mid-1640s. The Arnolds and Greenes moved to the Pawtuxet River area in 1638 and the early 1640s. Benedict Arnold eventually moved to Newport, and was the colony's governor at the time he sold Captain John the north Main properties.

The June 2004 photograph above (see also photograph on page 32) is of the present state of the four lots on Constitution Hill looking northeast from the northeast corner of Main Street and Star Street. This newly constructed single row of eight two-story condominiums stand at the bottom of a sharply rising hill, with Main Street to the left. The original Main (or Towne) Street was much narrower when the Whipples lived there.[105] The John Whipple house was long the oldest house in Providence, finally demolished shortly before WWII to allow for the widening of Main Street into four lanes. His house/inn, at 369 North Main, would have stood about 75 yards north of the south end of the condominium complex (on the right of the photograph) and toward the front, where Main street now traverses. The inn/tavern of Mary Whipple Olney (John's second daughter) was located about two blocks up this street. The ascending street to the right is Star Street, where Whipple Hall schoolhouse was located.[106] John Whipple Junior's house stood at this intersection. The street to the left is Mill (now Charles) Street, on which the John and Sarah Smith (Captain John's oldest daughter) gristmill, and home, were located, as well as the tavern/inns of John Junior and Joseph.

Previously in the possession of absentee landowners for well over a decade, their new acreage likely demanded much of the Whipple family. Restoration and expansion of the property was first priority. As a result, John appears infrequently in town records for the first three years or so. The first record of community activity in the settlement occurred in January 1660/61, when as a surveyor, he "laid out 5 acres of low land for Thomas Clemance." This was recorded on 27 January 1660/61.[107] He was called upon to serve on a committee to collect taxes later that year. At a town meeting 26 March 1660/1661, it was ordered that "a rate of 35 pounds after peage, 8 penny shall be levied upon this towne to pay toward the colony prison."[108]

Not until 1663 is John seen as more than tangentially involved in community affairs. In that year, he served as a juryman on two occasions, and was a committee member twice, one committee concerned with property boundaries and the other with building a new towne house.[109] The year 1663 saw the first of eight deeds recorded to

21

his sons, when he deeded to "my son John Whipple a houselot formerly owned by William Arnold excepting two acres, two shares of meadow, six acres of upland, sixty acres of land at Loquasqussuck…" The only known extant handwriting of John Whipple Senior appears in this document.[110]

In 1664, John again entered town records when his neighbors called upon his training and experience as a carpenter. Four years earlier, the town council had overseen the building of its first ever bridge. Three years later, the bridge had to be rebuilt. Then

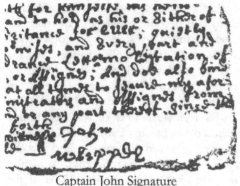
Captain John Signature

at a Quarter Court 27 January 1664, it was ordered that "John Whipple Senr. Be sent for to confer with the moderator, Mr. William Field, about mending the bridge." A subsequent agreement was made between Thomas Harris Sr. and Valentine Whitman, acting for the town, and John Whipple. With the help of two other men, John was hired to do the work.[111] Then three years later, 28 October 1667, five persons were chosen "to view the bridge…and to consider of the most easy and facill way to repair it so that the passage may not be lost." John Whipple and Roger Williams were members of the committee.[112]

It would be informative, as well as interesting, to know something of John's everyday experience as a carpenter. However, as seen above, only on rare occasions were the services of tradesmen required on public projects. Fortunately, the contract wages John charged, and some of the tools used, are known. Early town records include an undated estimate in John's own writing on constructing a leanto: "To making of ye leanto and work about it, 06-00-00. To making of ye seller roof and shingling it, 01-05-00. To making of a door and shelves in ye leanto, 0-80-6." Among his tools were a froe, a Rye bit, iron square, small jointer, carving tool, axe, clearing plane, whetting steel, wimble stock and bits, soding iron, compasses, and brass rule for a chalk line.[113]

The Captain John Whipple Inn

"Taverns, inns or ordinaries, were words used interchangeably in early New England to designate public houses where meals, liquors and lodgings could be obtained at reasonable prices. These places ranged from a single room with a bar, a chair and a hard board bed [like John's], to larger houses, with accommodations for a number of persons of both sexes, where meals and comfortable lodgings could be had, with a bar to supply all tastes with liquors of all grades. Taverns existed in England from the thirteenth century, and crossed the water with the Pilgrim and Puritan founders. Children and servants (and Indians) were not allowed to drink at taverns…profane singing, dancing, and reveling were forbidden."[114] A Bed and Breakfast Inn, with liquor privileges, would be its modern equivalent.

"John Whipple Senior was one of the most competent inn holders in Rhode Island. Because of the staid and sober character of the Whipple Inn and its central location it was a favorite meeting place for the Town Council and Court of Probate. The October 1690 session of the Rhode Island General Assembly met at the Whipple Inn."[115] As shown herein, present research reveals the above to be overstated, if not romanticized. The possibility has been broached that John may have acquired an initial pecuniary interest in licensing his own inn as early as 1670. At a town council meeting on 6 June 1670, John Whipple Senior "is paid 10 shillings for holding the town meeting in his house." By the next time the council met at his house, the amount paid was increased to 20 shillings.[116]

At least three of John Whipple's children (John Junior, Joseph, and Mary Whipple-Olney), as well as at least three grandsons (John III, James Olney, and William Hopkins Jr) and one step grandson (Sylvanus Scott), were actively involved in that business for a half-century and more. John Junior established his own inn by special request of the town, because the needs of its citizenry were not being adequately met,[117] three years before his father's death. Ostensibly, John Senior's inn, which had begun in 1674,[118] no longer actively operated and probably had not for sometime. This is understandable, considering the devastation that resulted from the Indian war that started within a year after he opened his doors for business. By the time the war had ended and residents began to trickle back late in 1677, and the long years of recovery required to rebuild or repair most of the houses in the settlement had passed, John had but five or six years to live. Although John's property was spared destruction, the Indians had stolen everything that was not burned. When he died in 1685, "he left a large property in land, but the means at his disposal 'for entertainment of strangers'...was scanty. He had one feather bed, seven pewter platters, five pewter porringers, three old spoons, one old red blanket, and [three chairs and a decayed old warming pan]..."[119] Most of what has been penned about the so-called "staid" Captain John Whipple Inn, located at 369 Main Street, should have been attributed to his children's taverns instead, John Junior's in particular, located approximately one block or so to the northwest on Mill Street. John Whipple III inherited his father's inn in the year 1700 and continued its history for several more years. The Olney Inn existed until after the Revolutionary War. The Joseph Whipple family continued in the business until at least 1740.[120] "Whipple's tavern...stood, one of the most conspicuous of the old taverns, to the middle of the eighteenth century---not a long life, but a notable one."[121]

Early Rhode Island innkeepers have been described as "a picturesque lot." Perhaps the ensuing description could have applied to the Whipples: "Usually stout, good-natured, good-looking, and well dressed, they were prominent public figures, enjoying all sorts of confidences, public and private, leading the singing in the meeting houses, running ferries, teaching the children of travelers, serving on the legislature of town council, acting as recruiting officers in times of war, as storekeepers, surveyors or story-tellers. Some were frugal and thrifty, some mean and penurious, while others were extravagant. Some were of bitter dispositions, but, as a rule, they were jolly enough."[122]

"As Providence increased in size and importance more strangers had occasion to visit the town, and it became necessary to provide for their comfort and entertainment. In the earliest days the only lodgings available for visitors were in private houses and, as the accommodations of few of those houses exceeded one room [as in the case of Captain John Whipple's tavern], the guest quarters were neither sumptuous nor particularly private. The first tavern on the Town Street of which there is record was the one opened by John Whipple in 1674, halfway up Constitution Hill. This was followed by another, immediately north of the home lots, maintained by Epenetus Olney. In a more secluded spot some distance to the north (Abbott Street) Roger Mowry had, for some years, conducted an 'ordinaire' in a house, erected in 1653" [bought by Samuel Whipple in 1671].[123]

"Even after settlements spread to Bristol, Rehoboth, Attleboro, Smithfield and Pawtuxet, the farmers and their wives would come into Sunday services and town meetings (both typically held at the inn). This Sunday ride or walk to and from the meetings was the one way both the men and women had, with their farms scattered one and two miles apart, to become acquainted with each other and to keep up their fund of information about their neighbors. Further, town meetings days also became shopping days. Crafty traders would circulate handbills making a bid for the handiwork of the housewife and adroitly calling their attention to those goods that would excite the curiosity of the farmer's wives as to the condition of their wardrobe...The merchants on these occasions engaged one or more rooms at the tavern and while tea was served in the room, a bowl of punch was in the other and there was trading outside of the house as well as inside. The merchants had a variety of goods wanted by the farmer's wives, from a bottle of snuff to a warming pan, and they would take anything from the farm in exchange."[124] A more in-dept discussion of the Whipple Inns is presented in the chapter on John Whipple Junior.

Dispute with The Reverend Roger Williams

"...John Whipple was received as an inhabitant in Providence, purchased a Proprietors' share and soon became a leading citizen and a zealous supporter of Harris and Olney. Williams says that he was a constant speaker in town meetings and evidently regarded him as one of his chief opponents...It seems probable that Williams addressed his letters to Whipple, that they might become more widely known in what was then the chief club house of the village..."[125] For over a century, this or similar statements have been iterated and reiterated in numerous publications by various antiquarian researchers. It may well be that The Reverend Roger Williams did not see eye to eye with Captain John Whipple Senior as to the logistics of ethical land acquisition. However, in the instance below his verbal conflict was not with the elder Whipple.[126]

Less than a decade after arriving in Providence as a teenager, the youthful John Whipple Junior became a major participant in a protracted verbal and legal conflict over Indian land. Early on, John Junior allied himself with his wife's father, Thomas Olney, his brother Samuel's wife's uncle, William Harris, and William Arnold, his sister Abigail Hopkins husband's uncle. These men were the leaders of a consortium of proprietors who had for years sought to extend the plantation's boundaries westward for some 20 miles, allowing them to create vast land holdings exclusively for themselves.[127] Roger Williams opposed the plan. The ensuing legal wrangling lasted well into the next century, long after the combatants had died.[128]

The letters in question, which Williams addressed to John Junior in July and August of 1669, were a virtual diatribe against the personality and moral rectitude of the young man, not his father.[129] Although the outcome of the various lawsuits went against the Harris, Olney, Arnold, and Whipple family syndicate, a great deal of land still came into the possession of their descendants. In the case of the Whipple family, by the year 1700, several descendants had moved onto the generally disputed areas of Cranston, Scituate, Coventry and West Warwick under such surnames as Arnold, Harris, Rhodes, Rice, and Whipple.[130] A more in-depth examination of these letters is attempted in the chapter on John Whipple Junior.

Honorary Military Rank

In the April 1676 meeting of the town council, John was elected moderator; he had been elected to the council at least twice before.[131] By that time, King Philip's War had been raging for almost a year. Less than one month earlier, Providence had been attacked and burned, its livestock stolen or killed, and its fields of spring crops destroyed. It is assumed that the April meeting was held at John's house, attended by some of the two dozen or so who were left in town, because his house was one of only a few that had been spared on the north end of Town Street. A few days before the attack, most of the town's residents had fled to Aquidneck Island for safety. Apparently each head of household was given the option to stay and defend the settlement; John Whipple Senior, Roger Williams, and two dozen others elected to stay.[132] The Indians had previously informed Williams, "Brother Williams, you are a good man, you have been kind to us many years; not a hair of your head shall be touched."[133] Apparently, that caveat applied to his sequestered colleagues in arms as well. Because of this act, John was listed among those who "stayed and went not away" and as such was entitled to Indian slaves.[134] He was subsequently appointed to a committee in October of that year to "demand & receaue at euery Garrison what was taken from yee Indians."[135] In 1679, the Rhode Island General Assembly, in which he served as a deputy that year, appointed him to a committee to give a final report on the Indian uprising.[136] The quasi-military designation "Captain" was used for the first time in this document.

Last Will and Testament

In his Last Will and Testament, dated 8 May 1682 and proved 27 May 1685, John Whipple Senior of Providence wrote:
Be it known to all persons to whom this may come, that I, John Whipple of the town of Providence, in the colony of Rhode Island, and Providence Plantations, in New England (Sen.) being in good measure of health, and in perfect memory, upon consideration of mortality, not knowing the day of my death, and having many children, and to prevent difference that otherwise may hereafter arise among them concerning my worldly estate, do see cause to make my will and do hereby dispose of all my estate in this world and do make my last Will and Testament.
Having formerly given unto three sons, all of my lands and meadows in Louisquisset, namely, Samuel, Eleazer and William equally to be divided among them three only; excepting thirty acres, which I give unto my son John, at the North West End.
I give unto my three aforesaid sons, namely, Samuel, Eleazer and William, each of them, a quarter part of one right of Common, for pasturing, cutting of timber, and firewood.

I give unto my son Benjamin a right of land in the late division which is already made out to him.

I give unto my son David a right of land in the late division which is already made out to him.

I give unto my son Jonathan twenty-five acres on which he now dwelleth, also I give unto my son Jonathan one division of land which is ordered by the town to be laid out between the 'seven-mile line' and the 'four-mile line' and papers already drawn for.

I give unto my son Joseph, my dwelling-house, and my three house-lots, and the garden next; also a six-acre lot lying on the southern side of the neck whereupon the town of Providence standeth; also twenty acres near Thomas Clemens, his dwelling; also I give unto my son Joseph my share of meadow near Solitary Hill, and the two six-acre lots, lying on each side of said Hill; also a six-acre lot, near William Wickenden formerly dwelt; also one division lying on the 'seven-mile line', which is already ordered by the town and papers drawn for; also I give unto my son Joseph, all other divisions which shall hereafter belong unto two rights throughout.

I give unto my sons, namely John, Samuel, Eleazer, William, Benjamin, David and Jonathan twelve pence every one of them.

I give unto my three daughters, namely, Sarah, Mary, Abigail, unto everyone of them, ten shillings.

I give unto my son Joseph, all of my right of land in the Narragansett country. I give unto my son Joseph, all my movable goods, of what sort soever and all my cattle, and all my tools; also I do make my son Joseph my executor; also my will is that my son Joseph do see that I be decently buried; this being the real absolute Will and Testament of me John Whipple Sen; as aforesaid, I do hereunto set my hand and seal, this eight day of May, in the year one thousand six hundred and eighty-two. Signed and sealed in the presence of

Thomas Arnold	Witness my hand
John Arnold	
Shadrach Manton	John Whipple L.S.[137]

I, Thomas Arnold, and John Arnold, the 27th day of May, in the year 1685, did upon these solemn engagements declare that they are witnesses unto the above will, and as these names so are there written do own it to be their hand. Shadrach Manton the 27 day of May, 1685, in the presence of the Magistrates and rest of the Council, full and truly declare that he is witness to the above will, and that he with his own hand wrote his name there unto, as, attest, Arthur Fenton, Assistant.

Joseph Whipple did upon the 27th day of May 1685 in the presence of the Council as he is Executor of the Testament upon his solemn engagement testify and declare that this is the last Will and Testament of his deceased father as ever yet perfected as he knoweth of and that he when he made it, was of sound mind, and of a good memory.

Taken before us   Arthur Fenner   Joseph Jencks

Thomas Olney deposed that he had gone to John Whipple, at his request, and obtained clarification of some of the bequests.[138] The inventory of Captain John Whipple Senior was taken 22 May 1685 and totaled a little more than £41, excluding real estate.[139] The unexpectedly penurious amount of £41 in worldly goods is informative if not enigmatic, until it is understood that almost everything John owned apparently had already been distributed to his children, who had long since established homes of their own. He had lived as a widower for almost two decades by then; accordingly his creature comforts were minimal---two beds, three chairs, and one old warming pan....[140]

Another unexpected revelation is the smallness of his residence, considering the size of the family. "The houses upon the 'towne streete' during the first generations were

369 N. Main, 1663

of a story or a story and a half in height, with a large stone chimney at one end. In the earliest days of the town its houses had but two rooms, called in the Probate documents, the 'lower room' and the 'chamber.' The space did not always permit the luxury of stairs, and the only ascent to the chamber was often by a ladder. These humble dwellings were nearly universal until the last decade of the seventeenth century---the poverty which followed the Indian war delaying the period of improvement. In such a house lived John Smith [and his wife Sarah, John's daughter] the miller and the Town Clerk. The house of John Whipple, one of the chief landholders of his day, stood near the foot of Constitution hill. It was one of the first which was rebuilt after Philip's war. It appears by the proceedings upon his will (which bears date 8th May, 1682) that his house had only a lower room and a chamber above.[141] This was also the primitive farm house of the Plymouth colony. A few houses had two rooms upon the floor, sometimes called in the inventories, the 'inner' and the 'outer' room. Thomas Olney, Senr., [father-in-law of two of John's children] had a 'parlour,' 'kitchen,' and 'chamber.' He had also a larger personal estate than most of his neighbours."[142]

Above is an artist's rendering as to how the exterior of the Whipple house would have appeared in the mid-1660s shortly after the family had settled into daily life in their new home. This interpretation is based on knowledge of mid-to-late seventeenth century construction practices and of John's inventory of movable goods. Due to the family's apparent wealth and John's carpentry skills, the house likely could have been more substantial than others on Town Street. The front of the house, which would have faced south, could have been more elaborate than was usual at that time. The photograph of the 1912 John Whipple house at the end of this chapter is part of an uncataloged collection in the Rhode Island State Archives.[143]

Death and Burial

Whipple Burial Grounds

Captain John Whipple died 16 May 1685. The inscription on his gravestone indicates that he was about 68 years old. John's first 15 years or so were spent at an unknown location somewhere in Old England; there followed a half century lived in New England, equally divided between Dorchester, Massachusetts and Providence, Rhode Island. His wife, whose place of birth is unknown, died in 1666 at the age of about 42. Their children had all reached adulthood by the time of John's death. John Junior was the oldest at 46, Jonathan, 21, the youngest. Only Joseph 85, and Eleazer 74, lived a longer life than had their father. Their children eventually produced 77 offspring: 37 grandsons and 40 granddaughters. Of the grandsons, 24 bore the Whipple name, making his Whipple descendants the most numerous of the three Whipple men who came to the Massachusetts Bay Colony in the 1630s.

John and Sarah were laid to rest in their own garden burial lot, as was customary at the time. "Every home-lot had its orchard, about haft way up the eastern hillside. There, but a few paces from their homestead, were the graves of the household. The family allotment soon became alike their birth and burial places. There was no

Capt. John and Sarah Whipple Headstones

anticipation of modern sanitary ideas, and the funeral march was a long and dreary one, for, until a comparatively recent date, the corpse was carried forth upon the shoulders of the neighbors. Whether through poverty or want of skill, or the early diffusion of Quaker ideas, no inscriptions were set over the earliest graves. This primitive custom of sepultare outlasted three generations."[144]

Nowhere else in the colonies was this cemetery custom prevalent. "The parish churchyard of England had been followed in the other colonies by common burial places, attached or at least near to the meeting-house. It was a feature of communal life and partook of the ecclesiastical sanctity descended from the Roman through the Protestant church. In Providence, death even could not end separatism and a common burial ground could not be attained until commerce began to relax the prejudices of the individuals whose ancestors had been driven from Puritan commonwealths."[145]

Although Providence was settled in the year 1636, the first mention of a public cemetery does not appear in town records until 1700. That year marked a departure from the individuality shown in the prior burial custom. At that time, the proprietors set aside the most useless sand hill in the area, located at the junction of the Pawtucket Road (Main Street) the "Country Road" to the Louquisset, for the burial of the dead. "The lot lying between Archibal Walker's southward to the brook that cometh out of Samuel Whipple's land, eastward with the highway, and westward and northwestward with the Moshassuck River, was voted to remain common for a training field, burying ground, and other public uses."[146] This land was next to the farm of Samuel Whipple, Captain John's second son, whose was its first interment in 1710/11. Providence at this time was a small town, very much in the shadow of Newport in terms of population and power; however, the time had come to develop a town cemetery as Newport had done more than fifty years previous.

Nevertheless, during the next 50 years few availed themselves of the opportunity. "While there were no interment records kept during the first 150 years of use, the study of the gravestone carvers who made the early markers helps us accurately date many gravestones carved long after the deaths they commemorate. Existing gravestones in the North Burial Ground mark only 18 burials here by 1725 and 29 by 1730. There undoubtedly were unmarked burials, but without records we have no way of knowing how many. An educated guess would be that ten percent of the burials were marked with gravestones. This would indicate that there were 180 or more by 1725."[147]

On 27 October 1746, a petition, signed by Stephen Hopkins and John Whipple (both Captain John Whipple descendants) and others asked for a street eastward of Town Street. It was to spare no ones houselot and imperiled all the household graves. Soon after, the first order was made for a new road to be called Benefit Street. It was to extend from Powers Lane on the south, so far northward as the great gate of Captain John Whipple. The John Whipple gate opened northwardly from his property into the Town Street at the head of Constitution Hill.[148] This Captain John Whipple, called the bonesetter, one of the largest landowners in Providence at the time, was the grandson of the first John through his son Joseph. The construction of this street required that household graves be relocated to the almost 50-year-old sand hill cemetery, by then called the North Burial Ground.

"Old habits die hard. Families did not immediately embrace the new town burial ground and abandon the family burial grounds on their own property where their parents and grandparents were buried. We know this by the dates on gravestones in those cemeteries when they were moved years later. There are two apparently earlier gravestones [than Samuel Whipple's] in this burial ground, those for Capt. John Whipple (1617-1685) and his wife Sarah (1624-1666) (see picture on P.13) but these do not in fact deserve the honor of being the first. Not only were they moved here from a Whipple family burial plot elsewhere in town, but they were not contemporary with the deaths they mark. We know this from evidence provided by gravestone studies. Both beautiful slate stones were carved by George Allen (1696-1774) of the part of Rehoboth, Massachusetts that is now East Providence, Rhode Island. Allen was not yet born when the Whipples died. His well-documented carving style would indicate that they were made sometime after 1750, possibly at the time when their graveyard was removed to North Burial Ground"[149]

29

To reach the burial area shown in the photographs above, drive north from downtown Providence on North Main Street. The cemetery is located on this street, approximately one mile north of downtown. Enter the main gate on the south side of the cemetery. Proceed northward on the street to the right named Eastern Street—stay on this street—a distance equivalent to two city blocks. Stop at the clearly visible small sign that marks an east/west walkway, which reads "Dahlia Path." The Whipple burial area is about 15 yards on the left along this path. There is a large white and gray monument to the east that has the name "TEMPLE" inscribed on it. [The Temples married into the Joseph Whipple Junior family.][150] Due to superstitions of the time, the headstones face to the west. The first two headstones to the left of the box tomb are those of Captain John and Sarah Whipple. Most of the 27 headstones present in this Whipple burial area represent the descendants of John Whipple, called the "bonesetter,"[151] eldest son of Colonel Joseph, the seventh son of Captain John Whipple. Actually, the majority of the burials are of the family of John's only son, Joseph of Smithfield, RI. Joseph[4] Whipple (John[3], Joseph[2], John[1]), his wife, seven daughters without their husbands, three sons and their wives, plus four grandchildren make up the majority of the burials. The remaining sites include the graves of Captain John and Sarah Whipple, Colonel Joseph and Alice Whipple, plus Mary Bardin, Colonel Joseph Whipple's youngest daughter, and Jeremiah, the infant son of John the bonesetter. There remains one unknown person, namely "Hannah wife of Samuel Whipple, c1819-1892."[152] George Allen, the above-mentioned carver, carved the headstones of Captain John and Sarah Whipple and the first four of the family to be interred, the fourth being Colonel Joseph Whipple in 1746. This indicates that the remains of Captain John and Sarah Whipple were, in all probability, reburied around the year 1750 or shortly thereafter.

The Captain John and Sarah Whipple headstones are among but a few with dates from the 1600s, and as such are among the oldest dated markers in the cemetery. Dozens of their generational cohorts were moved to the North Burial Ground in the mid-1700s, but few of their descendants had headstones made to mark their places of reburial. John's headstone is 36 inches high and 27 inches wide. Sarah's is 24 inches high and 20 inches wide. Both are three inches in thickness containing the following inscriptions:

In Memory of	In Memory of Mrs Sarah
Capt. John Whipple who	Whipple ye Wife of Capt
Was Born in England &	John Whipple She was
Died In Providence Town	Born in Dorchester in
Ye 16th Day of May Anno	New England & Died in
Dom 1685 about 68	Providence Anno Dom
Years of Age	1666 Age 42 Years

It has been remarked that some of the information inscribed on John and Sarah's headstones is inaccurate.[153] As previously noted, Sarah could not have been born in Dorchester, Massachusetts in 1624 as that town was not settled until 1630. Could not other information given be similarly inaccurate? It is improbable that the lives of John and Sarah Whipple, unlike others of the time, were originally commemorated with headstones. In view of the above sources, their inscriptions were likely carved some 65 to 85 years after they were originally buried, and could not have been based on information transferred from inscriptions carved on grave markers at the time of death. Colonel Joseph Whipple, who in 1682 was assigned the responsibility to bury his father, or more likely his sons, Captain John Whipple and/or Deputy Governor Joseph Whipple Junior, likely supplied the well-meant, but flawed, information.[154] Whipple descendants the world over are grateful to them, yet lament that seventeenth century burial customs proscribe a more informed glimpse into the memorable lives of Captain John and Sarah Whipple.

The first two photographs below are from the Preston Collection of the Rhode Island State Archives.[155] The third is of the same area taken in 2004. The 1912 house likely reflects additions built by Captain John's granddaughters and their husbands, the Crawford brothers, wealthy merchants, who lived there in the eighteenth century. The 369 property stayed in the Crawford-Whipple (and allied families) family for over 150 years. See the chapter on Joseph Whipple for details. The house was damaged in the New England hurricane of 1938 which devastated much of Rhode Island. It disappeared shortly thereafter.

369 N. Main, 1912

Main Street Looking North from Star Street, 1912
369 is the Sixth from Star on the Right Side. Its Roof Faces Camera

Main Street Looking North from Start Street, 2004
369 Would Have Been the Seventh or Eight Condo

End Notes

[1]Dorchester, the first and largest of the present day metropolitan Boston area settlements, was established in the summer of 1630 by 140 colonists arriving on the *Mary and John*, landed at Nantasket Bay about four miles south of present day downtown Boston. This ship, part of the Winthrop fleet of 17 ships, arrived on 30 May 1630 (6 June 1630) after a trip of 70 days from Plymouth, England. Dorchester settlers in general came from the southwest of England and, as such, were not forced to leave because of religious persecution. By the late 1650s, when John left, Dorchester's population was around 750. *History of the Town of Dorchester, Massachusetts* by a Committee of the Dorchester Antiquarian Society (Boston: David Clapp, Printer, 1859) 15, 18, 19 & 24. A mistake ridden one-paragraph discussion of John Whipple and family is given on page 140, and he is presented on a list of those in a "second emigration" on page 102.

[2] James K. Hosmer, ed., *Governor Winthrop's Journal, 1630-1649* (New York: Scribner and Sons, 1908) 1:92

[3] The Whipple name is Welsh originally meaning "one who came from Whimple (white stream) in Devonshire, *Dictionary of American Family Names*, 232. Whimple originally was the name of a stream, consisting of the words appearing in Welsh, as gwyn "white." and pwll, poll, "pool or stream," 513. A second interpretation from this source points out that it could be a topographic name for someone who lived near a Whippletree. Chaucer lists Whipple tree (probably a kind of dogwood) along with maple, thorn, beach, hazel, and yew. *The Concise Oxford Dictionary of English Place Names* 4th Edition, Eclert Ekwall, Editor, 513. The earliest record of its use was in a census of 1086 when it was spelled "Winple." Subsequent census spellings were "Wimpoll" in 1218, and "Wympoll" in 1296. In *The Early Records of the Town of* Providence, *21 vols, collected and compiled by the Record Commissioners* (Providence: Snow and Farnham, city printers, 1892-1915) [hereinafter ERP] the name was spelled Whippl, Whippelle, Whippell, Whippele, Whippel, Whippe, Whiple, Whipell, Whipel and Whipple. One author claimed, Charles H. Whipple, *Genealogy of the Whipple-Wright, Wagner, Ward-Pell, Mclean-Burnet Families* (Los Angeles, Privately Published, 1917) that the surname Whipple originated with Henri De V. Hipple, a knight from Normandy in the early 15th century. Subsequent research has not corroborated this contention. An alternative interpretation of the name is derived from "another Celtic word 'gwymp' meaning fine or fair, hence 'grymppwll' meaning 'fine stream.' ...In Saxon times Whimple had a small wooden two-cell church on the current slightly elevated site..." *Archive Information*, Whimple History Society, on line at www.whimple.org/ 4/2/2004. A recently published genealogy claims [without documentation] that an aunt of the Whipple brothers of 1638, named Marion, immigrated to Plymouth in 1621. As far is known, John of 1632 was the first verified Whipple in the new world.

[4] Blaine Whipple, *History and Genealogy of "Elder" John Whipple of Ipswich, Massachusetts, His English Ancestors and American Descendants* (Victoria, British Columbia: Trafford Publishing Company, 2003) vi. The Ipswich Whipples may have descended from Thomas Whipple in 1475 (Thomas, Matthew). William Fiske, "The Whipple Family of Bishops Stortford, Hertfordshire: Proposed Ancestral Origin of Matthew Whipple of Bocking, Essex," *The Genealogist*, Vol. 20, No. 2, (Fall 2006) 191-217. According to Fiske, the Captain John Whipple family may have descended from a brother, John, of the second Thomas.

[5] George F. Dow, *Every Day Life in the Massachusetts Bay Colony* (New York: Dover Publications, Inc, 1988) 101. "When the first considerable emigration ceased about the year 1640, of the 25,000 settlers then living in the Colony, probably ninety-five per cent were small farmers or workmen engaged in the manual trades, together with many indentured servants who had come over under the terms of a contract whereby they were bonded to serve their masters for a term of years — usually five or seven. The remaining five per cent of the population was composed of those governing the colony..."

[6] John O. Austin, *Genealogical Dictionary of Rhode Island*, reprint edition (Baltimore: Genealogical Publishing Company, 1969) 221. Nathaniel B. Shurtleff, ed. *Records of the Governor and Company of the Massachusetts Bay in New England, 6 Volumes in 5* (Boston: W. White, 1853-54) 1974. This very first record of John's behavior in the new world, though not flattering is very human. John and his fellow youthful indentured servant likely had never seen so much wild life before. Their exuberance, though immature, is understandable. At the least they learned a sobering lesson concerning Puritan discipline.

[7] Ralph M. Stoughton, "The Stoughton Families of Dorchester, Mass., and Windsor, Conn.," *The American Genealogist*, Vol. 29, No.4 (New Haven, October 1953). Stoughton was an often member of the

Massachusetts legislature where he undoubtedly met John Whipple of Ipswich, a fellow legislator. Perhaps they discussed Stoughton's young apprentice. Stoughton returned to England to fight with Cromwell where he was killed in 1645.

[8] Charles E. Banks, *The Planters of the Commonwealth,* reprint edition (Baltimore: Genealogical Publication Company, 1979) 99-100. The author states that John Whipple of Dorchester was from Bocking. A document entitled "The American Connection with Braintree District" published by the Braintree Council corroborates this contention, as does Winifred Ashwell who insists that both John and Matthew, from Bocking, were passengers on the Lyon. Winifred Ashwell, *Essex and the Lyon: The People Who Sailed in Her to New England in 1632 and the Land to Which They Went* (Braintree, England: 1979). The latest and most informed opinion is that Banks and others assumed incorrectly that John Whipple of Dorchester was from Bocking. A thorough discussion of this issue and a comparison of two lists of passengers supposedly on the 1632 Lyon can be viewed at www.whipple.org/docs/lyon.html. The nativity of John Whipple of Dorchester is unknown. In addition to Bocking, previous authors have given Milford, Wales as John's residence. There is but one Milford in Wales, located in the county of Pembroke at the parish of Huberston and Steynton. However, its earliest parish registers do not begin until 1637.

[9] Boyd's Marriage Index (London: Society of Genealogists, 1980)

[10] Debrett Ancestry Research Limited (Gordon Road, Winchester, SO23 7DD, England, March 1990) p. C

[11] Maude P. Kuhns, *The Mary and John* (Rutland, VT: Tuttle Publishing Company, 1943) 70. The weir was conditioned upon an agreement to sell fish at 5 shillings per thousand to the women of Dorchester, this being the first record we have of price ceilings in the United States. Perhaps as part of his indenture, John was given the responsibility to catch and sell fish.

[12] Richard P. Bonney, ed., Dorchester Tercentenary Commission, *Dorchester Old and New in the Old Bay Colony* (Dorchester: Chapple Publishing Company Ltd, 1930) 12-13. "The original mill was erected on the Dorchester side on land later occupied by the old stone chocolate mill." 32. [This was about 50 yards downstream from the bridge].

[13] "Bridge Project Digs Up History in Lower Mills," *Dorchester Reporter,* 27 February 2003.

[14] Bonney, 31. "Ship building commenced in 1640, small vessels of thirty to forty tons being built at Gulliver's creek." Also "The maintenance of a sufficient head of water in the Neponset has been a serious problem. In 1639, a canal was dug connecting the Charles and Neponset at a point in Dedham…and water from the upper Charles was diverted for the use of Stoughton's mill." 33.

[15] Dow, 107

[16] Sharon Sargent at www.genealogyfair.com. Personal communication with the authors 9 October 2004

[17] Dorchester Town Records, City Document 9, Report of the Boston Record Commissioners, No.4, 1880, p. 27. John "Whiplle" was the last of the Dorchester proprietors to sign his name to an agreement submitting to arbitration a dispute over the fencing and division of land, 79. In order to become a landowner, that is, a proprietor, John would have had to be a freeman and church member.

[18] Clarence A. Torrey, *New England Marriages Prior to 1700* (Baltimore: Genealogical Publishing Company, 1985) 803. It should not be presumed that Torrey's list is primary, accurate, or inclusive. "When a couple concluded to marry they made known their intentions to the town clerk, who posted a notice of their intended marriage in the meetinghouse. This was called being published. By law this notice had to be published three Sabbaths before the ceremony was performed…in addition to posting, the town clerk would rise in the meeting and read the intention to marry." Dow, 100. It is not known if they were married in this particular meetinghouse, which was located at the northerly end of Pleasant Street at Pond Street. This church building, one of America's oldest English churches (after Plymouth and Salem), in which the Whipples undoubtedly worshiped, was a crudely thatched small edifice with a stairway on the outside. It quickly became insufficient to meet the growing needs of the settlement.

[19] *Records of the First Church at Dorchester in New England,* 1636-1734 (Boston: George H. Ellis, 1891) 6. Eugene Aubrey Stratton, *Plymouth Colony, Its History and People* (Salt Lake: Ancestry Publishing, 1986) 213. "From yeoman on down the social scale, a man was called 'Goodman,' and a woman 'goodwife,' the latter familiarly shortened at times to 'goody'. Men above yeoman status were addressed as 'Mr.,' pronounced 'Master,' and their wives were addressed as 'Mrs.,' or 'Mistress.' A young girl coming from a higher class family would also be called 'Mrs.,' even though unmarried." Although her husband is not listed, Goodwife Whipple and eight of her nine children born in Dorchester are listed together in the name index on page 267, and on the appropriate pages, of the *Records of the 1st Church* referenced above. It is believed that the

record of John's admittance to membership was taken to Connecticut in 1635/6. "There is little hope of finding these ancient records either in Windsor or in Dorchester." xi.

[20] Shurtleff, 1:397. "In the spring of 1631…the magistrates decreed 'that for time to come noe man shalbe admitted to the freedome of this body polliticke, but such as are members of some of the churches within the lymitts of the same.'" *Records of the 1st Church at Dorchester,* iv.

[21] Thomas Bicknell, *The History of Rhode Island and Providence Plantations, 3 vols* (New York: The American Historical Society, 1920) 1:106.

[22] Perry Miller, *Orthodoxy In Massachusetts, 1630-1650* (Cambridge, Ma: Harvard University Press, 1933) 200. The children of Massachusetts church members therefore received baptism, "the seal of righteousness of faith." But it was still understood to be merely an "offer of righteousness from God"; it could not in itself make the recipients "partakers of that grace offered." Davenport-Page Controversy, Massachusetts Historical Society Proceedings XLIII: 52. Shurtleff, 2:155. "In 1646 the Cambridge Platform skirted the problem gingerly, affirming the conventional theory that only children of members were entitled to baptism…"

[23] On 24 November 1684, John Whipple Junior gave a deposition in which he stated that he was at that time 45 years old---making his birth to have occurred in 1639. ERP, XVII:53-4. Also ERP XV:231

[24] *Records of the First Church at Dorchester,* 267, Austin, 221-23. Henry E, Whipple, *A Brief Genealogy of the Whipple Families Who Settled in Rhode Island* (Providence: A. Crawford Greene, 1873). James N. Arnold, *Vital Records of Rhode Island, 1636-1850* (Providence: Narragansett Historical Publishing Company, 1892). Vital statistics of the children and grandchildren of John and Sarah Whipple are taken from the above and numerous publications that quote from them. To view more recent information consult www.whipple.org, Weldon Whipple, Webmaster. For John Junior's birth see Robert C. Anderson, *The Great Migration Begins, Immigrants to New England, 1620-1633* (Boston: NEHGS, 1995) 1972-73. The date of his birth was, "three days after his mother's baptism." The Providence children's nativity dates are estimates only. The birth of Abigail, in particular, likely occurred in Dorchester about 1657/58---the absence of a christening record resulting from the family's disfavor with church officials. James Blake, *Annals of the Town of Dorchester* (Boston: David Clapp, 1846) 1:20. "The records of Births & Deaths that was before this year [1658] is said to be accidentally burnt in Thomas Millet's house, and so are all lost, except a few Families that kept ye Account of their Childrens Births, entered them in ye next Book of ye Records of Births." Faulty memory may account for the problem with the births of John Junior and Abigail.

[25] Bicknell, 2:652. "When we remember that in English towns [Old England] there were no free schools and that reading and writing were accomplishments, obtained only at private expense, we can readily forgive the men and women, the founders of towns, who made their marks in their signatures to public documents and we may esteem those who gave us their autographs in almost unintelligible form, the privileged ones in English social life. It is evident from all we can gather that the first settlers were most anxious to give their children the rudiments of an education--that they should be able to read write, spell and cipher…"

[26] Breen, The *Character of the Good Ruler* (New York: W.W. Norton and Company, 1974) 420. The free school was established at Newport in 1640…was, so far as public records may be trusted, the first of its class in New England and possibly in the world. The only claimant for the honor that can support a worthy argument is Boston, [Dorchester] in the Bay Colony. So far as our studies extend, the Boston free school was not wholly free, while that at Newport required no fee of the pupils." Bicknell, 2:656

[27] *History of the Town of Dorchester Massachusetts,* 185.

[28] Dow, 102-104

[29] Bicknell, 2:660-61.

[30] Dow, 103

[31] Hosmer, Winthrop's Journal, 1:120, 152, 200

[32] http://www.dorchesteratheneum.org/page.php?id=82. It is the belief of some that John Whipple helped in the construction of the Pierce house on Oakten Street as well.

[33] Breen, 176-77

[34] Kuhns, 2-3.

[35] Breen 66-67, 72. *History of Dorchester,* 84.

[36]Henry C. Dorr, *The Proprietors of Providence, and Their Controversies With The Freeholders,* Collections of the Rhode Island Historical Society, vol. 6 (Providence: The Society, 1897). 58-59. "The earlier records (of

Providence) contain allusions to brawls and disturbances…and even to outbreaks, may charitably be ascribed to inexperience. In Massachusetts, none but members of Puritan parishes were voters…The graduates of the English Cambridge and of the American Harvard exacted the deference of the uneducated men, and those who did not yield it had small opportunity of a hearing in town meetings. These were ruled by the fortunate possessors of wealth, culture and sanctity, and a man of humble station had small opportunity to acquire political experience. When some of these withdrew to Mooshassuc it is not surprising that they lacked self-control in matters where their interests or their passions were concerned. The Legislature of Massachusetts was open only to the elect, and magistrates and elders permitted little adverse debate in parish meetings. The future rulers of Providence were left to pick up their political education in the rough school of experience. They did do but slowly in the first generation at Mooshassuc."

[37] William Orcutt, *Good Old Dorchester, 1630-1893* (Cambridge: University Press, 1893) 60-61.

[38] *New England Historical and Genealogical Society Record*, Vol. 6, 1852, p 41.

[39] James Savage, "History of Dorchester in the County of Dorset" 61-66, as quoted in *New England Historic Genealogical Society Register*, Volume 5 October 1851.

[40] Robert C. Anderson, *The Great Migration Begins, Immigrants to New England, 1620-1633*. 3 vols. (Boston: New England Historical and Genealogical Society, 1995) 3:1974

[41] Irving B. Richman, *Rhode Island, Its Making and Meaning* (New York: B.P. Putnam Sons, 1908) 292. In 1655, Providence had 42 freemen, Newport 96.

[42] Clifford Monahon, *Rhode Island: A Students' Guide to Localized History* (New York: Columbia University Press, 1965) 1. "The State of Rhode Island and Providence Plantations has a total area of 1214 square miles, of which 1058 are land and 156 inland water." Providence Plantations encompasses approximately 350 square miles most of which can be "used for small farms, dairy farms, poultry raising, and orchards, while the submarginal hilltops are suited only for the growth of timber." Six of the eight sons of Captain John Whipple subsisted on farms such as the above.

[43] Roger Williams wrote that in deference to John Smith, the miller, a resident of Dorchester (and John Whipple's oldest daughter's eventual father-in-law), he allowed another Dorchesterite a destitute boy named Francis Wickes to escape from Massachusetts with them. Perhaps Wickes, whose property Captain John eventually bought in Providence, was a fellow apprentice.

[44] Assuming the move took place in late 1658 or early 1659, the ages of the children at that time were: John 19, Sarah 17, Samuel 15, Eleazer 13, Mary 11, William 7, Benjamin 5, David 3, and Abigail 1.

[45] Edward Johnson, *Wonder-Working Providences* (London: 1654), 41

[46] Bicknell, 1:230-31.

[47] William B. Weeden, *Early Rhode Island, A Social History of the People, 1636-1790* (New York: The Grafton Press, 1910) 74. "They (Providence residents) framed the solid chests and tables, rude but strong, which stood on sanded floors." Welcome Arnold Greene, The *Providence Plantations for Two Hundred and Fifty Years*, 1886) 35.

[48] Florence Simister, *Streets of the City, An Anecdotal History of the City of Providence* (Providence: Mowbray Company Publishers, 1968) 47. "For over a century after it was founded, Providence really had only one street…" Henry C. Dorr, *The Planting and Growth of Providence. Rider's Tract #15* (Providence: Sidney S. Rider, 1882) 86. "The town street was continually flooded by currents of rain or melting snow from the abrupt hill side…At length, on the 4th of the 12th month in 1649, the town council ordered that every man shall mend and make good the highway before his house lot or lots…This is the earliest regulation of Providence streets. The duty of repairing them must have been but negligently performed…The Legislature granted a lottery in February 1761 for the first pavement of Town Street." Since John owned at least four lots on a steep incline of the street, his would have been a demanding obligation. One of John's last entries in colony records, 1682, concerned a law against galloping horses in front of his property. This was the first law in Rhode Island concerning traffic. Gertrude Kimball, *Providence in Colonial Times* (Boston: Houghton Mifflin Company, 1912) 123. "The Town Street was becoming so heavily traveled that in the same year the General Assembly enacted the first traffic regulation, forbidding riding a gallup on horse, gelding or mare, in the street lying against the great river…between the land of Pardon Tillinghast, and the northerly corner of John Whipple, Sen'r, where his dwelling house stands in the north end, under penalty of a fine of five shillings for each offense." John R. Bartlett, ed., *Records of the Colony of Rhode Island and Providence Plantations in New England* (Providence, 1856-1865) III:105

36

[49] Dorr, Rider's tract #15, 8. "Providence did not grow up around a Puritan meeting house as their center with the common graveyard, and separateness and independence showed themselves, even in the resting places of the dead. Nearly a century went by before the first steeple [Anglican] arose above the town." Baptists and Quakers held religious services in "house churches" until the early 1700s.

[50] Dorr, Rider's Tract #15, 98.

[51] Named in honor of Captain John's oldest daughter's husband and father-in-law. Bicknell, 3:383.

[52] Dorr, Rider's Tract #15, 57, 64. "In 1658, a year of scarcity and trouble, 'all commodities were drawn from the neighboring colonies, except produce.' There was no grain save Indian corn, and the vengeful Puritans of Massachusetts threatened to combine, and to sell that at their own rates. This was the year in which Rhode Island refused the demand of the United Colonies for the expulsion of the Quakers." Actually, there were at least one physician and three ordained ministers, plus some who had studied law among the "first comers."

[53] Dorr, Rider's Tract 15, 135. Fifty-two (or 54) original proprietor families were each assigned about 125 feet of land along Towne Street. By the late 1650s only half of these families had built houses on their properties, yet were still hesitant to sell to outsiders.

[54] Dorr, vol. 9, 11. Its citizens feared that Bay authorities were trying to take over by immigration.

[55] William G. Mcloughlin, *Rhode Island, A Bicentennial History* (New York: W.W. Norton & Company, 1978) 10

[56] Irving B. Richman, *Rhode Island, A Study in Separatism* (Boston: Houghton Mifflin and Company, 1905) 61.

[57] Richman, 159

[58] Genealogies of Rhode Island Families, (Baltimore: Genealogical Publishing Company, 1983) 2:414-15.

[59] Carl Holliday, *Woman's Life in Colonial Days* (New York: Frederick Ungar Publishing Company, 1922) 108.

[60] Dorr, vol. 9, 40. Providence leaders were worried that Massachusetts was trying to gain control by infiltrating their midst. "What could not be done by force might be effected by emigration."

[61] Dorr, vol. 9, 46. John's apprenticeship had ended by 1637. He sold approximately 43 acres of land in Dorchester, and bought over 200 acres in Providence, for £180, from the colony's longtime governor. This could have been partly the result of the difference in land values in the two towns. Bicknell, 1:206. "Males, married, heads of families, were the only persons eligible to membership to be elected by a majority vote of the whole body--after a name had been propounded for one month. Land could not be resold without consent of the land company (proprietors)."

[62] Dorr, Tract #15 67. The town tried to borrow a carpenter from Warwick in 1654.

[63] *ERP*, III:59. Dorr, (Tract #15) 68.

[64] Clara H. McGuigan, *The Antecedents and Descendants of Noah Whipple of the Rogerene Community at Quakertown, Connecticut* (Ithaca, New York: John N. Kingsbury, 1971) 36. The author contends that both of Samuel Whipple Junior's grandfathers, namely John Whipple and Thomas Harris, were non-conformists, and had removed to Rhode Island to escape persecution in Massachusetts. It is proven that Harris was a persecuted Quaker, however, only circumstantial evidence is available to show that John Whipple was as well

[65] An exception being a small settlement of Quakers on the east end of Long Island, New York.

[66] Carl Bridenbaugh, *Fat Mutton and Liberty of Conscience, Society in Rhode Island, 1636-1690* (Providence: Brown University Press, 1974) 4

[67] John could have been a member of the church doctrinally in good standing, yet have rejected the high handedness of the magistrates. Had this been the case, the Whipples likely would have moved (like their Dorchester neighbors of 1635/36) to Connecticut, which would have permitted them to maintain their Massachusetts religious beliefs yet be free from Massachusetts authorities. It was 1722 before a Congregational Church was started in Providence.

[68] McLoughlin, 23. "John Clark wrote the first tract by an American defending the Baptist persuasion and was the first Baptist to take a missionary trip into Massachusetts Bay (in 1652) to spread that persuasion (for which he narrowly escaped whipping)." Winthrop's Journal, 2:177. If John Whipple and family had been Baptist at that time they likely would have left in November of 1644 when Massachusetts ordered the banishment of all Anababtists. This 1644 law was most unpopular in England. The civil war in England, in which two-thirds of Cromwell's army were Separatists (i.e.) non Church of England or Puritan, created an unheard of tolerance for religious diversity. "Massachusetts replied to these criticisms by gathering her holy

skirts closer about her heels and proceeding on her unlovely way alone. From this time forth the colony turned aside from the main currents of English opinion…. Thus did the New England orthodoxy turn its back upon the greatest single religious advance of modern times, and exert itself to avoid making innovations in its thinking." See Chapter 8 in Miller. That is, for the next 25 years it became even more determined to weed out all non-Puritan elements in its citizenry, and the Quakers, who were in the wrong place at the wrong time, were the first to feel its wrath. "The first Baptist church to start in Massachusetts was at Rehoboth near the Rhode Island border in 1663." Bicknell 2:585.

[69] Edward Field, State *of Rhode Island and Providence Plantations at the End of the Century: A History* (Boston: Mason Publishing Company, 1902) 83. "While a considerable number of earnest Christian men and women joined Mr. Williams in the formation of the first church it is evident that a very much larger number of residents at Providence held themselves entirely aloof. It must thus be explained why the general religious condition of the State was, in early times, somewhat low and why traces of that chartered irreligion, which perfect liberty of conscience to a degree encouraged in certain sections, still subsist." Bruce C. Daniels, *Dissent and Conformity on Narragansett Bay* (Middleton, Connecticut: Wesleyan University Press, 1983) 111. "After the initial four settlements founded prior to 1663, some settlers were still attracted to Rhode Island by its dissent but many more New Englanders came for economic opportunities. Several areas of Rhode Island were settled by people who did not particularly care whether they were in Massachusetts, Connecticut, or Rhode Island as long as they had clear title to their land…" Dorr, vol. 9, "The majority manifested little sympathy with Williams…No religious society was organized until the autumn of 1638. Out of nearly sixty householders only twelve united with Williams in its formation. During the whole of the seventeenth century, its members were a small minority of the townsmen and numbered so few adherents that they met in the small dwellings of those days…"

[70] Wilfred H. Munro, *Picturesque Rhode Island* (Providence: J.A. & R.A. Reid, Publishers, 1881) 146.

[71] Bicknell, 3:1017.

[72] Mcloughlin, 27

[73] McLoughlin, 36

[74] Richman, *Rhode Island Its Making and Meaning,* 216

[75] Rufus M. Jones, *The Quakers in the American Colonies* (New York: W.W. Norton & Company, 1966) 70. Also page 81. His brother, William Harris, a close friend and John Whipple Junior's tutor for the profession of law, became a Quaker after Fox's visit to Rhode Island in 1672.

[76] Richman, *Rhode Island, Its Making and Meaning,* 351. Mcloughlin, 36. Beginning in October 1656, Massachusetts passed the first of a series of laws inflicting harsh penalties on Quaker and Quaker sympathizers. Starting with imprisonment, fines, and banishment, these laws subsequently included whipping, branding, ear cropping, and tongue boring. The final step, in 1658, was a law ordering death by hanging.

[77] Suffolk Land Records, Deeds, 14 vols. (Boston: 1880-1906) 3:204-05. Minot, a native of Safron Walden, Essex, England, was born 4 August 1594, and died in Dorchester 24 December 1671. He was a deputy 1635-36, one of the first signers of the church covenant in 1636, and a ruling elder for 30 years. He gave the Whipple property to his 32-year old son John. *History of the Town of Dorchester,* 67.

[78] www.usigs.org/libry/books/ma/braintree1879brntr-05htm

[79] ERP, II:11 & XV:127. "Att a Quarter Court July the 27th 1659 Mr. Ffeild moderator. This Day John Whipple Senior: is received into the Towne a purchaser." By this date, all purchasers were freemen so John automatically assumed that status. Dorr, 40. John's next-door neighbor's friend, Mary Dyer, was likewise hanged in Boston in 1660.

[80] Henry King does not mention the Whipple family in his history of the First Baptist Church. Henry M. King, *Historical Catalogue of the Members of the First Baptist Church in Providence, Rhode Island* (Providence, F.H. Townsend, Printer, 1908). "…Unfortunately, there are no minutes or records of First Baptist Church Prior to 1755. The first Whipple that appears on our membership lists (1764) was Bethiah Whipple, wife of John Whipple (the second son of Benjamin who was the fifth son of Capt. John Whipple)… Rarely did Baptist churches keep any records in the 17th century. They were small congregations and had no associations to report to." Email to the authors from J. Stanley Lemons, professor at Rhode Island College and historian for the First Baptist Church, 25 May 2004.

[81] McGuigan, 28. It must be recalled that Williams was a Baptist for only four months. His religion could be described in modern parlance as fundamentalist but "non-denominational." Later in life, he did not

38

require that adults be rebaptized. John Callender, *The Early History of Rhode Island* (Freeport, NY: Books for Libraries Press, 1843) 31. "Not withstanding so many differences, there are fewer quarrels about religion than elsewhere, the people living peaceably with their neighbors of whatsoever persuasion. They all agree in one point, that the church of England is second best." On page 110 Callender argues rather convincingly that Williams never joined the Baptist church at Providence. For a different opinion of Williams' conversion see, Richard Knight, *History of the General or Six Principle Baptist Church* (Providence: Smith and Parmenter, 1827) 255.

[82] John Junior's second wife was a Quaker, as were the spouses of Sarah and perhaps the second spouse of Abigail. Samuel's in-laws were likewise Quakers, as were those of Joseph Junior. Thomas Senior, son of Samuel, married a sister of Governor Jenckes. Eleazer's oldest daughter, Deborah, married into the prominent Wilkinson family of Quakers.

[83] "John Whipple on the Baptist Church," Rhode Island Historical Society Manuscripts, 10:35. "I found the folder for this letter in the Historical Society Library, but nothing was in it but a Warwick deed between two parties. I had the same problem last year. The technician and I checked the cross-references. They were all for the same folder, so the reference was correct. The librarian stated that the letter is either lost or misplaced." Personal observation of Barbara Carroll, 5 March 2004. "Probably the John Whipple who wrote this letter was admitted to the church on July 11, 1790. But, he was expelled from the church on August 26, 1808 for 'quarrelling with Wheeler Martin.' Martin was the chief judge of the Court of Common pleas in Providence." Email to the authors from J. Stanley Lemons, professor at Rhode Island College and historian for the First Baptist Church, 25, May 2004. Mark S. Schantz, *Piety in Providence: Class Dimensions of Religious Experience in Antebellum Rhode Island* (Ithaca, NY: Cornell University Press, 2000) 31. Record Book, First Baptist Church, August 26, 1708, Manuscript Collection, Rhode Island Historical Society. "The church did not countenance instances of assault on gentlemen."

[84] Representative Men and Old Families of Rhode Island, 3 vols. (Chicago: J.HJ. Beers and Company, 1908) III:1639. "He was received as a preacher at Providence in 1659..."

[85] Mcloughlin, 46. The Providence Baptist fellowship operated without a formal creed. During its first 75 years services were held in member's homes and under the trees in good weather. Its first meetinghouse was constructed in 1701. Rhode Island Quakers followed the Baptist in this regard. Fox complained in 1672 that Rhode Island Quakers did not have adequate places to worship.

[86] Dorr, vol. 9, 60. The Whipples did not marry into the Williams family for at least three generations.

[87] *ERP*, III:98-100. Charles W. Hopkins, *The Home Lots of the Early Settlers of the Providence Plantations* (Providence: Providence Press Publishers, 1886) 24.

[88] *ERP*, XX:281-284. Bicknell, 1:183.The 1663 document deeded to John Junior included the William Arnold lot with its apparent very expensive price tag. The first tax ever levied in Providence occurred in 1650 shows that Arnold was assessed a property tax of five pounds, by far the most of any lot owner. John Junior's son, John III, subsequently sold the property to his uncle Colonel Joseph Whipple, who in 1726 traded with a son-in-law, Stephen Dexter, for an additional three lots—Thomas James, John Greene Senior, and John Smith—immediately to the south of the Arnold lot. The Colonel's oldest son, Captain John Whipple, in 1738, bought from the heirs of Thomas Arnold the two house lots that had long been unoccupied on the north side of the 1661 purchase, which had originally been laid out in 1638 to Thomas Painter and Edward Manton. By this last purchase, Colonel Joseph and his son became the owners of nine consecutive house lots along Town Street that extended from about 100 feet of the top of Constitution Hill to within 150 feet or Roger Williams' fresh water spring. In addition to these, in 1728, the Whipples bought three lots toward the southerly end of the street, those of William Mann, William Burrows, and William Wickenden. By the time of Colonel Joseph Whipple's death in 1746, between 70 and 80 acres in the heart of the town were in the possession of one man and his son. Each lot granted the owner an additional six acres of farmland, thus the Whipples owned over 150 acres of highly coveted property. Hundreds of other acres were owned by them in the northern and central parts of the colony.

[89] John H. Cady, *The Civic and Architectural Development of Providence, 1636-1950* (Providence: The Book Shop, 1957) 11. The house could have been unoccupied since 1651. "Benedict Arnold paid the highest town rate and probably enlarged or rebuilt his father's house on the present Constitution Hill when he returned to Providence from Pawtuxet after his marriage. He lived there until 1651 when he moved to Newport, later becoming governor of the colony." Arnold was elected governor for the years 1657-58-59-60-62-63. It was

in 1661, the year he was not governor, that he sold his land to John. Captain John Whipple was first to build a house, next door on the former Wickes property, sometime before 1663.

[90] Dorr, Rider's Tract #15, 40

[91] In June of 2004, the present author measured the inclination of that part of the hill that was enclosed by John's property lines. Given that its topography has changed in 350 years, much of the incline still climbs almost straight up; the rest varies between 45 degrees and 60 degrees extending up the hill for over a quarter of a mile where it levels off toward Hope Street. It is indeed an understatement to describe it as a "steep" hill. Then as now it is fit for logging and orchards only. It is clear why John bought the property at such a cheap price. At present, houses standing on precarious ledges, most man-made, completely cover the hillside much in the fashion of Southern California—and nowhere is an orchard or corn stalk to be seen.

[92] Bicknell, 1:183. "During the life of [Roger] Williams, two men by their executive ability and personal influence ruled the proprietary as well as the town---William Harris and Thomas Olney, and at the death of both, the power was vested in the popular leader and town-proprietary clerk, Thomas Olney Jr." By marrying into these powerful families, the Whipples automatically became influential themselves.

[93] ERP, XV:127. "About ye middle of nouember, in the yeare 1660, Laid out unto John Whipple Senior, at the place Called Loquasqussuck: by William Carpenter Towne Deputye…"

[94] Publications of the Rhode Island Historical Society, New Series (Providence: Standard Printing Company, 1893-1900) V:127. "…to the west of Eleazer's farm on the cross road to 'Martin's Wade' was his son-in-law John Wilkinson's [husband of Deborah] farm. To the south of the Whipple and Wilkinson farms were those of William Whipple [Captain John's fourth son] and Stephen Dexter [first husband of Abigail Whipple]. Still farther south was the farm of Col. Sylvanus Scott [John Whipple Junior's stepson], which later became the home of David Whipple [Captain John's sixth son]. All these Whipples were the brothers of Col. Joseph Whipple [Captain John's seventh son], the early and most liberal of the founders of King's Church. West of Col. Scott was Eleazer Arnold [brother-in-law of Sarah Whipple Smith Arnold], while still further to the west was land of Samuel Whipple [Captain John's second son]."

[95] ERP, III:26

[96] ERP, III:72

[97] ERP, XV:115

[98] ERP, III:88

[99] ERP, IV:46

[100] ERP, IV:47

[101] ERP, IV:18

[102] ERP, III:9

[103] ERP, VIII:98. William and Benedict Arnold left the settlement early on and moved to the Pawtuxet. Benedict moved to Newport and served several years as governor of the colony.

[104] Samuel H. Brockunier, The Irrepressible Democrat: Roger Williams (New York: Ronald Press, 1940) 130.

[105] Simister, 21. "It was first changed from a path to a street in 1704, its width, 4 poles, its name to Towne Street." The hurricane of 1938 severely damaged the 369 N. Main (and adjacent) property.

[106] Whipple Hall was located about one block north of Star Street on Benefit Street. See the chapter on Joseph Whipple for details.

[107] ERP, I:8. Clemence's son, Richard, married Sarah Smith daughter of Sarah Whipple-Smith, Captain John's oldest daughter. Austin, Genealogical Dictionary, 382-83. ERP, XVII:25. He exchanged 20 acres of land with Joseph Whipple in 1685.

[108] ERP, II:144

[109] ERP, III:4 & III:47

[110] ERP, III:98-100. In a letter to the authors dated 5 August 2004, the Rhode Island Historical Society denied its permission to show John's signature on the Internet. His signature can be shown in book form only. Rhode Island Historical Society Manuscript, MSS #9003, 1:12.

[111] ERP, XV:109-10

[112] ERP, III:110

[113] ERP, III:591

[114] Bicknell, 3:887

115 Dorr, Rider's Tract #15, 184. Charles H. Whipple, *Genealogy of the Whipple-Wright, Wager, Ward-Pell, McLean-Burnet Families* (Privately Published, 1917) 12. McGuigan, 289. Samuel G. Arnold, *History of the State of Rhode Island and Providence Plantations* 2 vols. (New York: Appleton & Company, 1859) 1:523. "The regular session was held at Providence at the house of John Whipple [Junior]. The smallpox had broken out with great violence upon the island. The whole affairs of the colony were deranged by the prevailing sickness, and no business of general interest was transacted by the Assembly. So virulent was this formidable plague...that a letter from Boston written during the winter, says, 'Rhode Island is almost destroyed by the smallpox'. Newport was abandoned by the legislature for nearly a year."

116 *ERP*, III:148 & III:152.

117 *ERP*, VII:5-6. John Junior, for unknown reasons, refused a request to establish an inn the year before. It is doubtful that he would have started his own tavern had his father disapproved or was still in the business himself.

118 *ERP*, IV:8. Bicknell, 1:215. "In April, 1674, John Whipple, tavern-keeper was paid 'one shilen for house rent.' The Whipple tavern was central and seems to have been a favorite for town meetings."

119 Kimball, 127. Dorr, 182."In the early days very few travelers came to Providence. During two generations, all strangers were received in private houses---the most important, or those entrusted with public business---by Williams himself, or by Thomas Olney, the town clerk. After inns were duly licensed (in 1655) the reception of wayfarers was scarcely their chief employment.

120 Kimball, 128. Weeden, 221. Joseph renewed his license as late as 1732. Although confirming records have yet to be evidenced, it is believed that John III sold his father's tavern to his uncle Joseph sometime in the fall of 1710.

121 Richard M. Bayles, ed., *The History of Providence County, Rhode Island, 2 vols.* (New York: W.W. Preston and Company, 1891) 1:305.

122 John W. Haley, Old *Stone Bank, History of Rhode Island, 4 vols* (Providence: Providence Institution for Savings, 1931) II:92-93.

123 John H. Cady, *The Civic and Architectural Development of Providence 1636-1950* (Providence: The Book Shop, 1957) 15. A year 1700 map, on page 14, shows three taverns in Providence, those of Whipple, half way up Constitution Hill, Olney's, on the corner of Town Street and Olney Street [about two blocks northeast of Whipple's], and Turpin [about three blocks north of Olney's]. On a 1750 map in the same book, page 27, only the Olney and Turpin taverns remain. This author, like all others, seems not to differentiate between the John Senior and John Junior taverns. It appears that Joseph Whipple left the business around the year 1740.

124 Barbara Mills, *Providence: 1630-1800, Women Are Part of Its History* (Bowie, Md: Heritage Books, 2002) 79-80.

125 *Publications of the Rhode Island Historical Society, New Series,* III: 228. John Whipple Senior did not own a tavern in the late 1660s when the letters were written, so the dissemination argument is ill chosen. Dorr, vol. 6, 46. He was not alive in 1690.

126 Glen W. LaFantasie, ed., *The Correspondence of Roger Williams* (Providence: Brown University Press/University Press of New England, 1988) II: 603-604. Typical of the respect that early historians paid to John Whipple is seen in a lengthy paragraph from an 1897 book. It likewise does not differentiate between John Senior and Junior. Dorr, vol. 6, 81. The confusion that it, and similar earlier accounts, created is with us still.

127 Bicknell, 1:218. Differences soon arose between Williams and his associates in the corporation as to an extension of the territorial bounds...Williams held to the four-mile limit...and opposed any further extension. Had his policy been pursued, Providence in its narrow territorial domain [four square miles] would have lost existence to Massachusetts or Connecticut."

128 Bicknell, 1:181. "William Harris and Thomas Olney, clerk, were leaders of the landed class, while Mr. Williams was the head of the 'down-and-out' party... Mr. Williams had neither constructive, executive or diplomatic ability, while Harris and Olney had all these qualities. Then again, Mr. Williams had withdrawn after four months...from the society called Baptists and had thereby lost his influence as a religious teacher and guide...As late as 1669, Mr. Williams appeals to the land aristocracy in behalf of those who do not and others who will not come to town meetings, but the fact remains that the men of property, the proprietors, were able and organized and retained their control of town affairs during their lives and left

41

their heritage of wealth and power to their successors." As shown, the Whipples by marrying into these leading families shared in this largess.

[129] Williams had his own personality problems. "Historians urge that he (Roger Williams) was eccentric, pugnacious, persistent, troublesome; undoubtedly he was." Bicknell, 1:231. Dorr, vol. 6, 10-11. "The founder (Williams) and many of his associates had not much in common...His followers did not share his unselfish purposes. Their experience of the abuse of power in Massachusetts had made them impatient of all authority whatsoever...and provided homesteads only for themselves. The majority manifested little sympathy with Williams, except in his negative opinion as to what the State should not do."

[130] Harris and his allies received most of the shares supposedly at the expense of the rest of the plantation. John Junior's descendants in particular shared in this largess. A more in-depth analysis of this conflict is presented in the chapter on John Whipple Junior.

[131] ERP, 1670, III:150; 1674, IV:1; & 1676, VIII:11 & XV:149

[132] A list of the 27 names of such as stajd & went not away is given in the ERP, XV:151-52.

[133] George W. Greene, A Short History of Rhode Island (Providence: J. A. Reid Publishers, 1877) 75

[134] ERP, VIII:12. Welcome Arnold Greene, 42 & 99. "There were two houses in Providence deemed capable of serving as garrison houses. One was the fort whose erection on Stamper's Hill [across the street north from Capt. John's house]...and of this Roger Williams, who was captain of the train band, took command with a portion of the townsmen who remained. The other was that of William Field, near the present foot of Hopkins Street, where Captain Arthur Fenner with the other remaining men were posted...there appears to have been no actual attack upon either of the garrisoned houses...Exactly what was the number of houses destroyed cannot be determined. One account says all but five...At the time of King Philips War, 28 are recorded as 'men who staid and went not away,' others are known to have stayed..." Collections of the Rhode Island Historical Society (Providence: Knowles and Vose Printers, 1843) 103-07. During the attack on the town, the town records were thrown into the millpond--by John Smith and Sarah Whipple Smith-- to extinguish their burning. Later on John Whipple Junior was commissioned to find out how many pages were missing. The account enumerated a list several pages in length. Sixty-five leaves were missing from Book 1 and twenty from Book 2. Surely, much more would be known about the Whipples had the war not happened.

[135] ERP, XV:153

[136] Charles H. Whipple, 11. According to John O. Austin, 221, John was a deputy in 1676, 69, 70, 72, 74, 76, & 77. A different account lists his years of service as 1666,74, & 76. Rhode Island Historical Society Collections, 1918--1941, 2:645-49. John Whipple Junior's service as a deputy and assistant is usually given as the reason for the confusion. He also served as the town's treasurer in 1668 and in 1683. Bicknell, 2:642-43. "The Colonial officers were a Governor, a Deputy Governor and ten Assistants. These with sixteen deputies elected by the towns constituted the lawmaking power, styled in the charter, The General Assembly...The General Assembly met twice a year, in May and October.. .On the 6th of May, 1696, the Deputies voted to sit by themselves as a House of Deputies, choosing their own Speaker and Clerk, and the General Assembly thereafter met in two bodies, the Governor, the Deputy and Assistants constituting the Upper House, and the representatives of the towns, the House of Deputies or the Lower House. Col. Rec., p.313, Vol. III."

[137] Horatio Rogers, George Moulton Carpenter and Edward Field, Record Commissioners. The Early Records of the Town of Providence, Volume 6, Being Part of the Will, Book Number 1, otherwise called the First Book for Providence Towne Council Perticulior Vse. (Providence: Snow and Farnham, City printers, 1894) VI:126-128. ERP, VI:126-28. See Chapter 7 for a discussion of a flaw in this will.

[138] ERP, VI: 128-30

[139] ERP, VI:130-34

[140] He had perhaps been living with his oldest son for sometime by then. Volume IV of the Early Records of the Town of Providence provides interesting reading for those desiring to know about the private property of "city people" in the time of Roger Williams. Captain John's wearing apparel was valued at £2. Bicknell, 1:152.

[141] ERP, VI:130-134

[142] Dorr, 25

[143] 369 North Main Street, Providence, Rhode Island photo, circa 1912, Preston Collection, Rhode Island State Archives, 337 Westminster Street, Providence, Rhode Island 02903.

[144] Dorr, 44, 46. Jones 573.

[145] Weeden, 129.

[146] W. R. Staples, *Annals of the Town of Providence* (Providence: Knowles and Vose, 1843) 184.

[147] John E. Sterling, *North Burial Ground, Providence, Rhode Island, Old Section, 1700-1848* (Providence: Rhode Island Genealogical Society, Special Publication #5, 2000) xii.

[148] Welcome Arnold Greene, 53. "A street in the rear of the town street was advocated as early as in 1743, but such a street would run through all the ancestral burial grounds of the home-lot owners, and their souls rebelled against the proposition. After a stubborn contest, in February 1747, a committee was appointed to 'inspect and examine the land whether it was convenient to lay the new street' to be call 'Back Street' or Benefit Street…the street was ordered in 1747, but the land-owners contested so persistently against it that it was not finished till 1756, and its extension northward to the town street at the head of Constitution Hill was not made till 1758, and then only on condition that a gate be kept up at the north end. This gate was retained for half a century…"

[149] Sterling, xii.

[150] An Account of the Temple Family," New England Historical and Genealogical Register, Vol. 10, January 1856.

[151] Henry E. Whipple, 40

[152] Sterling, 12-13. The 27 burials are as follows: (1) In Memory of Capt. John Whipple first Son of Col. Joseph Whipple who departed this life the 18th of May died 1769 aged 84 years 5 mos & 19 days, (2) In Memory of ye Hon Col. Joseph Whipple who departed this life anno dom 1746 in ye 85th year of his age, (3) In Memory of Mrs. Alice Whipple ye wife of Col. Joseph Whipple born in Providence and died July 20th anno dom 1739 aged 75 years, (4) Jeremiah son of Capt. John Whipple & Abigail his wife died Jan 2d 1731 aged 14 mos 23 days, (5) In memory of Mary wife of Capt Charles Bardin youngest daughter of Col. Joseph Whipple died Dec 8 1733 aged 29 years & 8 mos, (6)In Memory of Capt John Whipple who was born in England & died in Providence town 16th day of May anno dom 1685 about 68 years of age, (7) In memory of Mrs Sarah Whipple wife of Capt John Whipple she was born in Dorchester in New England died in Providence anno dom 1666 aged about 42 years, (8) In memory of Capt William Whipple a Revolutionary Purist who died on the 5th of July. Suppress not your tears. This is a soldiers grave, (9) In memory of Mrs. Abigail Whipple wife of William Whipple who died Nov 16 1818 age 64 years, (10) Miss Susannah Whipple daughter of Joseph & Sarah 27 May 1797 in 23 year of her age, (11) Mrs Mary Olney wife of Capt Stephan Olney daughter of Josf Whipple died May 24 1798 age 27 years 4 mos, (12) Miss Freelove Whipple daughter of Joseph died Dec 4 1798 age 30 years 5 days, (13) Miss Mehitable daughter of Joseph Whipple died 3 Feb 1799 aged 17 years 11 mos, (14) Miss Elizabeth daughter of Joseph Whipple Esq. & Sara his wife who expired Feb 27 1800 age 21 years 3 mos 2 days, (15) In memory of Amy Hurd Wife of Ambose Hurd & daughter of Joseph Whipple died 17 Jan 1803 42 years & 19 days, (16) In memory of Miss Hatty Whipple Hurd adopted daughter of Gen John Whipple & Naomi his wife who died May 3 1827 in her 26th year, (17) In memory of Joseph Whipple, Veteran of the Revolutionary War, died Jan 6 1816 age 82, (18) In memory of Sara Whipple wife of Joseph Whipple died Apr 20 1820 age 85 years, (19) In memory of Mrs Abigail Jastram relic of Mr. John Jastram & daughter of late Joseph and Sara Whipple of Smithfield. She died June 31 1841 in her 83d year, (20) In memory of Gen John Whipple, veteran of the Revolutionary War, 21 Dec 1811, (21) In memory of Mrs Naomi Whipple relict of Gen John Whipple who died Feb 18 1837 in the 83d year of her life, (22) In memory of Pardon Whipple, Lieut, son of William, USN Veteran c1791-11 May 1827, (23) In memory of Hannah Whipple wife of Samuel, c1819-27 Jan 1892, (24) In Memory of Samuel Whipple Veteran of Revolutionary War, c1758-17 Oct 1809, (25) In memory of Deborah Whipple wife of Samuel c1757-1 Nov 1831, (26) In memory of Joanna Whipple 2d daughter of Samuel c1781-22 Oct 1784, (27) In Memory of Joanna Whipple daughter of Samuel and Deborah c1796-26 Aug 1832. Some of these headstones are no longer legible. The authors were unable to find either headstone number 23 in June 2004, nor number 23's relationship to the family. Also, headstone number 22, a box tomb, was found to be next to Sarah Whipple wife of Capt. John. At least five burial plots, scattered out among the Whipple headstones, are unused or the headstones long since have disappeared. All the headstones are in immediate need of repair.

[153] www.whipple.org/blaine/johnswife.html. "It is obvious that the information on Sarah is unreliable, and there is no way to know if the information on John is correct." There had been small, organized bands of Caucasians (primarily male fishermen) living in and around the later to-be-named Massachusetts Bay area

immediately before and after the settlement of Plymouth in 1620. The numbers were so infinitesimal, however, as to obviate a significant probability that Sarah had been born there. Blake, *Annals of Dorchester*, 77-78. More likely, since the Whipples had lived in Dorchester most of her adult life, those who had her gravestone carved naively assumed it to have been her place of birth.

[154] Dorr, 222. "By the fourth generation they sought to preserve the memory of their English lineage. There was, until late in the century, but little encouragement of such workmanship in the Plantations. The earliest headstones must have been wrought in Boston or Newport. They were made here by the middle of the century. These were probably all of Braintree slate, so enduring and so plainly sculptured, which abound in the old section of the North Burial Ground. But by 1760, there were monuments which might compare with sculptured stones which an earlier generation had imported from England. So late as 1796, the earliest marble slabs of no extraordinary pretension were ordered from Attleborough." The Whipple headstones are made of Braintree slate.

[155] Photographs from Kenneth Carlson, reference archivist, to Charles Whipple 16 September 2005; held in 2005 by Dr. Charles Whipple, 327 Sundance, Edmond, Ok. Three sixty nine North Main Street, Providence, RI, photos circa 1912, Preston Collection, Rhode Island State Archives, 337 Westminster Street, Providence Rhode Island, 02903. "I walked into the State Archives today [17 August 2005] on a different case, and staring me in the face were photographs of the 300 block of North Main Street. As you know, I've been searching for 369 for the past three years. Perhaps chance does favor the prepared mind. The archives staff is putting together a new photo display--Providence about 1912. They have them all in their Preston Collection, the contents of which I was unaware since these particular photos are unindexed. Just about every building on the block was in these photographs. In 1912, all this was a Jewish neighborhood. Much of the area was torn down as part of urban renewal from the 1930s to the '50s." Barbara Carroll, personal communication 18 August 2005. The Providence Preservation Society was chartered in the mid 1950s to preserve historic properties; however, it was too late for Captain John's home, for centuries the oldest house in Providence.

A close up look at the sign (in five lines) over the front door of 369 reads: 369 Providence 369, Remnant Store, Dry and fancy Goods, Remnants Direct From the Factory, B.F. Rosen. The windows show tablecloths, towels, headscarves, sheets, etc. with an unreadable sign on the right. The retaining wall is badly deteriorated and crumbling. It appears to be several decades old. As previously shown, in the Captain's day the house was but a story and a half. Obviously, the city dug out several feet of soil when it enlarged the street right up next to the houses. As a result, some owners apparently created basement "mom and pop" stores. This reveals that in the Captain's time, his house was several feet (yards?) from the original street, as well as several feet up an incline.

The second photograph is a panoramic looking north from Star Street [ascending on the right] where Whipple Hall had been located, and Mill Street [now Charles] Street to the left where John Jr. and Joseph had their Inns, and Sarah's mill was located. Captain John's house is the sixth up the right side of the street. The first five houses north from Star Street are newer additions with their doors leading directly on to the street. Captain John's house is the first one where the roof faces the camera, that is, south. Its front door, as it always had, opens to the south with the house oriented east/west, and looks like a house, whereas the others look like apartment buildings. Records show that the building next to 369 was a plumbing supply, then a grocery, a store front synagogue or Jewish reading room, bakery, barber shop, then at 327 N. Main (on the corner) was the Lee Sing laundry. Main appeared to be paved with cobblestones, with cable car tracts traversing Main and Mill streets. One can now understand why the city had to dig out the street so close to the old houses on the right (Captain John's and northward); it was to build houses on the left side of the street. There is a sheer drop off of from a few feet up to about 60 feet to the left of the left row of houses as Main ascends around the corner to the northeast to the top of the hill. The 2004 photograph shows that the left row of houses was not rebuilt. It is not likely that that row was there during Captain John's lifetime. His house would have been located where the seventh or eighth condominium is now standing. What a pronounced contrast the 2004 photograph reveals of this area. It was taken just outside the front door of the Roger Williams Tourist Information Center. The 1912 photo looks to have been taken about 25 or 30 yards to the northeast out into the intersection of Main and Star.

Chapter 2

The Whipple Children
1639-1746

On Living Close to Home

The ensuing chapters are a record of what is known with respect to the adult lives of the sons and daughters of Captain John and Sarah Whipple. The account commences with the christening of the oldest child in 1641 and ends with the death of the last surviving member of the second generation in 1746. Considerable information relative to the second generation was furnished in the previous chapter on their parents. Individual chapters extend genealogical data on each child, and his or her family, as each was impacted by the sociocultural milieu of that era. Contributions to developing American history by later generations are noted throughout the narrative.

The children of Captain John and Sarah Whipple lived out their adult lives within ten miles or so of the old home place on north Town Street in Providence. Five of the eight sons established homes on inherited "north woods" properties that had not as yet experienced the civilizing effects of the European axe and plow. The property of each was located to the north or northwest of Providence, a small settlement of between 200 to 300 persons, along the four principle rivers that flow past it into the Narragansset Bay.[156] In the 1670s and early 1680s, Eleazer and William had to travel eight miles or so up the meandering Moshassuck River to its headwaters to establish farms at what became known as the "Louquisset Meadows." Samuel received land at the same location, as did John Junior, although they lived and died closer to Providence's lone north/south street called "Towne Streete."

Specifically, at the time of his death, Samuel resided in the former Roger Mowrey house located just east of north Town Street about one-and-one half miles north of the freshwater spring that had, only a few years before, induced The Reverend Roger Williams to stake a claim to that parcel of untouched wilderness. Samuel's farm was located on the banks of the Moshassuck River next to the newly established town graveyard. Early on, David relocated from his Moshassuck farm, six miles north of Providence, to the Blackstone River, approximately two miles to the east. Benjamin established a home next to the Woonasquatucket River, roughly three miles to the north and west of Town Street. Jonathan's property, slightly more than two miles to the northwest of his birthplace, was beside the slow-moving waters of the West River. John Junior and Joseph lived and died within the environs of Town Street in Providence. The Whipple daughters took up residences in widely scattered areas to the north and west of Town Street. The approximate locations of the residences of second generation Whipples are known, with those of Samuel, Eleazer, and Jonathan yet viewable in photographic form. During the administration of Sir Edmund Andros, 1686-89, extensive tax records were maintained. A 1688 list of 182 male taxpayers, 16 years and older, was compiled. The sons, sons-in-law, and at least three grandsons of Captain John Whipple are listed in this document.[157]

Six of the Whipple brothers were consistently referred to as "yeomen" farmers in written records of the time.[158] Their oldest brother, John Junior, became an attorney, noted civil servant, and successful politician in Providence. But it was Joseph who alone became a member of that select society historians have since christened the "merchant princes"[159] of colonial Rhode Island. He and John Junior broke free from the soil to establish themselves as the more successful of second generation Rhode Island Whipples in the New World. Due to the growing success of the neophyte maritime industry in the late 1600s, "the people ceased to discuss their local troubles over toddy bowls at the Mowry and Whipple taverns, or to plan political schemes at the John Smith [husband of Sarah Whipple] gristmill, and now busied themselves at the wharves and warehouses on south Water Street, where the Tillinghasts and Crawfords [sons-in-law of Colonel Joseph Whipple] had set a new pace and a new way of financial venture."[160]

In all probability, the farmer brothers lived the life style of the typical Rhode Island farmer of the time. As it is in the twentieth-first century, so then, freedom of religion meant the possibility of freedom from religion. If their families were religious, they likely attended a local Baptist or Quaker house church, and as custom dictated, associated principally with those of like social and religious sensibilities. Rhode Island church attendance of the time appears likewise similar to the present,: women filled most of the pews. "Church was the one place where, despite not being allowed any say in its governance, wives could earn membership, whatever their social status, and hear sermons supporting their guardianship of sexual mores, elevating charity over commerce and neighborliness over trade. It was also a place where they could meet and socialize with their neighbors.[161]

"The indifference of the early villagers to religious matters extended also to those of education."[162] Ten of the 11 Whipple children could not write---or at least signed their names with an "x". "The widespread dislike for learning produced a general disinterest in education...education in that day being largely centered in scholarly debates about dogma. Since neither the Quakers nor Baptists, the two predominant groups in the colony after 1676, were interested in scholarly debates...few books were published. No one thought it necessary to found a college, and few sent their sons to Harvard or Yale. The first descendant of Captain John to graduate from college, Harvard University in 1749, was William, son of Joseph Junior. The absence of a professional clergy and an established church was also largely responsible for the absence of a public school system. The emphasis upon a spirit-filled, rather than head-stored, clergy left in the colony's intellectual and cultural life a vacuum that was not filled until the Anglicans and Congregationalists established churches."[163] "A small geography... has the following under the heading of 'Literature:' No provision is made by law for the establishment of town schools. There are probably more people in Rhode Island who are unable to read and write, then in all the rest of New England."[164] It was the oldest son and grandson of Joseph, after the family became Anglicans, who helped establish Whipple Hall schoolhouse in 1768.

Urban and Rural Family Conflict

The following vignettes of Rhode Island rural life, selected from an anthology of impressions penned by visitors (mostly European) to Rhode Island during the late 1600s and early 1700s, imparts insight into the everyday lives of the Whipple children during this period of time.[165] Of particular interest is one traveler's peculiar explication as to why Rhode Islanders died so young and teenage women lost their teeth.

"These husbandmen, more simple in their manners than our peasants, have also less of their roughness, and rusticity; more enlightened, they have neither cunning nor dissimulation; farther removed from luxurious arts, they are not so much attached to ancient usages, but are far more dexterous in inventing and perfecting whatever tends to the conveniency and comfort of life....

"They are descendant of Sectaries who were banished from Massachusetts...but now live in great Amity with their Neighbours, and though every man does what he thinks right in his own Eyes, it is rare that any notorious Crimes are committed by them which may be attributed In some Measure to their great Veneration for the Holy Scriptures, which they read from the least to the greatest, though they have neither Ministers nor Magistrates to recommend it to them... They have an aversion to taxes...They are very hospitable to Strangers; a Traveller passing through these Towns may call at any House with the same Liberty as if it were in an Inn, and be kindly entertained with the best they have for nothing...There is such a confidence in the public virtue that, from Boston to Providence, I have often met young women traveling alone on horseback; or in small riding chairs, through the woods, even when the day was far upon the decline....

"Scattered about among the forests, the inhabitants have little intercourse with each other, except when they go to church. Their dwelling houses are spacious, proper, airy, and built of wood, and are at least one story in height, and herein they keep all their furniture...They make use of wall-paper which serve for tapestry; they have them very handsome. In many of the houses there are carpets also, even upon their stairs. In general, the houses are pleasant and kept with extreme neatness... In all of them that I have seen, I never failed to discover traces of their active and inventive genius...I do not remember ever to have entered a single house, without seeing a huge family bible, out of which they read on evenings and Sundays to their household...the mildness of their character is as much owing to climate as to their customs and manners, for you find the same softness of disposition even in the animals of the country....

One visitor bemoaned the Rhode Island climate and wished to be elsewhere: "In general, the Air is infinitely more clear and serene than in England; and our nearness to the Sun occasions more frequent and loud claps of Thunder, and sharper Lightening, than you have. It is no unusual Thing for Houses, and Stacks of Hay, and Grain, to be burnt; and Men and Cattle are often killed by the sharp Lightening. In New England, the Transitions from Heat to Cold are short and sudden, and the Extreme of both very sensible; We are sometimes frying, and at others freezing; and as Men often die at their Labour in the Field by Heat, so some in Winter are froze to Death with the Cold. Last winter, in February, which begins the Spring with you, I rode 30 miles upon one continued Glaze of Ice to assist a neighbor who was sick. As I can see the Atlantic Ocean, I have seen it froze as far as the human Eye could reach; and 'tis common, in a beautiful Lake of salt Water to have the Ice three feet thick every Winter...As the Sun grows low, my Longings after Europe increases....

47

"Before I arrived here, I had no expectations of discovering traces of French modes and fashions, in the midst of wilds and forests...The head dresses of all the women, except Quakers, are high, spreading and decked profusely...and I cannot but reflect on the oddness of their taste...with manners at the same time so simple and pure, as to resemble those of the ancient patriarchal age. Pulse, Indian corn, and milk are their most common kinds of food; they also use much tea, and this infusion constitutes the chief pleasure of their lives...and upon entering a house, the greatest mark of civility and welcome they can show you, is to invite you to drink it with them...and perhaps this may be one of the causes, that with a robust and healthy constitution, their lives here are much shorter than those of the inhabitants of other countries. The loss of their teeth is also attributed to the too frequent use of tea; the women, who are commonly very handsome, are often, at eighteen or twenty years of age, entirely deprived of this most precious ornament....

However, one visiting clergyman from Massachusetts did not have as elevated an opinion of yeomen such as the farmer brothers, particularly as it concerned Sabbath day observance: "The inhabitants of this place, in general, are very profane, and exceeding famous for contempt of the Sabbath. Gaming, gunning, horseracing and the like, are as common that day as on any other. Persons of all professions countenance such practices." It should be emphasized that the foremost criticism of rural Rhode Islanders during the first two or three generations of Whipples and their confederates, repeated ad infinitum in these travelogues, was their lack of a school system, and consequent widespread illiteracy. A typical comment complains, "Arts and sciences are almost unknown, except to some few individuals; and there are no public seminaries of learning; nor do the Rhode Islanders in general seem to regret the want of them....

In stark contrast to the rustic lives of the farmer brothers and their immediate descendants in the frontier existence of primitive northern Providence Township, John and Joseph's families lived sumptuously in Providence and Newport. The estimated population of rural Cumberland Township was about 500 (100 families) in the year 1700, with the Louquisett and the Fruit Hill populations a little less. On the other hand, Newport's upscale urban inhabitants numbered over 2000. When Cumberland petitioned to become separated from Smithfield Township some 50 years later, it "consisted of one hundred and twenty families or thereabouts."[166] It is to be noted that the 6 January 1746 petition of Bristol County, Massachusetts (which included Cumberland) to become part of Rhode Island was addressed to "The honorable William Green Esqr Governor of Rhode Island and to the Honorable Joseph Whipple Esqr. Lieut. Governor...."[167] The petition included the names of several of the yeomen descendants of David and Eleazer; the petitioned was their cousin Joseph Whipple Junior, the family's second merchant prince.

It would be instructive to know what a family reunion of second and third generation Whipples would have looked like in the year 1743, the year Joseph Junior was elected Deputy Governor. It is not certain that such could have been possible. Only a few wealthy Whipple lime manufacturers, textile mill owners, politicians, and a handful of military officer descendants of the farmer brothers would likely have been invited to Newport for such an occasion--it would have violated social protocol. Early New England colonial society, like that of Old England, maintained strict social distinctions--

even to the extent of dictating the style of clothing that various classes of citizens (particularly women) could wear. The gap between social classes that had emerged in just one or two Whipple generations would have been striking.[168]

"Northern Rhode Island [where most second and third generation Whipples lived] was home to a hardy, resolute, independent yeomanry. The clearing of land of forests and rocks cost hard work and a constant industry, summer and winter. Agriculture was the sole dependence of the people, and a comfortable living and the raising of a family were the limits of the ambitions of the marriageable young men and women. The larger town life at Providence offered no special attraction to those born in the country and reared in its atmosphere of individualism and independency. The town had but few holiday attractions to country-bred people. Still more, the dress and learning of the towns-people did not comport and the manners and homespun of their country cousins. There was an air of superiority, of proud satisfaction of the townsman when he met his brother of the farm that built a barrier between the two of separateness and aloofness. Society and politics were of two species--the country reserved, quiet, conservative, and town progressive, assertive, and tending towards a low-grade aristocracy. A great gulf of variations divided the town and country of Providence Plantations. Not only so, but hostilities, family, financial, political, made members of the same family name hateful to and hated by each other."[169] Even in the mid twentieth century, those in the "outback" were still looked down upon by their Providence neighbors: "In the 1950s and early 60s, I and a couple of friends attended school in Providence. Many of our schoolmates thought of us as country bumpkins because we lived in Lime Rock."[170]

Wealthy Whipples

The merchant princes of Providence and Newport wanted an efficient economic order "but also well-paved roads, solid wharves, street lighting, fire protection…. Nor did men of property care to be accosted by drunkards, beggars, and cripples asking for alms as they passed by. So they combined enlightened self-interest and Christian benevolence….Elegant new churches were built, ostensibly to honor God. Parks and shady walks made Sunday strolls or carriage rides fashionable--and of course enabled the wealthy to demonstrate their status by their equipage and dress. The rich lost their pious Puritanism and decided to live well. Their wives were expected to entertain lavishly which necessitated large, well-appointed homes, many servants, fine plates and silverware and furnishings….Black slaves also had to dress in a manner befitting their master's station, and their uniforms became increasingly costly, until some wore wigs and buckled shoes."[171] Even the most perfunctory perusal of Joseph Whipple's Last Will and Testament and inventory of movable goods show a remarkable resonance with the above, even to the status of his seven slaves.

However, one traveling French nobleman was not all that impressed with the level of culture enjoyed by Rhode Island's nouveau riche merchants: "On the 15th, I was invited to a party to which I went. The purpose of the party was to eat a turtle, weighing three or four hundred pounds, which an American vessel had just brought from one of our islands. This meat did not seem to me to be very palatable; it is true that it was badly

49

cooked. There were some quite handsome women; before dinner they kept themselves in a different room from the men, they also placed themselves at table all on the same side, and the men, on the other. They danced after dinner to the music of some instrument which had been brought there expressly. Neither the men or the women dance well; all stretch out and lengthen their arms in a way far from agreeable....They all love money and hard money; it is thus that they designate specie to distinguish it from paper money, which loses prodigiously. Whilst I am writing, at Providence and Newport it loses sixty for one.

"They do not eat soups and do not serve up ragouts at these dinners; but boiled roast and much vegetables. They drink nothing but cider and Madeira wine with water. They do not take coffee immediately after dinner, but it is served three or four hours afterwards with tea; this use of tea is universal in America. These Americans are almost always at the table; and as they have little to occupy them, as they go out little in winter and spend whole days along side of their fires and their wives, without reading and without doing anything, going so often to table is a relief and a preventive of ennui (depression). Yet they are not great eaters."[172]

Favored Sons

It is significant that the name of each of Captain John Whipple's sons was associated during his lifetime and afterward with well-known local physical land features of late seventeenth century Rhode Island. The designation "Whipples from Fruit Hill"

has come down through the centuries synonymous with Benjamin Whipple and his immediate descendants. Jonathan and his sons, from the earliest times forward, were identified as the "Whipples of Wanskuck." Samuel lived his entire life in Providence Neck, and will forever be identified with the North Burial Ground, being the first ever to be interred there, in addition to having most of his estate eventually taken over by that cemetery. John Junior, like his father before him, lived out his adult

Whipple Burial Grounds

life on Town Street at the bottom of Constitution Hill. Eleazer and William became known as the "Louquisset brothers" having established farms in that well-known area. Solitary and Wolf Hills appear in association with Joseph Whipple and his sons, while Joseph Whipple Junior and family would have been known to their kinsmen as the unapproachable politically powerful inhabitants of "The Hill," the colony's capitol city of Newport. But without question, the most historically noted land purchase among second generation Whipples was the acquisition of "Study Hill" by David Whipple. Through this purchase, the Whipple name became inextricably linked with this land feature, to

50

one of early New England's most colorful characters, and a putative founder of the colonies of Massachusetts and Rhode Island.

It would appear that, for whatever reasons, Joseph was his father's favorite. In Captain John Whipple's Last Will and Testament, Joseph, age 20, received what seems to have been the choicest parcels of land in and around the town of Providence, including the highly coveted original property on north Towne Street.[173] In contrast, Benjamin and David age 28 and 26[174] each received in separately declared laconic sentences, "a right of land in the late division which is already made out to him." These properties and those of the other brothers were raw backwater forest and meadow approximately five to seven miles apart, which had been awarded originally by proprietary right to their father in the 1660s and 1670s. Each division amounted to about 100 acres although the brothers eventually increased their properties to encompass hundreds of additional acres. David essentially traded his original 65 to 70 acres for the Study Hill property that was located in another colony. He was thus the only member of the second generation to leave Rhode Island.

While Joseph and John Junior may have been the model sons of Captain John's old age, Benjamin and David could have been considered the bad boys of the family. Benjamin was arrested, approximately one month before Captain John drafted his will, and charged with "breaking the law and misbehavior." As a teenager, David became the father of a child out of wedlock. It does not appear that Captain John made any attempt to interfere with the criminal process or subsequent legal adjudication. And in the case of David, he chose not to bear the financial burden of the son's youthful indiscretion, although it was a tremendous financial hardship, which took David over a decade to repay.

Dozens of Whipple descendants are interred throughout the North Burial Ground. The photograph above shows Joseph's broken headstone on the first row of the original Whipple burial plot in that cemetery. It is believed that John Junior is also buried in this row, although his headstone was never made or has long since disappeared. The headstones of Captain John and Sarah Whipple are the fourth and fifth to the right of Joseph, next to the box tomb.[175] The box tomb is that of Lieutenant Pardon[6] Whipple (William[5], Joseph[4], John[3], Joseph[2], John[1]). Most of the 27 burials in this area are those of Colonel Joseph Whipple's branch of the family; even the large, gray and white monument in the background, which commemorates the Temple family, is part of his line through the marriage of a granddaughter.[176]

The farmer brothers differed from Joseph and John Junior in the above and other ways. John and Joseph were elected on numerous occasions to high political office in the colony. William, Benjamin, David, and Jonathan seem to have eschewed such involvement, although Samuel and Eleazer did represent their respective areas at the semi-annual assembly in Newport on a couple of occasions. Dying at ages 50, 54, and 55 respectively, Benjamin, David, and Jonathan were the shortest lived of the eight sons; at 85, Joseph lived the longest, with the other brothers dying in their 60s and 70s. The farmer brothers, with the exception of Eleazer, were buried in unknown graves, while Joseph was buried in a place of honor near his mother and father. As did ninety percent of colonial Rhode Island residents, they lived out their days on earth modestly as tillers of the soil. However, like his father before him, Joseph became a successful entrepreneur-- indeed, the family's first "merchant prince."

As culture dictated, their sisters became housewives and mothers. Each lost her first husband through death. The five families into which they married were financially successful and politically prominent. Sarah, the oldest Whipple daughter, married John Smith Junior the town's miller, and for several years the town clerk. They had 10 children. Her next husband was Richard Arnold, a wealthy Quaker. Sarah's granddaughter, Anne Smith, married her sister Abigail's grandson, Stephen Hopkins, in 1755, a few months before he became governor of Rhode Island. Mary, the middle Whipple daughter, married Epenetus Olney, and had eight children. She and her husband owned an inn about two blocks from her parent's house. The Olney family founded a splinter Baptist church in 1652. If the Whipples were Baptists, they were likely members of that group, rather than the church founded supposedly by The Reverend Roger Williams. Abigail, the youngest, married Stephen Dexter, the son of a Rhode Island governor. Her second husband was William Hopkins. Their grandson was Stephen Hopkins, governor of Rhode Island and signer of the Declaration of Independence.

Sectarianism and Missing Gravestones

It is generally agreed that the Whipples moved to Providence, Rhode Island from Dorchester, Massachusetts in order to enjoy freedom of conscience. Unquestionably, they shared in the unique religious and political diversity of their new community, and so were among a privileged few on earth to enjoy such freedom at that time. Joseph became a communicant in the Anglican Church. John Junior became a member of the Society of Friends, as did Sarah and Samuel. The remaining children likely were Baptist or nonreligious.

Most of the settlement's citizens were members of Baptist or Quaker communions, and due to this, the absence of a central parish church, with its ubiquitous graveyard, was part of their everyday experience. With the added bias against the use of grave markers, the nativity and necrology dates of most of the colony's earliest residents likely will not be retrieved. (It is fortuitous then that the birth dates of Abigail, Joseph, and Jonathan and the death date of Sarah are the only unknowns in that regard). "Whether through poverty or want of skill, or the early diffusion of Quaker ideas, no inscriptions were set over the earlier graves. This primitive custom of sepulture outlasted three generations."[177] Due to laws that mandated separation of church and state, churches of several denominations were built throughout Rhode Island. However, each was small, and none were known to have built its own cemetery because families, following a separatist tradition, buried their dead in family plots: "These small family cemeteries are private burial grounds that belong to and are the responsibility of the descendants. Most of them were reserved out of the deed when the farm was sold with words like 'I reserve my family burial ground 4 rods by 4 rods with rights of pass and repass forever.' ...Most are abandoned, overgrown, and generally decaying." [178]

Due to the above, the graves or monuments of only four second generation Whipple children are yet viewable: Samuel and Joseph in the North Burial Ground and

Eleazer in his family burial plot at Limerock.[179] The headstones of William and family were moved from their family plot at Lime Rock and taken to the Moshassuck Cemetery about three miles to the southeast, where a common monument now stands in their stead. Even then, the descendants of Captain John and Sarah Whipple are fortunate that their gravestones and those of four of their sons were preserved for future generations.

Four Whipple Generations

Number of Descendants of Captain John and
Sarah Whipple Through the Fourth Generation[180]

Second	Third	Fourth
John Jr.	1-4	37
Sarah	7-3	66
Samuel	3-2	16
Eleazer	4-6	51
Mary	4-4	40
William	2-1	26
Benjamin	3-3	23
David	4-4	46
Abigail	2-1	25
Joseph	5-7	47
Jonathan	2-5	24
	37-40	401

Of the 77 grandchildren (37 Males and 40 females), 55 produced at least 401 great grandchildren. There is scant information available on at least 15 other grandchildren. Conservatively estimating that eight of these produced an average of five children, each would increase the number of estimated descendants in the fourth generation to about 440.

Whipple Male Descendants of Captain John Whipple from the Second Through the Fourth Generation

Third Generation   Fourth Generation

John Junior [368]
John III   [6025]   Job, John IV, Hezekiah

Samuel [370]
Noah   [635]   Noah Junior, Enoch, Daniel

53

| Samuel [362] | Samuel, Samuel III, Daniel, Nathan, Zachariah, Zephaniah |
| Thomas [636] | Thomas Junior, Abraham |

Eleazer [371]

Eleazer [6107]	Eleazer III
Job [6111]	Job Junior, Simon, Stephen
James [6112]	Eleazer
Daniel [6113]	Daniel Junior, Joseph, Eleazer, Joel, Preserved, Job

William [373]

| William [380] | William III, Jeremiah, John, Anthony, Benjamin, Moses, Joseph, Eleazer |
| Seth [381] | Died at 28 no children |

Benjamin [374]

Benjamin [6125]	Andrew, Benjamin III, Daniel, Ephraim, Benedict, Beneger, Stephen, Joseph, Benedict, Jesse, John
Josiah [6128]	Died as a child
John [6129]	Josiah, Ezekiel, Jabez, John Junior

David [375]

David [6136]	Jonathan, David III, Silas, Anthony
Israel [6137]	Israel Junior, Nathaniel
Jeremiah [6139]	David, Jeremiah Junior.
William [10928]	William Junior, Peter, John, Samuel, Ibrook, Israel

Joseph [377]

John [6152]	Jeremiah, Joseph
Jeremiah [6153]	Died as a child
Joseph Junior [6154]	Joseph, Christopher, Joseph, William, Joseph III, Benjamin, Abraham, William
Christopher [6161]	Died as a child
Christopher [6163]	Died as a child

Jonathan [378]

| Jonathan Junior [6175] | Jonathan III |
| Thomas [6176] | Thomas Junior |

$$24-5 = 19 \qquad 74-5 = 69$$

Eight Whipple brothers produced a total of 24 Whipple grandsons, of whom 19 produced male offspring. These 19 fathered 74 Whipple great grandsons. Of the 74 names, five were repetitions, indicating that five of those individuals died in infancy, leaving a total of 69 Whipple males in the fourth generation. It can be but roughly estimated how many of these could have participated in passing on the Whipple surname to the fifth generation. (Estimate 45-50)

There is insufficient information on six grandsons to determine whether they fathered children: John IV, son of John III [6025]; Josiah, Ezekiel, and John, sons of John Senior [6129]; Job, son of Daniel [6113]; and Israel, son of William [10928].

An additional 17 grandsons died before producing children or did not father sons: William III, Jeremiah, John, Anthony, and Joseph, sons of William Junior [380]; Eleazer, son of Daniel [6113]; Enoch, son of Noah Senior [635]; Nathan, son of Samuel Junior [362]; Simon, son of Job Senior [6112]; Eleazer III, son of Eleazer Junior [6107]; Jeremiah, son of John [6152]; Peter, son of William [10928]; as well as Christopher, William, Joseph III, Benjamin, and Abraham, sons of Joseph Junior [6154].

With deletion of these 23, the total number of fourth generation Whipples who could have transmitted the surname is reduced to 46, with an additional six (those of insufficient information) who could have done so. These 46 produced 177 sons. Conservatively assuming that three of the six unaccounted for individuals above sired four sons each would suggest a number nearer to 190 total. The 46 Whipples in the fourth generation should be compared to the roughly 400 non-Whipple surnames of that generation who could have produced the fifth generation of Captain John and Sarah Whipple descendants.

Migration Patterns of the First Three Generations of the Male Descendants of Captain John Whipple

Preliminary data available on migration patterns of the first three generations of Whipple male offspring show that most appear to have retained a Rhode Island residence, though at least six moved from one township to another. It is noteworthy that of these, only one moved further south than Providence. That is, duplicating the demographic migration pattern of their ancestors, they stayed in the northern part of that state--the majority in Cumberland Township.[181]

Descendants of John Junior

Job [6026] and Hezekiah [9728], sons of John III [6025], lived out their lives in Rhode Island; Job in Providence and Glocester Townships, and Hezekiah in Providence.

Descendants of Samuel

Of the ten grandsons of Samuel Senior [370], only Enoch [10911] and Daniel [6490] stayed in Rhode Island. Enoch died young and Daniel lived and died in the township of Glocester, later named Burrillville, the most northwesterly of the townships. Because Samuel Junior [362] and Thomas Senior [636] moved to Connecticut before

1718, their sons lived in that adjoining colony. None of their immediate descendants are known to have moved back to Rhode Island.

Descendants of Eleazer

Daniel [6113], the youngest son of Eleazer Senior [371], moved about five miles north of his father's homestead across the Blackstone River into Rehoboth township in the colony of Massachusetts. This move took place approximately 30 years before Rehoboth was annexed to Rhode Island becoming Cumberland, the most northeasterly of its townships; subsequently, his six sons were born at that location. Of these, Eleazer [10917] and Job [10927] appear to have died without children. Preserved [10924] moved to Richmond, New Hampshire. His three brothers were living in Rehoboth when it was annexed to Rhode Island in 1746. Eleazer [75145], grandson of Eleazer Senior and son of James [6112] located from his father's farm in Smithfield Township about 15 miles south to the town of Warwick, RI, where he lived as a merchant and sea captain.

Descendants of William

Two of the eight grandsons of William Senior [380], Moses [396] and Eleazer [399], moved from their childhood home in Smithfield Township across the Blackstone River into the township of Cumberland, where they and the majority of their children lived out their lives. Jeremiah [390], son of William Junior, apparently died young while the remaining five sons lived and died at Smithfield in the town of Lime Rock.

Descendants of Benjamin

Four of Benjamin Senior's [374] grandsons moved out of state: Beneger [8209] to New York; Stephen [6199] to Massachusetts; and, Jesse [8235] and Joseph [8233] to Connecticut. Jabez [9739], son of John [6129], lived most of his adult life at sea as a captain while retaining a home in Providence.

Descendants of David

Of the four sons of David [375], who moved to Rehoboth Massachusetts in 1692, David Junior [6136] moved to Connecticut and there maintained a large family, including four sons. Nathaniel [10842], son of Israel [6137] moved to Richmond, New Hampshire. His other siblings and cousins were living in Rehoboth Township when it was taken over by Rhode Island.

Descendants of Joseph

It is lamentably noteworthy that of the 10 grandsons of Joseph Senior [377], eight of whom were born in Newport, only Joseph [6164], son of his eldest son, John [6152], fathered sons. He lived and died in Smithfield Township, about three miles north of Providence.

Descendants of Jonathan

Jonathan III [10105] and Thomas Junior [10108], and their three sons, lived and died in North Providence, as did their father before them.

In summary, by the fourth generation, at least fourteen Whipple male descendants lived in Connecticut: eight grandsons of Samuel Senior, [360], [644], [646], [647], [648], [19264], [13228], and [10162]; four grandsons of David Senior, [39296], [41713], [41714], and [48385]; two grandsons of Benjamin Senior, [8235] and [8233]. Two descendants lived in New Hampshire: one grandson of Eleazer Senior, [10924]; and one grandson of David Senior, [10842]. Two descendants lived in Massachusetts: one grandson of Benjamin Senior, [6199]; and one grandson of David, [10839]. One descendant lived in New York: a grandson of Benjamin Senior, [8209]. One descendant lived in Vermont: a grandson of Samuel Senior, [644]. Twelve descendants lived in Rehoboth, Massachusetts: seven grandsons of David Senior, [8192], [8206], [52679], [10933], [10934], [10935], [10903]; three grandsons of Eleazer Senior, [10915], [10916], [10923]; and two grandsons of William Senior [396] and [399] before it was annexed by Rhode Island. As stated, this is a partial list based on incomplete data. Later antiquarian researchers are encouraged to fill in the missing information.

Third through Fifth Generations of the Male Descendants Of Captain John Whipple

Fourth Generation	Fifth Generation
John III [6025]	
Job [6026]	Elijah 33136, John 6026
Hezekiah [9728]	Christopher 33137
John IV [9724]	Insufficient information
Noah Senior [635]	
Noah Junior [10162]	Abraham 3570, Samuel 46303
Daniel [6490]	Enoch 10267, Jonathan 10268
Enoch [10911]	Died at 25 no children
Samuel Junior [362]	
Samuel III [360]	Samuel IV 652, Timothy 358, Joseph 653
Daniel [644]	Jeremiah 14993, Ebenezer 14660
Zachariah [647]	Zephaniah 13505, John 13507, Zachariah 13509
Zephaniah [648]	Solomon 10036, Zephaniah Junior 15841, Elijah 15842, Isaiah 15847
Nathan [646]	Died at 21 no children

Thomas Senior [636]

Thomas [10264]   Thomas III 25983, Abraham 25085, Nathan 25087
Abraham 13228]   Abram15529, Samuel15531, Joseph13230,Luther
                 15532,   Calvin15534,   Daniel8344,   Thomas15536,
                 Daniel30262

Job Senior [6111]

Job Junior [16083]   Ephraim 9721
Stephen [15568]   Simon 50348, Arnold 50349, Stephen 15557
Simon [16090]   Died as a child

Eleazer Junior [6107]

Eleazer III [75146]   Died as a child

James [6112]

Eleazer [75145]   James 10309, Job 10312, Joseph 10313

Daniel Senior [6113]

Daniel III [10915]   Daniel IV 25100, Simon 13012, Amos 25102
Joseph [10916]   Gideon 33156, Amos 33158, Asa 33160
Joel [10923]   Bennett 37906, Leonard 37907, Knight 37908
Preserved [10924]   Otis 15330, Preserved Junior15331, Stephen15332,
                      Silas 15334, Russell 15338, James 15339
Job [10927]   Insufficient information
Eleazer [10917]   Died as a child

William Junior [380]

Benjamin [395]   Jeremiah 10166
Moses [396]   William 10189, Joseph 10190
Eleazer Senior [399]   Eleazer Junior 404, Joseph 405, Jesse 409
William III [388]   Died at age 77 no sons
Jeremiah [390]   Died as a child
John   [392]   Died at 83 no children
Anthony [393]   Died at 26 no children
Joseph [397]   Died at 29 no children

Benjamin Junior [6125]

Benjamin III [8224]   Gideon 30038, Ethan12725, James 26055, Elisha
                       30444, Cyrus 9755, Charles 9754
Daniel Senior [6556]   Ezekiel 9763, Richard 9765, Daniel Junior 9566

Ephraim Senior [8227]	Emor 9804, Benjamin 9805, Ephraim III 9806
Beneger Senior [8209]	Ezekiel 8283, Beneger Junior 8282, Reuben 8384, Barnett 8211 James 8286
Stephen[6199]	Asahel 6202, Andrew 6203, Samuel 6204, Oliver 6207, Nebadiah 6208, Benjamin 6213, Stephen 6211
Joseph [8233]	Benjamin 9857, Caleb 9858, David 53748, Ephraim 9859, John 9860, Thomas 9861
Benedict Senior [8234]	James 9902, John 9903, Benedict Junior 9905
Jesse Senior [8235]	James 9878, Jesse 9879, Benjamin 9881, Ethan 9880
John [8237]	Benjamin 9997, Samuel 9999, Nathan 10001, Stephen 10002, Joseph 10003
Andrew [8223]	Insufficient information

John [6129]

Jabez Senior [9739]	Jabez Junior 9750, Arnold 9751
Josiah [9535]	Insufficient information
John [10864]	Insufficient information
Ezekiel [9536]	Insufficient information

David Junior [6136]

Jonathan [41713]	David 41718, Jonathan 41719, Titus 42284, Titus 41722, Nicholas 41723
David III [41714]	David IV 41726
Silas Senior [39296]	Silas Junior 45411, Daniel 45412, Joshua 45414
Anthony [48385]	Anthony 48392, Jeremiah 48391

Israel Senior [6137]

Nathaniel [10842]	Israel 10846, Nathaniel Junior 10848, Ichabod 104847, Squire 10850, Rufus 10851, Dan 10853
Israel [10839]	Died at 47 no sons

Jeremiah Senior [6139]

David [8192]	Simon 8194, David 8195, George 8196, Otis 8197, Jonathan 8201, Benjamin 8174, Joseph 8202
Jeremiah III [8206]	Oliver 50064, Jeremiah IV 10302, Bela 10068, Jabez

William Senior [10928]

William Junior[52679]	Ezra 55989
John [10933]	Christopher10214, John Junior10215, Daniel22210
Samuel [10934]	William 22239
Ibrook Senior [10935]	Peter 15280, Ibrook Junior 15282
Peter [10903]	Died at 60 no children

Israel [10938]   Insufficient information

_____

            John [6152]
Joseph [6164]   William 10068, John 10069, Samuel 10070, George
                                        10071
Jeremiah [6153]   Died as a child

            Joseph Junior [6154]
Joseph III [26807]   Died at 36 no children
Christopher [80990]   Died as child
Benjamin [88061]   Died as child
Abraham [88062]   Died as child
William   [53819]   Died at 20 no children

_____

            Jonathan Junior [6175]
Jonathan III [10105]   Eleazer 16234

            Thomas Senior [6176]
Thomas Junior [10108]   Nicholas 10110, Levi 28259, Christopher 10111,
                                        George 10112, Thomas III 10113

        69- 24 = 45   177

End Notes

---

[156] Welcome Arnold Greene, *The Providence Plantations For Two Hundred and Fifty Years* (Providence: J.A. & R.A. Reid, publishers, 1886) 49. "To the north, west, and southwest, up the valleys of the Blackstone, the Moshassuck, the Woonasquatucket, and the Pawtuxet, venturesome pioneers had pushed their way, locating their scattered farms on the most available sites, and more than half of the inhabitants of the town lived in the country districts."

[157] Edward Field, *Tax Lists of the Town of Providence During the Administration of Sir Edmund Andros and His Council 1686-1689* (Providence: Howard W. Preston, 1895) 37-41.

[158] Eugene A. Stratton, Plymouth Colony Its History and People, 1620-1691 (Salt Lake City: Ancestry Publishing, 1986) 213. "From yeoman on down the social scale, a man was called 'goodman' and a woman 'goodwife'...Men above yeoman were addressed as 'Master'...and were considered gentlemen. Below the level of yeoman were laborers who hired themselves out for daily wages and apprentices. A few very wealthy farmers were addressed as gentleman."

[159] William G. McLoughlin, *Rhode Island, A Bicentennial History* (New York: W. W. Norton, 1978) 66.

[160] Thomas Bicknell, *The History of Rhode Island and Providence Plantations, 3 vols* (New York: The American Historical Society, 1920) 3:880.

[161] Barbara Mills, *Providence: 1630-1800, Women Are Part of Its History* (Bowie, Md: Heritage Books, 2002) 79.

[162] Wilfred H. Munro, *Picturesque Rhode Island* (Providence: J.A. & R.A. Reid, Publishers, 1881) 147.

[163] McLoughlin, 46

[164] Bicknell, 3: 906.

[165] Gertrude S. Kimball, *Pictures of Rhode Island in the Past, 1642-1833, by Travelers and Observers* (Providence: Preston and Rounds Company, 1900) 48, 54, 97-99.

[166] John G. Erhardt, *A History of Rehoboth, Seekonk, Mass. Pawtucket & East Providence, R.I. 1692-1812* (Seekonk, Mass. Privately published, 1990) 508

[167] Erhardt, 502

[168] George F. Dow, *Every Day Life in the Massachusetts Bay Colony* (New York: Dover Publications, 1988) 107. Rhode Island social classes were not quite so rigid but money, and lots of it, determined ones status in mid century Newport.

[169] Bicknell, 3:929.

[170] Personal conversation with Mr. John Cullen, whose family bought the property of Job Whipple, and has lived in the Lime Rock area for many decades.

[171] McLoughlin, 68

[172] Kimball, 82-84.

[173] Horatio Rogers, George Moulton Carpenter, and Edward Field, Records Commissioners, *The Early Records of the Town of Providence 21 Volumes*, Volume 6, Being Part of the Will, Book Number 1, otherwise called the First Book for Prouidence Towne Council Perticulior Vse, (Providence: Snow and Farnham city printers, 1894) 126-28.

[174] As of 1682, when the will was originally drafted. David took possession of his land early in 1683, Benjamin in 1681, John Junior in 1663, Samuel in 1665, Eleazer in 1670, William about 1680, and Jonathan in 1682.

[175] "Col. Joseph's headstone is in two pieces. Fortunately, the top piece with his name faces up, so I was able to get a photo of that. The other stones, except for those of his daughters, are very difficult to read. The whole cemetery is in a deplorable condition. Directional signs are torn down every thing looks like a haunted maze. Because of financial problems, the city of Providence cannot adequately take care of the property any more." Barbara R. Carroll, Exeter, Rhode Island, personal observation, 2 Nov 2003.

[176] "An Account of the Temple Family," New England Historical and Genealogical Society Register, Vol. 10, January 1856, pg. 77.

[177] Henry C. Dorr, *The Planting and Growth of Providence. Rider's Tract #15* (Providence: Sidney S. Rider, 1882) 46.

[178] John E. Sterling, designer. Rhode Island Cemetery Database. Rhode Island Cemetery Transcription Project, 1990-2001. On Computer at the Rhode Island Historical Society Library, 121 Hope Street, Providence, RI. 02906. Project Coordinator Comments.

[179] The Eleazer Whipple cemetery has been abandoned and neglected for many years. Large trees and other plant life are literally destroying it. Few inscriptions can be read, although Eleazer's name can yet be seen with difficulty on his headstone, which is lying flat on the ground. The cemetery is hidden behind a six-foot stockade fence and barn about 30 yards west of the 1000 block of the Great Road, across the street from the Lincoln Central Elementary School. Personal observation of the authors in June 2004.

[180] Abstracted from www. whipple.org , Weldon Whipple, Webmaster, and the many primary and secondary sources it quotes.

[181] 1824 *Providence, Rhode Island City Directory,* page 71. Arnold, a jeweler and Captain Jabez, descendants of Benjamin, Captain John's fifth son, lived at 319 N. Main (i.e. the northeast corner of North Main and Star Street), part of the land originally owned by Captain John Whipple. John Whipple, renowned attorney, a descendant of Joseph, Captain John's seventh son, address was listed as Market House, which was on Main Street. The antecedents of the other Whipple's listed in Providence are unknown (by this author). Cyrus, a machine maker; David a hat maker, lived at 31 Market Street; a yeoman, Eleazer lived at 283 N. Main; Ethan, operated a grocery at 156 N. Main; another grocer was Jeremiah at 181 N. Main; John H. Whipple, was listed as a town constable; and Leonidas a painter resided at 49 Broad Street. Mrs. Deborah, at 200 N. Main and Mrs. Nancy were listed.. Miss Zilpah Whipple lived at 18 Benefit Street. Thus, by this year (139 years after Captain John's death), only 11 adult Whipple men resided in Providence. Of the 14 individuals, over half lived, or had their business addresses, within a half mile or so of the original seventeenth century property of Captain John Whipple.

Chapter 3

Ensign John Whipple Junior
The Whipples From Constitution Hill

Children and Relatives

Ensign John Whipple Junior, the oldest child of Captain John, was born in1639, christened at Dorchester, Massachusetts, 1 November 1641, and died at Providence Rhode Island, 15 December 1700.[182] He married Mary Olney, the daughter of Thomas Olney and Marie Ashton, at Providence, Rhode Island, 4 December 1663, she dying in 1676. To this couple, three children were born:[183]

> i. *Mary Whipple, born 4 Mar 1664/5; died 12 Mar 1739/40;*
> *married James Carder*
> ii. *John Whipple, born 2 Oct 1666; died aft 3 June 1737; married Lydia Hoar*
> iii. *Elnathan Whipple, born 2 Jan 1675/76; died aft Aug 1753; married*
> *John Rice*

Following the death of his first wife, John married Rebekah Brown Scott, the widow of John Scott and daughter of John Brown of Portsmouth, New Hampshire, at Providence, Rhode Island, 15 April 1678. To this union, two children were born:

> i. *Deliverance Whipple, born 11 Feb 1678/9; died 5 Jan 1765; married*
> *William Arnold*
> ii. *Dorothy Whipple, born about 1680; died 19 Sep 1728; married*
> *Malachi Rhodes*

"Rebecca's first husband, John Scott, was said to have been killed by an Indian while standing in the doorway of his own house at Pawtucket Ferry in 1677…. It appears that the entire Quaker Moshassuck settlement went to Newport during that struggle [King Philip's War] and that John Scott and his family returned too soon for safety. The widow remained in Providence…and there married…John Whipple, Jr., who was one of the prominent men in Providence colony, and had held nearly every office in town, from constable to town clerk and moderator of the Town Meeting….The youngest child of John and Rebecca Scott, who was about six years old when his father died, lived with his mother in John Whipple's house. He became Major Silvanus Scott, and early in life entered into the politics of the town, becoming nearly as prominent in his generation as his stepfather had been before him. [Silvanus was given part of the land in the Louquisset that John Whipple Junior received from his father in 1663. Silvanus subsequently sold the land to David Whipple, his stepfather's brother]. He married, about 1692, Joanna, daughter of Joseph and Esther Ballard Jenckes. His wife was a sister of Governor Jenckes so noted…"[184] Silvanus' daughter, Sarah, married Governor Stephen Hopkins in 1726.[185] [As seen later, the second wife of Governor Hopkins was the granddaughter of Sarah Whipple Smith, John Junior's sister].

John, the brother of Silvanus, who likewise grew up in the Whipple home, married a daughter of Edward Wanton. This Wanton family furnished five colonial governors, and was known as the "Fighting Quakers." John Scott's father, Richard, was "the first convert in Providence... of George Fox, [founder of the Quaker religion] and the persistent enemy of Williams. It is singular that the bitterest foes of Williams, and who gave him annoyance equal to any which he had experienced from the elders of 'the bay' were those in closest contact [they lived next door] with him."[186] The fact that Quakers seldom married outside the faith gives credence to the assertion that John Junior may have been a member of the Society of Friends at that time.[187]

At least two letters written by Rebekah Whipple to her husband, John, are extant. Both were written from Newport, where she had gone in 1692, apparently to undergo a medical procedure (blood letting). The first letter was an accounting of items she had purchased. The second letter reads in part, "Loving husband my love to you and my children hoping you are all good. I am under the doctors hand. I have some incuragemont I hope...I must be loss blood before I can come home. I have been blooded once...Pray Mr. Crawford and Mr. Olney not to fail Robert...When Simon Davies comes in send your anser whether you have mollasos and rum pray send down some money if you please and love to all, at Newport, June 27, 1692. Your loving wife Rebekah Whipple."[188]

In 1635, Thomas Olney, the father of John Junior's first wife, a resident of Hertfordshire, Old England, came to Salem, Massachusetts, where he early became associated with those who accepted the views of The Reverend Roger Williams; on 12 March 1638, he was banished from the colony with a number of others. John Junior's wife's sister, Lydia Olney, married Joseph Williams, the son of Roger Williams. On 8 October 1638, Olney was one of twelve men to whom Williams deeded equal shares with himself in the Providence Plantation. He thus became one of the "Original Thirteen Proprietors of Providence."[189] In 1652, along with a minority of members, he separated from the First Baptist Church in Providence in order to establish his own Baptist church that continued to teach, among other ideas, the Calvinist doctrine of predestination. His church lasted for some 70 years.[190] He and his son, Thomas Junior, were minister/elders there until the latter's death in 1722. One wonders whether members of the John Whipple Senior family, if they were Baptist, might not have been communicants in this church instead of the larger and better-known congregation.

John Whipple Junior Inn

The two families were undoubtedly close, even to the point of witnessing marriages between two of their children. Mary, Captain John and Sarah's second daughter, married Thomas Olney's second son, Epenetus, on 9 March 1665. Epenetus and John Junior owned competing taverns in Providence: "Taverns continued to be places of great resort especially before the building of the county court house in 1729. Those of Whipple and Epenetus Olney were famous..."[191] It would seem that John Junior's inn was the more luxurious of the two. "Even at this early date a competitor had entered the field, and a rival hostelry now offered the town-meeting not house-room only, but 'fire roome and fireing and Candle at all their Towne Meetings and Council meeteings,' nor does it admit of doubt that the inner man might also be warmed and comforted should the necessity arise. This enterprising competitor was no other than John Whipple Junior. John Junior kept a tavern for many years on Mill Street and a brother, Joseph, was also at one time a licensed innkeeper within the town of Providence."[192] It is thus seen that at least three of Captain John Whipple's children (John Junior, Joseph, and Mary Whipple-Olney) were actively involved in that business for many years. At least four members of the next generation were innkeepers on Mill (now Charles) and Town streets: John III, Sylvanus Scott,[193] (John Junior's stepson), James Olney (son of Mary), and William Hopkins Junior (son of Abigail).

John Junior started his tavern at the special request of the town, because its citizens were not adequately being provided for,[194] three years before his father's death. Apparently John Senior's tavern, established in 1674,[195] no longer operated and likely had not for several years. This is to be expected, considering the devastation of the Indian war of 1675-76 and the long years of recovery needed to rebuild and repopulate the town. When John Senior died in 1685, "he left a large property in land, but the means at his disposal 'for entertainment of strangers'...was scanty. He had one feather bed, seven pewter platters, five pewter porringers, three old spoons, and (three chairs and a decayed old warming pan)...." [196]According to testimony given to the town council by John Junior involving his brother Samuel's niece, Howlong Harris, Captain John Whipple was apparently living with him by the year 1681.[197] Most information recorded about the so-called "prominent" Captain John Whipple Inn, located at 369 North Main Street, should have been attributed to his children's taverns—John Junior's in particular, built approximately one block to the northwest on Mill Street. It is known that John III, who inherited this tavern in the year 1701, continued as its owner for several years. The second brother to establish an inn (in 1710) was Joseph: "...Colonel Joseph Whipple, who at one time kept an inn on Mill Street, but is better known of local fame as a well-to-do merchant, and colonel of the militia raised on the mainland in 1719."[198]

The Olney tavern's address was just around the corner from Mill Street, on the northeast corner of the intersection of Town Street and Olney Lane. Mill Street led northward from Town Street across from the Whipple property to the gristmill located on the falls of the Moshassuck River. Sarah Whipple (Captain John's oldest daughter) and her husband John Smith Junior owned this mill. Sarah Whipple-Smith and her husband also owned the nearby sawmill: "The Proprietors granted to John Smith, the son of the old miller...the land next south of the gristmill for a sawmill... The inns and the 'gaol [jail] house' were... not far away, and the mill was thus the centre of the old agricultural town."[199] It is clear therefore that the businesses of the Whipples, Smiths, and Olneys constituted the very center of the old town. However, by the middle of the next century the center of the town had moved about one mile to the south. "Olney's Tavern, which shared with the Whipple's and Turpin's [brother-in-law of John III, their wives were sisters] a celebrity that endured well into the last century...enjoyed a longer life than either of the other two...In 1803, when the city was drifting away from it and it had seen its best days, Colonel Jere Olney built a house on the green before it, and it was a matter of a few years only before it passed away."[200]

"Throughout the colonial times, the inns of Olney... and of Whipple, while it lasted, were the centers of any unusual excitement, and the principal scenes of public events. Thus, 23d September 1696, the Town Meeting reciting an act establishing an annual fair in Providence, appointed places for setting it up. 'Stalls for the goods shall be in the highway against William Turpin's land, and in the highway at Epenetus Olneys house, near the stocks,' [paid for by John Junior's brother Samuel] ---no doubt an effectual persuasive to honest dealing---'and one in the highway against John Whipple's house,'...Captain William Hopkins [the second husband of John Junior's youngest sister Abigail] was appointed 'clarke of the Market' for the fair. Similar orders were made in 1697 and 1698."[201]

John Whipple Junior Estates

In the Last Will and Testament drawn by Captain John Whipple in 1682 and proved 27 May 1685, John Whipple Junior was bequeathed the sum of only twelve pence, "excepting thirty acres which I gave unto my son John at the northwest end."[202] This refers to a deed for a house and land drawn up some 19 years earlier, 23 November 1663. Within two weeks of receiving this property, John Junior and his bride moved in to their new house. Ostensibly, the rest of the John Whipple Senior family moved into their newly constructed house next door (369 N. Main) north on the former lot of Frances Wickes.

The photograph below is of the northeast corner of Main and Star Streets. The land that was deeded to John Junior was located approximately where the south end of the condominium building now stands. The house would have faced south (to the right

of the photograph), with its front door leading toward what was to become many years later, Star Street. William Arnold, father of the man from whom Captain John bought the property, was its former owner. In 1650, Arnold was taxed five pounds, twice the sum of any other owner on the street.[203] The land immediately to the right of Star Street is now the parking lot

John Whipple Jr. Property, 1663

of St. John's Episcopal Church and the Diocese of Rhode Island. Colonel Joseph Whipple, John Junior's brother, was the leading contributor to the building of the original church building in 1722. Whipple Hall, one of the earliest permanent schools in Providence, was located at the top and to the left of Star Street on Benefit Street, just to the left of the distant red sign in the photograph. John Whipple Senior's provisions for his son in this 1663 deed were detailed thus:

The enrolment of A deede, signed and sealed by John Whiple Senior. As followeth: Know all men by these presentes, That I John Whiple Inhabetant of the Town of providence in the Nanhiggansick Bay in New England (senior). Have ffreely given, granted, and confirmed; and by thes presentes doe ffreely give grant make over, and conffirme unto my sone John Whiple a howse lott, or home share of land which fformerly belonged unto William Arnold (Now inhabitant of Pautuxett) with all the howsing ffencing, ffruite Trees standing upon the said land or appertaineing thereunto: only Excepting so much of the East part of said lott which belongeth unto Thomas Olney…Also the aforesaid Lott, or sharae of land containeth in breadth Eight poles according unto sixteene ffoote & a halfe to the pole: Also Two shares of Meaddow lieing in one percell, they being in Esttmation six Acrs (more or less) the which shares of meadow are scituated lieing and being at the south End of the Meadow commonly called the great Meaddow; and on the East side of the fresh river called Moshosick River…I bought of M'Benedict Arnold Now of Newport on Roade Jland: Also six acres of upland lieing within the Tract of land called the Neck, and neere unto the Now dwelling howse of Arthur Ffener…Also sixty acrs of land lieing an being neere unto, or about the place commonly called by the name of Louquasqussuck and lieing a crosse the north East End of a percell of land or ffarme which I the said John Whiple due possess as my owne proper Right…I doe here unto putt my hand and seale, Signed John Whipple. Enroled, May the 14th 1667: by me Thomas Olney Jun': Clarke of the Towne of providence: by, & with the Townes order." [204]

The Thomas Olney mentioned in the phrase "only excepting so much of the east part of said lot which belongeth unto Thomas Olney," deeded his part of the lot to the young couple at the same time. The Whipple-to-Whipple deed can yet be viewed in the library of the Rhode Island Historical Society. It is interesting that John Junior and Mary were married in the same year that Rhode Island received its Charter, which unlike the other American colonies guaranteed freedom of religion, from the new king of England (whose father had been beheaded by Oliver Cromwell). The Whipples, like their recently adopted frontier homeland, were entering a new and challenging stage of life. John Junior and his bride, as seen in the deed, moved into the former house of William Arnold, ancestor of the notorious Revolutionary War trader, Benedict Arnold.

Dispute With The Reverend Roger Williams

Within less than a decade of arriving in Providence with his parents, at about the age of 18 or19, John Junior became a major participant in a protracted legal battle to acquire Indian land. His primary opponent in a battle of words and legal machinations was none other than The Reverend Roger Williams, the colony's founder. Indeed, it has been noted that John Junior was considered by the much-revered Williams to be one of his most formidable foes, particularly in the battle of words.

In brief, the youthful John Junior allied himself with his wife's father, Thomas Olney; his brother Samuel's wife's uncle, William Harris; and William Arnold, his sister Abigail's second husband's uncle. These men were the leaders of a consortium of the earliest settlers, called "Proprietors," who had for years sought to extend the plantation's boundaries westward for some 20 miles, allowing them to create vast land holdings exclusively for themselves.[205] Roger Williams, always the champion of the Indians, opposed this plan. The ensuing legal wrangling lasted well into the next century, long after the combatants had died.[206]

By virtue of two extant letters that Williams wrote to John Whipple Junior (others are known to have been exchanged between them) on 8 July 1669 and 24 August 1669, something is learned of John Junior's personality and character, at least from Williams' point of view. In the August letter, after discussing the inaccuracy of John Junior's unflattering pronouncements against him, and alluding to why the youth had been precipitously drawn under the supposed nefarious influence of his relatives,[207] Williams next addressed the issue of John Junior's own mental and spiritual inadequacies:

…Further, since You seeme so fair and innocent in Your owne eye, I pray you to consider Your face impartially…in the Glasse of these 2 or 3 particulars.

1. First in all our Towne meetings is it not notoriously knowne that You are so far from being Swift to heare and slow to speake (according to Gods command unto us:) that what ever is propounded or by whomsoever You are the first that lets fly upon it, and betweene Your selfe and Some other begins Dispute and Contention that other Neighbours (though able, ancient, and experienced) scarce find an Interim to utter their Thoughts in the Case and Busines. Whether this be out of quicknes of your mind, or Weaknes of Judgmnt; Out of an Itch of Contention, or Self Conceitednes and pride, let Your Selfe and others Consider it. However I am sure it is not the Badge and Character of a Sober and Peaceable Townsman, least of all a humble Christian.

2. Secondly How can you be an innocent and peaceable Christian, when Your Selfe (above others of William Harris' disciples) Continually and Voluntarily thrust in your Selfe amongst Your Adversaries, though you declaime agnst their Persons, Meetings and practices, and You to them be as welcome as Water into a Ship or a Moskeeto to the face or bozoome, and have gaind your Selfe The title of one William Harris' spies and Promoters…If it be a dutie for all of your partie to crosse and contend with your Adversaries why doe they all Neglect their Dutie?…how can you Wash your Hands amongst your neighbours in the Bason Of Puritie and Christian Innocencie? It is clear, that you beare up your selfe upon the Gentlenes and Patience of your Adversaries… for they have not feard the presence of any of William Harris's promoters, though no other good can be expected from their presence but Contention, Provocation; further Alienations, and catching hold of all Advantages, according to William Harris's his Machivillian Maxime 'All Advantages angst Adversaries.'

If you came as a Messenger from the other Partie with messages or Proposals for Peace and Accommodation, and leave Your Adversaries alone to Consult upon them and upon an Answer, what an Instrument and Angel of peace might be between them…how far is this from Christianitie, Yea from common prudence and Civilitie?

Lastly if my case were Yours and I were such a Companion, Councellor, and Conferderate of William Harris and such a Spie and Promoter of his Covetuous and ambitious ends so take notice of an cried out on by the Barbarians (Indians) for such Monstrous Stealing of their Countrey I know not how to escape that Thunderbolt Psalm, 50…"Now I humbly beseech the most holy and Eternall God to…punish William Harris and you…and beg of him to heale our Breaches, and for his Names

Sake to spring us Some Providences of Love and peace amongst us. Your unworthy neighbour, RW."[208]

This appears clearly to be a one-sided vilification of the character of an obviously gifted and highly motivated young man. From another perspective, in carrying out the example set by his father to "supplant" the wilderness, John Junior clearly exemplified those familial traits that soon enlarged the extended family's ownership of much of Providence and northern Rhode Island. There is no denying that his personality traits of driving ambition and thirst for land appear in others of the Whipple family, particularly in his younger brother Joseph and family, who by the mid 1700s were much-admired owners of some of the town's most highly valued property.[209]

From this perspective, the sons of Captain John Whipple became self-made men, like many others in the English colonies who were determined to take advantage of every opportunity that increased their status and wealth. However, it was this very acquisitiveness in John Junior, and his allies, that Roger Williams vilified in the above letters. Although the ultimate outcome (11 February 1712)[210] of the lawsuits went against the Harris, Arnold, Olney, and Whipple family syndicate, a great deal of land still came into the possession of their descendants. In the case of the Whipple family, several descendants moved into the generally disputed areas of Cranston, Scituate, and Warwick, living there for several generations under such names as Rice, Carder, Arnold, Harris, Rhodes, and Whipple.[211] If Williams had won the argument, Providence Plantations would have been but four miles wide; consequently, it would have been easy prey for other colonies to absorb. Later historians note that the family syndicate[212] was concerned, with good reason, about the intent of Massachusetts men as well as syndicates of land speculators to take over much of the Narragansett and possibly end Rhode Island's existence as a separate colony. Therefore in fairness, it should be noted that the motives of the syndicate were not entirely selfish. It should also be noted that Williams himself made money by selling land.[213] Moreover, "Near the end of his life... Williams lamented the bitter land dispute and his own role in it."[214]

The Indian War

One event caused a serious delay in the final disposition of the litigation: an Indian uprising during the years 1675/76. Though the conflict lasted barely 18 months, all but a handful of Providence's 300 to 400 inhabitants fled to Aquidneck Island for safety, while much of their town burned to the ground. John's father and his close relatives, John Arnold, and James and John Angell, "stayed and went not away," and as such were later entitled to the sale of captives.

The colony had forbidden servitude of Indians since 1674, but the incensed settlers were not willing to abide by that law so soon after the war. The captives were auctioned off as bondservants under the direction of a committee of five men: Roger Williams, Thomas Harris, Thomas Field, Thomas Angell, and John Whipple Junior. By early 1677, the committee, now composed of Arthur Fenner, William Hopkins, and John Whipple Junior, had concluded its work: "Wee whose names are here unto Subscribed having imployed Arther Ffenner, William Hopkins, and John Whipple Junior to make Sale of a Company of Indians to us belonging as by Act of the Comittey doth Appeare,

69

they having made Sale of the Same, and received a part of the pay for the Same, and having proportioned Each man his share of what they have received the which amovnted to Sixteene shillings and fower pence hafle peeny the which sayd svmm wee say wee have received, and Doe hereby fully Acquitt and disschareg the above named persons of the same as witness our hands this first day of January one thovsand, Six hvndred, Seventy and Seven."[215]

"The committee limited the time of servitude to varying periods of years. Thirty-six young Indians were sold and proceeds divided by the committee among the town's defenders, based on the list of twenty-seven who had stayed. Eight persons got fractional shares and it is not clear whether prowess in the fighting or property loss or other reasons governed the division...It prescribed a humane treatment of the prisoners. In view of the devastation wreaked by the savages, the limited terms of servitude which the townsmen accepted for their captives points to an enlightened leadership."[216] Whipples who received part of the "proceeds" were John Senior and his sons Samuel and Eleazer. Actually, the only Whipple brothers who appear never to have been mentioned in such awards in 1676-77 were William and David. Even the 12-year-old Jonathan was listed.[217]

John Whipple Junior played an important role in preserving the town's records. "By the time the good people of Providence had sold off their Indian prisoners, reinstated their house-hold goods so far as that was practicable, and settled down once more to a quiet life on the Towne Street...their first thought was for the preservation their 'Town Books and Records (saved by Gods mercifull Providence from fire and water).' Accordingly four men who had held the position of town clerk were appointed to 'view and search the papers, what is wanting or Lost, and make report to the Towne." This was done in October 1677, and the records were in due course delivered to the then town clerk, Daniel Abbott.[218]

This transfer actually took place almost a year later. "We whose names are here under subscribed, being empowered by an order of this town as before said, have this 23rd day of August 1678 received of John Whipple Jr. the former town clerk, all the said books, papers, parchments, and writing herein before mentioned and particularized, which belong to the town. And do there of in the town's behalf fully, clearly, and absolutely acquit and discharge the said John Whipple Jr. of and from all papers that concern this town. In witness whereof we do here unto set our hands this day and year above said. Signed, Roger Williams & Daniel Abbott."[219] The paid position of town clerk, which automatically meant the leadership of the proprietors as well, was a position of great influence and profit in those days-- indeed the most important office in Providence.[220]

An Influential Entrepreneur

The distinction of being the first resident of Providence to receive a grant of land on the west side of Town Street next to the cove and river, for the purpose of constructing a warehouse and wharf, has historically been awarded to Pardon Tillinghast in the year 1680. However, John Junior had received permission from the town a year earlier to erect such a structure which "...adjoyneth to the south part of Ware howse lot formerly laid out to John Whipple ffather of the said Now John Whipple (deceased)..."

70

See the 27 January 1703/04 entry below for details of the transaction. Although the descriptor "wharfe" was not specifically used, there would have been no use for a structure of that size, twice that of Tillinghast's, unless commodities in significant amounts were being imported/exported for sale. As noted below, John's warehouse was kept busy buying and selling for his clients and those of others. He was listed as one of Providence's leading merchants during the decade of the 1680s.[221] He subsequently sold this property to his brother Benjamin, 6 March 1692/93.

In addition to owning the equivalent of a modern Bed and Breakfast Inn,[222] like his father before him, in the days when the holder of such a position was one of the most important public functionaries, John Junior was one of Providence's leading attorneys.[223] In reality, the two professions were symbiotic: "A tavern keeper in these primitive days immediately radiated influence and power.[224] His place of business was like a club center or exchange…a permanent parliament in perpetual session, and minute regulation of town affairs was conceived and worked up in these friendly debates. As the Assembly, Courts, Town, and council meetings always sat in central taverns, the landlord often became the oracle of his neighborhood. Sometimes chief of local militia and representative in the Assembly, he enjoyed prominence which in Massachusetts belonged to the Puritan minister."[225]

It would seem that the profession of the law was similarly profitable, as evidenced in several references to John Junior's practice. At a time when newspapers were unheard of and back fence discussions carried the news of the day, scandal, slander, and gossip often filled the air and occasionally went on record. For example, "On 27 August 1684, Samuel Bennett was obliged to retain John Whipple, Jr., an attorney, to defend him against the suit of Bridget Price. In September, Bridget declared that the said Bennett charged her with being a thief and a vagabond." Even far-away Boston furnished him considerable tort business, for a "Thomas Clarke in his pewtour's shop there, had an altercation with one Mary Brattle. He followed her to Providence where he arraigned her through the busy attorney Whipple"[226] As an attorney, John Junior played a role in a later important occurrence in early town history. Joshua Verin was one of the five who had come in the traditional canoe with The Reverend Roger Williams on his first recorded voyage in 1636. He had received a home lot in the division and settled in Providence. However, he had immediately become involved in a"liberty of conscience" conflict that forced him to return to Salem, Massachusetts. Years later, he addressed a request to the town council to maintain his status as one of the original proprietors and to retain his property in Providence. Captain John Whipple and others were able to prevail in his favor in the ensuing adjudication. Subsequently, although an absentee owner, Verin was allowed to

John Whipple Jr. Signature

keep his land. "In 1674 he was represented by John Whipple Junior who held a power of attorney, he (Verin) having gone to Barbados to reside." [227]

The practice of the corporate side of the legal profession likewise appears to have been a profitable aspect of his busy schedule. Shortly before his death, John wrote to the town council on behalf of a client enquiring as to whether "rivers belonging to the towne are common and ffree to sett up any mill or mills, or Contrary to law so to do." [228] The General Assembly, in 1707, ruled that towns could determine the use of rivers, coves, etc., providing that they avoided abrogating property rights. "The Quakers usually confined their business to other Friends: at Providence John Whipple [Junior] acted for those in Boston, Bridgewater, Plymouth Colony, Rehoboth, and Newport. He bought rum through Daniel Gould on Rhode Island, and in turn looked after forwarding a trunk full of goods Edward Shippen wanted delivered to Newport. Frequently, too, a correspondent in a distant place made 'my good friend John Whipple' his 'Lawfull Attorney' to collect money or goods or estates due; Stephen Paine of Rehoboth used Whipple to recover what was owed to him from the estate of Leonard Smith of Providence in 1670. [229] The above has led some to think that John Junior may have been a convert to the Society of Friends. [230]

Furthermore, in 1672, John Junior and his brother-in-law, Thomas Olney Junior, were recipients of a letter from George Fox, the founder of that newly formed Christian sect, imploring the colony to continue to allow freedom of religion and speech. Fox had for two years been traveling in the colonies, and in that year spent the summer in Rhode Island. "Just before his departure he wrote a singular paper to Thomas Olney, jr. and John Whipple, jr., at Providence known as 'George Fox's instructions to his friends,' which was answered the following year, by Olney, in a lengthy article entitled 'Ambition Anatomised'." [231] It has never entirely been explicated why the letter was addressed to them in particular, unless they held positions of authority or were able to promulgate its message in some way. John Junior was at the time serving in his third consecutive year as town clerk, and Thomas Olney Junior was the long-time minister of a Baptist Church in Providence, former town clerk, and town council member. It seems also, at least at that time, that John Junior may have been Baptist. The above is a portion of a document thought to have been written and signed by John Whipple (Junior).

John Whipple Junior in Early Town Records

In addition to the numerous times John Whipple Junior was elected to town and colony offices, [232] he appeared in Providence town records on at least 400 other occasions. The following is a summary of a chronological representative sample extracted from *The Early Records of the Town of Providence*, 21 Volumes (Providence: Snow & Farnham, 1892-1915). Individual entries are noted with the volume number and page. Original spelling and punctuation are retained in some cases.

2 May 1666
    John Whipple Junior listed as a freeman. (XV:73)

27 October 1666

Neighbours I desire that you grant me Leave, for to comon my cattle, and cut wood for fireing, Timber for building and fencing upon your: common. John Whipple Junior (XV:113)

May 1669

To be payd unto John whiple Junior for attending at a gennerall Assembly (a deputy for the Towne of providence) at a Court of Election held in May in the yeare 1669, for 14 dayes…(XV:125)

29 July 1670

Recorded a deed, as town clerk, transferring ownership of William Arnold property to Henry Fowler (XV:131)

19 October 1670

John Whipple Junior and John Whipple Senior chosen to Serue upon a Grand Jury at a Generll:Curt of Tryalls to be held at newport…(XV:129)

27 October 1670

To the Towne my desire is that I may be Received a purchaser, John Whipple Junior (XV:130)

19 March 1671/72

John Whippull commissioned to collect certain monies for the absent Mr. Joseph Torrey (XV:133)

3 June 1671

John Whipple Junior, along with his father and brothers Samuel and Eleazer, were taxed. (XV:135)

3 June 1672

Ordered that the Towne Counsell shall receive from John Whipple Junior: and give him a ffull discharge for such wrightinges or Bookes as they receive of him…(XV:139)

16 October 1672

The Town of Providence paid John Whipple Jun. Over 5 £ in back wages for "runeing of a line in the yeare 1663; serveing as Towne Serjant in 1669; for attending a Deputy 1669; for attending a duputy in 1672 (XV:140)

7 January 1674

The town council voted & Granted vnto John Whipple Junr in the behofe of Joshua Veren…that the sayd John whipple may haue all such Lands as are dew to the said veren Layd out to him for the vse of the said veren…(IV:18)

12 April 1674
The town council voted that Joshua Veren hath no Right in this towne of prouidence and therfor denye John Whipple to draw a paper for the deuiding of any Land in the Behalf of the sayd Joshua Veren (IV:34)

1 June 1674
John Whipple Jr. chosen to ade to the Generall officer to make vp the Towne Counsell (IV:7)

13 June 1674
John Whipple Junr witnessed a deed between William Carpenter and John and Joane Shelton.

24 May 1675
Granted vnto John ffield that he may Chang 5 acres of Land: and pay his Chang mony...voated that whereas John Whipple Junr prefered 50 shilings in the behalf of joshua Veren the towne haue voated that the towne Conclud that the said veren hath no Right to Land in this towne therefor Refuse to Except of said veren his mony (IV:43)

1 June 1675
John Whipple:Jun and seven other men signed an agreement to mine for silver (XV:147)

X June 1675
John Whipple junior and Richard Arnold Chosen survaiores to Layout Land on the East side of the seauen mile Line. (IV:52)

15 August 1676
Five men including John Whipple Junior were appointed to a committee to decide the rules for dividing out Indian slaves (XV:152)

18 December 1676
Stepen Payne made John Whipple his lawfull attorney. (XV:159)

14 January - 25 December, 1678
John Whipple, Jr., performed eight marriages. (IX:188-9)

6 August 1679
Rebekkah and John Whipple Junior signed an agreement with Alexander Bolkcom to lease the land of her former husband John Scott, deceased. The lease was to end when her son, Silvanus Scott, reached the age of 21 years. (XV:194-95)

6 June 1680
To the town whereas there is many weighty matters which Conserne ye Counsell, and in the multitude of Counsell there may be safety, I do desire ye Towne would be

pleased to add to ye Counsell two person more, which may be so added by Election…
that we may have as large an Number as any other Towne in ye Colony. Signed, Your
ffriend, Joh: Whipple: Jun

16 June 1680
John Whipple Jun taxed for himself and the orphans of John Scott (XV:208)

14 October 1680
Whereas my husband is by a providence now a Captive in Turky…do hereby
appoint John Whipple of Providence (jun) my true & Lawfull Atturny…Susan Harris
(XV:215)

17 December 1680
Jonathan Whipple and John Whipple Junior witnessed the sale of a horse to
William Herndon (XV:217)

21 January 1681
In his Majestys name Charles ye Second Ectt: to require you [John Whipple as
sergeant] to arrest ye bodey of one sephor stanly…(XV :220)

7 September 1681
…I Walter Rhodes of prouidence…doo atherise my wel.belued firend John
Whipple Junior to bee my Lawfull Aturney…(XV:233)

7 October 1681
Edward Bennett and Thomas ffenner ki[   ] a woulfe …and Delivered [   ]
according to order of this Towne…John Whipple Clerke (IX:200)

8 November 1681
…Joseph Williames Did take up a stray mare upon ye Eight day of November:
1681, of a Browne Couler and Doct, with a starr in her forehead, and made proclamation
of ye same according to law. Entered upon record ye Day and ye year beforesd, me John
Whipple Clerke. (IX:195)

1 December 1681
That Thomas patey of providence Did take uup a Stray Beast…being a steere, and
as he judgeth about a yeare old …John Whipple, Clerke

8 February 1682
This discharge on ye other side was Delivered to yr Towne in ye face of the
Towne meeting February the eight: 1682: As Attest John Whipple junr Clerke (XVII:10)

1 July 1682

Stephen Sabeere of ye Towne of Newport in ye Collony afosd or his ordr to receive of ye Generall Treasurer Weston Clark forty shillings...Wittnes us John Whipple junr; Edward Smith (XVII:7)

28 January 1683/4

My request is whereas there is an order formerly made in this towne; of a Grant of a purchase right of land to be layd out in this Towne for ye use and Benniffitt of a Schoole; which hath nott bene yet done, my Humble request is that the same may be fulfilled or accomplished according to the tenour of the sayd order, Jon Whipple Junr (XVII:27)

April 1683

Benjamin Whipple brought the head of a wolf to John Whipple, Clerke, for recording. (IV:56)

April 1683

John Haukins brought the head of a wolf to John Whipple, Clerke, for recording. (IV:57)

27 April 1683

Honord Gentelmen, wee humbly Conceive: ye: it is in the power of our Towne, to Regulate all such things, as ar Amiss in our towne...And whereas theire are Divers persons, (to will Indians) Come into our Towneshipp: And doe both hunt, and ffish, without any Liberty of our Towne, the which is Contrary to a knowne Law of our Towne made unpon Matture Consideration, and Whereas wee judge, or at least are willing to Alow all such Indians as have served with ye English in our Towneshipp, here to Abide. And have ye same priveledgs in them Respects with uss, But not thereby to harbore any others with them, to Infringe our Rights, Therefore pray of ye Towne a full order to ye Contratrary, or elce wee must provide other ways for ours, and the Colloney's peace...Your Loueing: Neighbors: and Townes Men: Joseph Jenckes, Edward Smith, John Whipple Jounr, Eleazer Whipple, and Samuel wilkeson. (XVII:19)

May 1683

James Matuson brought the head of a wolf to John Whipple, Clerke, for recording. (IV:57)

10 June 1683

Attest John Whipple: Junr: Clerke of ye Towne of Providence (XVII:20)

31 July 1683

Whereas at or Towne Meeting July: ye: 27th: 1683: It was ordered by sayd Towne that I should receive of John Whipple junr late Towne Clerke all such books, records, writeings, and papors what soe Euer: as belong to ye Towne now in ye hands of ye sayd John Whipple: And Deliver them to the now Towne Clerke Thomas Olney: and

Whereas the sayd John Whipple having this last day of July 1683: Delivered up all such Books, Records, writetings, papors and parchments... (XVII:22)

27 January 1684
       To ye Towne mett Jan: ye: 27th 1684 whereas there was at ye last Towne meetiing an order for any receiveing: ye: 25: rate: these are to signifie to ye Towne now mett, That upon my further Consideration: see Cavse fully to De Cline the same: and leave it to some other. Yors to serve: Jon Whipple jun. (XVII:25)

20 June 1684
       The Depotion of John Whipple Junr of providence...Aged forty fower yeares or there abouts and David Whipple, of sayd Towne & Collony aforesayd, Aged twenty nine years or thereabouts...That upon ye first day of June, one Thousand Six hundred and Eighty fower: these Deponants Saw and heard Thomas Tery of ffretowne in his majestys Collony of new plymouth at The hovse of Alixander Bolkom in providence there tender the Delivery of a deed signed by Jabesh Cotterell, to Tho King, and Samuel Thrashar...(XVII:36-7)

27 August 1684
       Knowe all men by these presents that I Samuell Bennett, senr, nowe Liueing in este Greenewich...appoynte my well beloued and trustye ffreind John Whipple Junier of providence in sd Collonye, my lawefull atturnye...(XVII:40)

September, 1684
       Court of Tryalls held at Newport...Whereas by Bridgett price, Single woman, plantiff inhabeting at East Green witch in ye kings province, an Action of slander & Defamation was Comenct against Samuell Benjett, John Whipple, Jurn Atturney (XVII:42)

29 October 1684
       Rate levied upon ye inhabetants of ye Towne of Providence...John Whipple junr: 00-05-08 (XVII:47)

24 November 1684
       The Depotion of John Whipple of ye Towne of providence Aged forty five years: testifieth as followeth: That upon ye twenty fowerth day of November: 1684 being in ye shopp of Thomas Clarke: /peutour/ in boston where came in to sayd shopp: one called Mary Brattle, and Demaunded of sayd Clarke ye key of a house of office and ye sayd Clarke Denied to Deliver it, to sayd Brattle, whereupon sayd mary Brattle gave sayd Clarke very Taunting speeches: where upon sayd Clarke called sayd Brattle prateing hossey: where upon sayd Brattle called sayd Clarke Beggars Bratt, and Cheate: and sayd she'd kept a better man to wipe her shoes, the sayd Clarke speaking very mildly and patiently all the while: she alsoe Called ye sayd Clarke Rascal, the ye sayd Clarke bid her gett out of his shopp for yov are a pratteing hossey for you had need to have had a hundred pound Bestooed upon you at a boardeing Scoole: to learn manner & breeding:

then shee sayd Brattle called sayd Clarke Rouge and soe went out of ye shopp: This this Deponant, sayth is truth: and further sayth nott. Jon Whipple testimony abovte Tho: Clarke (XVII:53-4)

27 January 1685/6
    Wheras there was an order for a rate by ye Collony and Levie of ye same by ye Towne, out of which sd rate Eliaz whipple: and Jon Wilkenson was to have tenn pounds pr mann, ye which sd rate was to have bene payd, in march last past...was Twelve months, ye which is not yet Done nor any part of...These are to signify to ye Towne mett that the abovesayd Eliazur Whipple, and John Wilkenso or Either of them will receive Each of theire shaires therein...Yors John Whipple (XVII:70)

27 April 1685
    I desire yet yov wovld Grant mee liberty as others have had, that I may have ye bounds of ye six Acres of land belonging to the heires of John Throckmorton Deceassed, revised by ye Towne surveior or sorveiors: paying ye Charge:: Yoers John Whipple in: behalfe of John Throckmorton and them Conserned: (XVII:58)

3 August 1685
    Lickewise I doe in his maijesties naime, warne you, that you Cause ye freemen of yor towne to meet together, And in yor said towne meeting to Chuse so many Able discreet men of ye towne, to be yor deputies...Att ye house of mr John whiple. (XVII: 62)

3 November 1685
    Neighbors My Request is that you would Consider ye Townes bennefit in stateing of som Comon Continually so to remaine & also to Confirme...Jo:Whipple jr (XVII:64)

27 January 1686/7
    I desire to know if it may be, The Bounds of ye Towne of providence southerly, pautuxett Right Excepted, that I may know how much money to pay, and how much for a Towne Right, to defray ye Charge, to Answer if need Require, or make out before his Excelency sir: Edmund Andros what if ye Townes Claime, and I shall pay my Dve, Jon Whipple (XVII:77)

31 May 1687
    As allso you Thomas olney John whiple as grand Jury men...(XVII:89)

8 July 1687
    I doe Authorise & appoint mr John Whipple to Receive the whole Excise of all sortes of Drinke that shall be sould within the Towneshipp of prouidence by Retaile...(XVII:90)

16 July 1687

John Whipple is admitted allowed & lycenced...To keepe a Comon Ale house & victualling house & Entertainemt for Lodgers & travilers, & horsemeate & for retaileing of wine Brandy Rum beare or Ale; or any other sort of strong drinke whatsoever: By law to bee retailed: For the space of one whole yeare...To the best of his power shall: not suffer: or allow any misrule or disorder to bee...(XVII:91)

29 August 1687

There is a warrant Come for the Callinge of a Towne Meeting...at ye hovse of Jon Whipple. In order to the leavimg of a rate upon ye Inhabetance, for ye support of his majestys Goverment (XVII:97)

1 September 1687

A List of Names of those Rated in Providence...Jon Whipple 0-07-06 (XVII:102)

20 October 1687

John Whipple & William Turpin ...haue bin thought fit ...to keepe ordinary or houses of Entertainement....all proceedings made or intended to bee made against them on that account Doe cease at wch Cort they may apply for renewall of their seuerall Lycences...(XVII:105)

31 October 1687

Rate made...for ye payeing of Joseph woodward for takeing and bringing up ye Child of Thomas Waters...John Whipple 00-03-09...By us Tho:Olney; John Whipple, William hawkings (XVII:106, 111-12)

13 December 1687

Doe appoint you, the said John Whipple, to keepe a Publicke house of Entertainement: in the aforesaid: Towne: At the house where you now dwell: & not elsewhere; For victualling Lodging & Entertaineing of strangers & travilers; Both for people & horses; & for what other people the Law allows Entertainement for; The which shallbee for the space of one yeare next...said Towne of Providence Lycence & Liberty to victuall Lodge and sell out drinke by Retaile Either beer ale wine or Rum or any other sort of strong drink whatsoever...(XVII:113-14)

6 March 1688

Wee whose Names are here Vnderwritten his majesties Justice of the Peace of Rhode Island and Providence Plantations Sitting in Generall Quarter sessions in Rochester...Lycence Admitt and allow John Whipple of Providence a victualler to Keep A common Ale house ordinary or Victaling house for one whole year next ensueing Provided that the said John Whipple doe not suffer any vnlawfull Games to be vsed in his Said House butt doe vse and maintaine Good Order and Rule within the same...(XVII:115-16)

Samrell whipell Constabell or Ephram Pierce constabels...are required in his majesties name to atiche the body...of Nicholas brown and bring him befor me ...to ansr the Complent of John whippell in ane[ ] att not exciding fowrttie shillings for so doeing you [ ] shall be your warrant...(XVII: 120)

August 1688
    A List of Names of those who were Rated in Providence to a Country Rate...John Whipple 0-5-0

3 March 1690
    John Whipple junr witnessed a deed of sale between Joseph Smith and John Keene (IV:106)

27 May 1690
    You are here by in their Majstis names Requiered to giue timly notis vn to all the free inhabitantes of this towne to meet to gether at the dwelling house of Mr John Whippeles at nine of the Cloke in the morning ...to make Chois of Constabelles and town Counsell men and all other towne ofisers...(XVII:133)

4 July 1691
    ReQuiar you to atache ye bodey & for want thereof the goods of John Boorman Some time Resadent...Giuen vnder my hand this 4th day of July 1691 at ye house of John Whippell...Stephen Arnold, assistant (XVII:136)

21 September 1691
    Requiered to atache the body of John haiden and take bond Retornabell aCordinge to law...at a Coourte of maiestratts helld in prouideince ...at the house of Mr John Whippels(XVII:139)

16 December 1691
    Whar as theris Complaint made of on william jaratt that is Com in to this towne of prouidence with his famely with out the aprabation of said towne thes ar therefore in thair majs names to Requier you John whippele jurr towne sargant to giue notis and Requier all the Councell men of saide towne...to meet to gether at the hous of mr John whippeles the twenty first day of this Instant december...(XVII:141)

6 March 1692
    Whereas there is one william Ashley who formerly dwelt at the town of wells...haveing Removed himselfe & his family into this towne of Providence, where he hath been Entertained by Abraham Hardin in his house. ..he then proposedto ye towne for admittance, the towne haveing this day Considered his bill & Considering the Capacitye as the said Ashely is in have by this preasant act voated & declared that they doe not grant the said Ashley into our sd towne neither doe they take any speede to Remoove him out of the towne, But in Case the sd Ashley doe fall to eant or be

80

chargeable, then je shall be Relieved by him or them whome ye law detirmine shall Relieve Poore people...John Whipple Protest against ye abovesd Voate (IX:3)

6 March 1692

Know yee that the sd John Whipple for & in Consideration of a valuable sum of silver money in hand already Well & truely payd unto him by Benjamin Whipple (his brother)...It beareing the denomination of a Waare house lott...(IV:163-5)

5 June 1693

Ordered that Dan: Williams, Nath Mawrey & Silas Carpentr: who are Chosen Constables be by the Majestrats Summonsed in to Come before the town meeting by adjornment at ye house of Jon Whipple on fryday ye 16th instant to give their Engagemt to theire office (XI:5)

10 October 1693

Voated that for this year untill next Towne Election the Councill shall meete upon the second Tuesday in Each month: about 10 of ye Clock in ye day at Jon Whipples house (X:11)

22 May 1694

John Whipple witnessed a deed between Thomas Greene of Warwick and Robert Westgate of Providence (IV:158-9)

September 1695

I Present & indict Joseph Latham, Robert Kilton, William Harris, Richard Harris, Eliezer Whiple junr,: Samuell Bartlet, & Cornelius Walling, all of the Towne of Providence...for the Comiting of an outrage at the house of John Whipple of said Providence upon the Eleventh of September in the yeare 1695 in the Night time, by cutting a Hatt, & a Shoo, & a paire of Stockins belonging to one Joseph Bugben of Woodstock, who that night lodged at the house of the said John Whipple, which act of theirs is Contrarey to the peace of our Sovereigne Lord the King, & against his Crowne & Dignity. John Whipple. (XVII:156)

8 October 1695

I William haris abousaid do make my parsonall aperance att he next Courtt of goall deliury to be held att newportt...for that thar is strong suspition that I did vpon the Eleunth of septembar: 1695 latt in the night in the hoous of mr John whipples Comitt an out Radg by Cutting a hatte and a shoo: and a pair of stokings of on Joseph bugbues....(XVII:158)

27 January 1696/7

Joseph Whipple hath desired of the Towne that they would Grant him a small pece of land lieing on the north side of his lot where his now dwelling is...southwestern corner of the said Joseph Whipple's land next to John Whipple's land....(XI:30)

17 April 1699

I, Alexander Bryan of Milford in ye Colloney of Conecticutt for & in Consideration of ye sum of fifty pounds in silver mony Received of Mr John Whipple...all ye lands to Mr John Throgmorton in Providence...(IV: 232)

18 November 1699

John Whipple junior and Tho: Olney senr witnessed a document executed by William Hawkins, setting free a Negro man named Jack, whom he had purchased from William Mackollin in 1695. (IV:72)

27 January 1700

The town of prouidence to met at the house of John Whipples....XVII:178)

28 May 1705 referring to a 1674 action

Samuell Whipple of providence being of full age testifieth & saith that his Brother John Whipple he vnderstood had A Letter of Aturny from Joshua Verin to Challinge his deponent Asked Richarde Scott of sd towne whether he had bought all sd Verins Rights in Comon sd scott answered that he had bought his home Lote & his shere of salt medoe & farder this deponaant saith that sad scott said that he though he had bought allsd Verins Right in providenc but vpon search of his deed he found he had bought no more than his hows Lote & his medoe & Clamed no more than his deed mentioned...(XVII:206)

Death and Burial

Ensign John Whipple Junior, Esq., died 15 December 1700, and was most likely buried next to his first wife in a family burial plot on their household lot on Town Street. Whether his remains were subsequently moved, like that of his parents, to the town's common burial ground has never been shown (though assumed). He and his wives are not listed in North Burial Ground records, which began in 1848. "Existing gravestones...mark only 18 burials here by 1725...There undoubtedly were unmarked burials, but without records we have no way of knowing how many. An educated guess would be that ten percent of the burials were marked with gravestones. This would indicate that there were 180 or more by 1725."[233] It is known that the majority of reinterments did not occur until toward the middle of the 1700s; consequently, there is almost near certainty that John Junior's remains lie near his parents who likely shared a common burial plot (since their homes were next to each other, with bodies thus removed at the same time) and brothers, Joseph and Samuel, somewhere in Section A of the most ancient part of the cemetery. "John Whipple was licensed to keep an ordinary. His south windows looked down upon the 'Whipple burying ground' in the adjoining field."[234]

John Whipple III, A Family Skeleton?

John Whipple III was born 2 October 1666 at Providence, Rhode Island and died probably after 3 June 1737. He married Lydia Hoare 9 November 1688 at Taunton, Massachusetts. To this couple, 10 children were born:

  i. *Job Whipple, born 25 Dec 1688; died about 1777; married Lydia Harding*
 ii. *Mary Whipple, born 11 Oct 1690*
iii. *John Whipple, born 30 Aug 1692; died after 3 June 1737*[235]
 iv. *Lydia Whipple, born 6 Nov 1694*
  v. *Elnathan Whipple, born 19 Sep 1696*
 vi. *Patience Whipple, born 18 Feb 1699; married John Medbury*
vii. *Hezekiah Whipple, born 17 Feb 1701/02; married Katherine Olney*
viii. *Mercy Whipple, born 21 Jun 1703*
 ix. *Sarah Whipple, born 7 Apr 1705*
  x. *Mary Whipple, born 21 Jun 1708*

At the meeting of the Providence Town Council, 7 January 1701, "Rebeckah Whipple widow of the deceasd John Whipple presented unto the Councill a paper signed by John Whipple & sealed...as witnessed by ffoure pesons (viz)..." One of the witnesses was Joseph Whipple, his brother. After subsequent reading of the will, "John Whipple the son, & heir apparent...hath this day made objections against the said will by...reason that it is an Jllegall instrument...he having Rendred [his] reasons for the same to the council." The Town Council took depositions and heard testimony on February 11, and March 11 and 12. Finally, on April 8, it ruled the proffered will to be bogus and consequently invalid. The ruling was based on the reasoning that John Junior, being blind, did not know the actual contents of the will, he apparently having been read a variant version after the fact. When asked by four witnesses, at a later date, whether the will was his actual intent, it not having been read or heard by them either, John Junior replied affirmatively. Thus neither the deceased nor the witnesses had read the piece of paper presented to the Council on 7 January. In addition to this, two individuals testified that John Junior had told them personally that it was not his will to disinherit his son, but being blind, "he must doe as others [his wife and daughters?] have him doe..." When asked directly if he wanted to disinherit his son, "John Whipple answered no, no that is not my desire...."[236]

By the date of the next town council session, 22 April, all parties to the litigation had (amicably?) resolved their differences: "Differences have happened among relatives of deceased-now all considering that to bring it to law would be greatly troublesome to all parties, and great charge, and would cause animosities of spirit and alienation of affection-an agreement was made. To John Whipple, the homestall, dwelling house, barn, and certain lands. To Mary Carder, Elnathan Rice, Deliverance Whipple and Dorothy Rhodes, certain land. Movable estate to go one-third to widow, and the rest in five parts to five children..."[237] John III also inherited seven acres from his grandfather Thomas Olney at this time.

As part of the "certain land" above, John III apparently owned his father's property in the Louquisett meadows. John III sold part of this to his uncle Eleazer Whipple: "...I give (to my son Job) 120 acres in the district of Louquisset Woods and from part of the land bought from my cousin [nephew] John Whipple."[238]

By virtue of the agreement above, John III inherited the property, originally deeded to his father in 1663, seen below.[239] He sold the land in turn to his uncle Colonel Joseph Whipple in 1705.[240] The remainder of the original Captain John Whipple property, extending from the lot of Francis Wickes northward to that of John Green

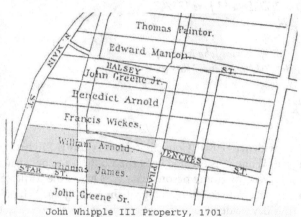

John Whipple III Property, 1701

Junior, each about 125 feet in width, had been willed to Colonel Whipple in 1685, who in turn willed it to his son John in 1746. "Beyond Scott, along nearly the whole east side of the present 'Constitution Hill' there was scarcely a house. The steep hill-side behind it did not invite purchasers. In 1659, came John Whipple, from Massachusetts. He purchased nearly the whole tract eastward of that part of the Town street."[241] The only street at the time was Main Street, or "Towne Streete," as it was then called. In the year 1798, this entire area from Star Street northward was still owned by John Whipple, S. Whipple, J. Whipple, and Joseph Whipple.[242] Note that the additional streets shown in the drawing above were constructed years later.

Regarding the controversy over John Junior's will, it is a conundrum why John III's sisters and stepmother would go to such lengths to have him disinherited. He does not appear in town records until late. He apparently was not living in Providence as of 15 April 1687. At that time, the village drew up a list of 27 men who were fit to serve in the militia. John III was not listed, although his father, seven uncles, and two cousins were.[243] The cousins were Samuel Junior and Thomas, sons of Samuel, and were yet teenagers, while John III was 21 years of age. On at least one occasion, seven months before his father's death, John III characterized himself, at age 34, as destitute. In response to a request, he was answered, "In Consideration of the Condition of the said John Whipple that he is destetude of land & in want of land to improve for a lively hood the Towne doe grant the said John Whipple Tenn Acres of land.[244]

What character flaws could have led to such a fiscal state? Records show that immediately following the death of his father, he attempted to confiscate the property of his deceased uncle Benjamin Whipple, which would have left his cousins, who were yet children, and their mother destitute.[245] Not only this, but due to an apparent flaw in Captain John's 1682 will, the inherited properties of three other of his uncles were challenged by John III as well. This forced them, in 1708, to buy off John III's uncharitable claims for an undisclosed sum of money: "...And lest that any

84

inconveniency or Trouble Should at any time arise by ye Meanes of any PerSon or PerSons WhatSoever Making Claime to any of the lands or Said house in Said Will Given and DeviSed unto any of ye abouve Named PerSons through any apprehension or Conjecture of any defect in Said Will, as they May, SuppoSe for want of Words or formality any Wayes; ffor the prevention therof, & the ye Said lands and HouSe by the Said Will...Be it knowne unto all PerSons to whome thsSe presents Shall Come That I John Whipple Now of the Towne of Providence...son of John Whipple & Mary his Wife, formerly of Sd Providence but now deceased. My ffather the Said John Whipple being Eldest son to John Whipple the above Sd TeStator; fffor. & in ConSideration of a Competent Sum of Money in hand to me Well & truly paid by ye above JoSeph Whipple, Samuell Whipple, & ye Heirs of the Sd Benjamin Whipple, & Jonathan Whipple, all of Sd Providence, the Recept whereof I doe owne & acknowledge; have RemiSed, ReleaSed, RelinquiShed, & forever quitt claimed...to their full & ReaSeable PoSseSsion & being...."[246] That John III makes a pointed reference to the fact that he was "now of the town of Providence" seems to indicate that he had resided somewhere else prior to receiving the ten acres described above. He appears to have returned to his childhood home just in time to claim an immense inheritance.

The controversy over the birth of his (or his wife's) first son sheds added light on the effects of John III's behavior on others. Though it is speculation, he could have lived a significant part of his adult life in another colony until at least the mid-1690s. As seen, he was not listed in Providence military records of 1687, and in December of 1688 his wife gave birth to a child in Taunton, Massachusetts. This child was born approximately one month after his marriage to Lydia Hoare, 9 November 1688. "In volume 44 of the American Genealogist appears an article entitled, Job Whipple of Providence, RI, by H. Minot Pitman, FASG of Bronksville, NY. The gist of the story is that Job Whipple was born prior to the marriage of his purported father, John Whipple and his mother, Lydia Hoar. Mr. Pittman says Job was born in Taunton, probably 25 December 1688...oddly there is no record in Taunton for the birth of a Job Hoar or Whipple. The vital records of Providence, giving the dates of birth and marriage for Job Whipple were not entered in the book (Vol.1 p.11) until the month of November 1719. The entry was probably made from information given by Job himself to the clerk and reads: 'Job Whipple, the son of John Whipple of Providence'...The facts are further supported by an indenture of apprenticeship to be found in the rebound volume now known as, 'Third Town Book B,' made between Job Liddeason [Lydia's son] John Whipple, Jr. and Lydia his wife, all of Providence on the one party and John Sayles of Providence...This shows that at the time Job had not taken the Whipple name. As apprenticeships usually began at about the age of 7 years and lasted until the age of 21 years, Job was probably born 25 December 1688." [247]

Could John III's relatives have been distressed at this treatment of his wife and son, and other such aberrant behavior? Due to cultural strictures of the time, he likely would not have married Lydia had the unborn child not been his. It is difficult to understand why, if he had loved and respected his wife, he would yet have allowed her child to live through life bearing the stigma of being considered a bastard, and she even worse. Such behavior would have hurt many people and caused great embarrassment to his father and sisters.

Unquestionably, this treatment of their daughter and grandson would have been an egregious affront to the Hoare family. Lydia was the daughter of Ensign Hezekiah Hoare, Esq., one of the original purchasers of Taunton, Massachusetts, who had served under Captain Miles Standish in the Dutch wars. They were the politically prominent and wealthy part owners of the first iron works in the colonies. The family lived on "Hoare's Lane" in Taunton, and traced its ancestry to 1093 England and its founding ancestor, Sir William Le Hoar. The castle and estate of Pole Hoar had ever since remained the property of the family of Hezekiah's cousin, Sir Philip Hoar.[248] The Hoare family probably would have maintained at best a rather strained relationship with the John Whipples, as would the families of his uncles, and his own sisters. His was not the first instance in which the only son of a rich and powerful father failed to measure up to familial expectations.

John Whipple III appeared in Providence Township records on several other occasions. The following is a chronological summary of these taken from *The Early Records of the Town of Providence, 21 Volumes,* (Providence: Snow & Farnham, 1892-1915). Individual entries are noted with the volume number and page.

[Note that there were at least four adult John Whipples living in Providence in the early to mid-1700s. In the year 1700, John III was 34 years old; his son was eight. John III's first cousin, Captain John Whipple, later known as the "bonesetter," and a Justice of the Peace, the oldest son of Joseph, was then 15 years old. John Whipple of North Providence, son of Benjamin, known as a cordwainer, had just been born. Town records only infrequently clearly differentiate them. Numerous entries merely state that an indeterminate "John Whipple" served as a juryman or committeeman, and such. Consequently, the authors of this work have attempted to make discriminations based on known historical data and particularities of circumstances at the time.

It is assumed that until the year 1705/06, the year that John son of Joseph became of age, entries refer to John III, particularly in the matter of town council meetings at his house/tavern. It is apparent that John III took over ownership, and the council continued to meet in the same location as it had during the late 1690s. Entries that mention the office of Justice of the Peace, or sea-faring commerce, or that refer to father, siblings, and in-laws, were assigned to John, son of Joseph. John, son of Benjamin, in the few cases in which he is mentioned, appears in connection with locations in North Providence and his siblings and in-laws.]

30 March 1696
    Indenture of Job Lideasson by John Whipple (IV:156-58)

27 April 1700
    Whereas John Whipple hath desired if the Towne that they would accomodate him with a percell of land lieing under the Southeasterne part of the hill Called the Wine mill hill to the quantetye of about Tenn acres, In Consederation of the Condition of the said John Whipple he is destitude of land & in want of land to improve for a livelihood the Towne doe grant unto the said John Whipple Tenn acres of land (XI:55)

27 July 1702

...And the said three persons (Tho:ffield senr; Elisha Arnold, and Tho:Olney senr) being desireous to have the knowledge of what Each mans Estate is that so they may make as Equall a levie as may be, Doe hereby give Notice to all the inhabitants of this Towne to bring in writeing, a true, full,& Exact account...to the sd three men at the hous of John Whipple (XVII:180-81)

27 January 1703/04

Whereas there was some time about the yeare 1689 a lot of land Called a waare howse lot laid out being forty foote square unto the then John Whipple, & in scituate lieing & being in the Towne of Providence, on the west side of the highway, or Towwne streete over against the dwelling house of sd John Whipple...the which sd was laid out & Rattified in the aforementioned Place, where, by the surveur laid out; the Time afore specified, laid out by me Tho:Olney Surveior.

Whereas at a Towne Quarterly meeteing ye January 27th: 1703/04 the Towne of Providence upon some Consideration did allow unto the now John Whipple so much land in sd Providence Towne as would make forty foote square, if laid out square; The which sd land some few dayes after the grant, Was by the Towne Surveior laid out unto the now John Whipple...adjoyneth to the south part of a Waare howse lot formeely laid out to John Whipple ffather of said Now John Whipple (deceased)...(IV:172)

21 March 1703

John Whipple witnessed a deed between Phebe Ffenner and Gideon Cruffurd. (IV:172).

26 March 1703

All the purchasers and proprieters of the Lands on the west side of the seven Mile Lign to meet to Geether Att the hous of John Whipple in this Town of prouidence on tusday the third day of Aperil 1705 by teen of the Clock In the morning then and there to rescue An Count of there Commitinars or trustees implied by said propieters to treet with the Gentlemen of warwick Concerning the souharn Lign of our plantation (XVII:203)

12 July 1703

...we giue notice to all ye free men in the township of prouidence to meete together on the 27th of this instant july at the hows of John whipples (XVII:185)

12 January 1704

...there is a great need for the building & Erecting a bridge ouer prouidence River (subscribers) John Whipple. (XVII:198)

6 April 1704

To all People to whome this Deede of sale shall come...know yee that I the said John Whipple for and in consideration of the sum of three pounds in silver Money, in hand already well& truly paid unto Me by Jonathan Whipple…a small Grassey Island, Containeing by Estemation about one acre…in the Northerne part of the salt water harbour…(IV:58-62)

17 May 1704
Samuel Williams, mariner, of Salem, Essex County, Mass. Bay, sold to John Whipple (Innkeeper): for twelve pounds, all the rights of lands formerly belonging to Joshua Verin, except the house lot of about 5 acres, and one share of meadow, which is salt marsh of about three acres lying along the south side of the Wanasquatucket. All other lands which belonged to Joshua Verin, uplands, meadows, groves, coppses, all Right in Common, to John Whipple. They were given to Samuel Williams by deed of gift from Joshua Verin. (XIV:276-78)

4 July 1704
…to Arest the body of Benjamin Dayly…and him in ssafe Custety to keep vnteel hee put in baiel…to make his persoanall Aperance before A Court of Majestrats held for her Majestie Att the hous of John Whipple… (XVII:189)

14 July 1704
…wee see Caues to Ajoyrne this Court Vntll the 25th of this instant at the hows of john whipples…(XVII:193)

22 July 1704
…Required to arrest the body of Jacob Clarke of prouidence …& him in safe Custety keep until he giue in bind befour the majestrats of sd tonwe on the twenty fift of instant july at the hows of John whipples…(XVII:179)

2 October 1704
David Sheppey, junr; of this Towne of Providence gave notice that he had taken up a stray Maare…Aprised Jon;Whipple & James Walling at 1 lb, 16 s (IX:185)

27 April 1705
…to be a towne meeting at the hous of John Whipple (XVII:204)

9 June 1705
The Towne council of Providence is warned to meete to Gether Att the hous of John Whipple on Tuesday of this instant june by teen of the Clock (XVII:207)

21 July 1705
John Whipple (Ordinary keeper) sold to Joseph Whipple: for eight pounds thirty and eight, my dwellinghouse and all my outhousing, together with all my lands adjoining which are standing in Providence in the row of houselots lying on the east side of the salt water harbor (XX:171-72)

4 October 1705

    To Richard Waterman Henry Harrris & Josep Mory Constables for the Towne of prouidence with his Mjsts Coloney of Rhoad island & ct Greeting. These are to Require you in his majsts Ann Quene of England &ct to go persons whose names are in ye Rate bill or list which I haue her with sent you & Demand of Each person the sum of money that is set to there Respecttiue names… and if any Person Refuse or neglect to pay his or there proportion of sd Rate when demanded then you are here by Empowered & Required to detan on ye Estats of such Person…John Whipple & ye Estate of Deliuereance Arnold, & Dortihy Rhoads 00-11-06. (XVII:212)

24 December 1707

    John Whipple (Tavernkeeper) sold to Joseph Whipple: for seventy and eight pounds and fourteen shillings and nine pence, 164 acres on the northern side of the Wanasquatucket and about five miles northwest from the salt water harbor in Providence (original right of Joshua Verin) and about a ninety one acres on the western or southern side of the Wanasquatucket and about four miles WNW from the salt water harbor (original right of John Throckmorton and Joshua Verin) (XX:235-36)

23 August 1708

    John Whipple, son of John Whipple junr., & Mary his wife, was borne at Providence upon the 2nd day of October, it being the 3th day of ye weeke, & in ye year 1666. Coppied out of Providence Records August 23, 1708. Tho: Olney, Clerk. Ffor John Whipple (XVII:242-43)

27 May 1709

    John Whipple sold to Freelove Crawford: for 8 pounds, 5 shillings, John Whipple gave to Frelove Crawford full right of Common, or undivided lands, on the eastern side of the Seven Mile line in Providence, originally the right of Joshua Verin (deceased), with timber, wood, stones, herbage, grass, water, and watercourses, mine, mineral. Providence Land Evidence, Book 2:135, City Hall-Division of Archives and History Providence, Rhode Island.

September 1709

    The Declaration and Complaint of Roger Burlingame Junr Of the town of Prouidence in the colony And Abovesd husbanman Against John Whipple of the town and Colony abovesaid Now a Late Vintner in an Action of Debt by one Bond obsisatoriey as writ Beararing Date 18 Day of May in the Eight Year of hes Madests Reign Anno Domin: 1709 Dept and Dammage Six Pounds Currant Silver Money at Eight Shillings per ounce. Now the Plantiff Complaineth that the Above named Dfendant Did on the nineteenth Day of march 1797/98 isgne seal and Diliver To the Plantiff one obligation for the full and Just sum of Six Pounds of Currant Silver money of new England at fifteen penny weight with Condition their Vuder written to Pay or Caus to be the Platiff the Sum of three Pounds of like money on or before the fistr Day of Nouevember…the Plantiff in fs't saith that the Deffendant hath wholy neglected or Refuse to Pay the Above said three pounds. Although often Requested therunto and

Doth still neglect or Refuse to Pay the same whith foreseth the Plaintiff to Bring this his Action of Debt for the Resouery of the Whole obligaitn as Justly forfeited. And Prays this Honred Court and Gentlmen of the Jurey for Justice and relief in the Case...(XVII:268)

22 March 1709/10
...Court of Magestrats to be held at ye Hous of John Whipple...(XVII:268)

7 August 1710
At a Councill metting called by Warrant, Granted unto John Whipple liberty to keepe a publike house of Entertainment for entertaineing of People & Retaleing of drinke; but by license. (X:113)

15 December 1711
John Whipple, son of John Whipple, gave notice that he had taken up a stray hors of Colour white Eare marked, with a halfe penny Cut out of ye left Eare (IX:171)

24 June 1714
John Whipple, son of ye deceased Jon Whipple junr; Gave Notice that hee had taken up a stray horse of Colour, a bay a Gelding Branded in the off buttok...the hinder feete white at the Edge of ye hoofe, no Eare marke (IX:165)

27 January 1723/24
...The verdict of this Jury is that the said Joseah owen was Killed Accidently by meanes of Josiah owen seniour his Carrte Whele Runing ouer his head...Witness our hands...John Whipple, John Whipple Junr. [and twelve other men] (IX:41-2)

Descendants of John Whipple III

Job Liddeason Whipple married Lydia Harding 2 December 1713[249] at Providence and there had four children, including Elijah and John. "On the 2d of June, 1721, Job Whipple received a deed of one hundred acres of land in Taunton North Purchase from Hezekiah Hoar of Taunton, acting as attorney of his brother Edward Hoar, then of Philadelphia, who was entrusted by his father with the duty of confirming to six of the latter's children certain tracts of land which he designed for them, Edward and Hezekiah having already received the property. This one hundred acres was the right of Lydia (Job's mother), daughter of Hezekiah, Sen. Job sold this property, as he made his appearance in Providence soon after this date."[250] As noted, he and his brother, John, bought the former property of their uncle Samuel Whipple. Job and Lydia's son John (1718-1767) was in Glocester Township, Rhode Island by 1742, where his 10 children, including seven sons, were born. Jonah (22 October 1761- 6 January1843), his youngest child, moved to Gilmanton, New Hampshire before 1793, and then to Quebec, Canada, Sheffield, Vermont, and finally to Chateaugay, New York. Jonah Whipple and his wife, Hepsibeth Melvin, had seven children, including Nathan, Jonathan, Daniel, and John J.

90

Jonathan Whipple was born in the year 1800 in Stanstead, Quebec, Canada and died in 1892. He and his wife, Lucinda Kentner, had nine children, including William, who was born in Chateaugay, New York 13 January 1841 and died there 21 October 1927. William and his wife, Mary Ward, had eight children including Jasper[9] Whipple (William[8], Jonathan[7], Jonah[6], John[5], Job[4], John[3], John[2], John[1]), who was born in Reese, Michigan 9 March 1883 and died there 10 February 1966. [251]

Jonah's third son, Daniel, was born in Gilmanton, New Hampshire, and died in Chateaugay, New York 1 August 1885. He and his wife, Agnes McClatchie, had nine children, including four sons: James (1835-1923), who died in Rogue River, Oregon; William (1839-1888), who died in Wadena, Minnesota; John (1849-1924), who died in Hartford, Connecticut; and Alfred (1853-1926).[252]

John J. Whipple, Jonah's youngest son, was born in Sheffield, Vermont and married Esther Bickford 20 December 1828. Six of their children were sons. He apparently moved back to Canada before his marriage, as at least four of his children (Daniel, Ida, Gordon, and John), several grandchildren, as well as his wife were born there. John Jr's grandson, Ira John[9] Whipple (John[8], John J[7], Jonah[6], John[5], Job[4], John[3], John[2], John[1]) was born in Hatley, Quebec, and moved to Iowa around the year 1885 where he married his second wife, Hattie Dunbar. He died at Cheyenne, Kansas 25 January 1940. This couple had three children: Dallas, who was born in Stratton, Colorado, and died in Parsons, Kansas 14 September 1956; Alan (1890-1946), who lived and died at Stratton, Colorado, as did his five children; and Ethel, who married William Armknecht and lived out her life at Colorado, Springs, Colorado, dying there in 1952. [253]

Robert Farquarh[8] Whipple (Nathan[7], Jonah[6], John[5], Job[4], John[3], John[2], John[1]) was the son of Nathan Whipple of Gilmanton, New Hampshire. Nathan, Jonah Whipple's oldest son, moved with his father's family to Chateaugay, New York, where he died in 1873. "He married Rachel Farquhar, daughter of Robert and Barbara Farquhar. She was a full blood Scot and came to America with her parents when she was 15 years old. The Farquarhs were very zealous Scots Presbyterians and Rachel brought her family up in the faith. When Robert F. converted in a Methodist revival meeting and joined that church his mother emphatically declared that he had started on the direct road to hell. Robert Farquhar Whipple, son of Nathan and Rachel Whipple, was born at Chateaugay, N.Y., April 2, 1840 and died at Brockport, N.Y., Jan. 10, 1914. He married Lucy C. Stevens, daughter of Linus and Susan Witherell Stevens, Jan. 1, 1861. She was born July 28, 1840, and died at Brockport, N.Y., Feb. 16, 1914... [They] began their married life at Chateaugay N.Y., but in the spring of 1862 moved to Fort Jackson N.Y. where they lived until 1872 when Robert began his life work as a Methodist Episcopal Minister....At that period it was the custom to move Methodist Ministers ever year or two...."

In a thirteen-year period, he served seven churches in the state of New York. "At the conference in April 1885 he assumed a supernumerary (retired) relation...Early in the summer he moved to Black River, N.Y. where he bought a lot and built a house on West Street, which he sold later. In 1886 he resumed his ministerial work...." In the next twenty years he served seven more churches in the state of New York. "He retired from active ministry and moved to Brockport, N.Y. and bought a small fruit farm, where he was living at the time of his death, January 10th, 1914. He was educated in the Common Schools and the Chateaugay Academy. He learned the shoemakers trade and was very expert, especially in the manufacture of 'Mens Fine Boots' for dress wear. He followed that occupation until he entered the ministry. He was a member of the Masonic and Odd Fellows fraternities. Robert and Lucy were the parents of five children including Charles, Robert, and Fred."

In addition to Job, John Whipple III and Lydia Hoare had nine other children, including John IV [noted above] and Hezekiah. Hezekiah was born 17 February 1701 in Providence, and there married Katherine Olney 14 July 1723. Katherine's maternal great grandfather was The Reverend Roger Williams through his daughter Mary.[254] Their son Christopher was born 19 March 1736. Christopher married Mary Proud at Providence on 27 July 1765. He died before 3 December 1796, and she on 13 July 1820 at Providence. They had four children, three who died young and Captain Christopher[6] Whipple (Christopher[5], Hezekiah[4], John[3], John[2], John[1]), born 5 March 1773 at Providence.[255] He died 29 September 1807.

End Notes

[182] *Records of the First Church at Dorchester in New England 1636-1734* (Boston: George H. Ellis, 1891) 267 and 172. The date of christening for John Whipple is listed as "9 1 1641." In the old Puritan calendar the ninth month was November. Non-members of the church could not have their children baptized or christened. Sarah was added to membership on (8-29-41), or 29 October 1641; thus her John could then be baptized immediately thereafter. In Robert C. Anderson, *The Great Migration Begins, Immigrants to New England, 1620-1633* (Boston: NEHGS, 1995) 1972-73, the date of his baptism is given as 1 November 1641, "three days after his mother joined the church." On 24 November 1684, John Junior made a declaration that he was 45 years old at the time, making his birth 1639. *The Early Records of the Town of Providence, 21 vols.,* collected and printed by the Record Commissioners (Providence: Snow and Farnham, city printers, 1892-1915) 17:53-4. [hereinafter ERP].

[183] John O. Austin, *Genealogical Dictionary of Rhode Island* (Albany, NY, 1887, reprint edition, Baltimore: Genealogical Publication Company, 1978) 221. Henry E. Whipple, *A Brief Genealogy of the Whipple Families Who Settled in Rhode Island* (Providence: A.Crawford Greene, 1873). James N. Arnold, *Vital Record of Rhode Island, 1636-1850* (Providence: Narragansett Historical Publishing Company, 1892). *Records of the First Church of Dorchester,* 267. Vital statistics on the children and grandchildren of John and Sarah Whipple are taken from the above and numerous publications that quote from them. To view more recent information consult www.whipple.org, Weldon Whipple, Webmaster.

[184] Stephen F. Peckham, "Richard Scott and His Wife Catharine Marbury, and Some of Their Descendants," *The New England Historical and Genealogical Register,* 60:174, April, 1906

[185] *The Pioneer Mothers of America: A Record of the more Notable Women of the Early Days of Country, and Particularly of the Colonial and Revolutionary Periods* (New York: G.P. Putnam's Sons, 1912) 3:86-88

[186] Henry C. Dorr, *The Planting and Growth of Providence. Rider's Tract #15* (Providence: Sidney S. Rider, 1882) 39.

[187] Rufus M. Jones, *The Quakers in the American Colonies* (New York: W.W. Norton & Company, 1966) 547. "Keeping company" with unsuitable persons (non-Friends) was looked into…The parties were expected to gain parental consent, and in some cases the approval of the Meeting…Committees of men and women Friends respectively were appointed to inquire into the "clearness from similar engagements" of the members, and the consent of parents was publicly given… The parties, flanked by the parents, then stood up in meeting and took each other as man and wife. No priest or minister intervened or dictated the words. No ring symbolized the union…."

[188] Rhode Island Historical Society Manuscripts, 1:69-70.

[189] "Olney Family" in *History of the State of Rhode Island and Providence Plantations* (New York: America Historical Society, 1920) pp. 408-409.

[190] Sydney V. James, *Colonial Rhode Island, A History* (New York: Charles Scribner's Sons, 1976) 42. The church that Williams co-founded at Providence is known today as the "Free Will Baptist Denomination." Olney founded a church that would have been today part of the world wide denomination as represented by the "Southern Baptist Convention." Many historians believe that Dr. John Clarke, of Newport, was the real founder of the Baptist denomination in America. His church taught the same doctrines as the Olney church.

[191] William B. Weeden, *Early Rhode Island A Social History of the People, 1636-1790* (New York: The Grafton Press, reprint, Bowie, Md. Heritage Books Inc.) 220.

[192] Gertrude Kimball, *Providence in Colonial Times* (Boston: Houghton Mifflin Company, 1912) 126. It is doubtful that he would have started his tavern had his father disapproved or was still in the business himself. *ERP, VI:115*

[193] Thomas Bicknell, *The History of Rhode Island and Providence Plantations, 3 vols* (New York: The American Historical Society, 1920) 3:888.

[194] *ERP,* VII:5-6, VI: 29 & VI:115. John Junior, perhaps because his inn was not finished being built, refused a request to establish an inn the year before. As a condition of approval, the town council required

that it be made available for all of its meetings. The town used John's inn long after his son, John III, took possession.

195 *ERP*, IV:8

196 Kimball, 127.

197 *ERP*, XV:231-33. From this entry is learned that John Junior smoked a pipe and liked to drink rum first thing in the morning.

198 Kimball, 128. Joseph renewed his tavern license as late as 1732.

199 Dorr, 50.

200 Richard M. Bayles, ed., *The History of Providence County, 2 vols.* (New York: W.W. Preston and Company, 1891) 1:306.

201 Dorr, 190-191.

202 Horatio Rogers, George Moulton Carpenter, and Edward Field, Record Commissioners. *The Early Records of the Town of Providence*, Volume 6, Being Part of the Will Book Number 1, otherwise called the First Book for Prouidence Towne Council Perticulior Vse (Providence: Snow and Farnham city printers, 1894) 126-28. Also, pages 129-30. A deposition of Thomas Olney that he had gone to Captain John Whipple, at his request, and obtained clarification of some of the bequests. In the latter, John Junior was given an additional 30 acres in the Louquisset.

203 Carl Bridenbaugh, *Fat Mutton and Liberty of Conscience: Society in Rhode Island, 1636-1690* (Providence: Brown University Press, 1974) 38.

204 *ERP*, III:97-100. John Whipple to John Whipple Junior Deed, 23 November 1663, *Rhode Island Historical Society Manuscript, Mss 9003*, I:12. It took four years for the deed to be recorded.

205 William G. McLoughlin, *Rhode Island* (New York: W.W. Norton, 1978) 14

206 Arnold died in 1677, Olney in 1682, Williams in 1683, and Harris in 1680. Harris sailed for London in 1679, was captured by pirates and taken to Algiers where he was auctioned off to the highest bidder. He wrote to his family that he would be killed if not ransomed. The letter concluded, "Tell John Whipple (Jr) that all the affidavits and protests against the only executions I pray may be sent to the sign of the peele in Wentworth Street near Spittlefields in London to John Stokes living there to remain there for me." He was released, but died in London three days after arriving there. Irving B. Richman, *Rhode Island, Its Making and Its Meaning, 1636-1683* (New York: G.P. Putnam's Sons, 1908) 482-483. *Collections of the Rhode Island Historical Society,* (Providence: Rhode Island Historical Society, 1902) X:324-325

207 John Whipple Junior was also related to Roger Williams by marriage. John's brother-in-law, husband of his wife's sister, Lydia Olney, was Joseph Williams, son of Roger Williams.

208 Glenn W. LaFantasie, ed., *The Correspondence of Roger Williams* (Providence: Brown University Press/ University Press of New England, 1988) II:603-604. Also, *Rhode Island Historical Society Mss, V*:13-15.

209 Floy S.Hyde, *Captain John Whipple of Rhode Island,* 1616-1685 (Mountain View NY: Privately Published, 1984) 10-11

210 Richman, 485.

211 See: genweb.whipple.org/d0312/I368.html and subsequent related entries for the vital statistics and migration patterns of John Junior's descendants. Also: http://www.whipple.org/descendants/john366_6.pdf

212 Bicknell, 3:900. It may be that Harris, a Quaker, was the mentor of John Junior's education in the law. Harris was a well-known legal authority. As revealed in the inventory of the movable estate of Harris, John Whipple Junior was in possession of some of the Harris books. "Books prized ye 14th: of July 1682: the which were in John Whipple junior: his handes when ye other Goods were aprized: Ye Statute booke by poulton, Declerations & Pleadings, The exsecutors office, The Exposition of termes of law, The lay mans lawyer, The law Concerning juryers, Justice restored, Dallons Countrey justice." Total value: £2, 12d. *ERP*:VI:89.

213 Clifford Alderman, *The Rhode Island Colony* (Crowell-Collier Press, 1969) 46. See McLoughlin, 32 for an opposing opinion as to his wealth.

214 Sydney V. James, *The Colonial Metamorphoses in Rhode Island: A Study of Institutions in Change* (Hanover, NH: University Press of New England, 2000) 74. Harris received several of the 13 shares, supposedly at the expense of rest of Providence and northern Warwick. John Junior's children and the families of their eventual spouses obviously shared in the Harris largess.

215 *ERP*, XV:161

216 George L. Miner, *Angell's Lane: The History of a Little Street in Providence* (Providence: Akerman-Standard Press, 1948) 22. The prices of Indian slaves, great and small, £8. Two for 22 bushels Indian corn. Two in silver £4, one, in silver £2.10, One, 12 bu. Indian corn. One, in wood 100 lbs. One for three sheep...

217 *ERP* XV:155-156

218 Kimball, *Providence in Colonial Times*, 123

219 *Collections of the Rhode Island Historical Society* (Providence: Knowles and Vose Printers, 1843) 103-107. This account enumerates a list several pages in length. Sixty-five leaves were missing from Book 1 and twenty from Book 2. Without doubt the destroyed 85 pages contained memoranda concerning the first settlers, their antecedents, family connections and such. How much more would be known about the Whipples had the war not happened?

220 Henry C. Dorr, *The Proprietors of Providence, and Their Controversies With The Freeholders*, Collections of the Rhode Island Historical Society, vol. 6 (Providence: The Society, 1843) 45, 66.

221 Bridenbaugh, 139

222 *ERP*, VII:5-6. On 16 June 1682, John received permission to "keep a publick house of Entertainment for victualling & lodging & selling of drinke for the Entertaineing of strangers & Travellers, both people & horses, and what other persons the law allowes Entertainment for. He was to be closed on the first day of the week, and after nine o'clock. He was not allowed to harbor undesirables or take stolen goods. He was to "keepe good & wholesome diet fit for travelers, wholesome beer & other drinkes at reasonable rates." His bond was set at tenn pounds. The town council continuously met at his place of business, as did the Rhode Island General Assembly in 1690.

223 The General Assembly passed an act for the licensing and encouragement of "one or two houses for ye entertainment of strangers in every town." In May 1661, it was enacted that, "Forasmuch as it appears that there is great complaint by reason that there is no place or places for strangers to be entertained, it shall be unlawful for any person to retail wine of liquors, unless such person will also provide at least one bed and victuals, under penalty of ten shillings..." *Rhode Island Colonial Records*, I:280, 313, 441. Richard Mowrey, in 1655, had been appointed to keep a tavern that was apparently no longer operating at this time.

224 John Junior was likewise a spirited public servant, involved in several projects for the betterment of the community. For example, see Welcome Arnold Greene, 52. "The first educational movement in the plantations was in 1663, when the proprietors ordered that 100 acres of upland and six of meadow be laid out to be reserved for the maintenance of a school. The land seems never to have been set apart, and in 1684 John Whipple prayed (petitioned the town council) that the same might be laid out, but it was not done...."

225 Weeden, 42, 220

226 Weeden, 107

227 Richard Bayles, *History of Providence County, Rhode Island* (New York: W.W. Preston & Company, 1891) 143

228 James, *The Colonial Metamorphoses*, 127. *Providence Town Papers*, 169 Volumes, 2nd Series 5:01070, John Junior to the town of Providence, nd.

229 Bridenbaugh, 96

230 The well-publicized "Letter of John Whipple on the Baptist Church" was not located. "I found the folder for this letter, but there was nothing in it but a Warwick deed between two other parties. I had the same problem last year. The technician and I checked the cross-references. They were all for the same folder, so the reference is correct. The librarian affirmed that, "The letter is either lost or misplaced." Personal observation of Barbara Carroll, 5 March 2004

231 Samuel Green Arnold, *History of the State of Rhode Island and Providence Plantations* (Providence: Preston & Rounds, 1894) 361

232 Austin, 221. He was town clerk for seven years, town moderator, assistant to the governor for four years, as well as a representative to the Rhode Island General Assembly in Newport for six years, in addition to serving as town sergeant. Bicknell, 2:642-43: "The Colonial Officers were Governor, Deputy Governor and ten Assistants [elected by the General Assembly]. These with sixteen deputies elected by the towns constituted the lawmaking power, styled in the charter, The General Assembly. Newport had six deputies elected by freemen; Providence four;...They met twice a year, in May and October. On the 6th of

May, 1696, the Deputies voted to sit by themselves as a House of Deputies, choosing their own Speaker and Clerk, and the General Assembly thereafter met in two bodies, the Governor, the Deputy and the Assistants constituting The Upper House, and the representatives of the towns, the Lower House. Col. Rec., p. 313, Vol. III." The Upper House, to which John Junior was elected on several occasions, developed into what is now known as the Senate.

[233] John E. Sterling, *North Burial Ground, Providence, Rhode Island, Old Section*, 1700-1848 (Providence: Special Publication 5, Rhode Island Genealogical Society, 2000) xiii

[234] Dorr, Rider's Tract 15, 184

[235] James P. Root, *A Record of the Descendants of John Steere Who Settled in Providence Rhode Island* About the Year 1600 (Cambridge: Riverside Press, 1890) 187. "The old 'Samuel Whipple' or 'Abbott' house, which first after Samuel Whipple's death passed into the hands of his son-in-law, Robert Currie, was bought by Job Whipple and John Whipple Junior, (likely John III) father and son, on the 3d of June, 1737. Subsequently by a division of the estate, Job Whipple became the sole owner of the house and contiguous lands, which he sold to John Whipple (likely son of Benjamin), who occupied it till his death in 1751. Levi Whipple and Thomas Abbott were the successive owners." It is unclear as to whether John III or John IV was recipient of the 1737 property, thus the confusion in death dates.

[236] *ERP*, X:55-64.

[237] Austin, 221. *ERP*, IV:235-243. *Providence Records*, Old Book, II: 307. The home stall that John III received was "originally the home lot of William Arnold ...and one-half of the adjoining home lot on the south (the home lot of Thomas James), purchased by John Whipple, Jr. of Alexander Bryant..." Charles Hopkins, *The Home Lots of the Early Settlers of the Providence Plantations* (Providence: 1886) 24

[238] *Providence Record of Deeds*, 2:426. Dated 27 April 1710. It was common at the time to use the term "cousin" to refer to anyone of close relationship. Eleazer's father, Captain John Whipple, did not have a known brother, which is the only circumstance that could have led to a Whipple "cousin."

[239] As previously noted, John and Mary were deeded half their property from her father. *ERP* VI:64. "I doe give unto my son in law John Whipple to possess...my right in the house Lott, or home share of land where he now dwelleth, the which Right is two acres of the East End thereof, As also my right of five acres of land which I bought of mr. Roger Williams...After the decease of my son-in-law John Whipple, Revert and belong unto John Whipple the son of my said son in law & my Daughter Mary..." John's children, Mary, John, and Elnathan were also given certain cattle in the will. John Junior added additional property immediately to the south of the 1663 deed, "three home lots known as the Throckmorton land & purchased in copartnershhip with Maj. John Dexter. These three lots were originally laid out to Thomas James, John Green, & John Smith." Henry R. Chace, *Part of the Whipples in Early Providence, R.I. City History,* 4.

[240] *ERP*, XX:171-72. "I John Whipple (Ordinary Keeper) sell to Joseph Whipple...my dwellinghouse and all my outhousing, together with all my lands adjoining which are standing in Providence in the row of houselots lying on the east side of the salt water harbor, 21 July 1705.

[241] Dorr, Rider's Tract 15, 40.

[242] Henry R. Chace, *Owners and Occupants of the Lots, Houses and Shops in the Town of Providence* Rhode *Island in 1798* (Providence: Livermore & Knight Company, 1914) Plate VI. On this map, the Whipple School stands immediately to the east of the Whipple property across from Benefit Street. The old Baptist meeting house was located immediately west across Main Street. The properties of other Whipples were also located near by on Main Street and others.

[243] *Publications of the Rhode Island Historical Society, New Series*, Vol. 7, Number 4, January 1900. 233-34

[244] *ERP*, XI:55.

[245] *Rhode Island Historical Society Manuscripts*, 1:109. See also, on line at http://www.whipple.org/charles/yeomanandprinces/index.html.

[246] *ERP*, XX:274-275. John III in turn sold his father's property on Main Street to his uncle Joseph according to ERP, XX:171-72.

[247] Philip J. Currier, *Currier Family Records of U.S.A. and Canada* (Concord, NH: Capital Offset Company, 1990) IV:10-11. James N. Arnold, *Vital Records of Rhode Island, 1636-1850*, Volume 2, Providence, Part 1 (Providence: Narragansett Historical Publishing Company, 1892) p 256. Two entries are given, with birth dates 26 December 1690 and 26 December 1692, (both in Taunton). He is also listed in Bristol County,

Volume 6, Part 1, with birth 26 December 1690. Job's sister Mary and brother John IV were born in 1690 and 1692 respectively, precluding the 1690 and 1692 dates for him.

248 Norton T.Horr, *A Record of Descendants of Hezekiah Hoar of Taunton, Massachusetts* (Cleveland, Ohio: Privately Published, 1907).

249 Arnold, Volume 2, Part 1:157

250 Root, 187.

251 Email from Raymond F. Whipple whip69@concast.net to Weldon Whipple at www.whipple.org, 5 November 2003

252 Fred E. Whipple, *Whipple Family Genealogy* (Privately Published, c1932) Transcribed by Ron Whipple at ronfox13@concast.net, and sent to Weldon Whipple 16 December 1998.

253 Email from Elizabeth Whipple at gewhipple@home.com to Weldon Whipple at www.whipple.org 14 February 2001. John J. Whipple was, "one of the original settlers in Ayer's Cliff, Quebec."

254 Arnold, Volume 2, Part 1: 198, 235, 256. Also, Gen.Web/Whipple.org/d0197/I16158.html

255 Arnold, Volume 2, Part 1:256

Chapter 4

Samuel Whipple
The Whipples From Providence Neck

This and the next two chapters present evidence as to the identities of Captain John Whipple's second through fourth sons, who are known collectively as the "Louquisett Brothers." Part of the Last Will and Testament of their father declared, "...I having formerly given to three of my sons, all of my lands and meadows in Louquisset, namely, --Samuel, Eleazer, and William, equally to be divided among them three only; excepting thirty-acres which I gave to my son John, at the northwest end."[256] These three were also given "a quarter part of one right of common." Neither John nor Samuel moved on to their Louquisett properties, electing instead to continue to reside on Town Street and Providence Neck. His remaining sons (Benjamin, David, Joseph, and Jonathan) were deeded and subsequently willed large estates to the west and northwest, but closer in to the original settlement on Town Street. By some estimates, John deeded, traded or sold, and willed over 1000 acres in his 26-year stay in Providence.

Louquisset and Lime Rock Village

Louquisset, an Indian name for a place or brook in the northeast section of the township soon to be named Smithfield, was located at the headwaters of the Moshassuck River about two miles west of the Blackstone River, the eastern border of the township. The Moshassuck River emptied into the Atlantic Ocean at Providence about one block west of Captain John's house. In the 1670s and early 1680s, when, as young men in their late 20s and early 30s, the Louquisset brothers settled on their new lands, they likely traveled by horse and oxcart up this meandering river to its headwaters called "the meadows," a distance of some eight miles north. A natural feature of the area, notable for Whipple history, was an area called the "lime rocks." Roughly the eastern half of Smithfield, including Louquisset, was made into the township of Lincoln in the year 1871.

"The land which now forms the town[ship] of Lincoln was included in Roger Williams' original purchase. A year after Williams' arrival a verbal agreement was confirmed by a written deed, through which the white settlers acquired the 'meadows upon two rivers.' With this deed the Providence proprietors got title to the land which is now, 'upland from the water, most of it rocky and barren without meadow.' But only a few settlers ventured into the interior reaches purchased from the Indians. The area remained a wilderness, designated in their records as 'Louquisset' or the north woods, an apt description since the land was heavily forested. After decisive battles of King Philip's War in the 1670s, settlement began in earnest. The most common surnames in Smithfield during its first one hundred years were: Sayles, Arnold, Mowry, Comstock, Scott, Steere, Whipple, Waterman, Jenckes, Aldrich, Angell, Winson, Inman, Ballou, Wilkinson, Paine, Harris, Jillson, Mann, Sprague, and Thayer."[257]

"The opening of the 'North Woods' for settlement by Providence's second generation was encouraged by the laying out of a road north through the region from

Providence to Mendon, Massachusetts. One of the earliest of colonial roads, the Great Road was blazed through the wilderness and opened in 1683; it probably followed footpaths and the Indian's Shawomet Trail for some of its length and was designed to connect the growing town of Providence with its agricultural hinterland. The village of Lime Rock was eventually located along this road. It is eight miles north of Providence, seven miles south of Woonsocket, and forty miles from Boston. Traffic along this route sustained a number of early taverns which provided bed and board for travelers. In 1710 Eleazer Arnold was licensed to serve travelers at his house on Great road and by the mid 1700s Jeremiah Mowrey operated a tavern in the old Eleazer Whipple House at Lime Rock."[258]

Lime Rock, RI

"Even today, Rhode Island is full of tiny villages and hamlets, some consisting of only a few houses. Lime Rock is one of those places. The Lime Rock School is now a residence. There is a Baptist church and a volunteer fire station and some beautifully restored homes on a few rural roads in a lovely rural setting. As late as one hundred years ago, it had a general store and a post office. For generations, the lives of the people of Lime Rock revolved around the church, the Mt. Mariah Lodge of the Masons, and the Lime Rock Grange."[259]

"The manufacture of lime has been carried on with great success, and continuously, by the Dexter Lime Rock Company, and the Harris Lime Rock Company, and their predecessors. The village of Lime Rock, which at one time was the location of the Lime Rock Bank, and the seat of considerable local business, is now, owing to the construction of the Providence and Worcester Railroad, and the tendency of the times toward centralization of capital, indeed a 'deserted' village."[260] Lime Rock was placed on the National Register of Historical Places in 1974 and its historic significance to the Whipples will be discussed later in greater detail.

Louquisset Meadows

Sons who Inherited Louquisset Meadow Estates

Among those whose farms were located along the Great Road were the sons of Captain John Whipple. Numerous references to this road are recorded in the land deeds of these men. This highway, referred to as "Lime Rock Road" as it passed through the village, cut directly through the inherited properties of two of the Whipple brothers. The photo above, taken looking southwest from the Great Road in Lime Rock shows part of the original Whipple property.

100

Although John Junior inherited a small tract of Smithfield land, it is known that he and his immediate descendants never resided on the property. It is also clear that few of the immediate descendants of Samuel, Eleazer, or William stayed on their inherited properties. To these men and their wives, 18 children were born, including at least nine sons, of which only four sons lived out their lives in the Louquisset meadows.

Samuel Whipple House, 1893

As shown herein, by the end of the third generation, Samuel Junior and his brother Thomas had moved to the colony of Connecticut, and Noah the third brother, died in Rhode Island several years before his father. Job, the second son of Eleazer, lived and died in Smithfield. His brother Daniel moved out of the township at an early age. Eleazer's other sons, Eleazer Junior and James, died in Smithfield, but without passing their farms on to a descendant. Seth, William Senior's son, who moved to Providence, died young without issue. This left the opportunity to carry on the Whipple name in earliest Louquisset Meadows history to the heirs of Captain William Whipple Junior and Captain Job Whipple.

The Venerable Samuel Whipple House

Samuel Whipple, the second son of Captain John, was christened at Dorchester, Massachusetts 17 March 1644/45[261] and died at Providence, Rhode Island 12 March 1710/11. He married Mary Harris in 1667. She was born in 1639 and died 14 December 1722. Their five children were born at Providence, where all were married. Samuel and Thomas died in Connecticut.

i. *Noah, born about 1667; died 10 Nov 1703; married Amphillus Smith.*
ii. *Samuel, born about 1669; died 19 Apr 1728; married Elizabeth Eddy.*
iii. *Thomas, born about 1671; died before 4 Nov 1730; married Abigail Jenckes.*
iv. *Abigail, born about 1683; married Robert Curry*
v. *Hope, born about 1685; married Robert Curry*

The father of Mary Harris was Thomas. It has been claimed that, like Captain John Whipple, he was a non-conformist who moved from Massachusetts to Rhode Island to escape persecution, and that the children of both men married into families whose views coincided with those of Roger Williams.[262] However, as seen herein, they married into Anglican, Quaker, and Baptist families. Thomas Harris was a well-known Quaker, remembered in literature for being whipped and imprisoned in Boston for his faith.[263] Because Quakers did not tend to marry out of the faith, it may be presumed that Samuel was a member of that church. Some of his descendants are known to have married Quakers, including Thomas, whose wife was a sister of Governor Jenckes.

There is no indication that Samuel ever moved to the Louquisset Meadows area. This included large tracts east and west of the "7 mile line," on both sides of the Moshassuck River. For over forty years, he lived at 30 Abbott-Whipple Lane near north Town Street in a house [willed to his daughters, and sold to their cousin, Job Whipple son of John III] known for many years as the "Abbott-Whipple House." [264] Samuel's Last Will and Testament shows the extent of this property in the Providence Neck vicinity: "Reaching from Towne Street and extending eastward to the land which belongs to the deceased Daniell Brown." Samuel Whipple Senior was not only a farmer; for at least 20 years of his life he owned a wharf "on the saltwater side of Providence," and thus was an exporter/importer of goods. His father-in-law owned a limestone mine at Lime Rock and in all probability found good use for Samuel's wharf. The Harris and Whipple families shared in that successful business enterprise for over one hundred and fifty years. (See the chapter on William Whipple for a more complete account of the limestone business.)

Samuel Whipple in Early Town Records

Samuel Whipple appeared in Providence town records on over 170 occasions, and in these records was consistently referred to as a farmer. The following is a summary of a representative sample of these extracted from *The Early Records of the Town of Providence, 21 Volumes*, (Providence: Snow & Farnham 1892-1915). Individual entries are noted with the volume number and page. As much as possible, original wording, spelling, and punctuation have been retained.

1 June 1667
    The names of those who have "Engaged Alegance to his Majestye King Charles the Second" included Samuel Whipple (III:101)

4 May 1669
    Samuel Whipple and Eleazer Whipple made freemen. (XV:73)

7 June 1669
    Samuel Whipple chosen to be a sergeant but refused to serve. John Whipple was the next choice-- -he was engaged. (III:147)

10 June 1669
    Samuel Whipple and John Whipple were among 12 men impaneled by a coroner's inquest to make an inquiry after the death of Samuel Belloo, child of widow Belloo. Their verdict was that the child who went into the river which ran to the mill in Providence was by a Providence of God drowned. (V:337)

28 February 1670
    John Whipple, Sr., surveyor, made return of two acres of land and also one acre which he had layd out for Samuel Whipple. These three acres are to make up for three house lots, which he sayd Samuel Whipple bought. (III:164)

102

27 January 1671
Layd out to John Arnold by John Whipple Sr., surveyor, sixteen acres of land in the right of Thomas Arnold, in the place call the World's End—bounded on the north side with the Common or with the land of Samuel Bennett, on the south side partly with land of Samuel Whipple and partly with the Common, on the east side the Common...recorded by John Whipple, Jr., clerk. (III:205)

2 September 1671
Record of a deed of sale. Stephen Paine of Rehoboth sold to Samuel Whipple three house lots, with a dwelling house, and all of the out housing standing upon the lots, which Stephen Paine purchased from Mary Mowry, executor of the estate of her deceased husband Roger Mowry. One lot originally belonged to Daniel Comstock, one to John Smith, and one to Richard Prey, all of Providence. Stephen Paine also sold to Samuel Whipple one purchase right of commoning, one 25 acre right of commoning both reaching westward as the seven mile line. (III:206-9)

21 September 1671
It was voted by the town that the two deeds, which Samuel Whipple received of Stephen Paine of Rehoboth, in the Colony of New Plymouth, be recorded in town records. (III:202)

21 October 1673
Samuel Whipple, constable, gave a deposition in the matter of a prisoner. John Whipple, Asst. took the deposition.

27 April 1674
Laid out to Samuel Whipple two shares of low land of meadow, 18 acres of it lying east and west of the land of John Brown, the other two acres lying east of his upland, Samuel Bennett, surveyor. Two shares of upland bounded in the west and north corner with the Stephen Harden. (IV:4-5)

27 January 1678.
Samuel Comstock requested that the towne grant the laying out of land which remains due to him of his father's right, which he bought from John Smith. Samuel Whipple objected to the request. The council suspended an answer until 10 February. The council on that date decided against Samuel Comstock. (VIII:68)

3 June 1678
Samuel Whipple was chosen constable and engaged. David Whipple chosen sergeant and engaged. (VIII:30)

3 March 1679.
Samuel Whipple chosen for trial jury in the General Court of Trials, held at Newport. (VIII:68)

27 April 1681

Granted to Samuel Whipple, with the permission of his father-in-law Thomas Harris, that he should have a piece of ground forty foot square and the privilege of a wharffe, also, within his father-in-laws lots. (XV:204)

7 December 1681.

Towne meeting voted that Samuel Whipple, if he sees cause, may change three acres of land that lies upon Observation Hill, adjoining the land of Nicholas Power, now deceased, for the advantage of the orphan of Power. (XV:235)

4 March 1683/4

Samuel Whipple chosen the Grand Jury for the General Court of Trials in Newport---Eleazer Whipple chosen for petit jury. (VIII:136)

20 March 1684

Nathaniel Waterman, Thomas Field, and Samuel Whipple were employed to audit an account on the town's behalf with Capt. Fenner, Capt. Hopkins, Sergeant Comstock and others concerning a 27 pound rate (tax) which was levied upon the town several years ago. The town's part was received into their hands, and they had to make their return to the town, and take discharge of the Colonies' thereof from Capt Fenner. (VIII:48)

17 June 1684

Towne voted the return of Samuel Whipple's four acres of land in the Neck. Returned under the hand of William Hopkins, surveyor. (VIII:140)

21 August 1684

There was a general order that a pair of stocks should be in Providence, but Providence was destitute. Samuel Whipple proposed to the town that if they would satisfy (pay) him, he would procure a plank and a pair of blocks to set the stocks on, and bring them into Dexter's Lane, against the dwelling house of Epenetus Olney, by the first of October. The town accepted his proposition. (VIII:142)

14 December 1685

Town layd out to Samuel Whipple on the right of Roger Mowry 15 acres of land at Nudaconacet (Neutaconkonet) Hill, 3 miles west of the town of Providence. The fifteen acres had eight corners, they being heaps of stones. (IV:137)

22 February 1687

Samuel Whipple took up a stray boar, black, white in the face, some of his feet white, no earmark. (IX:193)

30 March 1691

Samuel Whipple chosen to serve as a deputy at the General Assembly the day before the election. (VIII:177)

17 February 1693

Samuel Whipple Senior and James Brown asked for permission to erect a fence across the highway at each end, with a gate or inlet of bars. The Town Council granted them permission to do this for one year but the fence at the southern part of the highway had to be set on the north side of the spring at the east end of James Brown's land so that the spring could lie open all the way from Dexter's lane to it. (XI:83)

1 June 1691.

The Purchasers and Proprietors of the lands of Providence chose Samuel Whipple as a Way Warden. (VIII:178)

21 December 1691

Know yee that the said Samuel Whipple (Husbandman) for and in Consideration of ye sum of Thirty Pounds of Silver Money in hand...payd unto him by Eliezer Whipple (house wright)...ye upland being in Estemation about Sixty acres...and adjoyneth to ye land of Eleizer Whipple, Bounding Northeasterward with ye said Eliezer Whipple his land, And on ye South Easterne part of ye land of William Whipple...and on the Westerne part with ye River Called Moshausuck River... (XIV:207)

27 April 1695.

Samuel Whipple changed 60 acres which he bought from James Ashton near the place called nonpluss.(XI:16)

28 May 1695

Samuel Whipple sold to John Mowry sixty acres in the northern part of the township near to the place called Nippsachuck. (V:65)

29 April 1696

Joseph Goldsmith was given permission to set up a Smith's shop on the common between the houses of Thomas Harris and Samuel Whipple. (XI:23)

16 June 1698

Samuel Whipple was chosen as a highway warden. (XI:40)

27 July 1698

Daniel Brown informed the Towne Council that Samuel Whipple had taken in about 4 acres of the Town's common lying in the Neck. The town appointed Major William Hopkins, Capt. John Dexter, and Joseph Smith to inspect the matter and to make a report back to the council. (XI:43)

12 December 1700

Laid out to Samuel Whipple Senr., 20 acres lying in the northern part of the township, partially adjoining the land of Edward Inman and his partners, at and about the place called wesquadomeset, alias Crook Fall River (IV:143)

No date---between 1699-1703

Samuel Whipple and Daniel Brown acknowledged themselves to stand truly and lawfully indebted to each other in the sum of forty pounds sterling, payable upon demand. The condition of this obligation was such that there was a difference between them about a highway through their lands where the land joined together in a part of Providence called the Neck. Samuel and Daniel Brown mutually chose Samuel Comstock and Thomas Olney to be their arbitrators to make a determination and final issue thereof. (IV:177)

2 June 1701

Samuel Whipple was chosen for highway warden.(XI:63).

15 December 1701

Seventy three acres of land were laid out to the heirs of the deceased Edward Smith, which he changed with the town of Providence. There was a mistake in the matter. It was but 60 acres, the other 13 was purchased by Samuel Whipple and layd out in his right. (IV:227)

20 December 1701

Laid out to Samuel Whipple, two acres, lyeing in the part of the towne of Providence called the Neck, and at a place called the second opening of the Great Swamp.(IV:223)

21 October 1704

Be it known that I Samuel Whipple Senior for the sum of ten pounds, five shekels...sell to Gabrill Bernon [Samuel's brother Benjamin's father-in-law] my waar house lott: it being in breadth forty foote...(XIV:286)

11 December 1708

Samuel Whipple took up a stray steere, one year old, color brown, earmarked with a kind of slit in both ears, a part of his hair and his tail white.(IX:179).

Last Will and Testament

Here followeth the Record of the last Will & Testament of Samuell Whipple who dyed March ye 12th 1710: as followeth. I Samuell Whipple of the Towne of Providence, in the Collony of Rhode Island & Providence Plantations in the Narraganset Bay in New England being sick & weake of Boddy, but yet (through mercy) of sound & Perfect memory, Do make, Ordaine & appoint this to be my last Will & Testament; Revokeing making Null & voyd all & Every former Will at any time by me made Either by Word or Writing & this Will only to stand & be in force.

Imprimis, I Do Give & yield up my spirit unto God who gave it & my body to the Earth to be decently Buried.

Jtem. I do give & devise unto my two sons (as Namely) Samuell Whipple and Thomas Whipple my hundred & fifty acres of land being on the west side of ye seven mile line in said Providence Towneship, together with the Right or to say share of Meaddow unto the said hundred & fifty acres of land belonging as also one quarter part of a Right of Commons on the west side of ye said line to be all Equally divided betweene them two; & to be unto them & their heirs & Assignes for ever.

Jtem. I Do Give & Devise unto my two sons (as namely) Samuell Whipple & Thomas Whipple my share of Meaddow Which I bought of James Ashton lieing & being in the great Meaddow (so Called) and my Twenty acres of land lieing by ye Pond Called the broad Pond, & my seven Acres of land lyeing by hye southeasterne part of the hill called the Windmill hill to be Equally divided, and also Each of them one Right in the Thatch Beds, all to be unto them their Heirs and Assigned for ever./

Jtem. I Do Give & Devise unto my son Thomas Whipple my seven acres of land lieing in that Tract of land Called the Neck, & is betweene the swampe Called the Great Swampe & the land which did belong unto Mr. Dexter, to be unto my son his Heiars & assignes for Ever: And I do also Give & Devise untomy sd son Thomas Whipple, for and duireing the terme of his Naturall life, my warehouse lott of land lieing in said Providence Town by the water side; & after his dicease the said Wasrehouse lott of land to revert and be unto his Male Heir begotten of his body, & so successively to proceed and be./

Jtem. I Do Give & bequeath unto my son Thomas Whipple & unto my Grandson Noah Whipple, I do Give and Devise all my Commons on ye East side of the seven mile line in sd Providence Towneshipp, equally to be divided betweene them, to be unto them, their Heirs & Assignes forever.

Jtem. I Do Give & Devise unto my son Thomas Whipple all my lands on which he now dwelleth which lieth on both sides of the River Called Moshausuck River, both vpland, lowland, Meaddow & swamp land together with the house theron to be unto him his heirs & Assignes forever:

Jtem. I Do Give & Devise unto my two Grandsons (as namely), Enoch Whipple & Daniel Whipple, Three quarters of all my lands & Commons on the west side of ye seven mile line in said Providence Towneshipp, which is not yet laid out to be Equally divided betweene them two to be unto them their Heirs & their assignes forever.

Jtem. My home stedd or to say my dwelling place & out housing withal my land & Orchards thereunto adjoyneing Reaching from the Towne Street & Extending Eastward to the land which belong to the deceased Daniell Browne. I Give & bequeath unto my beloved wife Mary Whipple to be for her use & improvement for & duireing the Whole term of her Naturall life; and at her decease the said dwelling house, out houseing & all said lands and Orchards to Revert & be unto my two Daughters (namely) Abigaill Whipple, & Hope Whipple, and after their decease to Revert & be unto their Heirs begotten of their Boddyes; the which said house lands & orchards shall with what out housen there are shall be Equally divided betweene my said two daughters; But in case it shall so be that my said daughters neither of them have any children, then shall the said house & lands be Equally devided amongst all my Children; But if Either of them have Children or a child then shall the said House & lands Revert & be to that daughters Heir.

Jtem. I Do Give & bequeath unto my two daughters Abigaill Whipple and Hope Whipple Each of them a bedd & bedding & all the furniture to a bedd belonging; Each of them to Receive the same at my said wife her decease; And I do give also unto my said two daughters Each of them a Cow, to receive them also at my said wife her decease;

Jtem. I Do Give & bequeath unto my sd loving wife for her vse & improvement all my Goods and Cattell duireing her Natural life, & at her decease to be unto my two sons Samuell Whipple & Thomas Whipple Equally to be divided betweene them, Except what I have before disposed of.

And I do make & appoint my son Samuell Whipple to be my Executor of this my last Will & Testament; to 'receive all my debts & to pay all my debts & to see my body decently buried; and to Execute & performe this my will according to the true meaneing & intent thereof: In witness Whereof I have hereunto set my hand & seale the Ninth day of March Annoq: Domini, one Thousand Seven hundred & Tenn: 1710. Signed Sealed & Proclaimed, The mark of Samuell Whipple. In the presence of us, John Sayles, Henry Adams, and James Olney. Samuel's extensive inventory of moveable property, in numerated a few days later, included such items as: cowes, steeres one old horse, twenty six sheepe, hay, tenn bushels of Indian corne, grinding stone, a beetle & 4 wedges, plough sledge, two bells, three hoes, sithes porringers dreinging boule, pepper bowl, spoones trentchers & Earthen waare, warmeing pan, ffether beds, guns, pair of stilliards, porke & biefe, etc. His son, Samuel Junior, who was by then "dwelling within the prescinkes of New London in the Collony of Conitekut," was granted a letter of full power of Administration by the Providence Towne Councill on 22 March 1711 [265]

Death and Burial

Samuel Whipple died 12 March 1710/11 in Providence. His wife and daughters were buried next to him. Their graves are on the west side of Elm Street about 50 feet south of Summit Avenue. A marker at the foot of his headstone states that he was first to be interred in the North Burial Ground.[266] Henry E. Whipple, on page 55 of his

history, gives the interesting, and somewhat remarkable, account of the erecting of this identifying marble slab by a Mr. Thurber, at his own expense, long after Samuel's death. It is hoped that the full identity of this individual will someday be known. Whipple history, if not Providence history in general, owes a debt of gratitude to him.

As seen in his Last Will and Testament above, Samuel's sons, Thomas and Samuel Junior, were willed most of the land that he had inherited from Captain John Whipple in what were to become the townships of Glocester (west side of the 7 mile line), and Smithfield (east side of the 7 mile line), and in and around

Samuel Whipple Gravestone

the town of Providence. Thomas was also given the Louquisset Meadows property: "all my land on which he now dwells, which lies on both sides of the river called Moshassuck River, upland meadows…. together with the house…." When Thomas built this house or to whom he eventually sold it in about the year 1717 is unknown. Thus, after only 60 years (less than 10 years after Samuel's death) the proprietor's share in the meadowlands of the

108

Moshassuck River originally willed to their father, Samuel, after Samuel's death, passed out of the Whipple name. [267]

Samuel Whipple Junior
Iron Products Manufacturer

Samuel Whipple Junior, the second son of Samuel, was born about 1669 at Providence, Rhode Island.[268] He married Elizabeth Eddy 26 February 1690/91. To this couple, nine children were born, four of whom died young. The last two children were born in Connecticut. Only Daniel seems to have moved from that colony.

    i. Alice, born 10 Apr 1693.
    ii. Samuel, born 10 Apr 1693.
  iii. Samuel, born 8 Nov 1695; died before Jan 1760; married Ruth Card
    ii. Daniel, born 11 Oct 1698; died 16 Apr 1789; married Anne Hough
    v. Hope, born 12 Aug 1701; died before 28 Oct 1739; married Walter Capron
    vi. Nathan, born 5 Apr 1704; died 1 Apr 1725.
  vii. Zachariah, born 2 Feb 1706/07; died 1760; married Elizabeth Rogers
 viii. Zephaniah, born about 1709; died 8 May 1767; married Keziah Parke
    ix. Elizabeth, born Feb 1718; died Nov 1718

"Rhode Island had settled all of its lands by the end of the seventeenth century. Hence, it had no frontier to absorb its growing population. Many Rhode Islanders left for frontiers in other colonies."[269] "The opening years of the eighteenth century witnessed a rapid migration from the east to Western Rhode Island and Eastern Connecticut."[270] Due to this situation, if an individual wanted to buy a great deal of land, as Samuel Junior evidently did, he had to move out of state. Consequently, Samuel left for Connecticut in 1707 with his family of five children; two more were born after he arrived. He bought 1000 acres (over one square mile) of land approximately five miles south of the town of Norwich and about 10 miles up the Thames River from New London-Groton, Connecticut. New London-Groton is located next to the Atlantic Ocean, approximately 15 miles west of the southwest corner of the Rhode Island border. For the next two decades, Samuel carried on extensive business enterprises including a sawmill and iron works. At his river facility, he furnished the ironwork and timber for many of the first ocean-going vessels to leave New London.[271] Samuel Junior, Joseph Whipple Junior, and John Whipple the bonesetter were by far the most financially successful of the grandsons of Captain John Whipple.

Samuel Whipple Junior died 19 April 1728, and was buried at the Gallup-Whipple Cemetery in Old Poquetannuck, Connecticut. In his will, dated 1727, Samuel left the ironworks and saw mill to his son Daniel; his land with buildings was divided between his sons Samuel, Zephaniah, and Zachariah. The portion of Zachariah alone sold for over £1000 in 1734.[272]

At least one of Samuel's sons was a member of the Baptist church. The Reverend Daniel Whipple sold his portion of the iron works to his brothers and assumed the position of minister of a Baptist church in Brattleboro, Vermont. The first clear evidence that some of the family had become members of the so-called Rogerene "Quaker" Movement is seen in the marriage of Samuel's fourth son Zachariah to Elizabeth Rogers, the granddaughter of John Rogers, founder of that sect.[273] Anne Whipple, the daughter of Daniel, Samuel's second son, married William Rogers, the grandson of John Rogers. At least two of the daughters of Zachariah, Content and Hope, married members of the Rogerene church.

Content Whipple married Timothy Waterhouse (they shortened their name to "Watrous"), 17 June 1764. Timothy was the son of John Waterhouse, who by 1750 had become the leader of the Rogerene community. At his death, Timothy and Content became the recognized heads of the movement. They and their sons, Timothy Junior and Zachariah, wrote a book entitled *The Battle Axe*, which explained the movement and argued against war. Leadership eventually fell to Timothy Junior, then to his youngest brother Zephaniah. Zephaniah (who died in 1858) "was the last of the great religious leaders of Quakertown."[274]

Hope Whipple married her first cousin, Samuel's son Noah[6] Whipple (Samuel[5], Samuel[4], Samuel[3], Samuel[2], John[1]), 7 November 1762. At least three of their children married into Rogerene families, including Samuel Sterling Whipple. He and his brother Silas were the first known Whipples to become actual residents of the settlement at Quakertown. Samuel Sterling Whipple's son Jonathan,[275] and his grandson Zerah[9] Whipple (Jonathan[8], Samuel S.[7], Noah[6], Samuel[5], Samuel[4], Samuel[3], Samuel[2], John[1]) were major figures in founding the first American school for the teaching of the deaf and dumb in Ledyard, Connecticut (later moved to Mystic, Connecticut). He taught Jonathan's son Enoch, a deaf-mute. At his death in 1897, Enoch was the oldest recognized communicating deaf-mute in the United States. Enoch inspired his nephew, Zerah, to invent the "Whipple Natural Alphabet," and with the help of Jonathan, opened the Whipple Home School for deaf-mutes, later known as the Mystic Oral School.[276]

The Rogerene sect was active in social reform movements from its inception-- in particular the antiwar and abolition of slavery movements. [Two hundred years later, the descendants of Samuel Sterling Whipple were continuing this tradition]. The Connecticut Peace Society, as a branch of the Universal Peace Union, was organized in1869, with Jonathan Whipple as its president. For years, he and his sister, Content, published the magazine *Bond of Peace*, which was taken over by the Peace Union as its major publication, and is now entitled *The Peace Maker*, with its headquarters in Philadelphia.[277]

Thomas Whipple
From the Moshassuck River to Thomas Pond

Thomas Whipple, third son of Samuel, was born at Providence, Rhode Island about 1671. He married Abigail Jenckes, the sister of Governor Joseph Jenckes of Rhode Island, about 1697. Since the entire Jenckes family were well-known Quakers, it is probable that Thomas, like his mother and father, was a member of that faith. This couple had at least three children:

    i. Thomas, born about 1698; married Mary Gary
    ii. Abraham, born about 1709.
    iii. Patience, born about 1712

The lack of more land, and consequent high prices, caused Thomas, like his brother 10 years earlier, to relocate from his farm in the Louquisset Meadows to the village of Tolland, township of Bolton, Connecticut, approximately 25 miles northeast of downtown Hartford, about 50 miles north northwest of his brother's property. At a place called Thomas Pond, he bought a minimum of 150 acres, probably in the summer of 1718. Providence Land Records III:191 shows that Thomas had moved to Tolland by 29 November 1718. His last date of residence in Rhode Island was October 1717, according to Land Records II:595.

Thomas Whipple Senior had apparently died by 1726, less than eight years after this move. On 31 March 1726, his sons sold part of his estate, the deed reading in part "of our honorable father Thomas Whipple now supposedly deceased." It would be most enlightening to know what had happened to cause their father to be missing and presumed dead. The brothers sold off some of the rest of the property in absentia, 3 November 1730. This deed clearly states that Thomas was deceased.[278] At the time of this deed, the brothers were living in Enfield, Hartford, Connecticut.

Descendants Who Remained In The Colony of Rhode Island

In summary of those mentioned in Samuel's Last Will and Testament, only his grandson Daniel, and Daniel's descendants, lived and died in Rhode Island--in this case, Glocester and Burrillville Townships. Burrillville, which was the most northwesterly of the colony's townships, was set off from northern Glocester and incorporated as a separate entity in 1806. This property was willed to Daniel by his grandfather Samuel, and was approximately 10 miles west of the Moshassuck River.

Daniel, Grandson of Samuel Whipple

Daniel[4] Whipple (Noah B.[3], Samuel[2], John[1]), third and youngest son of Noah, was born in Glocester Township in 1703, and died there about the year 1790. His wife, Mary Smith, was the granddaughter of Sarah, the daughter of Captain John Whipple. They were parents to seven daughters and two sons; Jonathan, and Enoch. The descendants of Jonathan (1731-1805) founded the town of Whipple, Rhode Island, through his oldest son, Stephen. Stephen (1756-1811) had three children, including sons Ziba (1790-1867) and Smith. Stephen and Ziba were buried in the Whipple burial lot on Gazza Road in Burrillville, as were several other relatives. "He (Ziba) was a farmer and resided south of the present village of Mapleville, on land that is now owned by his grandson, Gilbert F. Whipple, and which has never been out of the family name." [279]

Seven sons of Ziba were successful mill owners and founded the town of "Whipple" Rhode Island, which is still shown on most maps of Rhode Island. Daniel S.[8] (Ziba[7], Stephen[6], Jonathan[5], Daniel[4], Noah[3], Samuel[2], John[1]) owned at least two mills. 55"A mill was reported started here about 1838. It burned down in 1845 and Daniel Whipple, who purchased the site, erected a new mill. Daniel opened another mill in nearby Mapleville in 1849, and devoted his interests there, while the rest of the Whipple family ran the Gazzaville mills for many years. In 1888, the mill burned and was never rebuilt. The former mill owners' house lived in by a Whipple descendant until the 1960s, still stands…. Along the Clear River and along Whipple Avenue, west of Oakland is the former mill hamlet of Plainville, later named Whipple…. Charles H.[8] (Ziba[7], Stephen[6], Jonathan[5], Daniel[4], Noah[3], Samuel[2], John[1]) purchased Plainview in 1856 and began the manufacture of woolen goods. The town was renamed Whipple in 1891 when a railroad and station were constructed. However, by 1929, most of the employed residents were employed outside of Whipple. A description in the brochure advertising the sale of the village in 1929, described it as a 'cozy and snug little village.' The mill was subsequently demolished. The mill site today is not visible from the road, but several of the old mill houses along Whipple Avenue survive." [280]Charles H. and Daniel S. had at least five brothers who also worked in the woolen industry: Enoch, Sterry, John, James, and George.[281]

Gilbert Whipple (12 April 1855- 1923), son of Charles H. (1823-1885), took over his father's portion of the family business after his father retired to Providence with an ample fortune. His son Charles H. Junior (1894-1953) and grandson Charles (1933-2005) continued the Whipple interest in that and other industries. With the latter's death, at least four Whipple generations were buried in the Swan Point Cemetery at Providence.

Whipple Avenue in Whipple Rhode Island

Frederick (1842-22 July 1904), son of Daniel S. (31 January 1815-12 September 1872), took over a portion of the family business, when his father retired to Providence with a sizeable fortune. Frederick graduated from Brown University with a degree in law. However, he spent his life in the family business. He eventually moved to New York City, where he was a stockbroker. He returned to Burrillville in 1897, where he died in 1904 after a lingering illness. Frederick was a colonel during the Civil War, and served several years in the state legislature.[282] His sons were Frederick Junior and Clarence. Clarence moved to Seattle, Washington, where he died in 1948. He was buried beside his parents in the Swan Point Cemetery at Providence.

Abraham Whipple, Commodore of the Continental Navy[283]

Samuel's grandsons by his deceased son Noah were Noah, Enoch, and Daniel. They were willed their father's share on the west side of the 7-mile line in Glocester. As noted, Daniel lived out his life in that township, and Enoch died young without issue. Noah Junior joined his uncles in Connecticut during the late 1730s. Of his descendants, the most noted in American history is Commodore Abraham Whipple.

Commodore Abraham[5] Whipple (Noah[4], Noah[3], Samuel[2], John[1]) was born in Providence, Rhode Island 26 September 1733 and died in Marietta, Ohio 29 May 1819.

He married Sarah Hopkins 2 August 1761. She was born in 1739 and died 14 October 1818. To this couple three children were born:

  i. John H., born about 1762; died before May 1819.
  ii. Catherine, born about 1759; died 1834; married Ebenezer Sproat.
  iii. Mary; born about 1767; died before May 1819; married Ezekiel Comstock.

The most notable descendant of Samuel was his great grandson, Commodore Abraham Whipple, of Cranston, Rhode Island. This property was located approximately five miles southwest of the town of Providence and was not part of the Louquisset bequest. Sarah Whipple was a niece (daughter of a brother, John) of Stephen Hopkins, a multi-termed Governor of Rhode Island and signer of the Declaration of Independence. Their son John Hopkins Whipple continued to follow the sea after leaving Marietta, Ohio, and apparently never married. Mary had three daughters and a son after marrying Dr. Ezekiel Comstock of Smithfield, all of whom were married in Smithfield Township. Catherine's grandson was Henry H. Sibley, the first Governor of the state of Minnesota. Several descendants of the female branches are living in the states of Michigan, Rhode Island, and Massachusetts under the names of Sibley, Comstock, and Fisher. Catherine was the only child mentioned in Abraham's Last Will and Testament.[284]

At 10 p.m. the evening of 9 June 1772, eight boats containing 64 angry, determined men of Rhode Island set out from Fenner's wharf in Providence Harbor to destroy his majesty's customs ship *Gaspe*, which lay aground on a sandpit near Namquit Point in Narragansset Bay. The ship had been a problem to colonial commerce and this was an opportunity long awaited.[285] The leader in this act of rebellion was Captain Abraham Whipple.

Abraham Whipple

News of the *Gaspe's* grounding came from Newport's Captain Benjamin Lindsey, master of the packet *Hannah*. He arrived in Providence about sunset and reported the incident to John Brown, one of Providence's most powerful merchants. Brown immediately ordered eight of the largest longboats in the harbor be fitted to engage the *Gaspe*, and named Whipple, one of his merchant captains, to lead the expedition. When close by to the grounded ship, they were challenged with a "Who goes there?" Whipple, resplendent in blue cloth coat, ruffled shirt, and hair neatly tied behind, stood and responded that he was the sheriff of the county of Kent and wanted to board. Lieutenant William Dudingston, the captain, waved them off and fired a pistol at them.[286] Whipple bellowed back he had a warrant " to apprehend you... So surrender, God damn you!" He was not a man to mince words. After a few shots, Dudingston was wounded and Providence men boarded with no casualties.

113

The longboats had been filled with paving stones and Whipple ordered them placed in the hold before they set the *Gaspe* afire. The gunpowder exploded and it burned to the waterline by dawn. Dudingston and his crew, put ashore at the Point of Pawtuxet, suffered no serious injury but lost all their personal possessions. The news spread like wildfire. Whipple and his men had committed an overt act of treason with a penalty of death if caught.[287]

The Crown's reaction was sharp and swift--a thousand pounds for information that led to the arrest and conviction of the perpetrators. Amnesty was offered to any participant who turned in the leaders. The reward was a fortune to most Rhode Islanders and might tempt even a strong patriot. But fortunately for Whipple, Brown, Hopkins, Mawney, and the other principals, mass amnesia broke out in Providence. After a year's trial, on 11 June 1773, the superior court, presided over by Stephen Hopkins, Abraham's wife's uncle, decided it "had nothing to go on."[288] To the relief of Whipple and his fellow perpetrators, the case was closed. This incident was a turning point in Whipple's life. He had been a privateer for England during the French and Indian Wars, built a successful mercantile career as trader and sea captain, and lived a peaceful life as a solid citizen of Rhode Island. Now his long, loyal, faithful allegiance to the crown ended and he became committed to a cause: revolution.

Born 26 September 1733 in Providence, Abraham Whipple was the fourth child and eldest son of Noah Whipple Junior[289] and Mary Dexter.[290] He had sisters Freelove, Susanna, and Mary, and a brother Samuel.[291] Records of his early life are skimpy but suggest he went to sea at an early age. Ancestors on both the paternal and maternal side were landsmen and it was common for the eldest son to follow his father's work so his link to the sea was probably influenced by the Hopkins family. His great great aunt Abigail Whipple married William Hopkins as her second husband. Their only son William fathered nine children, three who played an important role in Abe's life. Stephen, born in 1707, who presided at the *Gaspe* affair, served several terms as the colony's governor, and represented it in the continental congress where he signed the Declaration of Independence.[292] Esek, the first commander in chief of the continental Navy, and John, who also served in the continental navy, and was father of Abe's wife, Sarah. Two other brothers, William and Samuel, also followed the sea.

Sea Captains Carousing in Surinam, 1758

Privateering became a major business in the mid-1740s. Among the early privateers out of Providence was the 90-ton sloop *Reprisal* owned by Stephen Hopkins and several other investors. Stephen's brother John commanded the ship. Brothers William and Esek were captains of the *Prince Frederick* and *Wentworth*.

The business was profitable but dangerous. John, Abe's father-in-law, was killed in an

114

engagement with a large Spanish ship in 1746 when Abe was only 13 years old, leaving John's wife to raise several small children.

The French and Indian War dragged on in spurts for 19 years and embraced Abe's formative years. The West Indian trade flourished during this period bringing growth and prosperity to Providence. Abraham's introduction to the sea was likely on a privateer with cousin Esek when he was in his early teens. Since William didn't die until 1755, it is possible he also sailed under his guidance as well. He rose rapidly, commanding his first ship in his early 20s and earned a reputation as a successful privateer. His greatest success in that war came in 1759. On 10 September 1758, the schooner *Gamecock* was issued a letter of marque. Abe became captain in 1759 and sailed from Boston on July 19th on a record-setting cruise that brought fame and fortune. He captured 23 French prizes valued at over a million pounds sterling. His share was $60,000, a massive sum for the time. [293]

Surinam was a favorite gathering place of the Caribbean captains. Paramaribo, its principal port, offered them all the comforts of a home away from home.[294] A painting done in the winter of 1758 by English artist John Greenwood, now in the St. Louis Art Museum, presents a vivid picture of the captains at play and demonstrates their strong ties that benefited America during the Revolution. It is an evening scene in a tavern taproom. Esek Hopkins and Nicholas Cooke are seated at the far side of a table chatting. Quaker Captain Jonas Wanton is dozing at the same table oblivious to Stephen Hopkins playfully pouring wine over his baldhead and Ambrose Page vomiting into his pocket. Godfrey Malbone Junior and Nicholas Powers are in the middle of the room doing a dance. Abe, with an amused grin, is standing to the far right smoking a long churchwarden pipe. While slimmer than in later portraits (he was only 25), there is no mistaking his nose, his most dominant feature. In white shirt with frothy lace jabot at the neck and deep lace cuffs, an elaborately embroidered vest that reaches his knees, immaculate white hose, and gold-laced tricorn hat, he is the most fancily dressed man in the room, also the only one not wearing a surcoat.[295]

Historian Samuel P. Hildreth wrote in an 1852 biographical sketch that Abe was "short, thickset, and stout with dark grey eyes and great muscular strength." Though imposing stern discipline on subordinates, he was highly respected. In times of danger Hildreth said he "diffused courage into all around him so that no crew could be cowardly with such a leader." He performed best during times of great danger according to Hildreth and he spent a fortune of his own money, never repaid by the government, to provide for his crews. No one exceeded his contributions to the navy, he concluded.[296] Many of his letters survive and their fluency suggests he was well schooled. He was a stylish dresser and at ease in distinguished company. He was 28 and a well-to-do sea captain when he married Sarah Hopkins, a distant cousin, on 26 August 1761 in Providence. The union lasted for 57 years.[297]

After the Peace of Paris in 1763, privateers had to seek other employment. Abe's spectacular previous successes impressed the Brown brothers, Nicholas, John, Joseph, and Moses, Providence's largest and most powerful firm of merchants, so they hired him as captain of their sloop *George*. The British never caught him engaging in illegal trade and he became on the shrewdest of the Brown traders in the Caribbean. There is no evidence that he was ever involved in the slave trade as were other Brown captains.[298]

115

The relationship with the Brown brothers was a profitable association, ending after 12 years when Abe chose to serve his country rather than his private interest.

Beginning in 1774, the British sent more ships and soldiers to America believing their presence would curtail an ever-increasing level of discontent. However, by December 16 rebellious activity reached its high point of the year when Boston patriots threw tea into the harbor rather than pay the hated taxes. On 2 March 1775, Providence held its own "tea party." Tea was piled up in market square, tar poured over it to ensure a good blaze, one of prime minister lord North's speeches placed on top, and the pile set afire. Rhode Island didn't ignore what it believed to be British repression and on June 15th its legislature, at the urging of Stephen Hopkins, authorized the purchasing and arming of two sloops. Abe was named commander of the two-vessel fleet and commanded the 12-gun Katy, with captain Grimes commanding an 8-gunner. Abe's wages were set at "up to 9 lawful money."[299]

Abraham Whipple's commission was signed July 2nd, just two days before the bloody battle of Bunker Hill and two days short of the third anniversary of the Gaspe burning. Abe sailed the Katy into Narragansett Bay to engage the HMS Rose and her fleet of tenders which were blocking the bay. Sir James Wallace, commander of the fleet blockading the rebellious colonies, had threatened to hand anyone taking arms against king George. The threat meant nothing to Abe and he successfully engaged the Rose, capturing one of her tenders, disabling two others, and temporarily freed the Bay allowing a large number of homeward-bound vessels to enter port. Thus Abe was responsible for firing the first gun of the Revolution against the enemy on the water. With this act of open rebellion, it was no longer necessary to hide the identity of the Gaspe participants an Abe's role was made known to Wallace who immediately sent him this message. "You, Abraham Whipple, on the 17th of June 1772, burned his majesty's vessel Gaspe and I will hang you at the yardarm, James Wallace." Abe's terse reply: "Sir, always catch a man before you hang him, Abraham Whipple." Wallace tried his best to make good on his promise. But his best was not good enough to cope with the wily brain and brassbound nerve of Abe Whipple.

Heartened by Abe's success against the Rose and its tenders, the Rhode island assembly instructed its delegates, Stephen Hopkins and Samuel Ward, to the continental congress to work for the establishment of a continental navy.[300] Congress appointed a committee of three, which on October 30th recommended building a fleet "for the protection and defense of the United colonies." That morning, a letter from General Washington was read in congress describing how he had recently assumed command, at continental expense, of three schooners to cruise off Massachusetts to intercept enemy supply ships. This information weakened the opponents of a navy and congress acted favorably. On November 12, Governor Cooke, as captain general and commander-in-chief of and over the English colony of Rhode Island, ordered Abe to Philadelphia to join the fleet of the continental congress."

The first American men-of-war were converted from merchantmen to frigates. The flagship Alfred was commanded by Dudley Saltonstal of Massachusetts, Abe was named captain of the 300-ton Columbus.[301] John Burrow Hopkins (Esek's son) was given command of the brig, Cabot, third largest of the four-ship fleet, Nicholas Biddle of Philadelphia, was given the smaller brig Andrew Doria. Esek Hopkins reluctantly accepted the job as commander-in-chief.[302] Thus Stephen Hopkins made sure his kin were to control the country's first navy.

Initial doubts about the prospects of a continental navy were soon justified. Each colony, eager to protect its own shipping and ports, established small individual fleets outside of naval control. Lack of a unified command meant a less disciplined and effective navy to face the 100 warships cruising off the American coast by 1777. Nonetheless, the marine committee issued Hopkins orders on January 5th. He was to take his squadron of ships and clear the southern coasts and then sail north to do the same in Narraganset Bay. They captured two forts in the Bahamas and left March 17th, the same day the British evacuated Boston. Though successful, the mission also produced the navy's first court-martial trial of which Abraham Whipple played a central role. The fleet was almost home when they spotted the 20-gun HMS Glasgow with a crew of 150 commanded by Captain Tyringham Howe. A lengthy battle ensued in which the British ship escaped after several hours. The American fleet arrived at New London, Connecticut with prizes to a great welcome. The fleet was safe, if not sound, the prizes had been retained, and a British fighting ship had been crippled. The press declared an American victory and congress sent a congratulatory note. But when it was learned the cost included 10 dead and 14 wounded, ugly rumors began to circulate. Abe was accused of cowardice. He considered the charges scurrilous and demanded a court-martial to either clear his name or confirm the charge. The court-martial was convened in the cabin of the *Alfred,* May 6. After hearing Abe's account and "sundry evidences of those who were present in different vessels during the engagement," the court concluded that he "proceeded from error of judgment and not from cowardice."[303] A full account was published in the *Providence Gazette* newspaper May 18 so Abe achieved his goal: exoneration on the eyes of his peers and his neighbors.

After the fleet was back in Narragansett Bay, Admiral Howe dispatched a squadron to patrol the coast to make sure it stayed there. It also suffered personnel problems. George Washington took 175 of their marines to help in the battle to save New York and another 100 seamen became ill. Esek ordered Abe to superintend the final fitting of the *Warren* and the *Providence* in Newport and to take the *Columbus,* "which was very foul" there for cleaning. The ships were ready in early December but the British fleet arrived at Newport with 5,000 troops on the seventh and conquered it along with most of the other communities on Aquidneck Island. Abe and John Hopkins saved the ships by sailing them to Providence where they were protected by the American forces commanded by General Spencer. The occupation of Newport was a major disaster for the continental navy. The British now had a major base in the Bay giving them an even tighter noose around the American ships.[304]

Due to this, congress apparently no longer considered Esek Hopkins naval commander-in-chief. However, they did not tell him and the news came from Abe. In a letter to the marine committee February 14, he referred to instructions received December 10 directing him to get the ships "out cruising as soon as possible." He said when he issued orders to Captain Whipple, Abe told him he had direct orders from the committee with instructions not to take directions from Esek.[305] Despite John Adams' efforts, congress dismissed Esek Hopkins on March 26th. Hopkins became a delegate in the Rhode Island assembly and customs inspector after the war ended. A "board of command," acting under direction of the marine committee, assumed Esek's command.

When congress reached a decision on how it would attempt to bring France into the war, it turned to the only man who stood a chance of getting their dispatches through the British blockade. On 20 March 1778, he was ordered to carry dispatches "to our ministers in France." There were many Tory sympathizers and informers in Providence and his orders were soon known by the British naval commander in Newport who positioned a 64 gun man of war and a host of frigates in the Bay to prevent his departure. The odds were great against him. The British had at least a dozen ships in the Bay with 300 guns, mainly 18, 24, and 32-pounders. Abe had only 28 guns, mostly 12 pounders with a few long 9s. Success would depend on wit, guile, and bold surprise. They left the night of April 30 under the welcome cover of a violent northeaster and heavy sleet and rainstorm. This circumstance and his own experience resulted in success.

Congress hoped the dispatches Abe carried would convince the French government to join in the war against England. The consequences of the September 1777 American victory at Saratoga were enormous. Britain's arch-enemy France, received the news with "as much joy as if it had been a victory of their own troops over they own enemies," according to Benjamin Franklin, head of the American commissioners in Paris. French foreign minister count Vergennes, in sympathy with the American cause, had covertly aided America with munitions, money, and other supplies since May 1776. Tough crucial, the aid was not enough. The dispatches carried by Abe instructed our commissioners to prod Vergennes into a final commitment to war. The Providence docked at Nantes May 26. William Jones immediately took the dispatches to Paris. Franklin, playing the negotiating game, wrote Vergennes on June 4, "we have the honor of enclosing to your Excellency a copy of the letter form Captain Whipple of the *Providence*. As she brought no dispatches for us, the letter from the Captain is all her intelligence" It was a lie, as Vergennes undoubtedly knew, intended to make the French think congress was tending toward the British offer of home rule. The outcome was the one desired. France and Britain were officially at war on 17 June 1778.[306]

After three busy months in France, the commissioners notified Abe by letter July 13 that it had ordered Captain Samuel Tucker and Captain Simpson to accompany the *Providence* back to America. Abe's orders were to "...use all possible dispatch in getting to sea with the *Providence, Boston, and Ranger.*" It was August 26 before all details were completed and he set sail bearing his new title of commodore,[307] as a commander of a three-vessel fleet. As the fleet sailed home it captured six prizes and Abe celebrated his 46th birthday. They ran the gauntlet of British ships blockading Boston, arriving safely with their cargoes and prizes--arms, ammunition, and clothing--all badly needed on the home front. Abe sent an account of the voyage to George Washington at his Fredericksburg headquarters.[308]

Abe spent the winter in Boston, refitting the *Providence* and working on the sale of the prize ships. The news of the French alliance made him a hero in Providence and he made several trips there by land because of the British blockade of Narragansset Bay. On April 4th, he was instructed to provision for a longer voyage, and on June 12 he received orders that launched him on a feat labeled 150 years later by the conservative United

States Naval Institute as "unsurpassed in war annals." Together with the *Ranger* and the *Queen of France*, they were to intercept either the homeward bound Jamaican fleet or the fleet from Hudson's Bay and take, burn, sink, or destroy as many as possible. They sighted the Jamaican fleet about 7.a.m on July 24. The Americans were hopelessly outmatched. Since Abe couldn't match their gunpowder, he decided to match wits. He ordered his three-ship fleet to fly the Union Jack of the royal navy and join the convoy pretending to be ships out of Halifax, Nova Scotia. Abe quietly picked off the first prize and obtained the signals used by the British commodore. He and his captains took turns with various schemes. They invited the captain of a potential prize on board the "Halifax" vessels for a convivial evening, then sent his boat back filled with a prize crew who took it over with a minimum of commotion so the rest of the convoy sailed on unalerted. Noting that the *Holderness* hoisted a light to her mizzen-top to guide the fleet's course, Abe quietly slipped into the center of the convoy and when the fog hid the *Holderness* hoisted a similar lamp to the *Providence's* mizzen and decoyed the *Friendship* and *Thestis* into following him. By morning they were so off course he could easily capture them. When he got back to the convoy, he discovered the *Ranger* and *Queen of France* had captured the *Neptune* and *Fort William*.

The next day, Abe decided to run out their guns and go after any ship they fancied. It was a day of wild chases but they added three more prizes. At dawn, the *Providence* moved through the convoy until it was abreast of the unsuspecting ship, the gun ports flew open, and a shattering broadside poured into the *Holderness*. Before the gunners could reload, the large vessel hauled down her flags in surrender. When her captain was brought aboard as prisoner, they learned why he didn't resist the smaller and weaker ship. Yesterday's open chase and capture produced wild stories about Abe's fleet. There were reports there were as many as two dozen disguised warships bristling with guns. Abe's fleet took 11 prizes before heading for home. This was another record as usually one or two prizes were taken before the captor could reach harbor.

When Abe sailed into Boston harbor the afternoon of August 21, the town was thrown into a panic by the sight of eight topsails. The *Boston Gazette* newspaper reported the alarm "soon subsided, for between the hours of three and five in the afternoon were safe anchored in this harbor the continental ship of war and their laden prize ships." Abe's fleet had the richest capture made by the navy during the war--6, 000 hogsheads of sugar, ginger, pimento, and cotton and 113 guns valued at over $1,000,000. He accomplished this will little expenditure or loss and received the accolades of the navy and the marine committee. Abe's feat also provided an important boost to New England's morale. People throughout the colonies celebrated his feat by singing the following ballad:

Come listen and I'll tell you how first I went to sea
To fight against the British and win our liberty
We shipped with Captain Whipple who never knew a fear
The Captain of the Providence, the Yankee privateer. (An error, of course)
    Chorus:
We sailed and we sailed and kept good cheer
For not a British frigate could o'ercome the privateer
We sailed to the southward and suddenly did meet,

Three British frigates--convey to a West Indian fleet,
Old Whipple put our lights out and crawled upon their rear
And not a soul suspected the Yankee privateer
So slowly did we sail along, so silently we ran,
    Chorus:
The biggest British frigate bore round to give us chase,
But though we were the fleeter, Old Whipple didn't race,
Until he'd raked her fore and aft, for the lubbers couldn't steer
And then he showed the foe the heels of the Yankee privateer
    Chorus:
Then northward sailed our gallant ship to a town that we all know,
And then we lay our prizes all anchored in a row,
And welcome was our victim, to our friends and family dear,
For we shared a million dollars on the Yankee privateer.[309]

As commander Abe was entitled to one-twentieth or $50,000. Some of the money was invested in a house and lot on Westminster Street in Providence and for a farm in Cranston.

The news of John Paul Jones' success and increasing fame roused the competitive spirit in Abe and he welcomed the marine committee's order to get the Providence ready for sea. His orders were to "command the ships *Boston, Queen of France,* and *Ranger,* and...embrace the first fair wind and without any kind of delay proceed to sea, and when [you are] five leagues to the southward of the lighthouse you are to open the orders enclosed and follow the direction therein given you."[310] Upon opening the orders he learned that he was to place himself and his fleet under the command of Benjamin Lincoln, general in charge of the defense of Charleston, South Carolina. The voyage was an unhappy omen of things to come. En route they were hit by a 30-hour gale of such force it sprang the mizzenmasts of the *Providence* and *Ranger* and delayed their arrival until December 19. Several other warships were already there and Abe became commander of the largest American squadron assembled during the Revolution. However, his success or failure was not in his own hands. His fate depended on an unknown factor--major general Lincoln.

Lincoln's orders, to hold Charleston at any cost, were a departure from American military policy. Heretofore, when the enemy was too stong, the American withdrew and waited for another opportunity. Until there was a sign of General Henry Clinton whose army was reportedly on the way, Abe believed he could be more help to Lincoln at sea. As he was cruising along the coast to the north 23 January 1779, Abe fell in with a fleet sent to re-supply Clinton. He captured three transports, a 14-gun brig, and three armed sloops loaded with military supplies and a few troops. The cruise was cut short when he was chased back to port by four large men-of-war from Admiral Marriot Arbuthnot's squadron. The British then blockaded the harbor.[311]

Clinton's British army of 6,000 landed 30 miles up the coast from Charleston. He outnumbered Lincoln two to one but held off attacking, awaiting reinforcements from Lord Cornwallis. When fighting began Lincoln's response was to draw his entire army inside Charleston and order Abe to bring all ships to the wharves so their guns and men could join with the forces within the city. Clinton could not have wished for a better trap for only the neck, a narrow isthmus, connected city and mainland. Cornwallis arrived the 18th with 3,000 reinforcements enabling Clinton to expand his lines and cut off all supplies to the city. Even with Abe's armament and crews, Lincoln was greatly overmatched by artillery and outnumber by more than three to one. Provision and ammunition were in short supply by May 6, and it was apparent that the British would be successful. More than 30 houses were destroyed and countless others damaged by the British bombardment. Charleston's leading citizens successfully petitioned Lincoln to accept Clinton's surrender terms and firing ceased between 11 a.m. and noon May 12.[312]

Abe's crews became the responsibility of Admiral Arbuthnot, and Abe somehow talked the admiral into letting his officers go. He was also able to favorably influence the disposition of his crews and the *Providence* and *Ranger* became part of the British fleet. General Lincoln was immediately paroled and in the spring of 1781, exchanged, and rejoined Washington on the Hudson. At the end of June, Abe and his men were transferred to Chester, Pennsylvania where they remained as prisoners for two years and seven months. The British provided little to feed or care for the sick at Chester. Small pox was taking a deadly toll, so once again Abe, at his own expense, provided for them by renting a house and furnishing supplies and medicines to keep them alive. In late 1782, General Nathaniel Green of Rhode Island, marching to liberate Charleston, was able to arrange Abe's exchange for British naval officer Captain Gayton of the 44-fun frigate Romulus.

Subsequent to returning to Rhode Island, Abe discovered that he was almost broke financially. Spending his own money to provide for his crews, failing to collect his share of prize money, and limited income coupled with his family living off capital had depleted his once considerable fortune. His Providence home and small farm in Cranston were all that remained. He moved to the latter and the 1782 state census shows nine people in his household: one male under 22, his only son John, two females under 22, daughters Catherine and Sarah, one male under 50,himself, one female under 50, wife Sarah, two blacks, probably farm workers, and two mystery people, a male and female over 50.[313]

After the peace of 1784, Providence merchants resumed their foreign trade. Abe's old friend and employer, John Brown, launched the *George Washington* and asked Abe to assume command. Anxious to return to the sea and make some money, he accepted and became the first American to fly the stars and striped in England. Hundreds of curious Britishers visited the ship when she docked in the Thames. It was Abe's last sea voyage of the eighteenth century. He was 53 with at least 35 years as a sailor. The record doesn't indicate why but he retired from the seafaring life and returned to the farm at Cranston.

Abe's finances had reached such a low point that he sent a letter to congress 10 June 1786 asking for payment for his time in service and to be reimbursed for his payments on behalf of the government. He recited his service from 15 June 1775 to December 1782, and noted he had received no wages or subsistence for the period from December 1776 to the end of his service. He listed large sums he advanced to the government in France and Charleston (estimated at $7,000 in specie, exclusive of interest), and asked to be repaid all or part so he could regain his mortgaged farm and "snatch my family from misery and ruin." With interest, his claim would have been worth at least $10,000 to which should be added six years of captain and commodore pay of $6,000. His petition was referred to the commissioner of accounts in the marine department and on 10 October it reported in his favor. However, congress only authorized reimbursement of the money advanced in France and the payment, dollar value unknown, was not money or specie equivalent to his expenditure. It was in the form of securities that had the same face value. Because of the low credit of the country, its real value was only a fraction in cash. Because of his pressing debts, Abe had to sell the specie at a discount of 80 percent. "I either took the discount or let my family suffer for the necessaries of life," he wrote. Little though it was, the money made it possible to stave off financial disaster, at least for the time being.

While waiting for congress to act, Abe followed family tradition and entered politics and was elected to the state legislature to represent Cranston. His pocket may have been empty but he was a famous and respected figure and had no problem wining. The major issue of the time was paper money. Paper money advocates, Abe was not one, led by Othniel Gorton, speaker of the house, were in power. When presiding, Gorton, who favored chewing tobacco, faced his members making it difficult for opposition speakers on the other side of the room to get his attention. Once when seeking recognition to speak without success, Abe raised his voice to a gale-defying bellow startling Gorton who testily acknowledged him with, "I hear you, I hear you." Abe responded acidly, "I wish, Mr. Speaker, you would shift your quid of tobacco from your starboard to your larboard jaw, so that might give your head a cant in this direction, so that you could sometimes hear something from this side of the house."[314] After having spent hard money on behalf of the government and being repaid in depreciated paper money, it is easy to see why he opposed paper currency. Abe lost that fight in the legislature.

At approximately the same time that Abe was penning his desperate plea to congress, a group of men in Boston were exploring the possibility of acquiring and settling a large tract of land in Ohio. Reports indicated its potential was great, both for its natural resources and fertility of land along it river basins. Led by General Rufus Putnam and Dr. Manasseh Cutler they formed the Ohio Company and set about raising $1,000,000 in continental certificates. Putnam was named leader of the enterprise and Cutler successfully lobbied congress to sell the company 1.5 million acres along the Ohio and Muskingum rivers at just over nine cents an acre. Ebenezer Sproat, Abe's daughter Catherine's husband, was hired as official surveyor of the Ohio Company in 1787. He was to lay out the first permanent settlement for the company. This meant moving his family to the frontier. Abe was intrigued by his son-in-law's opportunity and it caused him to consider his own options. Should he stay in Rhode Island where his roots were deep or seek a new, unknown, and undoubtedly dangerous life far from his beloved ocean? He decided to follow the lead of Captain John Whipple, his first American ancestor, who twice opted for the frontier: first when he left England in 1632 to settle in Dorchester and again in 1659 when he left a settled Dorchester for the frontier of Providence.

The trip to Ohio via the "Wilderness Trail," which ran from the settled states west through the Cumberland Gap in trackless forests, was virtually impossible.

Consequently, the early settlers went by water. The journey began in early April 1788 with the little fleet carrying 48 men dubbed in the annals of Ohio as "The Forty-eight Immortals." Abe is included among them, but this is questionable. The historian Hildreth says Abe with wife Sarah, son John, daughter Catherine, and granddaughter Sarah Sproat arrived in 1789 when, presumably Ebenezer would have built a log cabin to house them. They left following Polly's July wedding to Dr. Ezekiel Comstock.

Indians attacked the Whipple's new hometown, named Marietta, 2 January 1791. Fourteen were killed, four taken captive. The Ohio Company responded by spending $11,000 on defenses. They completed a fort, dug an 80-foot well to insure a water supply, and built two other forts. As superintendent and paymaster for these projects, Sproat was often away from home so the care of the family fell to Abe. The family was assigned to blockhouse number 15 in the garrison at the Point. Once the area became safe, Sproat built a log cabin about midway between the garrison at the Point and the fort. Both families moved there.[315] After the peace treaty was signed with the Indians in 1795, Abe and Sarah moved to their new 12-acre farm on the banks of the Muskingum, two miles from its mouth. He was 63 and his only resources were what he could produce on the farm. Son John decided that frontier life was not for him and left to become a seaman. By then, Sproat's duties as sheriff required him to live in Marietta so he built a frame house with a garden noted for its beauty. He was involved in the town's growth, contributing handsomely to building Muskingum Academy and the church. Ground for the Academy was broken in 1797 and it opened in 1800. Abe does not appear on its contribution lists. His lack of farming expertise and small acreage meant he was never able to earn more than a minimum subsistence.

By 1799, enough "free male inhabitants" lived in the territory to justify a legislative assembly. Rather than food shortages, farmers were producing surpluses with little means of selling the excess. Abe had an intimate knowledge of the Caribbean trade and convinced his friends that the islands were the market for their surplus. It wasn't

long before they determined that the large trees growing in the area would make fine timbers to build square-rigged keelboats suitable for seagoing. They could sail the local products down the river system to the sea, then to the Caribbean where they would sell the cargo and get a new one, sail it to eastern ports, sell it and the ship, return by land, and start again. If it worked, it would open a whole new world of trade to the Ohio settlers. Named the *St. Clair* after the territorial governor, the territories first ship was ready for its maiden voyage in April 1801. The first cargo was flour and salted pork. The whole town turned out to see them off. News of their sailing had spread and as they passed Cincinnati its citizens crowded the banks to cheer them.

Governor Sibley

Commodore Abraham Whipple, aware of the massive undertaking, was 70 when he assumed command. He wasn't worried once at sea, getting to sea was the challenge. It took six weeks of slow cautions sailing before they reached New Orleans in early June. To avoid port charges, he anchored in the river while loading provisions for the sea portion of the journey. A New

Orleans' newspaper report said "Commodore Whipple thinks it is the greatest thing he ever did" and that "he deserves more credit for it than his going out of Newport with dispatches from congress after passing eleven British frigates."[316] For the first time in 17 years, Abe was at sea again. The destination was Havana, Cuba. He was the only one aboard who could navigate on the high seas that meant long watches and much anxiety. Fortunately no problems developed and he found the Havana market just as he had anticipated--goods in scarce supply and high prices producing a good profit. Before leaving for Philadelphia in late August, he added a new mate to his crew--his son John Hopkins Whipple. There is no record whether this meeting was by design or happenstance but it was the only time they sailed together and may have been the last time they met.

He probably returned to his Ohio home by way of Rhode Island in order to see his daughter Mary and his grandchildren, Sarah, Elizabeth Carter, and William Whipple Comstock, for the first time. At home in Marietta he received a hero's welcome. On his return, Abe learned his granddaughter Sarah Whipple Sproat was to marry Judge Solomon Sibley of Detroit in October. Sibley, 15 years Sarah's senior, was born in Sutton, Massachusetts in 1769, and was a prime mover in the incorporation of Detroit in 1802. He was a member of Michigan's first legislative assembly in 1799 and a mayor of Detroit.

By 1811, at 78, Abe was finding it almost impossible to operate his farm and a neighbor persuaded him to apply for a much-deserved Revolutionary War pension. This time, a more prosperous government awarded him $30.00 a month, which allowed the aged couple to live out their lives without the threat of poverty and hunger. Abe lived to see the beginning of the end of the Age of Sail, for Robert Fulton's first steamboat was launched in October of 1811. He also lived through the war of 1812. In 1813, he and Sarah moved in with their widowed daughter Catherine. Now, 80, he wrote his will. Sarah took sick in October of 1818, and died shortly after. Abe died 29 May 1819 after a short illness. All that remained from his days of youth and glory were his dress sword and quadrant. He left them to great grandsons Ebenezer Sibley and Henry Sibley, who became the first governor of the state of Minnesota. He was buried in Mound Cemetery beside Sarah. The following inscription was placed on the grave: "Sacred to the memory of Commodore Abraham Whipple whose name, skill, and courage will ever remain the pride and boast of this country. In the late Revolution he was the first on the seas to hurl defiance at proud Britain, gallantly leading the way to arrest from the mistress of the ocean her scepter, and there to wave the star-spangled banner. He also conducted at sea the first square-rigged vessel ever built on the Ohio, opening to commerce resources beyond calculation."

It is difficult to comprehend why Abraham Whipple, one of America's greatest patriots, is honored with but two modest memorials; a Providence street that bears his name, and a grave headstone some 700 miles from his native home. No citizen of any state could claim as many "firsts" in the War for Independence as he. Truly, he might be called the "forgotten man of the Continental Navy."[317]

124

End Notes

[256] Horatio Rogers, George Moulton Carpenter, and Edward Field, Record Commissioners. *The Early Records of Town of Providence*, Volume 6, Being Part of the Will, Book Number 1, otherwise called the First *Book for Providence Towne Council* Perticulior Vse, (Providence: Snow and Farnham city printers, 1894) 126-28. Also, pages 129-30. A deposition of Thomas Olney that he had gone to Captain John Whipple, at his request, and obtained clarification of some of the bequests. In the latter, John Junior was given an additional 30 acres in the Louquisset. Also, pages 130-34 are the inventory of Captain John Whipple's movable estate.

[257] Thomas Bicknell, *The History of Rhode Island and Providence Plantations, 3 vols.* (New York: The American Historical Society, 1920) 3:1191. The Whipples married into nearly every family name in ancient Smithfield. A longer list of over 100 surnames is given on page 926.

[258] Lincoln Rhode Island. Statewide Historical Preservation Report, P-L-1. RI Historical Preservation Commission, January 1982: 5-6.

[259] Barbara R. Carroll, Exeter, Rhode Island, personal correspondence, 29 September 2002.

[260] Thomas Steere, *History of Smithfield* (Providence: E.L. Freeman & Company, 1881) 142.

[261] *Records of the First Church at Dorchester in New England, 1636-1734* (Boston: George H. Ellis, 1891) 267 and 174. John O. Austin, *Genealogical Dictionary of Rhode Island* (Albany, NY: 1887, reprint edition. Baltimore: Genealogical Publication Company, 1978) 222. Henry E. Whipple, A *Brief Genealogy of the Whipple Families Who Settled in Rhode Island* (Providence: A. Crawford Greene, 1873) James N. Arnold, Vital *Records of Rhode Island, 1636-1850* (Providence: Narragansett Historical Publishing Company, 1892). Vital statistics on the children and grandchildren of Captain John and Sarah Whipple are taken from the above and numerous publications that quote from them. To view more recent information, consult www.whipple.org, Weldon Whipple, Webmaster.

[262] Clara H. McGuigan, *The Antecedents and Descendants of Noah Whipple of the Rogerene Community of Quakertown, Connecticut* (Ithica NY: J.M. Kingsbury, 1971) 36.

[263] Rufus M. Jones, *The Quakers in the American Colonies* (New York: W.W. Norton & Company, 1966) 70.

[264] Edward Field, State *of Rhode Island and Providence Plantations at the End of the Century: A History, 3* vols (Mason Publishing Company, 1902) III: 622-23. Samuel bought the Abbott house in 1671 and added substantially to it. It would have been one of only a few houses in Providence that was spared during the war of 1675-76. It was built by Roger Mowrey in 1653 and used as a tavern. Abigail Whipple, Samuel's deceased daughter's husband Robert Currie sold the property to her cousins Job and John Whipple Junior (III) (brothers, and sons of John, Captain John's oldest son) in 1737. It remained in the Whipple family until 1761, and it is from this ownership that it was given the name Whipple House. Thomas Abbott owned the house from then until 1826. Hence, it was commonly referred to as the Abbott-Whipple House. It was demolished around the year 1900 and replaced by a three-story tenement building. For over 90 of its nearly 250 years of existence it was owned by a member of the Whipple family.

[265] Providence Record of Wills, 1:181-182. City Hall, Division of Archives and History, Providence, RI. The Early Records of the Town of Providence 21 vols, collected and printed by the Records Commissioners (Providence: Snow and Farnham, city printers, 1892-1915) VII:20-28 [hereinafter ERP].

[266] Field, III:622.

[267] McGuigan, 36. Samuel Junior had land originally deeded to him by his father in 1695 also on both sides of the Moshassuck River, which he had previously sold. The land willed to his grandsons (sons of his deceased son, Enoch) continued in the Whipple name for at least 200 years.

[268] Henry E. Whipple, 53. Clarence Torrey, *New England Marriages Before 1700* (Baltimore; Genealogical Publishing Company, 1985) 803.

[269] Bruce C. Daniels, *Dissent and Conformity on Narragansett Bay* (Middleton, Connecticut: Wesleyan University Press, 1983) 113.

[270] Bicknell, 3:925.

[271] McGuigan, 17

[272] John R. Bolles and Anna B. Williams, *The Rogerenes, Part II, History of the Rogerenes* (Boston: Stanhope Press, 1904) 300

[273] The designation "Quaker" is a misnomer. John Rogers was a member of the Seventh Day Baptist Church before he founded his own sect in the late 1600s. The Rogerenes worshipped on Saturday and practiced adult baptism and took communion-- practices shunned by the Quakers. However, their style of clothing and silence during the worship services were Quaker in nature. Neither group participated in military activity, which in the case of the Rogerenes created a constant source of persecution by the civil authorities. Samuel's mother was a Quaker, and probably his father also. It would have been an easy transition to the Rogerenes for them considering their similarities. The settlement of Quakertown was only about seven or eight miles south of Samuel's property.

[274] Bolles, 21.

[275] Jonathan's brother Noah was the titled Whipple in the McGuigan book, and her direct Whipple ancestor.

[276] Bolles, 314. McGuigan was superintendent of this school for over 25 years, before it was taken over by the state of Connecticut.

[277]   Vinton   A.   Ackley,   The   Rogerenes   of   Ledyard,   online   at http://home.earthlink.net~dschultz6/vackley.htm
"Whipple Family History", *The Day*, New London, Connecticut, 2 March 1892, p. 8.

[278] Tolland Land Deeds, II:284 and II:391.

[279] *Representative Men and Old Families of Rhode Island, 3 Vols.* (Chicago: J. H. Beers and Company, 1908) 3:1699.

[280] Burrillville Rhode Island. Statewide Preliminary Historical Preservation Report. RI Historical Preservation Commission, 1982: 26 & 54. Abstracted from this publication and liberally summarized.

[281] *The Historian*, Burrillville Historical and Preservation Society, XIII:1. March 1996

[282] Representative Men, 3:1700

[283] Most of the following narrative on the life of Commodore Whipple was taken from the article, "Commodore Abraham Whipple of Rhode Island and Ohio" by Blaine Whipple. It was sent to the authors on 1 June 2005 for inclusion in this history.

[284] Washington County Ohio Probate Records, 2:139-140. Office of the City Clerk, Marietta, Ohio. This probably meant that Abraham's son was already deceased.

[285] A.J. Langguth, *Patriots The Men Who Started the American Revolution* (New York: Simon and Schuster, 1988) 166. (Hereinafter *Patriots*). The smuggling of tax-free Dutch teas was an open fact and the Gaspe was sent to Narragansett By to stop the illegal traffic and collect taxes rightfully due the crown. Local merchants complained it stopped ever kind of vessel, even small boats loading to market. Whenever challenged its commander refused to show authorization papers and when he found smuggled goods he order them shipped to Boston though the law required the ship-owner be tried in the colony where his goods were confiscated.

[286] Margot Arnold, *Captain Abe: A Biography of the Revolutionary War Hero and Ohio Pioneer, Commodore Abraham Whipple of Rhode Island*. Unpublished manuscript at the William L. Clements Library, Early Americana (Ann Arbor: University of Michigan, 1986) Chapter 1, p. 3. The pages in this manuscript are not numbered consecutively. "I came upon the deck and hailed the boat, forbidding them to come near the schooner or I should order them to be fired on. They made answer they had the sheriff with them and must come aboard and I told them that the sheriff could not be admitted on board at that time of night, on which they set up a hallow and rowed as fast as they could toward the vessels bows. I than order the men to come forward with their small arms to prevent them from boarding."

[287] *Patriots*, 169. At its last session, parliament had extended the death penalty for destroying so much as an oar on one of the king's boats.

[288] Arnold, chapter 1, page 8

[289] Noah Whipple Senior, grandson of Captain John Whipple, received 169 acres of land from his father Samuel 8 May 1695. This is about the time Noah married Amphyllis Smith. Noah Junior was born 18 December 1696 and was bequeathed land by his grandfather Samuel by his will of 9 March 1711.

[290] Mary Dexter was born in 1699, daughter of John Dexter and his first wife Mary Field. After Mary died in 1727, John married Mary Mason. He died in 1734, the only grandparent to live to see Abraham's birth.

291 Clara Hammond McGuigan, *The Antecedents and Descendants of Noah Whipple of the Community at Quakertown, Connecticut* Rogerene (Ithaca NY: John M. Kingsbury, 1971) 37. Abraham's birth date is incorrect here and Samuel's birth is not recorded in this publication,.

292 Some members of Congress called Hopkins "Old Grape and Guts." He was a key figure in the rough-and-tumble politics of Rhode Island for over 40 years, and was as astute and experienced a politician as eighteenth century America produced. He was always attired in a simple Quaker-like dress with a large broad-brimmed hat.

293 David Fisher, "Commodore Abraham Whipple. A Paper by his Great-grandson, David Fisher," *Ohio Archeological and Historical Quarterly,* 1883, 3.

294 Surinam was a Dutch possession on the South American mainland. Britain exchanged it for New Amstrdam (New York).

295 Courtesy of the St. Louis Museum of Art

296 Samuel P. Hildreth,, *Biography and Historical Memoirs of the Early Pioneer Settlers of Ohio* (Cincinnati: H.W. Derby & Company, 1852) 162-64.

297 Abigail Whipple Dexter Hopkins, daughter of Captain John Whipple, was Abe's great grandmother and Sarah's great great grandmother. Sarah was six years younger than Abe. Stephen and Esek Hopkins were her uncles.

298 Arnold, Chapter 3, p. 8-9.

299 Naval Documents of the American Revolution, Naval History Division, Department of the Navy (Washington D.C.: Naval Department, 1971) 1: 740, 805. (Hereinafter Naval Documents).

300 John R. Bartlett, *Records of the Colony of Rhode Island and Providence Plantation in New England* (Providence: 1856-65) VII:368-69.

301 It was armed with 18 nine-pounders and manned by 137 seamen and 83 marines.

302 At the time Esek Hopkins was a brigadier general of the Rhode Island militia and was reticent about becoming the navy's first commander. He was uneasy about leaving his military obligation in Rhode Island where he was working with his old friend Governor Nicholas Cooke and was surrounded by men he knew. The overwhelming odds--525 British men-of-war against four continental vessels--mitigated against accepting the command.

303 *Naval Documents*, 4:1419-21. The proceedings, which are in the National Archives in Washington, D.C., are included with the papers of the continental congress. There is speculation that John Paul Jones, avidly ambitious for his own command was not above backstabbing to achieve his goal, was the source charging Abe with cowardice. Arnold, 6:8-9.

304 Congress commissioned the Brown brothers to build two frigates, the Warren and the Providence. They were launched in May 1776, but were far from ready for sea. Congress had authorized privateering in March, and the Browns diverted most of their work force to building their own privateering vessels to the detriment of the navy.

305 *Naval Documents*, 7:1199-1200.

306 By this decision, America was committed to several more years of war, and France was set on a course that lead to bankruptcy and revolution. Without France's open support, the United States would not have her absolute independence and freedom.

307 The title "commander-in-chief" of the navy was never revived after Hopkins' dismissal. Thereafter the highest rank was captain. When a captain acted in command of a squadron of three or more vessels, it was customary to address him as "commodore" but this was merely a title of courtesy, and not a designation of actual rank.

308 Washington's reply of November 25 commented on "the gallant circumstances: of his escape from Narragansset Bay" and expressed pleasure the squadron was able to capture some prizes on his return voyage.

309 Oscar Brand, Songs of '76: *A Folk Singer's History of the Revolution* (New Your, 1972) 120-21,

310 Sealed orders meant a secret mission. This prevented the squadron's destination from being leaked to enemy agents around Boston or for signals being sent by enemy agents.

311 Dudley W. Knox, *A History of the united States Navy* (New York: G.F. Putnam's Sons, 1936) 4.

312 Arnold, Chapter 10, p. 10. The surrender was the worst American defeat of the Revolution with the British capturing 5,500 continental soldiers. The Americans lost 92 dead and 148 wounded; the British 76

dead and 189 wounded Lincoln's troops became prisoners of Cornwallis who imprisoned them in ships in the harbor where the unsanitary conditions took a heavy toll. Of the 1900 prisoners, only 740 survived the "hulks".

[313] Page 110 of that census. NEHGS, Vol. 129 (1974), 50.

[314] Arnold, Chapter 11, p. 10.

[315] Arnold, Chapter 12, p. 13.

[316] Arnold, Chapter 13, p. 6

[317] Perhaps the most complete narrative written on the life of Abraham Whipple is the Hildreth treatise, as previously listed.

Chapter 5

Eleazer Whipple
The Whipples From Louquisett Meadows

Eleazer Whipple, third son of Captain John, was christened 8 March 1645/46 in Dorchester, Massachusetts and died in Smithfield, Rhode Island 25 August 1719.[318] He married Alice Angell 26 January 1669.[319] She was born in 1649 and died 13 August 1743. They were parents to 10 children, all born and married in Smithfield:

i. Deborah, born 1 Aug 1670; died 24 Jun 1748; married John Wilkinson.
ii. Eleazer, born about 1672; died 17 Dec 1734; married Mary Sprague[320]
iii. Alice, born 3 Jun 1675; died after 19 May 1746; married Joseph Mowrey.
iv. Harriet, born about 1677.
v. Margaret, born about 1678; died about 1722; married John Mowrey.
vi. Elizabeth, born about 1680; married Gabriel Peacock
vii. Job, born about 1684; died 19 Apr 1750; married Silence Pray.
viii. James, born about 1686; died 3 Oct 1731; married Mary Williams
ix. Daniel; born about 1688; died 3 Oct 1768, married Anne Chamberlain
x. Hannah, born 5 Mar 1695; died 1 Apr 1727; married William Arnold

Towne Streete Courtships

Alice Angell was the daughter of Thomas Angell, who came to Providence with Roger Williams, his cousin, when still a boy. He was one of Williams' associates at the planting of the settlement around the spring where the Moshassuck emptied into the salt water. Like Eleazer Whipple, he was by trade a housewright. The Angell home lot was the second south of Gaol (jail) Lane, approximately one-half mile south of the Whipples. He actually owned two lots, living on the north lot, with the south given to an apple orchard. The letters "A" and "B" are the two houses he and his family lived in during this time. As the drawing opposite shows, the present First Baptist Church was built on this lot in 1775.[321]

Towne Streete Courtship

Eleazer's youngest brother, Jonathan, married Margery, the sister of Eleazer's wife. His brother, Joseph, married a granddaughter of the Angells. As seen on the drawing, the Thomas Olney house was next door to the north. Two of Captain John's children, John and Mary, married into that family. The wives of Thomas Olney and Thomas Angell were sisters, which probably accounts for their living next to each other. One can envision the continual parade between the houses of

129

these five young couples "courting up and down north Town Street" for a period of about 20 years. If the families were typical of the time, they shared Sunday meals on many occasions. Marriage was a civil affair conducted by the town clerk or assistant. Between the years 1660 and 1680, Thomas Olney Senior and Junior, and John Whipple Senior and Junior, as well as John Smith, the husband of Sarah Whipple, held these offices. Thus, it is likely that the five Whipple-Angell-Olney couples were married by one of them.

The following speculation on the Olney and Ashton wedding in the 1640s could have occurred at any of the weddings above: "Thomas we surmise had hung up for the day his leather working-breeches to appear in a handsome new suit of local homespun---wool doublet and hose---rather warm and baggy no doubt, but set off with a starched ruff and wrist bands. As for Alice, she had perhaps been torn between her new woolen petticoat and the old flowered tiffany gown she had bought from Hertfordshire in her sea chest. We hope she had a new silk bonnet and scarf---the Boston ladies were wearing them until the court in 1651 tabooed them as worth of utter detestation."[322] Alice likely reveled in the new freedom found in Providence to perform such basic womanly acts as kissing her children or cutting her hair, or cooking, making beds, or sweeping on the Sabbath, which, had they been done in Massachusetts, would have subjected her and all other women, including Sarah Whipple, wife of Captain John, to possible arrest and fine.

Eleazer Whipple in Early Town Records

Eleazer Whipple appeared in Providence records on over 70 occasions. The following is a chronological summary of a representative sample of these taken from *The Early Records of the Town of Providence*, 21 Volumes, (Providence: Snow & Farnham 1892-1915). Individual entries are noted with the volume number and page. Original wording, spelling, and punctuation have been retained in some cases.

1 June 1667
The names of those who have "engaged Alegance to his Majestye King Charles the Second" included Eliazer Whipple. (III:101).

8 January 1669
Eliazer Whipple and Alice Angell were both published in way of marriage by a writing fixed upon a public place in the town of Providence under the hand of Thos Olney Jr., assistant clerk. (V:328-9).

4 May 1669
Eleazer Whipple and Samuel Whipple made freemen. (XV:73).

October 1670
Eleazer Whipple asked that he be made a purchaser. (XV:131)..

11 March 1675/76
I Eleazer Whipple Received of the Towne of Providence The fulle and Just sume of six pounds sterling mony of New Englande being the full sume of what the Town Engaged to pay for careing of me...Eleazer Whipple, his mark

27 April 1675
Chosen at the town meeting for Petit Jury. (IV:35).

1 January 1676/77
The undersigned, having employed Arthur Fenner, William Hopkins and John Whipple Jr. to sell a company of Indians belonging to them by an act of Committee, who appeared and sold the Indians and received a part of the pay for selling them, and proportioned each man his share, which amounted to 16 shillings and four pence half penny per share, which the undersigned said they received, then fully acquitted and discharged Arthur Fenner, William Hopkins and John Whipple, Junr. Signed by Roger Williams and twenty-two men, including John Whipple, Samuel Whipple and Eliazvr Whipple. (XV:161).

16 August 1676
Town meeting, in reference to Indians taken captive during King Philip's War, 1675-76: Wee whose names are here unto Subscribed having right to the sayd Indians, as by an Act of Comitty doth Appeere; Do betrust impower, and fully Authorize Capt Author Fenner, William Hopkins, and John Whipple, Junr: to hire, and procure a Boate to transport the sayd Indians where they may be Sold, and to make Sale and Delivery Thereof as fully, and as firmly, as if we were all personally present, And to doe all Such things as shall any ways belong to the transporting, making Sale or Disposition of all and every of the sayd Indians as above said, and to See all Such Chargess as doth arise by the sayd Indians, after tow them committed/defrayd out of the product of the Same, and themselves reasonably satisfied for theire pains, and then to make return of the remainder of the product of the Indians to the sayd Company. Signed by Roger Williams and fifteen other men, including Eliasur Whipple. (XV:156).

27 July 1677
Stephen Saabeer of Newport..."desireth a small parcel of land by the water side below the Bridge, upon the acompt of the keeping of Eleazer Whipple when wounded..." (VII:18)

27 July 1680
I desire ye Town to take some Care speedily that I may haue ye money that I stand obliged to pay for my Diett when I lay under Cure, being wounded by ye Indians in ye late Troublesome war my nessesti calleth for it, being often Called upon for ye same, saying they have great need of ye same. Yor ffriend Eleazur Whipple (XV:214)

27 July 1681

Eleazer Whipple asked the town to settle on a day for the moving of the thatch beds which might be beneficial to all, so that some covetous persons wouldn't in the hast suddenly cut the thatch before it was grown. (XV:233)

19 February 1683

John Wilkinson and John Pray asked the town meeting to state a highway whereby a covenant road may be maintained for passage to Louisquisett. Their bill was granted and Ed Smith and Eleazer Whipple were deputed to state a highway through Louisqusett and make their returns to the next town meeting. (XVII:14).

2 June 1684

"voated That ye deede of gift from John Whipple senr: to Eliezer Whiple his son beareing date ffebruarey ye 24: 1774 may be Entred upon ye Towne Records." (VIII:140)

27 January 1685

There was an order for a rate by the Colony and a levy of the same by the town. Eleazer Whipple and John Wilkinson were to have 10 pounds each out of this rate which was to have been paid the previous March by order of the General Assembly sitting at Warwick last October and this was not yet done. They will receive their shares, having satisfaction for their troubles. Signed by John Whipple. (XVII:70).

8 June 1685.

Eleazer Whipple requested of his neighbors that he might have thirty acres of land layed due to him on the east side of the 7 mile. (XVII:61).

27 April 1691

Eleazer Whipple requested that he may have a lot of forty square feet on the common, desiring the same privileges that his neighbors had. (VIII:170)

8 February 1692

Eleazur Whipple and John Inman made an exchange of land, both pieces exchanged, in the woods called Loquasqussuck woods, and near the dwelling of John Inman: each piece of land about three acres. (IV:123).

12 April 1693

Eleazer Whipple chosen as Deputy to serve in the General Assembly the day before election and at the election assembly. (XVII:144).

24 April 1697

Eleazer and Samuel Whipple and others were appointed "to endeavor to expulse, kill and Destroy them (Indians)"...(XVII:163-64)

15 February 1700

Eleazer Whipple and Samuel Wilkinson acted as appraisers of the inventory of the estate of Valentine Whitman. They signed the inventory of this estate on 15 February 1700, and appeared before the town council on 11 March 1700 and under oath attested to the inventory. (VII:204)

28 April 1701

Eleazer Whipple was chosen to be one of the deputies in the General Assembly at the Court of Election in Newport on the first Wednesday of May and at the General Assembly the day before the election. (XI:62).

4 December 1704

Joseph Woodward gave notice at the town meeting that he had taken in a stray steere, about 2 years old, black, with an ear mark. Proclaimed and entered 4 June 1704 by Thomas Olney, town clerk. The steere was appraised by Eliezer Whipple at thirty and four shillings. (IX:181).

11 May 1705

Eleazer bought 150 acres of land, which already adjoined his property in Louquisset, from his nephew John Whipple III "ordinary keeper" for £105 of silver money. (XX:44-47)

8 June 1719

Town meeting voted and order that the Poundkeeper in the northern woods shall at all times leave the key to the Pound at the house of Eleazer Whipple so that it may be there ready for any officer or person who has proper use of the Pound for the present year. The keeper lives remote from the Pound. This is intended only for the Pound in the northern woods. (XIII:66).

9 November 1719

Letter of Administration was voted and ordered that Mrs. Alice Whipple, Relick, widow of Mr. Eliezer Whipple, deceased, (who died intestate) with her son Ensign James Whipple shall have administration granted upon them of the moveable estate of the deceased Mr. Eliezer Whipple. (XII:10)

1 October 1719

"A true inventory of all & singulior of the Goods, Chattles & Creadits of Mr. Eliezer Whipple who departed this Life august the 25th 1719. Taken and apprised this 1 day of October:1719 by us the subscribers as followeth." (XVI:114).

The sum total of Eleazer's movable estate was over 495 pounds, a considerable sum in early 18th century rural Rhode Island, and included such items as: sheetes, pillo bears, powder horns, cissers, egg turner, chamber pott, linen whele, wool cards, ax & old plaines, hatchet, silver pint pott spoones, old lanthron, iron potts & copper kettle, mettle skillets, driping pan, trammel fire shovel & tongs, etc. (XVI:114-122).

The Venerable Eleazer Whipple House

Eleazer, as noted above, was an injured veteran of the King Philip's War of 1675-76, and the first to receive a war pension of £10 per year (the first pension granted for military service).[323] He was the only one of Captain John's sons to participate in that war, and was, so it would appear, a hero to his fellow townspeople. Eleazer was also a widely known housewright who built his own long-standing home in about 1680. This house was deeded to his third son James. The house (seen opposite, faced to the southwest) was located in the 1000 block of the Great Road. Some of the row of rocks in the foreground can still be seen in 2007.

Eleazer Whipple House

James Whipple was born about 1687 and died 3 October 1731.[324] He and his wife Mary Williams are known to have had at least one son, Eleazer. Eleazer owned a large tract of land at Warwick, Rhode Island and engaged in the mercantile business. He was also a sea captain, and died at sea in 1760. He and Deliverance Rhodes, whom he married in 1744, had eight children.[325]

In 1733, James' widow and her second husband, John Rhodes, were awarded the administration of Eleazer's estate. Eleazer's widow was still residing on the property and after her death in 1743, it was sold to Jeremiah Mowrey.[326] Two of James' sisters had married Mowrey brothers in the early 1700s. Regrettably, this homestead estate willed to Eleazer by his father, like so many others of Captain John's original properties still held by his third and fourth generation descendants, fell into the hands of those who did not bear his name.

Eleazer's homestead, as designated in the 1743 deed of conveyance, was "land that lieth on both sides of the highway from Providence towards Wensoket at Louisquesset brook near Lime Rock."[327] The Mowreys made a tavern of the house, which was demolished in 1964.[328] A later commentator wrote that, "The view from the old Whipple house (Mowrey Tavern) was a commanding one. Below to the eastward the Blackstone River winds…only a few rods distant are the white cliffs of the lime pits. The Whipple house was built between 1676 and 1684, for in that year he purchased of his brother Samuel five acres of land 'a little northward of ye said Eleazer Whipple his dwelling house' the bounds of which show that it was in the Loquasqussuck country. There is a continuous line of references to it in deeds to the present day. It was a grand old mansion house in those times, and there is even now a stately dignity to it that cannot but attract the attention of those who reverence and respect these old relics of former days."[329] This general area became known as "Montalto," or the highlands, and could be seen from any point in Providence.

Mr. John Cullen, whose family bought the nearby Job Whipple homestead, played there as a boy. "In the 1950s I played with my boyhood friend Ray Taylor Junior in the ancient Eleazer Whipple house that appeared more like a haunted house to two young boys. The house was in great disrepair, had not been lived in for many years, and was finally dismantled by Ray Taylor Senior who used some of the timber to add an addition to his own house, which is across from the site where the Whipple house stood. Mr. Taylor celebrated his 90th birthday this past fourth of July."

The oldest child of Eleazer and Alice was Deborah, who married John Wilkinson a next-door neighbor. The Wilkinson family was highly esteemed as Quakers. Their youngest son, Jeremiah, married Elizabeth Whipple II, daughter of William Whipple Junior, Eleazer's nephew. One of their twelve children was Jemima, whose life was remarkable. "Exceptionally beautiful, dress, amusement and pleasure were her sole consideration....In 1774 she suddenly abandoned her gay life and became deeply interested in religious subjects...[Some say she came under the influence of the evangelist George Whitfield]. She professed to have strange visions and visitations from white figures and celestial forms...Her friends were astounded by her arrogant assumptions and the great change in her voice and manner....Than began her career as head of the self-styled sect she created, the 'Universal Friend of Mankind'. She began to travel around New England on horseback seeking converts....The acquiring of money being her chief object, she managed to ensnare several wealthy persons who found their association with her both costly and disastrous. Jemima claimed to work miracles, accrediting any failures to lack of faith.... She was entirely unscrupulous and overbearing and ruled her converts with an iron hand.... She carried on her Ministry from the end of 1776 until July 1819 when she died. At the time of her death Jemima was living in the small community she had founded in 1790 in western New York. She never returned to Rhode Island."[330]

Eleazer and Alice's second and third daughters, Alice and Margaret, married Joseph and John Mowry respectively, and Hanna, their youngest daughter, married William Arnold. These men were descendants of Edward Inman, John and Nathaniel Mowry, and Stephen Arnold. In the 1660s, the Inman, Mowry, and Arnold syndicate, whose member families intermarried extensively, bought approximately six square miles of land, with Woonsocket at its northeast corner and Eleazer Whipple's property at its southeast corner. Eleazer's three daughters thus married into northern Rhode Island's most wealthy and influential families. And as earlier noted, the Eleazer Whipple property and name disappeared when the Mowry's bought out his descendant in 1747.

Eleazer Junior, Eleazer's oldest son, was born about the year 1672 and died 17 December 1734 in Smithfield. He married Mary Sprague 12 June 1719. She was born 1 October 1692 and died, as a widow, in Smithfield 26 July 1784.[331] They were parents to Eleazer, who died 2 March 1733 without issue.[332] At her death, Mary willed the homestead to her husband's relatives.[333] Eleazer Whipple Junior has been confused on occasion with his nephew Eleazer of Warwick, the son of James. [As noted, that Eleazer died at sea in 1760]. He and his descendants will be discussed later.

Eleazer's youngest son, Daniel, left the Louquisset Meadows about 1715/16. He and his descendants are also discussed later.

Eleazer was buried on his own farm, which is now near an area called Molasses Hill. "...Eleazer Whipple died, being then seventy-three years of age. A life of hardship and sufferings was ended, and he was laid away in the grave down in his meadow in front of his house." At present, this burial lot is called the "Whippple-Mowrey Cemetery." His wife, sons Job and James, plus several others of his Whipple and Mowrey descendants were buried beside him.[334] Of his sons, only Job contributed descendants who carried on the Whipple name in early Louquisset Meadows history.

Job Whipple
Louquisett's Wealthiest Whipple Family

Captain Job[3] Whipple (Eleazer[2], John[1]) was born about 1684 in Rhode Island and died in Smithfield, Rhode Island 19 April 1750. He married Silence, daughter of Ephraim Pray, about 1703. She was born in 1682 and died 7 January 1757. Job and Silence had 11 children, all born and married in Smithfield:

  i. *Job, born about 1703; died 25 Feb 1730; married Ruth Jenckes*
  ii. *Sarah, born about 1705; died 1781; married David Smith*
  iii. *Dorcas, born about 1708; married Oliver Mowry*
  iv. *Abigail, born about 1711; died 25 Feb 1730; married John Aldrich*
  v. *Simon, born about 1713; died 14 Mar 1730.*
  vi. *Alice, born about 1715; died 12 May 1736; married Abraham Angell[335].*
  vii. *Hannah, born about 1716; died 6 Mar 1792; married Nathaniel Eddy.*
  viii. *Mary, born about 1718; died 27 Feb 1810; married John Waterman.*
  ix. *Anna, born about 1718; died 3 Dec 1723.*
  x. *Amey, born about 1724; died 27 Dec 1747; married Thomas Mowry*
  xi. *Stephen, born about 1726; died 27 May 1795; married Phebe Ballou*

Job Whipple lived and died on his estate in the Louquisset meadows. He was born about 25 years after his grandfather Whipple immigrated to the Providence Plantations, and shortly after his father rebuilt their house near Lime Rock, about one mile west of the Blackstone River. Job was chosen to be a constable in 1712 and served on a jury of inquest in 1716.[336] He served on the town council in the 1720s. Job was mentioned in Smithfield township records of 1733 when the town built a road (likely what is now the Old River Road) next to his house. Also in 1733, Job filed a paternity case against his daughter Alice's lover as father of her newborn child. The courts denied the suit, and Alice named her son Job Whipple. Nevertheless, in his will of 1750, Captain Job referred to Alice's son as "Abraham Angell." Captain Job was mentioned a third time in town records of 1748. He and his youngest son Stephen and grandson Ephraim (Job Junior's son) were listed in District 5 of the Smithfield "Highway Act," in which every able-bodied man at least 21 years of age was required to work six days each year on the township's right-of-ways.[337] Job died two years later, and was buried near his father and sons Job and Simon in the Whipple-Mowrey Cemetery. His headstone reads, "Capt. Job Whipple died April 19, 1750 in his 66th year." His will, written 12 April 1750, was proved 19 July 1750.

Eleazer Whipple, on 27 April 1710, transferred by deed of gift, "...for and in consideration of the well being and settlement of my son Job Whipple of the Town of Providence, aforesaid, and for good affection which to him I bear... give 120 acres in the district of Louisquisset Woods and from part of the land bought from my cousin [nephew], John Whipple."[338] The house

Job Whipple House, 2004

that Job built on this property immediately afterward, located approximately one-quarter mile east of his father's house, is listed on the National Register of Historic Places. Its National Register description reads: "Whipple-Cullen Farm. The Whipple House is a standard, two-and-one-half story, 5 bay, center-chimney house. The entrance porch is a later addition, as is the Victorian porch on the side. Well preserved on the interior, it still exhibits the heavy cased corner posts and fireplaces typical of its date; an elegant Adamesque swag detail at the cornice of the right front chamber is a Federal addition. The house was probably built by Job Whipple, member of an important early family in Lime Rock."

The farm remained in Whipple hands until the 1870s; of particular interest are owners Stephen Whipple and Simon, his son, both of whom were extensively involved in the local lime industry and in Smithfield town affairs. Simon Whipple was also connected with the Smithfield Woolen and Cotton Manufacturing Company, whose mill was located on the nearby Blackstone Canal. In the late 19th century, the Cullen family converted the farmstead and its lands into a dairy farm; the dairy continued to operate into the mid-20th century, and the farm buildings are still surrounded by open fields. North of the house stands the Cullen barn---a long gable-roofed structure, still well preserved. [NR].[339] At present, the house is a Bed and Breakfast Inn located at 99 Old River Road in Lincoln. Mr. Cullen states, "Regarding the time line for Job Whipple's ownership of my property, my sources state, of which I have viewed personally in Book One, page 257 that in 1736 my ancestor Woodward Lovet deeded his grandfather's (Joseph Woodward) homestead farm (about 100 acres) to Job Whipple, 9th year of the reign of King George II'." It is thus apparent that the Cullen family maintained a relationship to that part of the 250-acre property as far back as the middle of the eighteenth century.

Job Whipple Junior was born in 1703 and died 25 February 1730, perhaps as a consequence of an epidemic, since he and his brother Simon and sister Abigail died within a month of each other. He was the father of Ephraim (1725 – 1805), who had 11 children. It is estimated that Ephraim moved to central Cumberland Township about 1768. His cousins, Moses and Eleazer, sons of William Junior, in a move eastward across to the other side of the Blackstone River, joined him about the same time. His first cousin Stephen Junior joined them about five years later.

Captain Job's youngest son, Stephen Whipple, born in 1726, died 27 May 1795, the only son whose children stayed in Smithfield, lived out his life in the Louquisset, as did his sons, Colonel Simon (1760-1829), and Arnold (1769-1804). His oldest son Stephen Junior (1750–1822) moved to Cumberland Township about the year 1773. A 1774 Smithfield census revealed that Stephen Senior's household consisted of 14 persons: four adult men, three adult women, along with two boys, four girls, and one slave.[340] "Mr. Whipple was a man of large wealth, influence, and respectability in Smithfield, RI, where he held many responsible town offices. He left by will to his children, much real and person estate."[341] "He was a member of the town council and its treasurer for three years. He also served intermittently in the Rhode Island General Assembly from 1763 until 1790. As noted, he and his son Simon were extensively involved in the lime production and woolen businesses. "In 1809, Simon Whipple, a large landholder in the area, sold thirteen acres to a group of local investors ,including George Olney, George Smith, Thomas Arnold, and William and Joseph Whipple (son and grandson of John Whipple the bonesetter), near the historic river ford then known as Pray's Wade or Landing. Operating as the Smithfield Cotton and Woolen Manufactory, this group began building a small mill estate....[342]

"About 1767, a bridge was built at Woonsocket Falls. A story of what happened to Simon Whipple while it was being built was told to E. Richardson by Mr. Stafford Mann: Col. Simon Whipple and Mr. James Arnold, as young men, were enroute to an unknown destination and tarried at Judge Peleg Arnold's inn before departing. They only had one horse so in the custom of the time rode double, the Colonel in front and James behind. On their way from the inn to the bridge, James requested that he be allowed to dismount at the riverbank. The Colonel agreed but forgot by the time they got to the bridge and spurred his horse for a fast trip over. The planks gave way and they fell into the water below. According to Mann, the imbibing at the inn caused the Col. to believe he was 'astride the charger of Napoleon' while James equated the fall with 'a hideous nightmare'."[343] Colonel Simon Whipple and Abigail Vey had six children, among them Anna who married Benoni Cooke. Anna's daughter, Anna, married James Whipple who sold off the property (about 250 acres) in the 1870s. It was finally bought

Job Whipple Headstone, 2004

by the Cullen family in 1881 and is presently the Whipple-Cullen B&B."[344] Stephen Senior, Simon, and Arnold were buried with their ancestors in the Whipple-Mowrey Cemetery. Some of their descendants were known to be living in and around Smithfield-Lincoln, some even in twentieth century.

It may be instructive to know that more Whipples resided in Cumberland than in any other township in Rhode Island in the year 1800, a total of 22 heads of households. The overwhelming majority of these were descendants of Daniel Whipple,[345] the youngest of Eleazer's sons. This population density statistic remained static throughout the late 1700s into the middle of the nineteenth century.

Descendants Who Settled in
Cumberland Township

Daniel, son of Eleazer Whipple

Daniel[3] Whipple (Eleazer[2], John[1]), the fourth son of Eleazer, moved to north Cumberland Township about 1715/16: "By the end of the seventeenth century, a number of families, some returning to rebuild, had settled in Cumberland. These

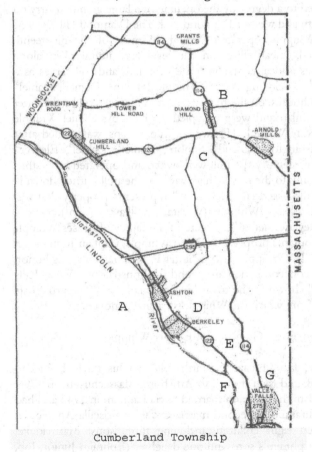

Cumberland Township

included the Ballous, Bartletts, Cooks, Jillsons, Whipples, and Towers. Unlike most New England towns, Cumberland settlers did not immediately erect a meetinghouse (Baptist), but until 1700 met in each other's homes to conduct religious services."[346] Daniel preceded his two nephews, described below, and two cousins, sons of William Junior, to Cumberland by 40 to 50 years. His property near Diamond Hill Road, north of the present Nate Whipple Highway [Highway 120 formerly Sneech Pond Road] was approximately five miles northeast of his birthplace.[347] He was born on the family homestead in 1688 and died 3 October 1768 in Cumberland. Daniel and several family members were buried in the Whipple burial lot southeast of Diamond Hill, on the map opposite.

He married twice, to Mary about 1715, and to Anne Chamberlain about 1735. He had 13 children by these two marriages, including six sons: Daniel, Joseph, Eleazer, Joel, Preserved, and Job. Daniel Senior, who could be considered to be the founder of the village of Diamond

139

Hill, is widely remembered as the founding father of the north Cumberland branch of the Whipple family tree. He had 57 known grandchildren, of whom 10 males carried the Whipple name. At least three sons, Daniel, Joseph, and Joel, lived and died in Cumberland. Among later descendants, Reuben, a grandson of Daniel Junior moved to Ohio about the year 1800. Albert, Edwin, and Stephen, grandsons of Joel, moved to San Francisco, California during the mid 1800s. They are considered the founders of the Whipple name in northern California. Another grandson of Joel, Arnold, moved to New York about the same time. Preserved moved to New Hampshire between the years 1790 and 1800, and Preserved Junior moved to Ohio around the year 1800.

The land area of Cumberland is less than twenty thousand acres. "The town has been called the 'Mineral Pocket of New England' on account of the variety and richness of its ore deposits of iron, copper, granite and other minerals."[348] Diamond Hill "...evolved into a small commercial center in the first half of the nineteenth century. Growth of the village was spurred to a degree by the opening of a large granite quarry on the east slope of Brush Hill, north and west of Diamond Hill. The Diamond Hill Quarry, principally owned by Amasa Whipple, operated throughout most of the nineteenth century.... The loosely arranged, linear village in the level agricultural plain along Diamond Hill Road continued as a local center into the twentieth and still serves as a focus for this part of town...."[349] Including Amasa[6]Whipple (Simon[5], Daniel[4], Daniel[3], Eleazer[2], John[1]), at least a dozen houses, on the map above, and represented by the letter "B," in the northern half of Cumberland were occupied, or built by, Daniel Whipple descendants. Highway 20, the Nate Whipple Highway on most maps, was named after Nathan[9]Whipple (Nathan[8], Washington[7], David[6], Simon[5], Daniel[4], Daniel[3], Eleazer[2], John[1]). "In the early years of this century the mill was owned and operated by Nathan W. Whipple, Jr., who gave his name to the nearby highway."[350] The mill burned down in January of 1988. As will be discussed later, letter "C" represents property that was owned by the descendants of Eleazer[4]Whipple (William[3], William[2], John[1]). Several structures and sites in the Berkeley area, letter "D," were of the family of Moses[4]Whipple (William[3], William[2], John[1]). The original property of David Whipple, Captain John's sixth son, is represented by the letter "E," Whipple Bridge "letter F" was named in his honor, and David's descendants mostly concentrated in an around the Lonsdale and Valley Falls areas, letter "G." The letter "A," shown in the township of Lincoln, is the approximate location of Lime Rock, the area from which the Whipple's originally moved.

Ephraim, Great Grandson of Eleazer Whipple

Ephraim[5] Whipple (Job[4], Job[3], Eleazer[2], John[1]) followed his uncle Daniel to Cumberland about the year 1768, and then moved to Attleboro, Massachusetts in 1796. He was a farmer and later a goldsmith. Ephraim married Silvia Lapham in 1745 and had three sons: David, Job, and Ephraim. His second marriage was to Priscilla Appleby in 1754, a marriage that produced eight children, including three sons: Marmaduke, Barneville, and Jencks. Four of Ephraim's sons and one daughter (Ephraim Junior, Job, Marmaduke, Barneville, and Anne Carpenter) moved to Washington County, New York. "Union Village was incorporated in 1809. Before then, it was called 'Whipple City' and originally grew from the fact that Job Whipple was the most prominent and successful

140

among the early settlers in 1775....Whipple, a Quaker, prospered and determined that water power was able to support a cotton factory....After his children were grown, Job moved west....The cotton factory founded by him closed in the 1840s. By the 1890s, the Whipple name had practically disappeared."[351] His daughter, Priscilla Bishop, is the only known child buried in Cumberland. Ephraim is known to have had at least 36 grandchildren scattered across the states of Massachusetts, New York, Illinois, and Pennsylvania, including seven who bore the Whipple surname

Stephen, Great Grandson of Eleazer Whipple

Stephen[5] Whipple Junior (Stephen[4], Job[3], Eleazer[2], John[1]) migrated to Cumberland about the year 1773. He was father to 11 children and had at least 19 grandchildren, including four known Whipple grandsons. At least four of his children were buried in Cumberland: Olney, Nancy, James, and Betsy.

Descendants Who Settled
In Warwick, Rhode Island

The Rhode Island census report quoted above additionally revealed that only three Whipples resided south of Providence County in the year 1800. This is in keeping with seventeenth and eighteenth century Whipple land deeds. With the exception of Joseph Whipple Junior, son of Captain John's seventh son, and his family, very few Whipple males in the first several generations moved to the central or southern areas of Rhode Island. The Whipples below, descendants of Eleazer Whipple, were among those few.

Eleazer[4] Whipple (James[3], Eleazer[2], John[1]) is the only known child of James Whipple.[352] In his early years, he moved approximately 15 miles south of his birthplace, becoming a merchant in Warwick, Rhode Island. He was also a sea captain and died at sea in November of 1760. He and Deliverance Rhodes, whom he married 24 June 1744, had at least eight children, at least two of whom were sons who settled on farms in Warwick and Coventry, Rhode Island. Eleazer's son Job, whose twin brother was Joseph, had five daughters and at least three sons, including John and Resolved. Resolved's son was Job R., who had Henry, and was buried in the Swan Point Cemetery in Providence, as were most of Job R's descendants.

Lieutenant Governor Thomas Whipple

Joseph, the twin of Job, sons of Eleazer, had two daughters and seven sons. He settled in Coventry, Rhode Island, and was a farmer. Judge Thomas[6] Whipple (Joseph[5], Eleazer[4], James[3], Eleazer[2], John[1]) son of Joseph, was a manufacturer, and served as Lieutenant Governor of Rhode Island from 1850 to 1852.[353] Judge Thomas Whipple's son, Henry, served for many years as the sheriff of Washington County. Everett Whipple, son of Henry, served for over 20 years as the city clerk for the town of Westerly, Rhode Island.[354] William, Joseph's fourth son, lived and died in Coventry. Christopher, youngest son of Joseph, lived on the homestead farm in Coventry. He had six sons and at least 10 grandsons who lived out their lives in Rhode Island. Of Joseph's other sons, John, the oldest, settled in Pennsylvania; and Eleazer became a Methodist minister in Utica, New York.[355]

Fred Lawrence Whipple
Pioneer Iowa Descendant of Eleazer Whipple

A notable twentieth century descendant of Eleazer Whipple Senior, the third son of Captain John Whipple was the astronomer Fred Lawrence Whipple. "Fred L.

Fred Whipple

Whipple, a pioneer in astronomy who proposed the 'dirty snowball' theory for the substance of comets, has died. He was 97. Whipple died Monday at a Cambridge hospital, the Harvard-Smithsonian Center for Astrophysics said Tuesday.

"Whipple proposed the theory in 1950, saying that comets consisted of ice with some rock mixed in, rather than sand held together by gravity, as was widely believed. Whipple's theory was an attempt to explain why some comets seemed to arrive at a destination earlier or later than predicted. Whipple believed that as a comet approached the sun, its light vaporized ice in the comet's nucleus. The jets of particles that resulted acted like a rocket engine that either slowed or accelerated the comet. He also theorized that the glowing comet tails contained particles that originated from frozen reservoirs in comet nuclei. Whipple's theories were proven correct in 1986 by close-up photographs of Haley's comet by the European Space Agency's Giotto spacecraft.

"Charles Alcock, director of the Center for Astrophysics, said Whipple had revolutionized the study of comets. 'Fred Whipple was a truly extraordinary person among extraordinary people. He was gifted with great scientific imagination, superb analytical skills, and excellent management acumen,' Irwin Shapiro, a former director of the center, said in a statement.

"Whipple was born in Red Oak, Iowa, in 1906. He received his bachelor's degree in mathematics at the University of California, Los Angeles, but didn't turn to astronomy until a bout with polio ended his dreams of being a tennis champion. He completed his doctorate in astronomy at the UC-Berkeley in 1931 and accepted a position at Harvard that year.

"In 1946, in anticipation of the future of space flight, Whipple invented a thin outer skin of metal to protect spacecrafts. Meteors disintegrated when they hit the shield, known as a meteor bumper or Whipple Shield, leaving only vapor to hit the spacecraft. The technology is still in use today. He was also ahead of the curve in 1957, when the Soviet Union launched the Sputnik satellite. At the time, Whipple was setting up a network of cameras to track it and one station was already operational. President Kennedy honored Whipple with an Award for Distinguished Public Service in 1963 for the project. "Whipple was director of the Smithsonian Astrophysical Observatory in

Cambridge from 1955 to 1973, when it merged with the Harvard Observatory and was renamed the Harvard-Smithsonian Center for Astrophysics, was 90. The license plate on his car was 'Comets'."[356]

End Notes

³¹⁸ John O. Austin, *Genealogical Dictionary of Rhode Island* (Albany, NY: 1887, reprint edition, Baltimore: Genealogical Publication Company, 1978) 222. Henry E Whipple, *A Brief Genealogy of the Whipple Families Who Settled in Rhode Island* (Providence: A Crawford Greene, 1873). James N. Arnold, *Vital Records of Rhode Island, 1636-1850* (Providence: Narragansett Historical Publishing Company, 1892). *Records of the First Church at Dorchester in New England, 1636-1734 (Boston: George H. Ellis, 1891) 267* and 176. Vital statistics on the children and grandchildren of Captain John and Sarah Whipple are taken from the above and numerous publications that quote from them. To view more recent information, consult www.whipple.org, Weldon Whipple, Webmaster.

³¹⁹ *The Early Records of the Town of Providence, 21 vols, collected and printed by the Records Commissioners* (Providence: Snow and Farnham, city printers, 1892-1915) V:328-9 [hereinafter *ERP*]. Eleazer's youngest brother, Jonathan, married his wife's sister, Margaret, in about 1680.

³²⁰ There is confusion as to the birth date of Eleazer Junior. His name is seen on a list of Providence taxpayers, age 16 and older, in 1688. To make that list, he would have had to be born no later than 1672. Edward Field, *Tax Lists of the Town of Providence, 1686-89* (Providence: Howard W. Preston, 1895) 40.

³²¹ George L. Miner, *Angell's Lane: The History of a Little Street in Providence* (Providence: Akerman-Standard Press, 1948) 26.

³²² Miner, 12.

³²³ Edward Field, *State of Rhode Island and Providence Plantations at the End of the Century: A History*, 3 vols (Boston: Mason Publishing Company, 1902) 1:403. Captain Benjamin Church chased King Philip to the great swamp at Pocasset. Philip and his Indian braves escaped at low tide and proceeded north toward what is now Brookfield, Massachusetts. They were overtaken just to the west of the Eleazer Whipple farmhouse. The pitched battle that ensued lasted from dawn to about nine in the morning of 1 August 1675. Thirty-two of the Indians were slain and several of the troopers wounded. The Indians retreated and the pursuit was abandoned. The wounded were taken to Providence, where they arrived about twelve or one o'clock that night, and later were sent to Newport; all of them received grants from the Colony for wounds received. "It is believed that the first recorded evidence of the granting of a pension was for wounds received in this encounter, and Eleazer Whipple was the first pensioner."

³²⁴ According to his gravestone

³²⁵ Henry E. Whipple, 60. The author mistakenly concluded that Eleazer's immediate parentage was of England. This was corrected in an article published in 1997. A reprint is available from the New England Historical Genealogical Society, item #P3-59493.

³²⁶ Richard Bowen, *Early Rehoboth* (Rehoboth, Mass., 1948) 3:98. Also, Field states that, "The Eleazer house was located near Limerock Lincoln, near the Loasquisset Brook, and that from the doorstep you could look right off upon Nipsachuck (where Eleazer was wounded)…The house was built by Eleazer Whipple between 1677 and 1684. His heirs sold the house to Jeremiah Mowrey." Field, I:402 and III:606-608. As late as the year 1895 it was called the "Ben Mowrey" house. Norman Isham, *Early Rhode Island Houses*, (Providence: Preston & rounds, 1895), 40.

³²⁷ Bowen, III:87

³²⁸ E. Richardson, History *of Woonsocket* (Woonsocket: S. Foss, printer, 1876) 69. "Jeremiah Mowry was licensed to operate one near Lime Rock on 1 January 1747. It was built by Eleazer Whipple. A prohibition against the sale of liquor seems to have been in effect in earlier days. On 10 January 1728/29, Henry Mowry was summoned to appear and testify concerning Eleazer Whipple's selling of strong liquor at retail."

³²⁹ Field, III:608. This would have been Eleazer's second house. The first had been destroyed in King Philip's war in the year 1675."I used to play as a young boy in the abandoned Whipple house until it became a danger. Raymond Taylor finally tore it down in 1964. Some of its timber was used to build the house across the street." Personal communication to the authors from John Cullen of Lincoln, Rhode Island, whose great grandfather bought the Job Whipple house in the late 1800s.

³³⁰ Extracted and liberally summarized from Barbara Mills, *Providence, 1630-1800: Woman Are Part of Its History* (Bowie, MD: Heritage Books, 2002) 226-28. Israel Wilkinson, Memoirs of the Wilkinson Family In

America (Jacksonville, Ill: Davis and Penniman, 1869) 92-93, 132, 136. "…eighth child…to whom this family is indebted for the celebrity of its name."

331 Robert S. Wakefield, *Mayflower Families Through Five Generations* (Plymouth: General Society of Mayflower Descendants, 1999) part 2, 18:65.

332 "Smithfield Rhode Island Deaths," *New England Historical and Genealogical Society* 146. (1992): 351. Online at http://www.newenglandancestor.org. Printout 9 Sep 2002.

333 Smithfield Rhode Island Probate Records, 1765-1797, 229-30. City Clerk's Office, Central Falls, RI.

334 Whipple-Mowrey Lot, Lincoln, Historical Cemetery #LN025, Gravestones in Natural Order, Providence County. *Rhode Island Historical Cemetery Database*, on computer at the Rhode Island Historical Library. Printout 12 Sep 2002. Location: 200 feet west of Great Road at Telephone Pole #129, 64 burials with 50 inscriptions from 1719 to 1903, 50 feet X 100 feet in poor condition enclosed with granite posts, sign missing. Lot contains some of the oldest and most beautiful stones in the town of Lincoln. Neighbors apparently don't think much of the lot, it is the neighborhood dump… "He, (Eleazer) was laid away in the grave down in his meadow in front of his house." Field, III:608 His headstone, which is in a deteriorated condition after 300 years, reads: Here lieth interred ye body of Eleazer Whipple aged about 74 years departed this life August 25, 1719. In 2004 Eleazer's headstone was found to be lying flat on the ground, crumbling, and practically illegible.

335 See the below discussion of Alice and Abraham Angell.

336 *ERP*, IX:21 and XI:162.

337 Thomas Steere, *History of the Town of Smithfield* (Providence: E. L. Freeman, 1881) 28. The Alice incident is described in an email to Whipple.Org by Clark Edwards in an article entitled "How to Get Whipples Out of Angells," 23 March 1998.

338 Providence Record of Deeds, 2:426. City Hall, Division of Archives and History. Providence, RI. Job and his descendants are extensively discussed in, Frank V. McDonald, *Inquires Relating to the Ancestors and Descendants of Job Whipple of Cumberland, RI, and Greenwich, Washington County, New York.* (Cambridge: University Press, 1881). *ERP* XX:401-02. Eleazer bought the property 11 May 1705 for the sum of £105.

339 Pamela A. Kennedy, Lincoln, Rhode Island, Statewide Historical Preservation Report, P-L-1, January 1982, page 66

340 John R. Bartlett, *Census of the Inhabitants of the Colony of Rhode Island and the Providence Plantations, 1774* (Baltimore: Genealogical Publication Company, 1969) 112

341 Ariel Ballou, *An Elaborate History and Genealogy of the Ballous in America; Carefully Compiled and Edited by Adin Ballou* (Providence: E.L. Freeman & Son, State Printers, 1888). 99.

342 Kennedy, 25.

343 Richardson, 63

344 Personal communication with Mr. John Cullen the fourth Cullen owner of the property, quoting from a brief history he wrote on the house, 28 June 2004.

345 Ronald Jackson, ed., Rhode Island 1800 Census (Providence: Accelerated Indexing Systems, 1972) 210-11.

346 Virginia A. Fitch, *Historic and Architectural Resources of Cumberland, Rhode Island* (Providence: Rhode Island Historical and Preservation Commission, 1990) 6.

347 Ray, personal correspondence, 9 Sep 2002.

348 Thomas Bicknell, *History of Rhode Island and Providence Plantation, 3 vols.* (New York: The American Historical Society, 1920) 3:1181.

349 Fitch, 13.

350 "Cumberland Landmark Destroyed," *The Call*, Woonsocket, R.I., 9 January 1988.

351 Abstracted from Grant Tefft, "The Story of Union Village," *The Greenwich Journal*, Greenwich, N.Y., 2:1943. Elmire Conklin, 1999, *Evidence for Believing Barneville Whipple was descended from John and Sarah Whipple of Providence Rhode Island, and that Sarah Ann Whipple who married Thomas Mosher was his Daughter*, an unpublished manuscript submitted to Blaine Whipple for inclusion into the Capt John Whipple history, and transferred to the present authors in 2003. Also, McDonald.

352 Henry E. Whipple, 60-61. As Noted, the author maintained an incorrect provenance for Eleazer Whipple of Warwick.

[353] Field, 1:356. "In 1849 the Whigs placed Henry B. Anthony, editor of the Providence Journal, in nomination for Governor, with Judge Thomas Whipple of Coventry for Lieutenant-Governor."

[354] Charles Carroll, *Rhode Island, Three Centuries of Democracy, 4 vols.* (New York: Lewis Historical Publishing Company, 1932) 4:338-39.

[355] Henry E. Whipple, 59-63.

[356] Associated Press Release, 31 August 2004.

Chapter 6

William Whipple
The Whipples From Smithfield

William Whipple, the fourth son of Captain John, was christened 16 May 1652 in Dorchester, Mass., and died in Smithfield, Rhode Island 9 March 1711/12.[357] He married Mary (maiden name unknown), her birth and death dates unknown. William lived and died on his farm in the Louquisset meadows, took the Oath of Allegiance to King Charles II in 1671, and was taxed on at least three occasions: 1684, 1687, and 1688. His Last Will and Testament included the names of three children:

> *i. Mary, born about 1689; died after 14 Aug 1749, married Richard Sprague*
> *ii. William, born about 1691; died 16 Nov 1776; married Elizabeth Sprague*
> *iii. Seth, born about 1696; died 13 Nov 1724.*

William Whipple in Early Town Records

William is the least documented of the Whipple brothers. In addition to his Last Will and Testament, the following lists a summary of these records, inclusive of the years 1671 to 1712, taken from *The Early Records of the Town of Providence*, 21 Volumes, (Providence: Snow & Farnham, 1892-1915). Individual entries are noted with the volume number and page. Original spelling and punctuation have been retained in most entries.

Last Monday of May 1671
    William Whipple and Benjamin Whipple took an Oath of Allegiance to King Charles the Second. (III:200)

18 January 1678
    William Whipple made Proclamation of a stray horse he had taken up, color bay, branded on the foreshoulder with an X, the two hind feet with a white in the forehead, with a small white on the nose, somewhat short of stature, something small. (V:338)

9 February 1679/80
    William paid to have his horse shoed. (XV:201)

13 March 1681
    It was voted that William Whipple may change eleven acres of land which his father gave him at "Louassqusuck," the said eleven acres lying at the eastern or northeastern end of his other land, and being parted from his other land by a highway between them layed out by the surveyor to go up into ye country and take it up elsewhere upon the Town's Common, he having paid his change money.(VIII:113).

27 April 1682
William Whipple requested that he might change eleven acres of land that he had of his father, John Whipple, which was divided by a highway from the rest of his land. He ended his request with "your neighbor, William Whipple." The Bill was granted by the towne, as attested to by John Whipple, Junior, Clerk. (XVII:1).

9 September 1685
William's property line was recorded on a deed transferring ownership of 30 acres of land from his brothers, Eleazer Whipple to Samuel Whipple.(XX:10)

9 September 1685
William's property line was recorded on a deed transferring ownership of 20 acres of land from Eleazer Whipple to Christopher Smith [his granddaughter Hannah's mother-in-law's father]. (XIV:150)

20 February 1688/9
William witnessed a deed transferring 25 acres of land from Valentine Whittman to William Hopkins [His sister Abigail's second husband]. (XIV:200)

21 December 1691
William's property line was recorded on a deed transferring ownership of 60 acres of land from Samuel Whipple to Eleazer Whipple.(XIV:207).

20 February 1699/1700
This day William and Mary Whipple his wife hath exhibited a bill of demand of Tenn pounds and 10s new England silver which the said Mary saith shee committed into Providence Williams his hand, for to be returned to her againe when she demanded it. But said Providence Williams dyeing, her money is not yet returned, therefore that some way may be considered that they may receive the same. Order that Daniel Williams be sent for to come now to the Councill to give them an account of the estate of Providence Williams which the Councill formerly put into his custody until further Order: but the said Daniel Williams hath refused to give the Councill any account of the said Estate; saying that he judged that the Councill hath nothing to doe to take an account of the said Estate. (X:52-3).[358]

11 November 1703
William Whipple and Richard Arnold [His sister Sarah's second husband] witnessed a deed of sale made between Thomas Arnold [Richard's father] and Shadrach Manton [Sarah's sister-in-law's husband]. (V:162).

17 June 1707
William Whipple of the town of Providence gave notice to the town council that he had taken up a stray brown mare, which was earmarked, docked, and branded with a blaze in her face. (IX:180).

28 July 1707
  Whereas William Whipple hath this day preferred a bill to ye Towne desireing the
Town to gratifie him with fifty acres of land, or more, for service, which (he saith) he
did ye Town in the Indian Warrs about Thirty yeares since; ye Towne having Considered
ye bill, their Ans: to it is, that they doe not yet see cause to gratifie his Request. (XI:119).

5 May 1710
  William's property is mentioned in the Last Will and Testament of Richard
Arnold. [Second husband of his sister Sarah] (VII:4)

Last Will and Testament

  Upon the 25th day of March 1712 the last will & Testament of William Whipple of this
town of Providence (deceased) was Exhibbitted to the Towne Concill & was by them
Examined & Proved; The Record of sd will is as followeth./
  In the name of God amen, I William Whipple of the Towne of Providence in her
Majestyes Coloney of Road Island & Providence Plantations in new England, being weake in
body yet by the Blessing of God of sound & perfect memory; And I knowing that all men
are subject to Mortallitye, and not knowing how soone it may please god to Remove me out
of this life, I do make this my lat Will & Testament, hereby making voyd all former Wills by
me mad either by Word or writeing & this only to stand in force as my last will & Testament.
  Ffirst, I bequeath my spirit to god that gave it and my body to the Earth to be decently
buried at the will of my Executor hereafter Named,
  Secondly. I Give to my loveing son william all my lands & house & improvements
whatsoever; hee paying such Legacies as I shall obleidge him to; Thirdly. I give to my loveing
son Seth Whipple Thirty Pounds, to be paid to him after he shall attaine to the age of one &
twenty yeares, to be payd by my Executor as he shall be able. Ffourthly, I give to my loveing
Daughter Mary Sprague Ten pounds to be paid to her by my Executor as my   Executor
shall be able, which Ten Pounds is besides what I have already given to her, which is one
Cow & Calf & Eight Sheepe & Eight lambs, besides what household stuff I have already
given to her:
  Ffiftly, my Will is that my son william shall maintaine his loveing Mother mary whiple
my wife with all such nessecary things as shee shall have Ocation for duireing her Naturall
life; And if shee se cause to dwell with Either of my other Children then my said son William
shall allow to his sister or brother where my loveing wife shall make her aboad according to
her Nessesity, & his ability. Sixthly, I Constitute & Appoynt my loveing son William
Whipple my Executor to Execute my last will & Testament, to pay all my just Debts, &
Receive all my just debts, and to se my Body decently buried; And in Confirmation of this
my last Will & Testament I have hereunto set my hand & seale this Twenty & Seventh day
of ffebruarey in the yeare of our Lord one Thousand Seven hundred & Eleven or Twelve
And Eleventh yeare of the Reign of Our Sovereign Lady Anne, by the Grace of God Quene
of Great Brittan./ Signed, Sealed, published and declared in the presence of us Job Whipple,
Thomas Hopkins, & William Hopkins. William Whipple, his mark. (VII:94-95)

  An inventory of his movable estate was submitted by the Town Subscribers on
15 March 1712, and included such items as " two beds and furniture, thirty pounds of
wollen yarne, cotton & wooll cloath, one chest, ten pounds of fethers, saddles & panel,
old iron tooles, cart & wheeles, grindstone, beetle & wedges, old lumber, meat & butter,
Indian corn, two oxen, five cowes, hefers, yearelings, 3 maares, four swine, twenty seven
sheepe, looking glass, etc." The sum total of his movable estate was just over £110,

which was about average for a Rhode Island farmer at that time. (VII: 94-99). Of those who signed his Last Will and Testament, Job Whipple was his nephew (son of Eleazer), and William Hopkins was the second husband of his sister Abigail, with Thomas being the father of William Hopkins.

Considering that much is known about his brothers, it is surprising that so little of his life is preserved in written records. Unlike his older brothers, he does not appear in pre-1675 Indian War accounts. As seen above, the town council rejected his claim that he fought in that war. His earliest recorded activity in the colony was in 1671, when as a teenager he was forced to take an oath of fealty to the king, and in 1678, when he found a stray cow. Even then, it is not clear as to whether he was still living in Providence town, with or near his father, or had moved to the Louquisset. Not until 13 March 1681 is it clear that he had done so.

It would appear that William lived a rather uneventful, bucolic life. He was not a formally educated man, and, like six of his seven brothers, could not read or write ---or at least could not write his name. His preference of religion is unknown.[359] He apparently paid his taxes on time, was respected by his neighbors, and in the end, willed a modest estate to his children. His brothers continually bought and sold land, took an active part in town and colony politics, and assumed positions of public responsibility, but not William--- although history did record that William was "a good neighbor."

The record of his marriage has never been found. His wife Mary (apparently much younger than William) is not mentioned in town records until the year 1699, and although most unusual in the seventeenth century, it may be that he married rather late in life. It may even be that he married more than once. It is known that his first child was not born until he was about 40 years of age.

William and Mary's youngest son, Seth, a minor at the time of his father's death in 1712, died intestate in 1724, without known issue. Providence town proprietors granted property to Seth on 24 January 1717, which was subsequently sold by William Junior. Considering that land could not be owned in Rhode Island until an individual was 21 years old, this grant would likely place Seth's date of birth close to the year 1696. As far as is known, Seth never married. William Junior married Elizabeth Sprague, and possibly was married a second time to a woman named Esther, who died 29 July 1757 and was buried in the North Burial Grounds.[360]

Mary Whipple Sprague

William and Mary's oldest child, Mary, also married into the Sprague family. She married Richard Sprague in about 1710. Mary was born around 1689 and died after August of 1749 when her husband's Last Will and Testament was drawn. Nine children were born to this couple:

i. Ruth, born about 1713; died after 1749
ii. Zerviah, born 1716.
iii. Obadiah, born 1717; died 12 Jun 1800
iv. Abigail, born about 1719; died after 1806
v. Urania, born about 1721; died after 1780

vi. Lydia, born about 1723; died after 1806
vii. Amos, born about 1725; died 1806
viii. Enoch, born about 1727; died 10 June 1810
ix. Daniel, born about 1729; died after 1748

This family descended from Edward Sprague of Upwey, Dorsetshire, England. His sons William, Ralph, and Richard immigrated to America in 1629 on the ship *Lion's Whelp*, settling in the Bay area. One wonders if the Sprague brothers were acquainted with Captain John Whipple, living as they were but a short distance from his home in Dorchester. William moved to the Hingham settlement, which is approximately half way between Boston and Plymouth, in the year 1634. Of William's five sons, three lived and died in the immediate area, leaving his two youngest, Jonathan and Captain William Junior, to move on westward, Jonathan settling in the Providence, Rhode Island area in 1670, with William joining him about two decades or so later. Two of their nephews eventually joined them: Anthony Junior in 1690 and Richard around the year 1710, after which he met and married Mary Whipple. There is no record of their marriage. As noted, Anthony Junior married Mary Tilden in 1689, and had one son and six daughters, including Elizabeth, who married William Whipple Junior. There is no record of their marriage.[361] (That is, Mary was married to the uncle of William Junior's wife). William and Mary produced 26 grandchildren to William Whipple Senior, most of whom lived and died in Smithfield Township.[362]

As noted, the first known Sprague to reside in Rhode Island was Jonathan, around the year 1670. He was the uncle of Mary's husband Richard, and the great uncle of William Junior's wife, Elizabeth. The Reverend Jonathan Sprague was one of the founders of the Rhode Island Baptist denomination: "It appears that Jonathan Sprague had commenced preaching, and received his ordination in said Providence church, and that he frequently visited and preached the word to this distant branch of brethren (Smithfield), which increased in numbers, until they were organized into a distinct church [the first in the Smithfield area] at the above date (1706), under the pastoral care of said elder Sprague...he was a very pious and judicious man, an able and faithful minister....This church erected a meeting house about one mile north of the Smithfield Academy.... Elder Sprague lived and labored with this church, until he was called to his reward in January, 1741, aged ninety-three years...."[363] Other Spragues to pastor this church were Peter, Jonathan's nephew, son of William, in 1780, and Elisha, grandson of Mary Whipple Sprague in 1795.

Captain William Sprague, Jonathan's brother, was the ancestor of two Rhode Island governors. "Those who recognize an overruling Providence in human affairs are wont to see the special Divine Hand in the election of William Sprague to the governorship...in the spring of 1860. He sprang from an old Massachusetts and Rhode Island family which had won merited honors in civil and military affairs. His ancestor, Jonathan Sprague, first mentioned in Rhode Island history in 1681, was for many years a member of the General Assembly, and speaker of the House of Deputies in 1703... [Governor] William's grandfather, William, was the first calico printer in Rhode Island and one of the first in America."[364]

151

Sixth Generation Male Whipple Descendants of Captain John Whipple Through His Son William

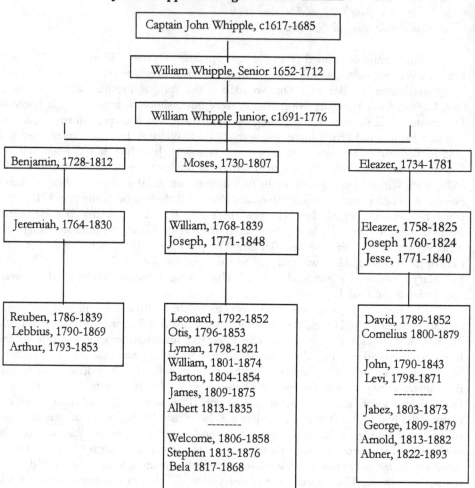

| Captain John Whipple, c1617-1685 |
| William Whipple, Senior 1652-1712 |
| William Whipple Junior, c1691-1776 |

| Benjamin, 1728-1812 | Moses, 1730-1807 | Eleazer, 1734-1781 |

| Jeremiah, 1764-1830 | William, 1768-1839
Joseph, 1771-1848 | Eleazer, 1758-1825
Joseph 1760-1824
Jesse, 1771-1840 |

| Reuben, 1786-1839
Lebbius, 1790-1869
Arthur, 1793-1853 | Leonard, 1792-1852
Otis, 1796-1853
Lyman, 1798-1821
William, 1801-1874
Barton, 1804-1854
James, 1809-1875
Albert 1813-1835

Welcome, 1806-1858
Stephen 1813-1876
Bela 1817-1868 | David, 1789-1852
Cornelius 1800-1879

John, 1790-1843
Levi, 1798-1871

Jabez, 1803-1873
George, 1809-1879
Arnold, 1813-1882
Abner, 1822-1893 |

The above descendancy chart shows that the three Whipple grandsons of William Senior produced a total of six great grandsons and 21 great great grandsons who are known to have lived to adulthood, and who bore the Whipple name. The oldest, Reuben, son of Jeremiah, was born in 1786. The last of the sixth generation to die was Abner, son of Jesse, who died in 1893. Because of insufficient information, only 35 Whipple males of the seventh generation have been identified, 21 of those through the four sons of Jesse. Names and dates were abstracted from www.whipple.org, and the sources it quotes.

Captain William Whipple Junior
Rural Constable

Captain William[3] Whipple (William[2], John[1]) was born about 1691 in Rhode Island and died in Smithfield, Rhode Island 16 November 1776. He was made a freeman 6 May 1712.[365] In about 1713, he married Elizabeth Sprague, born 26 May 1694 and died after 1735. William may have married a second time to a woman named Ester, who died 29 July 1757, and was buried in the North Burial Ground.[366] William and Elizabeth had 17 children, all born in Smithfield--- and with the exception of Jeremiah and Amey of whom nothing is known, in addition to Anthony, Joseph, and Elizabeth I, who died young, all were married in Smithfield.

    i. Mary, born 28 Feb 1714/15; died after 1752; married Stephen Olney.

    ii. Elizabeth I, born 26 May 1716; died before 24 Oct 1718

    iii. Jemima, born 1 Oct 1717; married Benjamin Davis.

    iv. Elizabeth II, born 24 Oct 1718; died 1764; married Jeremiah Wilkinson

    v. William, born 11 Oct 1719: died 16 Nov 1796; married Mary (_)

    vi. Mercy, born 15 Mar 1721; married David Arnold.

    vii. Jeremiah, born 19 May 1722.

    viii. Hopestill, born 28 May 1723; died 12 Oct 1793; married Nicholas Brown.

    ix. John, born 7 May 1724; died 20 Mar 1807.

    x. Anthony, 9 Apr 1725; died 11 Jul 1751.

    xi. Sarah, born 10 Oct 1726; married Solomon Aldrich.

    xii. Benjamin, born 2 Jun 1728; died 12 Jun 1812; married Jerusha Peck.

    xiii. Moses, born 31 Jan 1729; died 3 Sep 1807; married Patience Mathewson

    xiv. Joseph, born 18 Apr 1731; died 27 Dec 1760.

    xv. Amey, born 31 May 1732.

    xvi. Eleazer, born 20 Jan 1733; died 22 Mar 1781; married Anna Brown.

    xvii. Hannah, born 2 May 1735; died 22 Nov 1825; married Christoph Jencks.

Among the Whipple daughters, Mary, (the oldest) married Stephen Olney, who was the grandson of her great aunt Mary Whipple Olney. Elizabeth II married Jeremiah Wilkinson the son of Deborah, daughter of Eleazer Whipple, her great uncle. The Whipple's sixth child, Mercy, married David Arnold, who was the grandson of John Arnold, Mercy's great aunt Sarah Whipple's stepson. Mercy and her husband lived and died in Glocester Township, about ten miles from her place of birth. The youngest Whipple daughter, Hannah, married Christopher Jenckes, whose grandfather's brother was Joseph Jenckes, governor of Rhode Island. Hannah's mother-in-law's grandfather's sister was married to Colonel Joseph Whipple, Captain John Whipple's seventh son. Jemima and Sarah Whipple married Benjamin Davis and Solomon Aldrich respectively.

Lost Gravestones

William Whipple Junior was buried in the "Whipple Burial Lot, on the Whipple farm on Lime Rock Road,"[367] as were his sons John and Benjamin. The headstones of these men, and those of Jerusha and Sarah (wives of Benjamin) and Hopestill Brown (daughter of Hopestill Whipple who married Nicholas Brown in 1744), were later moved approximately three miles southeast to the Moshassuck Cemetery in Central Falls--by Phebe Whipple, wife of Arnold of Providence. The gravestones of Emily and Millie Aldrich (granddaughters of Sarah Whipple who married Solomon Aldrich in 1751) were moved to the Mineral Spring Cemetery at the same time. George Hawkins, Mary Whipple (William's oldest daughter) Olney's grandson through her daughter Sarah Hawkins, died as a child "by falling on the ice at Lime Rock," in 1831; accordingly, if the markers were moved immediately thereafter, William Junior would have already been deceased for 55 years. The uncertain date of 1697 could indicate that those responsible for the removal, two or more generations later, were even less aware of the facts than those who had the marker inscribed sometime after 1776.

The inscription on his headstone read, "Captain William Whipple, Died 16 Nov 1776, aged 79 years." [368]   William was addressed as "Captain" on at least one other occasion.[369] His eldest son, Ensign William, likewise died on a November 16 date—an

unlikely historical coincidence. His brother Seth was born about 1696, and it is possible that Seth's date was attributed to William Junior. William would have had to be at least 21 years of age to have served as executor of his father's Will.[370] This fixes his birth in 1691 at the latest, not 1697. William's wife Elizabeth was born in 1694, and they were married in 1713. This would make Elizabeth 19 years old and William Junior 16 (using the 1697 date) when married--- another unlikely scenario. He was made a freeman in 1712 at the age of 21, again showing that his year of birth was around 1691.

It may be assumed that the gravestones of William's wife and children Elizabeth, Jeremiah, Anthony, Joseph, and possibly Amy, who all died young, disappeared before the removal. It also seems logical that William Senior, his wife Mary, and others of their children and grandchildren would have been

Whipple Monument

buried in this family burial plot, but this question likely will not be answered because the plot was "plowed up" after removal of the stones. The headstones removed to Moshassuck Cemetery no longer stand, having been replaced by a communal monument.[371] Indeed, it is probable that the headstones of a number of the William Senior and William Junior families were moved at that time. It appears that the "list" supplied by L.A.Sayles was corrupted or otherwise inaccurately transferred to cemetery records. The headstones of at least two other family members not on the Sayles' list are known to have been removed at that time,[372] and the wives of William Senior and William Junior were undoubtedly buried beside them. In the rural Rhode Island of that day, it was typical for two or more generations of the same farm family to be buried on a particular farm. For instance, the farm burial lot of William Senior's brother, Eleazer, (Whipple-Mowrey) was a mile down the road, and was normative for rural families. The

154

final resting place of at least four generations of the William Whipple Senior family was apparently uprooted by the construction of a road in the mid-1800s. It is regrettable that their remains now lie under six inches or more of asphalt, and that their headstones never again will be viewed by their descendants. From another perspective, it is fortuitous that the headstones were moved to a large multifamily cemetery. Had they remained where they were they likely would be in the same regrettable condition now as the Eleazer Whipple cemetery.

William Whipple Junior lived and died on the Louquisset estate handed down to him by his father in 1712. "This property was located in Smithfield Township (now the town of Lincoln) on the road that leads from Providence to Worcester, Massachusetts. William lived in a small house that stood a little east of the road not far from a place called Lime Rock. He had the largest family of any of the Whipples on record."[373] This house was adjacent to the Moshassuck River, approximately eight miles north of the town of Providence, and a mile west of the Blackstone River. It was passed on to William's eldest son, Ensign William III. He in turn deeded it to his nephew Jesse Whipple, who subsequently sold it in the year 1807 and moved out of state in 1817.

William Whipple Junior in Early Town Records

William appeared on a few occasions in *The Early Records of the Town of Providence, 21 volumes* (Providence: Snow and Farnham, 1892-1915). Individual entries are noted with the volume number and page. Original spelling has been retained.

2 June 1718
Att a Towne meeting held att Providence this 2d day of June Anno Dom: 1718. It being the Townes Election day the choice of Towne officers...Col. Joseph Whipple [William's uncle] chosen Towne councilleman...William Whipple chosen hog constable and ingaged. (XXX:14

29 October 1718
[William and his first cousin, James, son of Eleazer Whipple, allowed the town to use their properties.] "The commette Chosen to appoint the place for ye building a pound in the Northern parte of our Towne ship this day made Return of a place they have pitched upon: which is by the highway side betweene James Whipples and William Whipples where they the said Whipples have promised to allow Land so long as it is Improved upon for that use. The which returne is by Town Accepted where upon it is voated and ordered that Sam. Wilkinson Junr. [James Whipple's nephew] and Ensign James Whipple shall Build a Poound vpon said place or spot of Land pitched vpon: and have theire satisfaction out of the Townes Treasurey for there Labour and servis there in." (XIII:8)

155

6 June 1720

It Being the first munday in said month and the Townes Election day for the Choce of theire Towne officers ... Col. Joseph Whipple, elected councilleman...William Whipple chosen pound keeper and ingaged. (XIII:37)

5 June 1721

....Joseph Whipple elected Moderator...William Whipple elected pound keeper, but refused to serve. (XIII:53)

19 June 1721

Saturday ye 10th day of June 1721, the meeteing againe in being--Col Joseph continues as moderator...Ensign James Whipple is Chosen pound keeper in the roome of William Whipple (XIII:54)

3 June 1723

...Col. Joseph Whipple chosen councilleman...Job Whipple [William's first cousin] chosen ffences uiewer...William Whipple chosen pound keeper and ingaged (XIII:63)

17 June 1725

...Col. Joseph Whipple chosen councilleman...Leiutt. Job Whipple chosen ffences uiewer...William Whipple chosen pound keeper and ingaged. (XIII:27)

"On 28 September 1733, John Whitman of Smithfield, blacksmith, and wife Sarah (Sprague), sold to William Whipple of Smithfield their rights in the land of their father Anthony Sprague (Jr) [William's grandfather] of Attleboro, dec.."[374] The Whitman mansion in Lime Rock is extant, and listed in the National Register. Valentine Whitman, John's father, is mentioned prominently throughout the *Early Records of Providence*, as a friend and associate of Captain John Whipple. Another Sprague Aunt, Lydia Sprague Harris, was married to Richard Harris, William's business partner in the lime manufacturing business. And as noted later, two other Sprague aunts, Phebe and Mary, married Whipple cousins.

William Whipple Junior and three of his oldest sons were listed in Smithfield records of 1748. The town had earlier passed a "Highway Act." This act provided for "surveyors who made it their duty to inspect the roads within the limits of their respective districts, and enough were appointed to care for the highways...specific provision was made, and every male inhabitant of the town, twenty-one years or older and able bodied, was required to work on the highways six days per year."[375] At that time, the Smithfield population was 450. The township was divided into 16 highway districts to be worked by the persons listed, the first person on the list being the surveyor. William and his sons Anthony, William, and John were assigned to District 4, with William Junior serving as surveyor. District 4, "began at Locusquesset Brook to the Providence line, beginning at the old highway by the lime kiln, to end where said highway intersects with the highway that goes by Dr. Jenckes'---also, the Cross Road from Abraham Scott to Pawtucket River."[376] As previously noted, Captain Job Whipple, William Junior's first cousin, son of Eleazer Whipple, as well as Job's son, Stephen, and

156

nephew Ephraim (son of Job Junior) were listed in District 5. His brother-in-law, Richard Sprague, and sons were also listed.

It is thus seen that by the year 1748, 63 years after the death of Captain John Whipple, only seven adult (16 years or older) Whipple men resided in the Louquisset meadows, each a descendant of either William or Eleazer, Captain's John's third and fourth sons. By the time of the Smithfield census of 1774, the Whipple population had decreased to five male heads-of-household: Benjamin, John, William, Joseph, and Stephen. The first three were sons of William Junior, and he, now in his mid to late 80s, was apparently living with one of them. Stephen, William Junior's second cousin, was the youngest son of Captain Job. This decline in Whipple residents is reflected in a paucity of elected town officials from the family. In 1731, the town of Smithfield was set off from Providence, and in March of that year its first town officers were elected. Whipple town officers from its incorporation in 1731 until its division in 1871 were Job in 1735 and 1736; Stephen (Job's son) 1755, 1761, 1772, 1780, 1782, 1785; and Jeremiah (son of Benjamin, grandson of William Junior), 1822, 1824, and 1827.[377]

The Joseph Whipple in the 1774 census was the grandson of Colonel Joseph Whipple, the seventh son of Captain John. Joseph (1734-1816) had moved to south Smithfield (not the Louquisset Meadows) about the year 1755, and had four sons, William, John, Samuel, and George. (Joseph and his sons are buried in the same burial plot as Captain John and Sarah Whipple). The only other known descendant of a non-Louquisset Whipple brother in Smithfield Township before the mid-1800s was Ephraim, the great-great grandson of Benjamin Whipple, the fifth son of Captain John. Ephraim (1800-1875), who moved to Greenville, in southwest Smithfield Township in about 1825, had three sons: Andrew, William, and John.[378]

A Mayflower Family

William Whipple Junior married Elizabeth Sprague about the year 1713. She was the daughter of Anthony and Mary (Tilden) Sprague of Cumberland Township. "They [the Spragues] lived in the west central part of Cumberland on the Blackstone River. Smithfield was just on the other side of the river. Apparently when Elizabeth married William Whipple Junior she moved to Smithfield, but obviously kept close ties with her parent's family. Two other daughters of Anthony and Mary married Whipples. Mary Sprague was married at Providence (probably Smithfield) to Eleazer, eldest son of Eleazer (Captain John's third son). Phebe Sprague married Peter Whipple, son of William, who was the son of David (Captain John's sixth son). Peter and Phebe lived in Cumberland."[379]

Elizabeth Sprague Whipple was a documented descendant of a Mayflower family. Her great great grandfather Richard Warren, who was christened in London in 1580 and died at Plymouth in 1628, was a signatory to the Mayflower Compact. Thus, Elizabeth and William's 17 children, all of whom were born on their Louquisset farm, including eight sons, claimed the Mayflower as their heritage.[380] The photograph of the Warren Plaque below was taken behind the First Parish Church at Plymouth, founded in 1620. The plaque is located just outside the main entrance to the cemetery immediately to the south and behind the church. Plaques honoring the other Pilgrims are seen on this

157

wall. Warren was buried in this cemetery but, like so many others, his gravestone was never erected in order not to alert the Indians as to how many Pilgrims had died.

Mayflower Whipples descend from Richard's oldest child, Mary, who married Richard Bartlett in 1628. The Bartlett's daughter, Elizabeth, married Anthony Sprague. Anthony Sprague Junior married Mary Tilden. Their daughter, Elizabeth, married William Whipple Junior. Richard Warren's English origins have been the subject of a great deal of speculation, and over a dozen undocumented ancestries published about him. It has long been known of his marriage to Elizabeth Walker on 14 April 1610 at Great Amwell, Hertford. In the will of Augustine Walker, dated April 1613, he mentions "my daughter Elizabeth Warren wife or Richard Warren", and "her three children Mary, Ann, and Sarah." The Warrens had seven children, five daughters and two sons. Little is known of his life at Plymouth. His wife and daughters came to America in 1623, and he and his wife had sons Nathaniel and Joseph at Plymouth. He received land in 1623 and

Richard Warren Plaque

shared in the division of cattle in 1627. The only record of his 1628 death is Morton's 1669 account, *New England's Memorial*, in which Morton writes: "This year died Mr. Richard Warren, who was an useful instrument and during his life bare a deep share in the difficulties and troubles of the first settlement of the Plantation of Plymouth." Warren's descendants include such notables as presidents Ulysses Grant and Franklin Roosevelt.[381] Several Whipple descendants are card-carrying members of the General Society of Mayflower Descendants, including the present author who is a twelfth generation descendant of Mr. Warren through Eleazer, the youngest son of William Whipple Junior and Elizabeth Sprague.[382]

It is unusual that only three of Elizabeth and William Junior's sons produced children. Jeremiah apparently died as a child. Anthony died at the age of 27, and Joseph at 29. Both died intestate, with their father serving as administrator; neither fathered children.[383] John died, apparently childless, at the age of 83.[384] In the 1774 Smithfield census, he was listed as head of household with two adult women living with him. William Junior's oldest son, Ensign William, who died at the age of 77, was father to one daughter. Benjamin lived out his life in the Louquisset meadows, dying at the age of 84. His son, Captain Jeremiah Whipple (1764 – 6 August 1830), had three sons: Reubin (1786 – 1839), Libbeus (1790 – 1869), and Arthur (1793 – 1853). Of these, Reubin died childless, Libbeus had two daughters, and Arthur was father to one son, Jeremiah[7] Whipple (Arthur[6], Jeremiah[5], Benjamin[4], William[3], William[2], John[1]), who it is thought died childless in 1866.

In summary of the descendants of the Louquisset brothers, the sons of William Junior who lived and died in Louquisset, Jeremiah, Anthony, Joseph, John, Benjamin, and William fathered only one daughter and one son among them. As previously noted, none of Samuel's (second son of Captain John) descendants stayed in Smithfield. Thus, with the possible exception of Scott, the great great grandson of Eleazer, after two

158

centuries the surname inherited from the three original Louquisset brothers was no longer heard in the meadows of the Louquisset. In time, Whipples from other than the three original families eventually moved into both the southern and northern sections of Smithfield-Lincoln. These later descendants of Captain John's other sons, and a few descendants of those families described below have lived for centuries even in the environs of Lime Rock.

This eventual state of affairs was quite unlike earlier days in the Louquisset settlement. "Below is a tax record levied by the town of Providence, 16 June 1713. The source is E. Richardson, *The History of Woonsocket, 1641-1876*, 51-53. Whipples in the list of taxpayers on that date were: Daniel, 116; Eleazer, 15; Eleazer Junior, 16, James, 18, Job, 17; Seth, 119; Thomas, 5; William with mother, 38. The number behind the name was the dwelling place along the roads. Eleazer and four of his sons, Eleazer Junior, James and Job, who lived in dwellings 15 through 18, and Daniel who lived in dwelling 116 comprised the Eleazer Whipple family"[385] As noted previously, Thomas, in dwelling 5, was the only known son of Samuel to take up residence on his inherited land in the Louquisset meadows. He moved to the state of Connecticut approximately four years after the date of this tax. Descendants of William Senior, who had died the year before, were his widow and William Junior in dwelling 38, and his youngest son, Seth, in dwelling 119. This is the only known record that lists members of all three families in the same Louquisset document.

A Cousin Controversy

On 24 June 1734, William Whipple Junior, brother of Seth Whipple, sold to Philip Smith of Providence, a plot of land in Providence on the east side of the Mill River.[386] William's wife Elizabeth Sprague signed the deed with an "x". The town proprietors had formerly granted this property to Seth, 24 January 1717.

A controversy as to the identities of two William Whipple cousins has been ongoing for several years. However, this 1734 deed, and William Junior's recently discovered nativity and necrology dates, provides compelling evidence that he was the son of William, not David, Captain John's sixth son. He was designated on the 1734 document as "Junior," and signed his name "William Whipple Junior," which would not have been the case were he David's son. The fact that Elizabeth's name and mark appeared on the deed, and that he clearly was stated to be the brother of Seth, is unequivocal evidence as to his identity.[387]

Only one other William Whipple was born in the 1680s or 1690s in the New England Colonies. He was Captain William Whipple, born in Ipswich, Mass. 28 February 1696, and died in Kittery, Maine, 17 August 1751. His eldest son was General William Whipple, a signatory to the Declaration of Independence from New Hampshire. No proven relationship exists between the early Ipswich, Maine, and New Hampshire Whipples and the Rhode Island Whipples.[388] The only other known Rhode Island William Whipple to be born before 1710 was William (1704) the illegitimate son of William, and grandson of David.

Uncle William's Gift

Smithfield records document the deaths of four of Captain William Whipple Junior's sons in the eighteenth century: Anthony, Joseph, William, and Eleazer. As stated, William Junior's oldest son, Ensign William, was the father of only one child, a daughter. Consequently, on 4 June 1791, he deeded his homestead to his nephew Jesse Whipple, the youngest son of his deceased brother Eleazer.

> Know all men by these presents that I William Whipple of Smithfield...for and in consideration of the love and good will which I have and do bear toward my dutiful and well beloved nephew Jesse Whipple of Cumberland but now residing in Smithfield, son of Eleazer Whipple of Cumberland...do freely, clearly, and absolutely give and grant unto the said Jesse Whipple...four separate tracts of land. The first tract containeth by estimation forty acres be the same more or less, and is the homestead farm whereon I now live. With two dwelling houses, one barn, one coopers shop, one corn crib, and outhouses....The second tract of land is a woodlot being by estimation fourteen acres that did belong to my honored father William Whipple deceased...The third tract being a two-thirds part of a boggy meadow...I do likewise give unto the said Jesse Whipple one –half of the lime kiln. In witness whereof I the said William Whipple have hereunto set my hand and seal this fourth day of June, Anno Domini, one thousand seven hundred and ninety one.[389]

This land description is virtually identical to the 1756 property deeded from William Junior to William III.[390] Apparently, William III did not add appreciably to his estate in thirty-five years. In return, Jesse signed an affidavit affirming that "both my honored uncle and aunt William and Mary Whipple may live on the land for the rest of their natural lives." [391]Also, on this same date, Jesse, with his brother Eleazer Whipple Junior as surety, borrowed £400 from his uncle William.[392] On 1 March 1795, Jesse was deeded by his uncle "one-half of a certain hill or quarry of lime rock" in Smithfield.[393]

The Lime Manufacturing Trade

William Whipple Junior became extensively involved in the lime mining trade in the early eighteenth century, when "he gave a lease of a portion of his farm in Providence (afterward Smithfield) for mining purposes to John and James Alford (merchants) of Boston, on 10 October 1715."[394] William Senior apparently took little interest in the large limestone deposits on this farm; most likely he sold limestone to his sister Abigail's in-laws, the Steven Dexters, as well as to the Harris family, in-laws of his brother Samuel.

"Throughout the seventeenth century and the first half of the eighteenth century, the lime-mining industry was carried on in a part-time and intermittent fashion, an important though small-scale exploitation of the resource. In the hundred years following 1750, however, lime quarrying and processing became a major industry and led to the development of a substantial village."[395] William Senior's next-door neighbor, Steven Dexter, who married William's youngest sister, Abigail, began "burning lime" at what became known as "Dexter's Ledge" in the late 1660s. The Dexter family and the David Harris (nephew of Mary Harris Whipple, wife of Samuel Senior) family owned the largest lime manufacturing facilities in the area until the mid-1800s, at which time the advent of Portland cement largely put an end to the demand for the product. Thomas Harris, one of the first settlers at Providence and father of Mary Harris Whipple, originally opened the Harris quarry in the early 1700s.

"The village of Lime Rock centered around and was named for its lime-mining industry, one of the oldest quarrying operations in North America. The availability of such natural limestone had a significant impact on the early building traditions of Rhode Island. If not quarried, lime could be obtained only by the burning of shells gathered on the beaches after a storm had washed them ashore. The ability to make burned lime mortars allowed for the development of strong masonry, most evident in the 'stone enders,' a form which dominated northern Rhode Island building for centuries. As recently as the 1960s, the Eleazer Whipple House, a fine 'stone ender' in Lime Rock, was demolished and its material scattered to several sites. [As earlier noted, the sons of Eleazer Whipple, William Senior's brother, were likewise successful lime producers]. Only a very few of these dwellings still remain, less than a dozen in the entire state. They are an architectural legacy shared by every Rhode Islander. Each demolition and fire has made the remaining stock of seventeenth-century houses more precious and rare."[396]

As previously shown, William Junior deeded away most of his mining interests to his sons in the 1750s. It is clear that from the year 1791, when Ensign William III deeded his lime rock property and business over to him, Jesse Whipple continued in the profitable manufacturing trade that had been established by his grandfather and carried on by his uncles. Anthony and Joseph Whipple, his uncles, died in 1751 and 1760 respectively. Anthony's estate of over £500 showed large sums of money owed to him by Richard Harris and the Mowrey family. The inventory of Joseph's estate, valued at £3979 (an enormous amount of money at the time), revealed that he was owed over £2000 pounds by such fellow mine owners as John Dexter, Joseph and Christopher Jenckes, Richard Harris, and three of his own brothers.[397] As late as the mid-1790s, William Junior's son Ensign "William and his nephew Jesse Whipple, who lived on Great Road in the eastern part of the village, (still) owned lime rock, part interest in a kiln, and a coopers shop; but their product was undoubtedly sold to David Harris (son of Richard) who delivered the Whipple lime along with his own to market. This arrangement permitted the farmers of Lime Rock to supplement their income and David Harris to develop a monopoly over the lime business in the years prior to the Revolution. When Harris died in 1797 [one year after Ensign William III] Smithfield lime was being sold from Boston to Nantucket to the southern states and the West Indies."[398]

"Each stage of lime production was labor-intensive from quarrying stone and making barrels to producing charcoal needed for processing, loading and firing the kilns, regulating them, packing the finished product into barrels, and carting the casks into Providence where the lime was sold. Though Lime Rock's glory days ended…The slow but steady market for its product since then has served to keep it a stable community. Its work force and population are still virtually the same size….The monopoly which the Dexters, Harrises, Whipples, Jenckeses, and Mowreys held for so long over industry and ownership, the community leadership kept Lime rock a close-knit community; the interconnections among these families were labyrinthine and contributed to the social and physical stability of the village. Many of Lime Rock's handsome houses dating from the eighteenth and early nineteenth centuries still stand, and, in our age of mobility and change, a surprising number are owned by families who trace their origins to the early settlers of the village. The unique character of Lime Rock, and, in particular the antiquity of its lime-producing industry have been recognized by the village's inclusion in the National Register of Historic Places." [399]

The Venerable William Whipple House

Among the 29 individual Lime Rock properties listed on the Register is the ancient Whipple home. Part of this property dates back to the time of William Senior and the 1660s. Its National Register description reads: "The Jesse/William Whipple House. The Whipple House is a good example of the Greek revival style---one and one half stories, 5-bays, with a center door; it has paneled pilasters, wide cornices, and a heave Doric portico. Together with his uncle, William Whipple, Jesse Whipple owned interests in limestone deposits, part interest in a kiln, and a coopers shop. [NR-LRHD]." [400]

The William/Jesse Whipple House [address 1073 Great Road] is located on the northeast corner of the intersection of Great Road and Simon Sayles Road (Structure 1). Next door to this (not shown) was the house (demolished in 1964) of Eleazer Whipple. Today, the Lincoln Central Elementary School stands in its place. Across the Great Road west is the Whipple-Mowrey cemetery, called in the Register "Lime Rock Cemetery," noting "that it is one of the oldest in the state and further the variety and good condition of the headstones." [Unfortunately, the present author found this cemetery to be in a badly deteriorated condition in 2004]. To the immediate north of the cemetery are the remains of the Nathaniel Mowrey Tavern (Structure 2). The Whipple and Mowrey

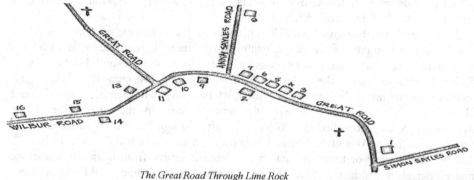

The Great Road Through Lime Rock

families intermarried on numerous occasions across the generations. Structures 8 and 10 were Mowrey homes. Other families that claim the Whipples in their genealogies lived in structures 12, 13, 15, and 16; the old Whitman, Aldrich, Harris, and Smith homes. [401] Structure 7 is the Masonic Lodge, whose membership included several Whipple men. The town's single worship center, the First Baptist Church, is Structure 14. [This church is now located next door to the Jesse Whipple house]. [402] Just off the map, about one fourth of a mile east on Simon Sayles Road at the intersection of the Old River Road, stands the mansion house of Captain Job Whipple, the son of Eleazer. As previously noted, this house is also on the National Register.

"The Limerock Historic District comprises twenty architecturally or historically significant buildings, three lime quarries, and the ruins of three lime kilns. These structures reflect the history of Limerock during its prominence and form the center of this old village. The district begins on the east at the intersection of Simon Sayles Road with Great Road to include the Greek Revival house built by the Whipple family and distinguished by a fine Doric portico, wide corner pilasters, and heavy cornice. The district proceeds for about one mile north and east. Within one square mile there are in the village good examples of New England vernacular architecture from the late seventeenth through the nineteenth century." [403]

Beginning in 1807, Jesse Whipple sold the estate deeded to him by his uncle (plus other properties) and moved, in 1817, approximately 800 miles southwest to the county of Franklin, Indiana, about 30 miles northwest of Cincinnati, Ohio. The land and buildings that he sold[404] had been in the Whipple name since the year 1660--over 150 years. Why would he abandon such original virgin land, land that had never been held by a European before his great-great grandfather Captain John, land that had been in his family name for more than a century and a half? It is impossible to know the full circumstances, but considerable economic pressure to leave the area is known to have existed in the early 1800s.

Jesse/William Whipple House

Two situations may have been among the deciding factors. It is the understanding of one of Jesse's descendants that… "The usable limestone on the property was running out and no one was willing to sell him additional deposits. About that same time period, a syndicate of local mine owners bought most all the mining rights and apparently Jesse was excluded. Several of his wife's family, mostly Quaker farmers, were moving west at the time, so they just packed up and joined them."[405]

Also, by the early 19th century, the Rhode Island state legislature, "believing that industrialization served the public interest, allowed mill owners to take precedence over those of farmers and fishermen. Farmers could sue for compensation when mill dams flooded their land but they could not stop the dams from operating…within a short time most rivers became polluted by industrial waste…by 1815, there were a hundred cotton spinning mills in the state employing seven thousand workers…the decline in the farming and maritime trades left the common people no other source of gainful employment…twenty-one of the state's thirty-one towns found some river capable of sustaining a spinning factory…agricultural employment declined to only about 10 percent."[406] These pressures apparently forced Jesse Whipple and many of his

163

Louquisset neighbors, as well as several relatives in Smithfield and Cumberland townships, to sell and move out of state.

Descendants Who
Settled Cumberland Township

Moses, Grandson of William Whipple Senior

Moses[4] Whipple (William[3], William[2], John[1]), the sixth son of William Junior, was born 21 January 1729 and died 3 September 1807. It is estimated that he left Louquisset no later than 1767, at the age of 38. He lived the last 40 years of life on his new property, located just east of the Blackstone River on the road [Mendon Road] that leads to Cumberland Hill, about two miles from his father's farm. He and wife Patience Matteson had four children who in turn produced 27 known children, of whom at least 10 continued the Whipple name. Moses was buried in the Ballou Cemetery on Mendon Road in Cumberland, as were two of his children and at least 12 grandchildren. His oldest son, William, inherited the family property, which he kept until his death in 1839. He had 11 children, including seven sons. He, in turn, passed the farm on to his son William III. "He resides in Cumberland, on the farm formerly owned by his grandfather, near the Blackstone River." [407]

Eleazer, Grandson of William Whipple Senior

Eleazer[4] Whipple (William[3], William[2], John[1]), eighth and youngest son of William Junior, was born 30 January 1733/34 and died 22 March 1781.[408] He was married in about 1757 to Anna Brown, who was born 21 August 1736, and died at Cumberland

between the years 1800 and 1810.[409] Anna was a great great granddaughter of The Reverend Roger Williams.[410] To this couple, nine children were born. In 1769, Eleazer bought the property of Joseph Razee, a tract of 104 acres in north central Cumberland Township near the community of Diamond Hill, about one block south of the intersection of what is now called "Little Pond Country

Eleazer Whipple House, 2004

Road and Sneech Pond Road." [Its present address is 274 Little Pond Country Road. The addition on the right of the above photograph is not part of the original house]. As previously noted, several of his Whipple cousins, descendants of Daniel, virtually founded the area in the early 1700s. Eleazer, like his ancestors, was a farmer, and was well esteemed in the community. He was elected to the position of Justice of the Peace in 1777. Eleazer Whipple also served in Captain Enoch Weatherhead's Company of Colonel John Mathewson's Regiment in the Revolutionary War in service to the United States in the alarm at Providence, Rhode Island, 23 July 1778.[411]

Eleazer, his wife, and two sons were buried in the Ira Peck Cemetery (R.I Historical Cemetery-Cumberland #19). "It contains headstones of early families including Ballous, Pecks, and Whipples, as well as a handsome granite-block fronted receiving tomb built for Joseph Whipple in 1825."[412] His sons Eleazer, Joseph, and Jesse inherited the farm, although, as previously noted, Jesse sold his interest to his brothers when still a teenager and moved to Smithfield to live with his uncle, William Whipple III. This tract of land was divided into five-acre lots, each brother owning alternate fields of five acres each.[413] Joseph (1760-1824) and Eleazer (1758-29 July 1825) continued to farm this homestead all their lives. Eleazer Junior died in Cumberland, as did his sons David and Cornelius. The sons of David, Pardon and Eleazer, lived out their lives in Cumberland, as did many of their descendants. Joseph lived and died in Cumberland, as did his five children, including sons Benjamin, Charles, and Joseph Arnold. As late as the year 1908, Joseph Arnold Whipple was in possession of the original Cumberland farm of his grandfather Eleazer. The author of this book, Dr. Charles Whipple Junior, is a lineal descendant of Captain William Whipple Junior through his son Eleazer and grandson Jesse. The author's great grandson, Joseph, is the thirteenth American generation from Captain John Whipple.[414]

End Notes

[357] John O. Austin, *Genealogical Dictionary of Rhode Island* (Albany, NY: 1887, reprint edition, Baltimore: Genealogical Publication Company, 1978) 222. Henry E. Whipple, *A Brief Genealogy of the Whipple Families Who Settled in Rhode Island* (Providence: A. Crawford Greene, 1873), James N. Arnold, Vital Records of Rhode Island, 1636-1850 (Providence: Narragansett Historical Publishing Company, 1892). *Records of the First Church at Dorchester in New England 1636-1734 (Boston: George H. Ellis, 1891)* 267 and 181. Vital statistics on the children and grandchildren of Captain John Whipple and Sarah are taken from the above and numerous publications that quote from them. For more recent information, consult www.whipple.org, Weldon Whipple, Webmaster.

[358] Providence Williams was the son of The Reverend Roger Williams. He died at Newport on 22 Jul 1686. His brother, Daniel, was appointed executor of his will on 14 Sep 1686.

[359] William Whipple Senior likely was Baptist. William Junior and Mary married into a staunch Six Principle Baptist family, the Spragues. Mary's husband, Richard Sprague, helped build the Baptist Church of North Smithfield in 1738. The first Baptist church to be built in Smithfield was in 1706.

[360] Henry E. Whipple, from a corrected copy of the book found in the Rhode Island Historical Society Library, call no. CS71. W574, 1873, RIHSL, 10.

[361] Warren V. Sprague, *Sprague Families in America* (Privately published, 1913). Warren V. Sprague, A *Supplement to the Sprague Families in America*, 1941. This source includes the many Sprague genealogies published in the 1800s and early 1900s. The most complete source presently available is the Sprague Database-The Composite Sprague Database-Richard E. Weber, Project Developer, and A. Arnold Sprague, Webmaster, 2004. On line at www.sprague-database.org. Unfortunately this source has William Junior and Mary incorrectly descended from the David Whipple line.

[362] Warren V. Sprague, 139. In 1712, Mary and Richard Sprague bought land with a new house upon it from Thomas Comstock, about one mile north of Mary's childhood home, in a place called Woonsocket and shown to be near the Branch River and Woonsocket Hill in North Smithfield where they were taxpayers from 1713 until 1748. Richard Sprague is mentioned in a deed from Captain William Sprague, his uncle, as having helped to build a meetinghouse in Smithfield, in 1738. In his last will and testament, dated 14 August 1749, Richard mentioned his wife Mary, sons Obadiah, Enoch, Amos, and Daniel, and daughters Ruth Whiteman, Zerviah Comstock, Abigail, Urania Aldrich and Lydia. The two Sprague governors of Rhode Island, William 1838-39, and his nephew William, 1860-62, were descendants of the above Captain William Sprague.

[363] Richard Knight, *History of the General or Six Principe Baptists, in Europe and America* (Providence: Smith and Parmenter, 1927) 267.

[364] Thomas Bicknell, *The History of Rhode Island and Providence Plantations, 3 vols* (New York: The American Historical Society, 1920) 3:1152. The first Sprague governor was his uncle William, in 1838.

[365] David Jillson, "Descendants of Capt. John Whipple of Providence, R.I.," *New England Historical and Genealogical Register* 32 (1878) 405. Henry E Whipple, from a corrected copy of the book found in the Rhode Island Historical Society Library, call No. CS71. W574, 1873, RIHSL, 3.

[366] Henry E. Whipple, from a corrected copy of the book found in the Rhode Island Historical Society Library, call number CS71.W574, 1873, RIHS, 10.

[367] Nellie M.C. Beaman, ed., "Lincoln Cemetery Inscriptions," *Rhode Island Genealogical Register* 19 (1996): 74-75. See also: Whipple Lot, Lincoln, Historical Cemetery #LN075, Gravestones in Natural Order, Providence County. *Rhode Island Historical Cemetery Database*, on computer at the Rhode Island Historical Society Library. Printout 3 Oct 2002

[368] Beaman, 74. "On the Whipple Farm, stones now taken up and removed, lot plowed down. List of names given by Mr. L. A. Sayles. (Handwritten in: 'Now in Moshassuck Cemetery')."

[369] William A Mowry, *The Descendants of Nathaniel Mowry of Rhode Island* (Providence: S. S. Rider, 1878) 74.

[370] In most states in the 18th and 19th century, the "age of legal action" required to serve as an executor for males was 14. In the states of Massachusetts, Rhode Island, and Missouri the minimal age was 17. In Rhode Island, land could not be owned until age 21. Judge Tapping Reeve, *The Law of Baron and Femme, of Parent and Child, Guardian and Ward, Master and Servant, and the Powers of the Courts of Chancery, With an Essay on the Terms Heir, Heirs, and Heirs of the Body*, 3rd ed. (1862 reprint, New York: Source Book Press, 1970).

[371] "The earliest presently listed burial at Moshassuck Cemetery is 1868, but records don't start until 1909. The cemetery caretaker referred me to the librarian at the Central Falls Library, who keeps a database of old burials at the cemetery. He told me where the earliest burials were located, so I went back to the cemetery and searched the gravestones. I came across only one common gravestone inscribed: Whipple-Sprague-Salsbury, 1766-1885. There was no other information, and no way to get an interment list since the records are filed by date of death, not by surname, and do not start until 1909." Barbara R. Carroll, Exeter, Rhode Island, personal correspondence, 26 October 2002. It must be recalled that William's wife's maiden name was Sprague, as was his sister's married name.

"Phebe Whipple, who died in 1879, was the great granddaughter of William Whipple Junior, and the granddaughter of Benjamin his son. Her grandmother, Jerusha Peck Whipple, died 21 May 1766 (probably giving birth to her mother Phebe Whipple Dexter, daughter of Jerusha and Benjamin, who was born on 20 May 1766). The first date on the common monument at Moshassuck Cemetery is 1766. Also, her husband, Arnold Whipple, son of Jabez, was the grandson of John Whipple and Bethiah Salsbury. The third name on the common monument is Salsbury." Barbara R. Carroll, Exeter, Rhode Island, personal correspondence, 5 Jan 2003. Arnold Whipple was the great grandson of Benjamin, Captain John Whipple's fifth son. See Henry E Whipple, 16-17, for the ancestry of Arnold.

[372] "Cemetery records state that Phebe Dexter was the wife of William, born 21 May 1766, died 21 June 1821. Entry for William Dexter states that he died 31 October 1795. A note on the database record states that Phebe and William were also removed from the burial ground in Smithfield. John E. Sterling, Compiler, Rhode Island Historical Cemeteries Database. On computer at the Rhode Island Historical Society Library, Providence, RI." Barbara R. Carroll, Exeter, Rhode Island, personal correspondence, February 27, 2003.

[373] Henry E. Whipple, 48. William Junior, between the years 1755-59, deeded land to six of his eight sons: Benjamin, Eleazer, John, Joseph, Moses, and William. Several of these deeds place the original Whipple property on both sides of the Moshassuck River. Smithfield Record of Deeds, 4:74-76.

[374] Robert S. Wakefield, compiler, *Mayflower Families Through Five Generations*, 18 vols. (Plymouth: General Society of Mayflower Descendants, 1999) 18:67.

[375] Thomas Steere, *History of the Town of Smithfield* (Providence: E. L. Freeman, 1881) 26

[376] Steere, 28.

[377] E. Richardson, *History of Woonsocket* (Woonsocket: S. Foss Printer, 1876) 33-38. Steere, 183, 194-95.

[378] Henry E. Whipple, 41.

[379] Judith Ray, *Founders and Patriots of the Town of Cumberland Rhode Island* (Baltimore: Gateway Press, 1990). Personal correspondence, 24 Sep 2002.

[380] Wakefield, 18:66-67. Richards's father was Christopher Warren, born 1558, died 7 Dec. 1587.

[381] Summarized from Edward Davies, "The Marriage of Richard Warren of the Mayflower," *The American Genealogist* 78 (April 2003) 81-86.

[382] Membership certificate number 75,238.

[383] Smithfield Probate Records, 1749-68, 2:68 and 2:352. City Clerks Office, Central Falls, RI.

[384] Nellie MM.C. Beaman, ed., "Abstracts of Smithfield Wills," Rhode Island Genealogical Register, (Princeton, Ma, 1991) 14: 85. In his Last Will and Testament, John mentions his niece Phebe and nephew Jeremiah, children of his brother Benjamin.

[385] Norma A. Combs, at nacombs@ntelos.net, correspondence to Whipple.Org and the authors, 11 February 2003. This is the only known record that enumerates members of the three families in the same document.

[386] Providence Record of Deeds, 9:316-17. City Hall, Division of Archives and History. Providence, RI
The Early Records of the Town of Providence, 21 vols., collected and printed by the Records Commissioners (Providence: Snow & Farnham, city printers, 1892-1915)[hereinafter *ERP*] XX:83.

[387] Charles Whipple Junior, "Captain John Whipple's Two Grandsons Named William: A Reply," online at www.whipple.org/twowilliams/charles.html 1 November 2002.

[388] Blaine Whipple, *History and Genealogy of "Elder" John Whipple of Ipswich, Massachusetts, his English Ancestors and American Descendants* (Victoria, British Columbia: Trafford Publishing Company, 2003) vi.

[389] Smithfield Record of Deeds, 8:175. Central Falls City Hall, Central Falls, RI.Inventory, Probate Records, wills, Smithfield 1769-1797, 526-27.

[390] Smithfield Record of Deeds, 4:74-76, 15 December 1756, Cental Falls City Hall, Central Falls, RI.

[391] Reiteration is noted in the William Whipple Will (1796), Smithfield Probates 13:132, City Clerk's Office, Central Falls, RI. See also: Smithfield Record of Deeds, 8:203-204.

[392] Smithfield Record of Deeds, 8:204, Central Falls City Hall, Central Falls, RI.

[393] Smithfield Record of Deeds, 8:321, Central Falls City Hall, Central Falls, RI.

[394] Jillson, 405. *ERP*, XX:11.

[395] Lincoln Rhode Island Preservation Report P-L-1: 13.

[396] Lincoln Rhode Island Preservation Report P-L-1: 9

[397] Anthony Whipple Inventory. Smithfield Probate Records, 1749-1768,.2:68-69. Central Fall City Hall, Central Falls, RI. Joseph Whipple Inventory. Smithfield Probate Records, 1749-1768. 2:361-363. Central Falls City Hall. Central Falls, RI.

[398] Mrs. Richard P.Sullins, Grants Administrator. National Register of Historical Places Nomination Form, Lime Rock Historic District, 1974. (Washington D.C.: US Department of the Interior, National Park Service): 5.

[399] Lincoln Rhode Island Preservation Report, P-L-1: 15.

[400] Lincoln Rhode Island Preservation Report P-L-1: 60.

[401] The Smith family descended from William Whipple's oldest sister, Sarah Whipple Smith. William Junior's daughter, Sarah, and her husband Solomon Aldrich owned the Aldrich mansion. William Whipple's sister-in-law, Sarah Sprague Valentine, owned the Valentine mansion.

[402] According to a typewritten 15-page 1981account researched and written by Bertha Crompton, long-time church historian, the church, which began in 1831, was relocated from the Wilbur Road to the Great Road location in 1964. The one reference to a Whipple occurs on page 6, "February 1898 quote, 'Death has gathered into the heavenly garner our oldest member, Mrs. Eliza Whipple Thornton, who like ripened grain was ready for the reaper.' She was not one of the original 24 members but joined in 1833." Some of her listed descendants were Northup, Curtis, Speight, and Watt. Her mother, Silence Arnold, was the youngest daughter of Eleazer Whipple and Anna Brown...married first a Whipple than a Thornton.

[403] Sullins, 1.

[404] Smithfield Record of Deeds, 13:171. Central Falls City Hall, Central Falls, RI. In June of 1817, Jesse and Anna sold "part of a farm or tract of land with all buildings there on in Smithfield containing about 160 acres of land formerly belonging to John Ballou." This was the last transaction of land that appears on the records that Jesse Whipple sold in Smithfield.

[405] Joseph Whipple, Edwardsberg, Michigan, personal written correspondence, 5 November 1980. "My grandfather, Levi Whipple, was always talking about his grandfather Jesse and his move westward."

[406] William McLoughlin, *Rhode Island: A Bicentennial History* (New York: W.W. Norton, 1976) 118-120.

[407] Henry E. Whipple, 51.

[408] James N. Arnold, Vital Records of Rhode Island, 1636-1850, Vol. 3, Smithfield, Part 6 (Providence: Narragansett Historical Publishing Company, 1892) 13, 43, 120.

[409] She appeared for the last time in the Cumberland Rhode Island Federal Census of 1800 (as Anna Whipple, Widow) listed next to her sons, Eleazer and Joseph. U.S. Census 1800 for Rhode Island, Roll 45, Page 429. Not listed in the 1810 census.

[410] Anthony, Bertha, *Roger Williams of Providence* (Cranston, RI: B.W. Anthony and H Weeden, 1949) 190.

[411] Eleazer Whipple Entry, National Society of the Daughters of the American Revolution, Patriot Index, (Washington, D.C.: National Society of the Daughters of the American Revolution, 1966) 1:734.

[412] Virginia A. Fitch, Historic and Architectural Resources of Cumberland, Rhode Island. Rhode Island Historical Preservation Commission, 1990. 23.

[413] *Representative Men and Old Families of Rhode Island*, 3 vols (Chicago: J.H. Beers, 1908) 3:1677

[414] Charles M. Whipple, Jr., *A History of William Whipple of Dorchester, Massachusetts and Smithfield, Rhode Island: His Antecedents and Descendants* (Vancouver, B.C.: Trafford Publishing Company, 2006). The line of descent is: Captain John, William, William, Eleazer, Jesse, Jabez, William, Charles, Charles, Charles, Christian, Collyn, Joseph.

Chapter 7

Benjamin Whipple
The Whipples From Fruit Hill

Benjamin Whipple, the fifth son of Captain John, was christened at Dorchester, Massachusetts, 4 June 1654, and died at Providence, Rhode Island 11 March 1703/04. He married Ruth Mathewson, the daughter of James Mathewson and Hannah Field, 1 April 1686 at Dedham, Massachusetts, she dying after 1740. To this couple, six children were born:[415]

i. Benjamin, born 11 Nov 1688; died 27 Apr 1788; married (1) Sarah Bernon (2) Esther Millard

ii. Ruth, born 12 May 1691.

iii. Mary, born 3 Mar 1694.

iv. Josiah, born 29 Jul 1697; died before Mar 1704.

v. John, born 25 Feb 1699/1700; died 13 Nov 1751; married Bethiah Salsbury

vi. Abigail, born 12 Jun 1703; died 1787.

Descendants of Benjamin Whipple and Ruth Mathewson trace their ancestry back for well over a millennium. "The ancestor of the Field family, the first of whom there is any record, was Hubertus de la Feld, who went to England with William the Conqueror in the year 1066 from near Colmer in Alsace, on the German border of France. He was of the family of the Counts de la Feld, who trace back to the darkest period of the middle ages, about the 6th century."[416]

"I give unto my son Benjamin, a right of land in the late division which is already made out unto him." This sole succinct sentence in Captain John Whipple's Last Will and Testament of 1685 is all that is known of thirty-one year old Benjamin's relationship with his father. The farms inherited by Benjamin and his younger sibling, David, were the smallest of those left to the eight brothers. And at their respective deaths, they seem to have been able to bequeath a modest legacy to their children. Perhaps in the case of Benjamin, this paucity of worldly goods can be explained by his early death at the age of fifty; the shortest life span of any of the brothers. He waited rather late in life to get married, resulting in his children's under-age status at the time of his death—the second son, Josiah, being already deceased.

Benjamin Whipple in Early Town Records

Benjamin Whipple appeared in Providence Township records on over 30 occasions. The following is a chronological summary of some of these taken from *The Early Records of the Town of Providence, 21 Volumes,* (Providence: Snow & Farnham, 1892-1915). Individual entries are noted with the volume number and page.

Last Monday in May 1671
    Gave Engagement of allegiance to his majesty Charles the Second. The sixth name on the list was William Whipple, the last name on the list was Benjamin Whipple (III:200)

16 August 1676
    Benjamin Whipple along with his brothers Eliezer, Jonathan, Samuel, and others were listed as recipients in the sale of Indian captives. (XV:156)

15 August 1679
    Benjamin Whipple chosen to serve on a "coroner's inquest." (XV:196)

Last of August 1679
    Benjamin Whipple was a member of the coroner's jury that found that Elizabeth Pierce, daughter of Ephraim Pierce and Hannah his wife, aged about one year and a half, accidentally fell into a well and drowned. (VIII:58)

15 November 1679
    Benjamin Whipple, along with his brothers, Samuel, John, Eleazer, and their father voted against the town council's election of three men to represent Providence at a trial in Newport in a lawsuit between William Harris and partners and the town regarding land purchases. (XIII:60-61)

2 February 1681
    Benjamin Whipple's land mentioned in a neighbor's will. (XIV:43)

6 June 1681
    Benjamin Whipple chosen Town Sergeant. (VIII:97)

14 December 1681
    Town Council voted the return of land laid out to Benjamin Whipple in the Right of his father be recorded, according to the return made by Capt: William Hopkins, Surveyor. (VIII:102)

April 1683
    Benjamin Whipple of this Towne: Brought to me the head of a Woolfe that he killed. John Whipple Clerk (IV:56)

1 April 1686
    "Upon the first day of April Anno: 1686: Benjamin Whipple and Ruth Mathuson (after lawful public) were both joined together in marriage by Richard Arnold Assistant." Also the births of their children are listed. (V:270-71)

23 August 1697
    Benjamin Whipple chosen to serve as a "Pettey Juryman." (XI:35)

6 March 1692/93

Deed of Sale between John Whipple and Benjamin Whipple. John sold to Benjamin, for a valuable sum of silver money, a forty-foot square Warehouse lot that had been granted to him by the town of Providence. It was situated on the side and brow of the bank against the salt water, on the south side of the highway, or the place that is a cart way from the waterside into the street, being against the house lots that belong to John Throckmorton, formerly of Providence. (IV:163-65).

12 August 1703

Benjamin Whipple's property mentioned in connection with a road laid out by the colony. (V:143)

12 April 1704

Last Will and Testament of Benjamin Whipple was examined and approved by the town council. Inventory of Benjamin Whipple, who died 11 March 1703/04 was examined by the council and approved. Ruth Whipple, widow of Benjamin Whipple, posted a bond as the Executrix of his will. The council gave her a Letter of Administration to execute the will. (X:76-7)

19 May 1707

"It is granted unto: Jonathan Whipple (and two others) that they may have use of a percell of land by the salt water side in the Towne for the loading of Boates…southward from the house belonging to ye heirs of ye deceased Benjamin Whipple…" (XI:116)

It may be assumed that Benjamin earned his livelihood as a farmer. It is true that he bought a small ocean front warehouse lot from his eldest brother John. But at his death, a decade later, this land and dwelling house, "being by the salt water side in the towne of Providence," bequeathed to his five year old son John, was not yet shown to have been developed into a wharf for commercial purposes. His inherited land was at "Fruit Hill," about four miles northwest of his father's property in what is now the town of North Providence.

The Benjamin Whipple Homestead

"The Eighteenth-century settlement was sparse with most of what is North Providence today divided into five farms held by Richard Pray, John Smith, Epenetus Olney, John (Benjamin) Whipple and Thomas Angell…. Villages, as such, did not come into being until the early nineteenth century. There were only two eighteenth-century settlements in present-day North Providence: one, a small cluster of farmsteads at Fruit Hill; the other, a mill site with a few residences located at Centerdale on the Woonasquatucket River. A dam had been built there as early as 1702 and several sawmills and gristmills were constructed nearby…. Fruit Hill was settled in the eighteenth-century by the Olney Family [Benjamin's sister Mary's family]. It was a rural community containing both a church and a school, when residential suburban development began after the Civil War. The vicinity is named for the many fruit trees, especially cherry trees that abound. The construction, in 1891, of the Fruit Hill Reservoir…and the area's proximity to Providence made it a popular residential neighborhood by the turn of the century, quite fashionable with successful businessmen…The area has maintained its quiet, well kept residential quality with a good mix of 18th-century and mid-19th century dwellings."[417]

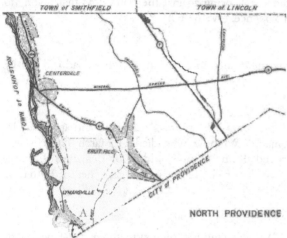

Benjamin Whipple Property

It is noteworthy that the four families named above were related to Benjamin Whipple. The Prays married into the family of Job Whipple, the son of Eleazer. John Smith III was the son of Sarah Whipple Smith, and Epenetus Olney Junior was the son of Mary Whipple Olney, Benjamin's sisters. Two of Benjamin's brothers, Eleazer and Jonathan, married sisters of Thomas Angell Junior. (Consult individual chapters for further details on these relationships).

One can imagine the immensity of any Sunday dinner the five siblings, their in-laws, and North Providence descendants may have shared in the early 1700s. Add to this that Benjamin's brother, Jonathan, lived about one mile east of him on the West River.

"The area known as Lymansville was first settled by Benjamin Whipple, who built a house c1684 on what is now Metcalf street. The farm that the Whipple family owned extended from the Woonasquatucket River to the site of the St. James Episcopal Church on Fruit Hill Avenue. [A distance of about 1½ miles northeast from his house]. On November 9 1807, Daniel Lyman of Newport purchased an 80 acre farm off Fruit Hill Avenue from William F. Megee, who had purchased the property from Richard Whipple, great grandson of Benjamin Whipple."[418] The house on Metcalf Street, no longer standing, (letter A on the map above) was located just west of Fruit Hill Avenue near its intersection with the Providence County line, about one block east of the river. Richard[5]Whipple (Daniel[4], Benjamin[3], Benjamin[2], John[1]) sold what was left of the house and property, 80 acres or so, which had been kept by Benjamin Senior until his death in 1788, and which Richard's father had inherited at that time. His father, Daniel, died four years later. Richard sold the farm soon after and moved to Massachusetts.

Last Will and Testament

I Benjamin Whipple of the Towne of Providence in the Coloney of Rhode Jsland & Providence Plantations in the Narraganset Bay in New England; being sick & weake of Body, but of Sound & perfect Memory, doe make this my last will & testament; making Null & Revokeing all & every other Will at any time heretofore by me made either by word or writeing, & this Will only stand in force. Jmprimis. I do Comit my spirit unto God who gave it, & My body unto the Earth, to be Decently buried, by my Executrix herein-after named:

Jtem. I doe Give & Devise all my lands at my home dwelling, (to say) my whole ffarme unto my two sons (namely) Benjamin Whipple & John Whipple, to be Equally devided betweene them, to be unto them their Heirs & Assignes for ever.

Jtem I doe Give & Devise unto My son John Whipple my dwelling house & land standing & being by the salt water side in said Towne of Providence, to be unto him his Heirs and Assignes for ever.

Jtem. I doe Give & bequeath unto my loveing Wife Ruth Whipple, all & whole My Moveable estate, Goods & Cattell out of which sd Estate my said wife shall deliver & pay unto my aforesd two sons (to wit) Benjamin & John, Each of them three milch cowes, to be delivered unto them, as each one of them attaine to the age of Twenty & one yeares, & at that time: The which sd Cowes I doe Give & bequeath to Each of them.

Jtem I do Give & bequeath unto My three daughters (namely) Ruth Whipple, Mary Whipple, & Abigail Whipple, Each of them three Tenn Pounds, and by their said mother, my said wife to be paid unto Each of them at the day of Each of their marriage, or within one month after, or at the age of Twenty & one yeares; the which shall first be; And that all the Remainder of my sd Moveable Estate, after or besides the aforsd Legasyes shall whole be at the dispose of my said wife for her owne.

Jtem. I doe order & dispose all my aforesd Children to my said wife, unto her Tuission, care, Custody, bringing up & Provideing for, until their marriage; or the time of the age of Twenty one yeares, the which first Cometh; and that all my said Children shall be in subject unto their Mother my said wife;

Jtem I doe Give unto my sd wife the whole Proffitts & management of all my sd lands & houseing until my sd sones attaine unto ye age of Twenty & one yeares; and when ye Eldest of my sd Sones (to wit) Benjamin doth attaine to the age of twenty & one yeares, then shall the sd land be devided unto Each of My sd sones his part; yet not withstanding I doe give unto my sd wife the one third part of all the proffitts of my sd lands duireing the Time of her widowhood: the which shall be one halfe of it out of one of my sons part, & the other halft out of the other of my sones part; but if my said Wife doe againe, Marrie, then at her Marriage, then her sd third part of the Proffitts of sd lands, as to her shall wholly Tirminate & Cease, & be unto my sd two sons.

Jtem I doe give unto my son Benjamin Whipple my dwelling house in which I doe now dwell to be unto him his Heirs & Assignes for ever; And at the Time of his attaineing to the age of Twenty & one yeares, he shall & may Enter & possess the Westerne Part of said house; but all the Easterne part of the said house shall be unto my said wife for her vse dueiring of her Widdowhood; but when shee doth marrey, or depart this life, whichever; then my said son shall Enter & possess that End of said house also.

Jtem I doe also give & bequeath my Barne & all my out houseing unto my sd son Benjamin whipple, his heirs & Assignes for Ever, to enter Possession & Take it into his hands & improvement at Twenty & one yeares.

Jtem. But in Case it shall so fall with my wife that shee fall to Poverty & be not Capable to maintaine herselfe with what I have left her, then shall my sd two sons take care of her, & supply her wants with suteable maintenance; And that the aforesaid Teen Pounds to be paid unto Each of my three Daughters, is to be paid unto Each of them Tenn Pounds in money, or in other good pay which may be Equall with money.

Jtem I doe Constitute & appoint my said loveing Wife Ruth Whipple to be my sole Executrix, who shall receive all my debts to me from any Person due, & to pay all debts from me due to any Person, and to see my body decently buried, & truly to Execute and performe this my last will and testament according to the true meaneing & intent thereof; Jn witness thereof I doe hereunto set my hand & seale the Ninth day of March Annoq Domini, one Thousand, seven hundred and three; 1703/04. Benjamin, his mark.

The Flaw in Captain John Whipple's Will

Approximately four years subsequent to Benjamin's death, the widow Whipple was brought to court. "You are hereby required in her majesties name Anne Queen of Great Britain to arrest the Body of Ruth Whipple Widow & relickt of Benjamin Whipple [?] ...to answer the complaint of John Whipple of sd providence in the Colony aforesaid eldest son and heir of John Whipple of sd providence...for wrongfully withholding from the plaintiff the possession of certain tract of parcel of land laying within the township of sd Providence...being upland arable land meadow and orchard by estimation twelve acres with the mansion house fences and edefies...plainly set forth damage four hundred

pounds currant money of New England.[419] Due to an apparent flaw in Captain John's will, Benjamin's nephew, John Whipple III, claimed that when Captain John willed his property to Benjamin in 1682 he gave it to him only, not to his heirs. Therefore, he, the son of John Junior, owned the land. On those grounds, he accused Ruth of wrongfully withholding the property that belonged to him. In this same suit, John III sought to obtain ownership of the properties of three other uncles. This forced them to settle with him for an undisclosed amount of money.[420] See the chapter on John Junior for further details.

Benjamin Whipple was also indicted for a breach of law, on 28 March 1682. "Newport Court Book A – General Court of Trials held in his Majesty's name at Newport: Benjamin

294 N. Main

Whipple of Providence was indicted by the general solicitor for breach of law and misbehavior. He was mandated to appear in Court. He 'put his exceptions' to the bill." The court considered the matter and sided with the defendant. [421]

John Whipple, Cordwainer

The youngest son of Benjamin Senior was John, called a cordwainer. He lived to be approximately the same age as his father. "March 15, 1736, John Smith sold the farm (in Centerdale) to John Whipple [his cousin], who probably bought it on speculation, for he soon afterwards, on January 6th, 1737, sold the same to Nathaniel Day...."[422] John apparently used this profit, and the money he received from the sale of the house and property seen above at 294 North Main Street near the waterfront,[423] which was willed to him by his father,[424] to purchase the former property of his uncle Samuel Whipple. This house was constructed by Benjamin Whipple in the 1690s and subsequently enlarged by John. The house and a one-acre island [called Whipple Island] located about one-half block to the west in the salt-water cove are shown on maps of the time.[425] "The old 'Samuel Whipple' or 'Abbott' house, which first after Samuel Whipple's death passed into the hands of his son-in-law, Robert Currie, was bought by Job Whipple and John Whipple Junior [actually John III] father and son, on 3d of June, 1737. Subsequently by a division of the estate, Job Whipple became the sole owner of the house and contiguous lands, which he sold to John Whipple [the cordwainer], who occupied it till his death in 1751. Levi Whipple and Thomas Abbot were the successive owners."[426]

John married Bethiah Salsbury, a distant Whipple cousin, 17 June 1722 at Providence.[427] To this couple six children were born:[428]

i. Josiah, born 8 May 1723
ii. Ezekiel, born 14 November 1725
iii. Abigail, born 19 February 1727/28
iv. Amy, born 15 April 1731
v. Jabez, born 15 August 1734; died 4 December 1833
vi. Ruth, born 15 December 1740; died abt 1827

Their youngest son, Jabez, was a sea captain, who, like his uncle Benjamin Junior, lived to be 99 years old. He was married five times. Of his five children, two were sons Jabez and Arnold. Jabez died at age 17 on the Isle of Martinique, without issue. Arnold[5] (Jabez[4], John[3], Benjamin[2], John[1]) married Phebe Dexter[6] (Phebe[5], Benjamin[4], William[3], William[2], John[1]) 12 September 1812. "Phebe Whipple, who died in 1879, was the great granddaughter of William Whipple Junior, and the granddaughter of Benjamin his son. Her grandmother, Jerusha Peck Whipple, died 21 May 1766 (probably giving birth to her mother Phebe Whipple Dexter, daughter of Jerusha and Benjamin, who was born 20 May 1766). [Phebe had the above ancestor's gravestones moved to the Moshassuck cemetery.] The first date on the common monument at Moshassuck Cemetery is 1766. Also, her husband, Arnold Whipple, son of Jabez, was the grandson of John Whipple and Bethiah Salsbury. The third name on the monument is Salsbury."[429] This monument's testimony is illustrative of the typical later intermarriage patterns of descendants of Captain John's children, in this case sons four and five, William and Benjamin. A photograph of this monument is seen on page 154.

Benjamin Whipple Junior, Centenarian

Benjamin Whipple Junior was born at Providence, Rhode Island, 11 November 1688, and died in his 100th year 27 April 1788, still residing on the last 80 acres remaining of the original 300 located in North Providence, where he had been employed as a currier, farmer, tanner and shoemaker. He and his wives were buried next to their house in their garden burial lot. "At the age of 75, he accidentally spilled shoemaker's wax, which burned his foot so severely that his entire leg had to be amputated. After that, he was said to have grown two new teeth."[430]

Children by his First Wife, Sarah Bernon

  i. *Andrew, born 3 Feb 1724*
 ii. *Benjamin, born 5 Jan 1725/26; died Oct 1803; married (1) Ann Brown (2) Deborah Damon*
iii. *Content, born 30 Aug 1727; died 11 Oct 1811; married Ezekiel Olney*
 iv. *Daniel, Born 7 Sep 1728; died 6 Jul 1792; married Abigail Comen*
  v. *Ephraim, born 7 Nov 1729; died 1800; married Mary Hawkins*
 vi. *Benedict*
vii. *Esther, born 12 Mar 1731*
viii. *Mary, born 28 May 1732*

Children by his Second Wife, Esther Millard

  i. *Beneger, born 17 Jun 1734; died 1812*
 ii. *Stephen, born 19 Jul 36; died 28 Feb 1813; married Zilpha Angell*
iii. *Joseph, born 1 Jan 1737; married Katherine Greene*
 iv. *Benedict, born 13 Oct 1739; died 16 Jun 1819; married Eliza Mathewson*
  v. *Jesse, born 16 Sep 1744; died 10 Feb 1823; married Freelove Olney*
 vi. *Freelove Whipple; born 8 June 1750*
vii. *John, born 9 Dec 1751; died 11 May 1824; married Lydia Irons*
viii. *Abigail, born 12 Oct 1754*

Benjamin was married first in 1722 to Sarah Bernon, daughter of Gabriel Bernon and Esther Elroy, wealthy and erudite French Huguenots, who had fled to the colony of Massachusetts on revocation of the Edict of Nantes.[431] Bernon and his family moved from the comparatively cultured environment of Boston to Rhode Island where, "By contrast the cultural strivings were weak. Though the French immigrant, Gabriel Bernon, praised the intellect of his new neighbors in the 1720s, and a few people of cultivation were on the scene in subsequent decades, they amounted to a small coterie. A few physicians with diverse interests, a lawyer or two...."[432]

Bernon's influence is credited with raising the initial sums of money to build the first Anglican Church in Providence, to which the major contributor was Benjamin Junior's uncle, Colonel Joseph Whipple. Perhaps it was the Joseph Whipple family who introduced Benjamin to his first wife. "Tradition refers to Gabriel Bernon, a French Huguenot, who came to this country at the revocation of the Edict of Nantz, as one of the earliest members of the Church of England, in this town. It is supposed that it was through his influence that the missionary at Newport occasionally visited and preached at Providence, and that it was at his house that the meetings were holden. This house occupied the site of the brick house, No. 149 on North Main Street, and a part of it is still standing in the rear of that house."[433]

Records of North Providence town meetings show that Benjamin Junior, on 24 October 1768, paid for keeping Hannah Field, and paid for making a coffin for Elizabeth Pain. On 5 June 1769, he was again paid for keeping Hanna Field. "3 June 1776 Benjamin Whipple of North Providence, yeoman, will take the indenture of Freelove Martin, a poor child, daughter of Rachel Shaw until she becomes 18." On 28 August 1787, Benjamin Whipple was paid for supporting Abigail Fletcher in her last sickness and for digging the grave.[434]

Benjamin Junior and his two wives had a total of 16 children, eight by each wife. Eleven of the children were sons, of whom Andrew and Benedict did not live to adulthood. Five sons (Beneger, Stephen, Joseph, Jesse, and Benedict II) left North Providence; the remaining (Benjamin III, Daniel, Ephraim, and John) lived and died on property inherited from their father. Benjamin Junior's nine sons appear to have earned their livelihoods as farmers. Portions of his 300-acre farm were parceled off over a period of several years as his sons came of age. Benjamin III settled on a part of the homestead farm about a half-mile south from his father's house. Of his four sons, Ethan and James moved to Vermont and Charles to New York; only Cyrus lived and died in North Providence. Benjamin Junior's second son, Daniel, was a farmer and lived at Fruit Hill. As previously noted, he inherited the remains of his father's house and adjacent 80-acre property, which his son Richard later sold and moved to Massachusetts. His other sons, Daniel Junior and Ezekiel, lived and died in North Providence. Ephraim, the third son of Benjamin Junior, was a farmer, and settled on a part of the homestead farm near Fruit Hill. He was a man noted for his piety and sound judgment. He was a leading member of the church. Ephraim's son, Captain Emor, and at least six subsequent generations, lived and died on their North Providence property. [435]Benjamin's youngest son, John, like his father, became a farmer, tanner, and currier. He owned a farm near

Whipple-Angell-Bennett House

Fruit Hill, where his father first settled. He was a deacon in the Baptist church at Fruit Hill for many years. John's sons, Benjamin and Stephen, lived and died in North Providence.

Of the sons of Benjamin Junior who left North Providence, Beneger settled on a farm in the town of Gloucester, Rhode Island, then moved to Cooperstown, New York. His four sons lived and died in that vicinity. Benjamin Junior's seventh son, Benedict, settled on a farm in the town of Scituate, Rhode Island. He was a farmer and blacksmith, and served during the Revolutionary War. Joseph was a farmer, and settled in the town of Plainfield, Connecticut. Most of his children were born in Kent County, Rhode Island. At least two of his sons moved to New York, residing in the same county as his brother, Beneger. Descendants are in Wisconsin and Illinois. Jesse, Benjamin Junior's eighth son, was a farmer, and moved to Killingsly, Connecticut. His immediate descendants lived in Newport, New York. Stephen lived about twenty years at Fruit Hill, and then removed to Massachusetts, settling in the town of Cheshire. At least four of his children moved to Rutland and Shaftsbury, Vermont. Two others moved to the same county as Stephen's brother Beneger. At least one child moved to Illinois, and one to Canada.[436]

The house that Stephen Whipple built at 157 Olney Street before moving to Massachusetts is listed on the National Register of Historic Places. "Facing south-southwest on a plateau near the top of Fruit Hill, the Whipple-Angell-Bennett House is a rectilinear z-plan dwelling with three distinct sections....The Whipple-Angell-Bennett Hous is significant to the history of architecture because of its ability to document vernacular architecture of the third quarter of the eighteenth century...as its setting changed from open farmland to suburban residential neighborhood.

"History of the property's ownership helps to illuminate the evolution of the house. On 30 July 1766, Stephen Whipple (1735-?), a shoemaker, purchased approximately fifty-five acres of the family farm at Fruit Hill from his father Benjamin (1688-1788), and soon began construction of his 'Home Stead Farm.' (Pawtucket Land Evidence Records, Book 1, Page 45, and Book 2, Page 6). In 1776 he moved to Chester, Massachusetts, and sold the property to his first cousin Jabez Whipple (1734-1833). William Angell bought the property in 1822, and his son William H. Angell...sold the property in 1872, and the property changed hands five times in the late nineteenth and early twentieth centuries until purchased by the Reverend Edmund C. Bennett in March 1921. By 1921, the property was reduced to approximately 7500 square feet, its current size. It remains in Bennett ownership until 1995. The more intact of only two surviving gambrel-roof farmhouses in the Town of North Providence, the Whipple-Angell-Bennett House is typical of modest rural Rhode Island farmhouses of the mid-eighteenth century. The story-and-a-half, gambrel roof, center-chimney form commonly occurred across the state throughout the eighteenth century, and a number of examples are listed in the National Register. The property nominated includes all of North Providence Tax Assessor's Plat 8 Lots 451 and 698. These two parcels are all that remains of the land historically associated with this property."[437]

"By the turn of the nineteenth century, the characteristic two-and-a-half, five-bay gable-roofed, center-chimney farmhouse was the most common form of dwelling---as can best be seen in the Stephen Whipple House at 430 Fruit Hill Avenue, built c. 1778."370 Fruit Hill Avenue. Whipple-Hawkins Homestead (c1778). Originally a two-and-one-half story Federal style dwelling with a gable roof and center chimney; the house has been enlarged by the addition of several wings and the entrance is now surmounted by a Victorian door hood, flanked by oriel windows. 430 Fruit Hill Avenue. Stephen Whipple House (c 1778). A two-and-one-half story dwelling with a gable roof, a large center chimney, and a central doorway with side lights. Stephen Whipple owned this house and the house at 370 Fruit Hill Avenue in 1835. This structure was sold to Whipple's son-in-law Francis Mann, in 1842. It is now part of St. Mary's Home for Children."[438]

As seen above, over one-half of Benjamin Whipple Junior's nine sons and 40 grandsons moved to other colonies/states. The rest lived and died in Rhode Island, and made lasting contributions to Rhode Island. Walter[8] Whipple (Weston[7], William[6], Daniel[5], Daniel[4], Benjamin[3], Benjamin[2], John[1]), a typical example of later descendants of the four brothers who stayed in North Providence, a wholesale commission merchant, was one of the few young men who made fortunes for themselves in early life. Considering his many and varied adversities in starting out, his success was phenomenal. He was the son of Weston and Mary (Watson) Whipple. He was brought up on the old homestead place in North Providence, where he remained, assisting his father on the farm and attending the district school until 14 years of age. When 17 years of age, he sought and obtained employment in a grocery store owned by Mr. H.S. Sharpe (now bookkeeper for Mr. Whipple), but soon afterward became a member of the firm of Brown, Whipple & Company, retail grocers.

On 8 April 1878, Mr. Whipple married Mary E. (daughter of Palmer) Tanner, of Providence, and located in that city. In the meanwhile, having somewhat recovered from his financial problems, he went on the road with a horse and wagon, trading in butter, eggs and poultry. This was the beginning of what became a mammoth industry. In 1882, when 24 years of age, he found himself in a store of his own at 104 Canal street. In 1884, he was obliged, for the want of sufficient room to move to larger quarters. In 1888, he established a large packinghouse in Oskaloosa, Iowa, operated under the style of Whipple & Company. In the year 1890, a business of $400,000 was done.

In 1885, Mr. Whipple moved back to North Providence and located on Fruit Hill, where he lived for the rest of his life. His was a magnificent property, which he improved at great expense, making of it an elegant residence. In 1889, Mr. Whipple was elected as a representative of his town to the general assembly of Rhode Island and re-elected several times afterward. He likewise served as a senator in the state legislature. He had three children: Mabel, Gertrude, and Florence. He died in 1928 and was buried in the Swan Point Cemetery at Providence.[439]   Other descendants of Benjamin Junior to serve in elected office in North Providence were Ezekiel, Olney, Stephen, and Emor.[440]

End Notes

[415] *Records of the First Church at Dorchester in New England 1636-1734* (Boston: George H. Ellis, 1891) 267 & 182. John O. Austin, *Genealogical Dictionary of Rhode Island* (Albany, NY: 1887; reprint edition, Baltimore: Genealogical Publishing Company, 1978) 222. James N. Arnold, *Vital Records of Rhode Island, 1636-1850* (Providence: Narragansett Historical Publishing Company, 1892). *ERP*, V:270-01. Henry E. Whipple, *A Brief Genealogy of the Whipple Families who Settled in Rhode Island* (Providence: A Crawford Greene, 1873). Vital statistics of the children and grandchildren of Captain John and Sarah Whipple are taken from the above and numerous publications that quote from them. To see more recent corrections and additions see, www.whipple.org, Weldon Whipple, Webmaster.

[416] Ruth Whipple Kapphahn , *Genealogy of Whipple, Paddock, Bull Families in America*, 1620-1970 (Columbus, Ohio, UMI, 1992) 5

[417] Preliminary Survey Report, Town of North Providence, Rhode Island Historical Preservation Commission, April 1978. 3-5.

[418] Thomas E. and Barbara Greene, *Images of America, North Providence* (Hanover NH: Arcadia Publishing, 1996) 83.

[419] Warrant for the Arrest of Ruth Whipple, 16 July 1708, Rhode Island Historical Society Manuscript, 1:109.

[420] *ERP*, XX:274-75.

[421] Jane Fletcher Fiske, transcriptionist, *Rhode Island General Court of Trials 1671-1704* (Boxford, Mass: Privately Published, 1998) 112

[422] Frank C. Angell, *Annals of Centerdale, In the Town of North Providence*, 1636-1909 (Central Falls, RI: E.L. Freeman Company, 1909) 12

[423] Providence Deed Book, 10:170. " John Whipple cordwainer, son of Benjamin, sells for 420L current money truly paid by William Antrim, distiller…a lot of land on the west side of the Town Street a little Southward of the Baptist Meeting house. Bounded on a highway that is between that and the said Baptist Meeting House; south by Steven Dexter, and east with the said Town Street holding by breadth of the 40' to the channel of said Providence River, together with all of the housing, buildings and improvements." Antrim subsequently sold the property in1765. Deed Book 18:125. Obviously, by the time the photograph was taken the house had undergone many changes. Mary A. Gowdey and Antoinete Dowling, compilers, records of #294 North Main Street, Providence Preservation House Histories, vol. 9, Providence Preservation Society, 21 Meeting Street, Providence, RI, 02822

[424] *ERP*, VI: 240-43. Early Records of the Town of Providence, Deed book A:240. I do Give and Devise unto my son John my Dwelling house and land standing by the salt Water side in said town of Providence…"

[425] Henry R. Chace, *Owners and Occpants of the Lots, Houses, and Shops in the Town Of Providence, Rhode Island in 1798* (Providence: 1914) plate 10.

[426] James P. Root, *A Record of the Descendants of John Steere Who Settled in Providence, Rhode Island About the Year 1600* (Cambridge: Riverside Press, 1890) 187.

[427] "Unfortunately, there are no minutes or records of the first Baptist Church prior to 1755. The first Whipple that appears on the membership rolls is Bethiah Whipple (wife of John) in 1764…" Email to the author from J. Stanly Lemons, historian of the 1st Baptist Church, Providence, 25 May 2004.

[428] James N. Arnold, *Vital Records of Rhode Island, 1636-1850*, vol. 2, part 1 (Providence: Narragansett Historical Publishing Company, 1892) 198. Henry E. Whipple, 15-16

[429] On line at <http://www.whipple.org/charles/louquisset/index html> See, Henry E. Whipple, 16-17 for the ancestry of Arnold. Arnold and Phebe were childless.

[430] Kapphahn, 2

[431] *Representative Men and Old Families of Rhode Island* (Chicago: J.H. Beers 1908) 3:2162

[432] Sydney V. James, *Colonial Rhode Island, A History* (New York: Charles Scribner's Sons, 1976) 263.

[433] William R. Staples, *Annals of The Town of Providence* (Providence: Knowles and Vose, 1843) 445

[434] Alden G. Beaman and Nellie Beaman, Rhode Island Genealogical Register, 20 Vols. (Princeton, Massachsetts) 6:170, and on-line at <http:www.genalogy.com>. Some of these entries could refer to Benjamin III, particularly the last.

[435] Representative Men, 3:2153-54.

[436] Description of Benjamin Junior's sons extracted from Henry E. Whipple, 17-34, and Kapphahn, 3. See *Representative Men* for additional biographies, 3:2162-3 and 2153-4, of Benjamin Junior's sons Ephraim and Daniel's later descendants.

[437] William McKenzie Woodward, Architectural Historian, RI Historical Preservation and Heritage Commission, National Register of Historic Places, Registration Form, April 1995. Section 7 & 8

[438] Preliminary Survey Report, Town of North Providence, RI Historical Preservation Commission, April 1978, pgs. 25-26. The authors have been unsuccessful in determining a relationship between these two houses and the property at 157 Olney Street.

[439] Richard M. Bayles, ed., *History of Providence County* 2 vols. (New York: W.W. Preston, 1891), 2:197-98. Liberally summarized.

[440] Bayles, 1:182-84

Chapter 8

Ensign David Whipple
The Whipples from Study Hill

Ensign David Whipple, sixth son of Captain John Whipple, was christened 28 September 1656, at Dorchester, Massachusetts, and died 18 December 1710 at Rehoboth, Massachusetts. He married first Sarah Hearnden Gregory 15 May 1675, at Hingham, Plymouth Colony. She died 2 April 1677. Their child was David Junior, born before 30 October 1674. David Junior was living in New London, Connecticut at the time of his first child's birth in 1692 or 1702; as such, he seems to have been the first of several Captain John Whipple grandsons to move to that colony.[441] David Junior had at least five children: Jonathan, David, Silas, Anthony, and Rebecka.

Court Trial of David Whipple and Sarah Gregory

David became the father of this first child at about the age of 18, while the mother was married to another man. The record of the resulting trial shows that both were punished under strict colonial law. They endured the prescribed alternate punishment of paying a hefty fine rather than being whipped. A divorce was granted to her, allowing them to wed when the child was about nine months old.

"The jury found David Whipple guilty of having a child by Sarah Gregory. The Court sentenced David Whipple to be whipped on October 30 with fifteen stripes, or to pay a fine of forty shillings to the General Treasurer and pay officer's fees. Upon indictment by the General Attorney against Sarah Gregory for fornication committed with David Whipple of Providence, she being in court called and being asked whether or not she was guilty, she owned that she had a child by David Whipple, who she said was her husband, and referred herself to the Court's mercy.

"The Court sentenced Sarah Gregory, referring herself to the bench concerning her indictment, knowing that her husband was a filthy man before he went away from her and strayed from her, not intending to be a husband, he broke that bond. However, the Court did not permit that it was lawful for her to be married, or to live as married, or to commit whoredom with any man, and therefore her sentence for having a child with another man, as for fornication, was to be whipped with fifteen stripes or to pay forty shillings to the Treasurer. If her husband did not come home in twelve months time, she may have liberty to marry as soon as the law permits, but she was not prevented from marrying sooner if lawful cause appears. She also was to pay officer's fees.

"David Whipple and Sarah, the daughter of Benjamin Hearnden, both of Providence, were sentenced to pay four pounds to the General Treasurer for not attending to the Court's order, and if they marry before the Court it will be a lawful marriage. They were married by Court the 15th of May 1675."[442]

David and his new wife apparently paid their fines with borrowed money. In November of 1686, John Sanford wrote to John Whipple Junior, David's brother and the Providence town clerk, concerning various overdue accounts. He charged that David's debt was 12 years over due: "To Ensign John Whipple at Providence and respected friend kind salutations promised your former kindness and realety, hath so much incouraged me that I am hereby inboldened to give you further trouble so that concerning those particulars relating to myself when I was last with you.... He (David) conscientiously knows that he promised me true and faithful payment both for himself and his wife, the due fees on both to me being about four and thirty shillings, was due in October 1674 twelve years past, and I hope my patience and long forbearance thereof will not encourage him not to be willing to pay me at all. And although my due be as aforesaid, yet for my promise safe to you I will now be content to take thirty shillings provided it may be forthwith sent to me in money or good currant pay equivalent for his asserting he paid my due to Sergeant Rogers I conceive there can be no truth therein for I am satisfied in my own mind I never gave him order to so do, neither did I give him an account of what was my due, and therefore admire how he should demand and receive mine, And I am certain he never gave me account thereof...Postscript. Please remember that the winter is come and we must expect frost and snow, pray let me hear from you by the time."[443] The resolution of this case and David's defense is not known.

"In contrast to the historical stereotype, at least of the Puritans, Smith claims in her women's history that 'premarital love making was a generally accepted practice. If she is correct, it would help explain the obvious 'vitality, virility and fertility' of both the men and women founders of Rhode Island, despite all the demanding circumstances of the day. Smith asserts that although fornication 'outside of a precontract might be punishable if discovered, for the most part it was accepted as a practical utility.' Pre contracts of marriage were regarded as legitimizing the 'folk custom of bundling' and a 'permissive attitude,' in general, was accorded 'sexual irregularities, provided they did not imperil good order in the community.' Thus, for a couple destined to get married to encounter each other in a direct physical way seems to have resulted in marriages in which the sensual aspect was of considerable if not primary importance. "In consequence, there was about Puritan society, and perhaps especially in Rhode Island, directness, a practicality, a lack of hypocrisy and subterfuge, an absence of prudery in matters that affected sexual relations and the functions of the body that is unique, certainly, in American history. Much could be tolerated as long as the social nature of marriage was generally acknowledged." [444]

A Massachusetts Resident

The second wife of David, whom he married 11 November 1677, was Hannah, daughter of John and Margaret Tower of Hingham, Plymouth Colony. She was born 17 July 1652, and died in 1722. To this couple seven children were born:[445]

i. Israel, born 16 Aug 1678; died 13 Jun 1720; married Mary Wilmarth
ii. Deborah, born 12 Sept 1681; died 1755; married Benjamin Tower.
iii. Jeremiah, born 26 Jun 1683; died 14 May 1721; married Deborah Bucklin
iv. William, born 27 May 1685; died 12 Nov 1746; married Mary (_)
v. Sarah, born 18 Nov 1687; died 27 Sep 1727; married Joseph Razee.
vi. Hannah, born 9 Jan 1690/91.[446]
vii. Abigail, born 20 Oct 1692.

In the Captain John Whipple Last Will & Testament of 1685, David's legacy is announced in one terse sentence: "I give unto my son David, a right of land in the late division which is already made out to him." This refers to the 4 March 1683 "deede signed by John Whipple Senr & Sealed. Be it knowne unto all people by these presents That I John Whipple, Senr of ye Towne of Providence in ye Colleney of Rhode Island & Providence plantations in New England for divers good causes & considerations me moveing: and namely for the Settling of my son David Whipple, for his Comfortable livelihood have given…sixty acrs of land (be it more or less) and also a percell of Boggy or Tussickey Meaddow in Esteemation five acrs (more or lesse).. .."[447] This property was located approximately two miles south of the farms of his brothers Eleazer and William next to the Moshassuck River.

David and Hannah, and their growing family, lived uneventfully on this farm for the next nine years, at which time they bought the property of John Blackstone, the son

Blackstone Monument

of William Blackstone, a farm approximately two miles east and along the Blackstone River in the township of Rehoboth. By virtue of moving to Massachusetts Colony, David became the only child of Captain John to leave Rhode Island. Because of its significance to historians in general, this deed is presented here in its entirety.

"To all Christian people before whome this deede shall come, I John Blaxton of Rehoboth in the County of Bristoll formerly in the Colony of New plimouth; but now of Massachusetts in New England. (Shoemaker) sends greeting. Know ye that the said John Blaxton for a valuable consideration of currant pay of this country in hand already will & truly paid unto him by David Whipple (husbandman) inhabitant of the town of Providence in the Narragansett Bay in New England:

"The receipt whereof to the said John Blaxton does owne & adlknowledge & …to be fully satisfied contented & paid Hath given, granted, Bargained, sold, enforced, assigned, and confirmed: And by these presents for him and his heirs, Executors, Administrators…fully and Absolutely Give, grant, Bargain, Sell, and Assign and Confirm unto David Whipple to Him and his heirs, Executors, Administrators & Assigns for ever, his house & lands (that is to say) his mansion house & misusage on the East side of the River called Pantucket River, and lying and being within the provinces of Rehoboth aforesaid. The misusage or parcel of land being by information one hundred and fifty acres (more or less) being layd out & bounded & is situated on the playne called the right playne, & the land adjacent; and is bounded to the northward to the land of Isaack Allin, to the southward the land of John Harreson; to the westward Pantuck River; to the Eastward, part of it to the land

185

of John Stevenson, and part of it to the highway, and part of it the undivided land, There running a countrey highway through it to Pantucket River. In recompense, or satisfaction for which highway allowed and layd out; two acres adjoining to the aforementioned land, being bounded by the highway Eastwardly and the aforementioned land westwardly, and southwardly by a small run of water; the which said two acres of land on the northwardly side of the Country highway next the house. The other part of the said twenty acres of land is bounded round, by the undivided land. The said hundred and fifty arcres of land is upland, swamps and meadow ground, With all and singular the privileges to the said house and hundred and fifty acres of land belonging. And all the estates, right, title, interest, use, property, possession, clayme and demand whatsoever of him the said John Blaxton in or to the same or any part of To Have and To Hold the said mansion house and said hundred and fifty acres of land as aforesaid unto the said David Whipple his heirs, executors, administrators and assignes forever."[448]

William Blackstone was the first Englishman to settle permanently in what is now the township of Cumberland, Rhode Island. He was an Anglican clergyman from Boston who raised fruit trees, farmed, and preached to the Indians. At one time, he was

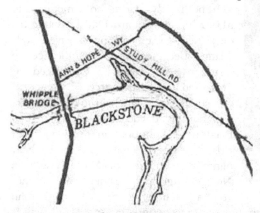

Study Hill Area

reputed to have held the largest library [about 250 books] in New England. Blackstone was ostensibly quite misanthropic. Asked why he had moved to the wilderness, he retorted, "I left England to get from under the power of the Lord Bishops, but in America I was fallen under the Lord Brethren (Puritans)."[449] In 1635, he moved to the extreme southern end of the township and established a home, which he called "Study Hill." At present, the Ann and Hope Shopping Center occupies the old property in what is now the town of Valley Falls. "Study Hill was leveled in the nineteenth century to make way for the railroad yard near Valley Falls."[450] Roger Williams moved into the area the following year, about five miles to the south. A few historians have insisted that Blackstone is the true founder of Rhode Island. Notice the Whipple Bridge on the map above with Study Hill Road (no longer there) and Ann and Hope Mill Way immediately to the north. David Whipple built on to the Blackstone house, which was located approximately at the intersection of these two roads. "Old Whipple Street" is approximately two blocks northeast of there.

"Occasionally he [Blackstone] went to the village of Providence, sometimes to expound the teachings of his church. To attract an audience, at first he tossed apples to passersby. He attained minor fame riding a [tame white] bull, for want of a horse, on these journeys to town or his rarer excursions to Boston."[451] The Whipple family children undoubtedly enjoyed Blackstone's entertaining irregular visits to Providence.

On 4 July 1659, Blackstone married Sarah Stephenson of Boston, which resulted in the birth of their son, John. Subsequent to Blackstone's death in 1675, the courts of Plymouth Colony appointed a guardian for the child. It was this son who sold this parcel of history to the Whipple family.

The inventory showed that John inherited considerable property, "...title to the property recognized because of this long occupancy. Amongst other land, it included 60 acres and two shares of meadow in Providence, the meadow called Blackstone Meadow, 200 acres of land about the house and orchard. His personal property included books....On October 27 1675, the same records note that the courts appointed Nathaniel Paine and Daniel Smith as guardians of John Blackstone. Since he was then apprenticed to Whipple in Providence as shoemaker, it must have been their doing...In 1692, David Whipple...bought Study Hill and passed it on to his descendants. Was this not, most likely, the Whipple to whom the property's rightful owner [a half brother, John Stevenson, occupied the land until then], John Blackstone, was apprenticed?"[452] The circumstances whereby the property changed hands were apparently as follows: "...When having become addicted to liquor, and intemperate in many things, John was compelled to sell his estate and it was bought by David Whipple. He soon after removed to Providence where he engaged in the trade of boot and shoe making. He eventually moved to New Haven, Connecticut."[453] According to George Carroll Whipple III in his 1999 book, *The Illustrated History of the Whipple Family in America, 1631-1987*, "Study Hill" stayed in his branch of the Whipple family until the year 1871, at which time the railroad took it over. As noted, it is presently a shopping center.

David Whipple in Early Town Records

David Whipple appeared in township records on several other occasions. The following is a chronological summary of a representative sample of these taken from *The Early Records of the Town of Providence*, 21 Volumes (Providence: Snow & Farnham, 1892-1915). Individual entries are noted with the volume number and page.

2 April 1676.
    Sarah Whipple died, wife of David Whipple. (XV:187)

3 June 1678
    David Whipple chosen Town Sergeant and engaged. (VIII:30)

27 July 1678.
    Voted by the Town that the clerk shall, on behalf of the Town be sent by David Whipple, sergeant, write to John Whipple, the former clerk, to demand the books and records of the Town. (VIII:32)

1 July 1679
    A rate levied upon David Whipple of 7 pence. (XV:187)

29 January 1680/81
   A rate of 9 pence levied upon David Whipple. (XV:225)

2 February 1680
   David Whipple and Edward Inman Jr. came to the office with the head of a wolf that they killed while deer hunting. (V:274)

27 July 1680
   A rate levied upon David Whipple of 2 pence. (XV:210)

4 March 1683
   Ordered that the deed of gift from John Whipple Senior to his son David Whipple, bearing the date of 4 March 1683, be enrolled in our town book. (VIII:137)

17 March 1683
   John Whipple deeded a gift of sixty acres of land (more or less) and also a parcel of boggy meadow of about five acres to his son David Whipple. (XIV:79-80)

13 August 1683
   David Whipple requested that a piece of meadow land lying at or about the place called Keyes be laid out to him when the surveyors may be at leisure. (XVII:23-24)

20 June 1684
   John Whipple, Jr., age forty-four years, and David Whipple, age twenty nine years or thereabouts, gave depositions that on 1 June 1684, they saw Thomas Terry of Freetown, colony of Plymouth, at the house of Alexander Bolkom in Providence, tender the delivery of a deed signed by Jabesh Cotterell to the King, and Samuel Thrasher dated 18 June 1683. (XVII:36-37)

29 October 1684
   David Whipple paid a rate 00 pounds, 01 shillings, 03 pence. (XVII:45)

1 September 1687
   David Whipple paid a rate of 00 pounds, 3 shillings, 0 pence. (XVII:99)

September 1687
   Fifty acres of land was laid out to David Whipple on the right of John Steere on the eastern side of the Wanasquatuckett River by Arthur Fenner, surveyor. (XIV:203-4)

31 October 1687
   David Whipple paid a Rate of 00 pounds, 1 shilling, 2 pence so that the town of Providence could pay Joseph Woodward for taking and bringing up the child of Thomas Waters and to pay for the pound and other things. (XVII:108)

August 1688.
     David Whipple paid a rate of 0 pounds, 2 shillings, 6 pence. (XVII:124)

10 September 1692
     David and Hannah Whipple sold 60 acres of land to John Blaxton near a place called Quadmesett, and ffive acres of a Boggy Meadow upon the branch of ye river Wanasquatucket. (IV:185-89)

18 February 1694/5
     Hannah Hayman, a vagrant woman from Boston, great with child, who said that her husband went to sea in July and hadn't been back since, was brought from Renton, [Wrentham] to David Whipple's house. David Whipple took two shillings from her for his sons to take her to Providence. (X:22)

8 June 1706
     Deed recorded between John Blaxton and James Phillips, both of Providence. Blaxton sold to Phillips fifty acres of land in Providence, on the eastern side off the Wanasquatucet River, which he had purchased from David Whipple. (XX:107)

Undated c1709
     "David Whipple of Providence & Hanna Towers of Hingham in the Province of Massachusetts were both joined together in marriage at Hingham upon the 11th day of November 1677." Their children's births are listed. (V:263-64)

     David Whipple continued to live an apparent non-descript, bucolic life in his newly adopted colony for the last 18 years of life. He was noted in township records on at least five occasions.[454] Original wording and spelling have been preserved.

6 October 1693
     The town appointed David Whipple, Dan: Jenke and Isrerall woodcock, Jury men to attend county court. (I:61)

7 November 1699
     David Whiple and 132 other proprietors divided-up township land. Other Whipples [of unknown relationship] listed were: William, Ebeizer, and John. (I:84)

7 November 1699
     David Whiple and Joseph Brown were appointed as land surveyors.

1 January 1700/01
     Leftenant Browne and David Whiple were chosen to serve on the Jury of Trialls. (I;87)

18 March 1705/06

David Whipple, Frances William, and Benjamin Fuller were named to serve on a Grand Jury. (12:103)

Early Cumberland Township Whipples

One year before David left Rhode Island by moving to the east side of the Blackstone River, Plymouth Colony had been merged with Massachusetts. Although there were at least three families of Whipples concurrently living in the general area (see the above 7 November 1699 entry), they were likely descendants of the Ipswich, Massachusetts Whipples (no common English origin has been proven for the two families). This shows that early on members of the two great families of Whipples in America likely first commingled and intermarried in this area.

The next descendants of Captain John Whipple to move to Cumberland were

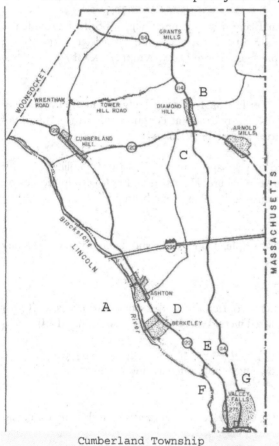

Cumberland Township

those of his third and fourth sons. Descendants of Eleazer, through his youngest son, Daniel, settled in the north, represented by the letter "B," on the map below, as early as the year 1716; and in the central part, represented by the letters "C" and "D," those of William in the mid-eighteen century. However, David was the first (by at least 25 years) to move back to the colony, represented by the letters "E" and "G," that his father had abandoned thirty-three years earlier. In time, "members of these three families intermarried creating a great deal of confusion for later generations of genealogical researchers." [455]

The David Whipple family settled in every part of the township, but primarily in and around the towns of Valley Falls and Lonsdale. Daniel Whipple descendants were concentrated in the area north of Highway 20, presently called the "Nate Whipple Highway"---Nathan Whipple Junior, for whom the highway was named, was a descendant of Daniel. Daniel himself is buried in the Diamond Hill Cemetery, just east of Diamond Hill. Descendants of William lived in area "C," on Little Pond Country Road, and at Ashton and Berkley. The David Whipple Bridge, photographed below letter "F," is located at Lonsdale. The letter "A" represents the area that most all the Whipples who settled in Cumberland came from. "The Whipple family figured so prominently in the settlement of this area that it is surprising that it [Cumberland] wasn't known as Whippleville. Ensign David Whipple was the first of this name to arrive in Cumberland...and settled near the present Ann and Hope Mill. Whipple Bridge, which crosses the Blackstone just west of this area, is named for this family.... Perhaps one of the most interesting buildings in the area was the 'Tower' or 'Biscuit' house, built by Benjamin Tower. In 1698, Benjamin Tower married Deborah Whipple, the oldest daughter of Ensign David Whipple....The term 'Biscuit' house is said to have referred to the number and nature of the additions to the building."[456] Tower Hill Road at the top of the map was named for this family.

David Whipple Bridge

"Located on a steep south-north slope on the east side of Diamond Hill Road, just north of the intersection with Fairhaven Drive, the Whipple-Jenckes House is a mid-eighteenth-century, one-and-one-half story, weathered-shingle-sheathed house with an asymmetrical four-bay façade (entrance in second bay from west), flank-gable roof, and parged brick, off-center chimney...Early maps, deeds, and other sources indicate that an earlier house, referred to as a blockhouse and later used as a boatbuilding shop, was sited a short distance north and east of the house into the nineteenth and early twentieth centuries....

"The Whipple-Jenckes House is significant as a well preserved example of mid-eighteenth-century rural vernacular domestic design, and illustrated the evolution of the half house to a full center chimney form. It is also of local historical interest for its broad associations with the development of the town of Cumberland. Built by a member of one of Cumberland's early settlement families, the house remained in that family for several generations, and became one locus of two of the town's important nineteenth and twentieth century economic pursuits: small-scale boat building and farming. Although its setting has been altered by mid-twentieth-century residential development, the Whipple-Jenckes House possesses integrity of location, design, materials, workmanship, and association. It meets National Register criteria C at the local level.

"The Whipple-Jenckes House was constructed by Samuel Whipple beginning about 1750, when he inherited this property from his father, William Whipple. At that time, the property also contained an earlier house, which is sometimes referred to in deeds as 'Samuel Whipple's old house' and in secondary sources as a 'blockhouse.' Its construction date is not known, but it stood immediately northeast of the present house well into the nineteenth century. Diamond Hill Road was one of the area's first primary north-south roads and is described in early deeds as the road between Providence and Franklin, Massachusetts.

"Although William Blackstone had built a house in Cumberland about 1635, consistent settlement of the town did not occur until the cessation of active hostilities between the Native Americans and the European settlers at the end of King Philip's War in 1676. Ensign David Whipple of Dorchester, Massachusetts, and the grandfather of Samuel Whipple, was one of the earliest settlers of the Diamond Hill area. In 1692, he purchased land on the Blackstone River from William Blackstone's son John Blackstone, and built a house in the vicinity. Upon his death the land passed to the next generation, and about 1750, Samuel Whipple (1718-1780), inherited the land on which the Whipple-Jenckes House stands from the estate of his father, William Whipple of Attleborough. No actual deed of inheritance has been found, but the transfer is referenced in a deed of other lands from Israel Whipple to Samuel Whipple in 1752 (Book 2:83, 10 /4/1752).

"Samuel Whipple built the house standing today in two phases between about 1750 and 1780. Expansion likely occurred in response to the growing size of the family, which numbered seven daughters at his death on 19 August 1780…In his will, he left the use of his personal and real estate to his wife, Elizabeth Whipple. Further pieces of the estate were bequeathed to seven daughters and two grandsons (Probate Records 5:385, 388-389, 1780). The main portion of the property passed to Hannah Whipple

Whipple-Jenckes House

Wilkinson…and her husband. In 1797, they sold all their rights to…their son-in-law David Sheldon….By 1812, David Sheldon had purchased the remains of the estate from the heirs of Samuel Whipple…and deeded the property to his son James Sheldon for $600….In 1847, Liberty Whipple Jenckes (1829-?) whose relationship if any to Samuel Whipple is not known…owned the property until 1903. His name has been commonly associated with the house, as it appears on nineteenth-century maps and remained in oral tradition well into the twentieth century…. In 1903…the property was purchased by Owen and Maggie Murphy for $1530. Between 1940 and 1988, the property changed hands several times and in the mid-1950s was subdivided, creating the present small lot. The house has lost its agrarian outbuildings and setting, but remains valuable as a simple, relatively unaltered, mid- to – late-eighteenth-century, vernacular house, and as an excellent example in Cumberland of its type and period. The Whipple-Jenckes House ably illustrates the kind of houses built by the town's yeoman farmers and settlers in the first century of town formation…The nominated property boundaries are defined as Town of Cumberland Assessor's Plat 24, Lot 126."[457]

Last Will and Testament

Ensign David Whipple died 18 December 1710. His will was dated 24 March 1709 and proved 8 January 1711, his wife being named executrix. To sons David, Israel,

192

Jeremiah, and William, he left money, having individually deeded certain lands previously. Jeremiah was deeded the Study Hill property. His wife, Hannah, was left land, and "best bed, the rest of household goods, money, cattle and personal property. To Joseph Cowell, 10 pounds; to son Jeremiah Whipple 20s; to daughter Deborah Tower, a feather bed, chest and half her wearing apparel; to daughter Sarah Razee, feather bed, and half of wearing apparel: to four children, Israel and David Whipple, Deborah Tower and Sarah Razee, the rest." The property inventory included such items as wearing apparel, plates, books, 5 beds, arms and ammunition, 2 trunks, purse, 2 wheels, 14 gray churns, hogg fatt, 28 barrels of cider, cattle, goats, horses etc.; and also "a 50 acre lot that had belonged to Solomon (unknown last name), and land and meadow on the south side of the way, and land that lyeth by Benjamin Towers." The total value of the inventory, including the above land, was just over £292.[458]

Sons of David Whipple

Israel Whipple

The eldest of David and Hannah's children was Israel, who died in 1720. A guardian (Mr. Henry) for his four children was subsequently appointed in 1727, ostensibly his widow's new husband.[459]   "Israel's son Nathaniel and five of his sons moved to Richmond, N.H. in 1767 as first settlers. Nathaniel's son Ichabod had a son Ichabod Jr. who was our Mason Whipple's father....Mason was born May 3, 1796 in N.H. and died April 14, 1880 in McDonough, N.Y. Mason left N.H. May 3 1819 (so says his son Mason Jr. in a letter) to come to McDonough. There he took up a piece of land on a road now known as the 'Chapel Road' near the first intersection. He began to clear a place for a log house. His granddaughter Mrs. Lucius Deeming of Syracuse says that 'the original log house was still standing some years ago.' One sometimes thinks that the present generation little knows or cares for the sturdy strong characters who built up our country...."[460] Israel's son, Israel, became a leading citizen of the town immediately after it was annexed to Rhode Island in 1746: "The freemen of the town assembled in town meeting, in February 1746-47, for the purpose of electing town officers. Job Bartlett, Israel Whipple and Samuel Peck were elected deputies to represent the town in the General Assembly [at Newport]. Job Bartlett, Joseph Brown, David Whipple [son of Jeremiah], Jacob Bartlett, Jr., Nathaniel Ballou, and William Walcott were chosen councilmen."[461]

William Whipple

The youngest son of David Senior was William. It is he who often has been confused in genealogical literature with his first cousin William son of William.[462] William's oldest child was apparently born out of wedlock.

i. *William, born 23 September 1704; died 20 February 1785; married Sarah Bowen*

At the Court of General Sessions held at Bristol on 13 October 1704, and on the second Tuesday of January 1705, the Court took the following action: "William Whipple of Rehoboth (being accused of being the father of a bastard child). Eliza wilmoth, not capable to appear, William was ordered to come to the next Court. Elizabeth wilmarth of Rehoboth, Singlewoman was bound to appear at the court and found guilty of Fornicating. She was ordered to pay 40 shillings. William Whipple, the reputed father was ordered to pay her 3 shilling per week and post a bond of 50 pounds."[463] There is no record of a marriage between William and Elizabeth. Their child, William Junior, who was not mentioned in his father's Last Will and Testament, was a respected citizen of Providence, dying there in 1785. The only son of William Junior, Ezra[5] Whipple (William[4], William[3], David[2], John[1]), was mentioned in his father's will as "living with the enemies of this country;"[464] that is, he had fought for the British in the Revolutionary War. William Senior married Mary Ibrook about 1708. They were the parents of nine children:

   i. Peter, born 25 May 1709; died 13 August 1769; married Phebe Sprague
   ii. Jemima, born 1 May 1711; married Israel Woodcock
   iii. Abigail, born 10 March 1712/13; married Richard Bickford
   iv. John; born 13 March 1715/16; married Sarah Peck
   v. Samuel, born 26 September 1718; married Elizabeth Jillson
   vi. Ibrook; born 15 September 1720; died 1790; married Mary Perkins
   vii. Mary; born 26 August 1723
   viii. Penelope; born 6 August 1726
   ix. Israel; born 5 February 1730/31

     The actions of Ezra Whipple as a partisan of the British appear to be an exception in that other known William Whipple Senior descendants lived out the American dream with honor and justice. An example of this is the line of Ibrook, the sixth child listed above. Adin Ballou[8] Whipple (Willard[7], William[6], Peter[5], Ibrook[4], William[3], David[2], John[1]) lived in Cumberland Township southeast of Woonsocket, Rhode Island during most of his adult life. He was born and lived on the old Whipple homestead on Ballou Meeting House Road, dying 8 May 1883. He was engaged in general farming and dairying, selling his products in Woonsocket. He married Lucilda Smith in 1858, and they had at least five sons born between the years 1861 and 1874: Henry, Walter, Adin, Lester, and Leander. Adin Whipple died 22 December 1904, and was buried in the Ballou Meeting House cemetery. "Honest and honorable in all of his dealing with his fellow man, full of kindness and charity for all, courteous and genial to those with whom he came into contact, Mr. Whipple was universally esteemed and respected."[465]
     Moreover, enumerable Whipples fought in the Revolutionary War on the American side, many with distinction and uncommon valor. A representative example from the family of John Whipple, the half-brother of William Junior, was Daniel Peck Whipple[5] (John[4], William[3], David[2], John[1]). Daniel, a physician, was the son of John and Sarah Peck Whipple. He was born in 1752 in Cumberland and died there 19 May 1814. "He served as a surgeon on the sloop 'Katy' ...under the command of Commodore Abraham Whipple...(and) as an assistant director in the General Hospital of the RI Second Continental Battalion...."[466] Many of these veterans, and their immediate

descendants, went on to make extraordinary contributions to the American way of life. Such was the case with another descendant of David, Cullen Whipple[7] (Welcome[6], John[5], John[4], William[3], David[2], John[1]): "He resided in the city of Providence, and was a ...great mechanical inventor. To him the American Screw Company is indebted for many of their valuable machines for making screws. He died Oct. 23, 1858 aged 67 years." [467]

The children and further descendants of David Whipple Senior and his nephew, Daniel Whipple, founders of the Whipple clans in southern and northern Cumberland Township respectively, were elected to political office on numerous occasions over the first few generations. Cumberland's first election of township officers was 10 February 1746/47. "Among the early [Whipple] officers were: treasurer; Col. Simon Whipple, 1790 and William Whipple in 1852--- sergeants; Ariel Whipple, 1842---president; Jeremiah Whipple, 1754 and William Whipple, 1819---second district councilmen; Stephen Whipple 1789, Amos Whipple 1824, William Whipple, 1829, Stephen, 1801, Stephen Whipple Junior 1816---third district councilmen; David Whipple, 1746, Stephen Whipple, 1786, William Whipple, 1815, Bennett Whipple, 1816, Amos Whipple 1823, Joseph Whipple Junior, 1824, Jeremiah Whipple, 1830---fourth district councilmen; David Whipple 1750, Stephen Whipple, 1779, Captain Amos Whipple, 1785, Amos Whipple 1786, Stephen Whipple 1796, Reuben Whipple, 1815, Amos Whipple 1821, Joseph Whipple Junior 1823, William Whipple 1826, Jeremiah Whipple, 1828, James Whipple 1829---fifth district council; Simon Whipple, 1782, Captain Amos Whipple 1784, Joseph Whipple Junior, 1811, Amos Whipple, 1818---sixth district councilmen; Samuel Whipple, 1776, and Christopher Whipple, 1785." [468]

Ensign Jeremiah Whipple

The second of David Senior's sons was Ensign Jeremiah Whipple, who was born 26 June 1683 and died 13 May 1721. He married Deborah Bucklin 22 November 1711, and they became parents to five children, all of whom lived and died locally. Three of these lived long enough to witness the take-over of their land by the colony of Rhode Island.

   i. Hannah, born 14 Jul 1712.
  ii. David, Born 1 May 1714; died 6 Oct 1766; married Martha Read.
  iii. Jeremiah, born 5 Mar 1715/16; died 1799; married Hannah Bowen
  iv. Amy, born 21 May 1718; died 27 Apr 1721.
   v. Sarah, born 8 Dec 1720; died after Aug 1762; married John Dexter.

"The General Court on 29 November, 1707, sent the following Company to Port Royal (5 p.689 and 690). The officers were: Jared Talbot of Taunton, Captain, Samuel Peck of Rehoboth, Lieut. Jeremiah Whipple of Cumberland, Ensign. This company was partly composed of Indians." [469] In 1709, Jeremiah was appointed to the position of surveyor of highways. He is last heard of when he petitioned to the court, "praying that he may have the Liberty of Ercting a fence with a good convenient gate acrosse ye country Rhoad that leads from Attleboro to providence Dureing that space of Time that the Bridge over Patucket river stand and is passable...." [470] As will be discussed

195

in more detail later, two of Jeremiah's grandsons graduated from Harvard University: Bela, a surgeon, in 1774, and Oliver in 1766.

Bishop Henry B. Whipple
Pioneer Minnesota Descendant of David Whipple

Of the many other notable descendants of Jeremiah, through his oldest son David, perhaps none has received more notice in genealogical literature than Bishop Henry Whipple. Henry B. Whipple[7] (John[6], Benjamin[5], David[4], Jeremiah[3], David[2], John[1]) was Episcopal Bishop of Minnesota from 1859 until 1901. "Except for churchmen, the name of Henry Benjamin Whipple now means little. But for almost 40 years this

energetic square-jawed, hard traveling Episcopal Bishop of Minnesota was a U.S. figure to be taken seriously; a man of affairs who exerted his influence from the poverty stricken, remote frontier post of Faribault, Minn.; a missionary who was denounced by Senators and generals for his defense of the Indians after the Sioux outbreak in 1862; an ecclesiastical leader who conferred with Queen Victoria and Abraham Lincoln, preached in most of the cathedrals of England and turned down the bishopric of the Sandwich Islands because he thought his work in Minnesota needed him more."[471]

"Right Reverend Henry Benjamin Whipple, Bishop of Minnesota; b 15th February 1822, at Adams, New York; d 16th September, 1901, at Faribault, Minnesota...Received his theological training under Rev. Dr. W.D. Wilson later of Cornell, University. 26th

Bishop Whipple

August 1849, was ordained Deacon by Bishop Delancey in Trinity Church, Geneva, New York. The following February ordained Priest in Christ Church, Sackeet's Harbor, and immediately thereafter called to Zion Church, Rome, New York. In 1856 was called to establish the first Protestant Episcopal Church in Chicago, Illinois. Among his parishioners were Generals Burnside and McClellan...1859, was consecrated first Bishop of Minnesota at St. James Church, Richmond, Virginia...He was loyal and fearless in protecting the rights of the Indians in Minnesota, against unlawful aggressions on the part of unscrupulous whites. He stood preeminently as the most rational, just and enlightened man who had any dealing with Indian affairs and for his sincerity and directness the Indians gave him the name of 'Straight Tongue.' He gave clear warning of the Indian massacre that occurred in 1862. Was appointed on many commissions by different Presidents of the United States. In 1888 by request of the Archbishop of Canterbury, Bishop Whipple preached the opening sermon of the Lambeth Conference at Lambeth Palace, London. From the Universities of Oxford, Cambridge and Durham he received the honorary degrees of D.D. and LL.D., and D.D. from Hobart College. One 3rd June, 1897, by a request of the preceding year, he preached in Salisbury Cathedral at the great service in commemoration of thirteen hundredth anniversary of

196

the baptism of King Ethelbert, the first Christian Saxon king, with a congregation of seven thousand persons, a procession of seven hundred bishops and vested clergy and fourteen hundred choristers...It was said by many...that Bishop Whipple seemed to have reached the zenith of impassioned out pouring of spiritual truths, striking the keynote of everything most needed in the Christianization of the world...M. (firstly) 5th October, 1842, Cornelia Wright, b 10th November, 1816, d. 16th July 1890, dau. of Benjamin and Sarah (Ward) Wright of the families of Pell and Ward of New York; m. (secondly) 22 November 1896, Evangeline (Marrs) Simpson only dau. of Francis and Jane (Van Poelien) Marrs of Massachusetts, and widow of Michael Simpson."[472]

It is not known why Bishop Whipple married a second wife who was almost 40 years his junior, nor would he likely have approved of her later behavior. "Evangeline Simpson, a wealthy widow, was the long time lesbian friend of Rose Cleveland, the spinster sister of President Grover Cleveland.... Several letters between them have been preserved.... When bishop Whipple dies in 1901, Evangeline waits the required year, and then abruptly leaves for Europe and never returns to the bishop's Minnesota....The two women lived together in Italy... until Rose dies in 1918. Evangeline dies 12 years later, having directed her executors to bury her in Italy beside Rose and another woman friend...."[473] After the bishop's death, Evangeline paid for the expensive chime of bells in the Cathedral Tower in his memory.

Bishop Whipple was laid to rest under the Altar of the Cathedral of our Merciful Savior, Faribault, Minnesota, on Friday afternoon September 20th, 1901. On the outside of the tower built in his memory are these words: "This tower is the Thanksgiving of many People for Henry Benjamin Whipple, the first bishop of Minnesota, and is the Symbol before men of the Supreme value of a Righteous Man."

Bishop Whipple and his first wife, Cornelia, had six children, including Charles Henry Whipple and John Hall Whipple. John died early, without issue. "Brigadier-General Charles Henry Whipple, U.S.A., retired, of Los Angeles, California; b. 12th June, 1849, at Adams, New York; m. 5th December, 1871, at Cincinnati, Ohio, Evelyn McLean, b. 5th July, 1851, dau. of Gen. Nathaniel Collins McLean, b 2d February, 1818, d 4th January, 1905, m 5th September, 1838, Caroline Thew Burnet, b. 26th August, 1820, d. 15th April, 1856, and gd.dau. of Justice John McLean of the United States Supreme Court. Charles Henry Whipple was educated at St. Paul's School, Concord, New Hampshire; from 1871 to 1881. Cashier Citizen's National Bank of Faribault, Minnesota; 18th February, 1881, appointed Mayor and Paymaster, promoted Lieutenant-colonel and Colonel in the Pay Department of the United States Army; appointed Paymaster-General of the Army with rank of Brigadier-General 1st January, 1908; retired 15th February, 1912."[474] General Whipple was the author of The Whipple-Wright, Wager, Ward-Pell, McLean-Burnet Families, a genealogy published in 1917. He died in Los Angeles, California, 6 November 1932, at the age of 84.

End Notes

441 William R. Cutter, *Genealogical and Family History of Western New York, vol. 1*, (S.L, S.N., 1911). The 22 February 1692 date would place his age at about 19. The next of his siblings was born in 1707 in Connecticut.

442 Jane Fletcher Fiske, transcriptionist, "Newport Court Book A," Rhode Island General Court of Trials, Boxford, Massachusetts: privately published, 1998, p. 43.

443 Letter from John Sanford to John Whipple, Junior, 15 November 1686, Rhode Island Historical Society Manuscript 9003, Volume 5, p. 27.

444 J. Smith, *Daughters of the Promised Land* (New York: Little Brown and Company, 1970) 50-56.

445 John O. Austin, *Genealogical Dictionary of Rhode Island* (Albany, NY: 1887: reprint edition. Baltimore: Genealogical Publishing Company, 1978) 222. *Records of the First Church of Dorchester in New England, 1636-1734* (Boston: George H. Ellis, 1891) 267 and 188. John N. Arnold, *Vital Records Rhode Island, 1636-1850* (Providence: Narragansett Historical Publishing Company, 1892). Henry E. Whipple, *A Brief Genealogy of the Whipple Families who Settled in Rhode Island* (Providence: A Crawford Greene, 1873). Vital statistics of the children and grandchildren of Captain John and Sarah Whipple are taken from the above and numerous publications that quote from them. To see more recent corrections and additions consult www.whipple.org, Weldon Whipple, Webmaster.

446 Hannah and Abigail likely died young. Richard M. Bayles, ed., *History of Providence County, Rhode Island, 2 vols.* (New York: W.W. Preston and Company, 1891) 2:479.

447 *The Early Records of the Town of Providence, 21 vols., collected and printed by the Record Commissioners (Providence: Snow & Farnham, city printers, 1892-1915)* XIV:79-80 [hereinafter *ERP*].

448 Deed, John Blaxton to David Whipple for "Study Hill," 10 September 1692, Rhode Island Historical Society Manuscript 378, Deed Book 3, p.2.

449 Samuel Green Arnold, *History of the State of Rhode Island and Providence Plantations*. 2 vols. (London: D. Appleton & Company, 1859) 1:98.

450 Charles Carroll, *Rhode Island: Three Centuries of Democracy, 4 vols* (New York: Lewis Historical Publishing Company, 1932) 1:20. The old railroad yard is now a shopping center.

451 Sydney V. James, *Colonial Rhode Island, A History* (New York: Charles Scribner's Sons, 1976) 2

452 Mills, 50-5l.

453 Albert Wright, printer, *History of the State of Rhode Island, with Illustrations* (Philadelphia: Hong, Wade & Company, 1878) 12.

454 John G. Erhardt, *A History of Rehoboth, Seekonk, Mass. Pawtucket & East Providence, R.I. 1692-1812* (Seekonk, Mass.: Privately Published, 1990) Volume number and page are taken from township records.

455 Judith Jenks Ray, *Founders and Patriots of the Town of Cumberland Rhode Island* (Baltimore: Gateway Press, 1990). Personal Correspondence, 24 September 2002.

456 Robert V. Simpson, *North Cumberland, a History* (Privately Published, 1975) 21 & 47

457 Virginia H. Adams, Architectural Historian, National Register of Historic Places Registration Form, Rhode Island Historical Preservation Commission, Providence, RIHPC, 1990.

458 Inventory, 30 January 1710/11, Registry of Probates, Bristol County, Taunton, Mass. Will, 1 January 1710-11, Bristol County Courthouse, Taunton, Mass. Note: the probate envelope containing his Inventory and the Letter of Administration for Hannah Whipple was found at the courthouse; however, David's will was missing.

459 Letter of Guardianship for Abigail, Hannah, Nathaniel and Ruth Whipple, Attleboro, Ma., 1727, Registry of Probate, Bristol County, Taunton, Massachusetts.

460 Extracted from a privately published history written by Lucy Whipple Burrows, date unknown. Letter and mss transferred from Blaine Whipple to the authors in July of 2003. The history records the descendants of Mason Whipple to the present.

461 Wright, 111.

462 Charles M. Whipple, Jr., "Captain John Whipples Two Grandsons named William: A Reply," on-line at <http://www.whipple.org/charles /louquisset /index.html> November 1, 2002. Charles M. Whipple, Jr. Sons and Daughters of Jesse (Oklahoma City: Southwestern Press, 1976) 5.

463 Erhardt, 97-98

464 Abracts of Providence Willis, Rhode Island Genealogical Register, 15:15.

[465] The description of Adin Ballou Whipple was extracted and liberally summarized from *Representative Men and Old families of Rhode Island*, 3 vols. (Chicago: J.H. Beers and Company, 1908) 3:2242-43.

[466] Ray, 8

[467] Henry E. Whipple, 52. See also: on-line at<http://genweb.whipple.org/d0286/I10231.html.> "Mr. Whipple invented and patented 6 other machines for improving the manufacturing of screws."

[468] E. Richardson, *History of Woonsocket* (Woonsocket: S. Foss printer, 1876) 20-24.

[469] Erhardt, 117

[470] Erhardt, 127 & 221

[471] Time Magazine, December 27, 1937

[472] George Mackenzie, *Colonial Families of the United States of America* (Baltimore: Genealogical Publishing Company, 1966) V:468-469

[473] Jonathan Katz, "The President's Sister and the Bishop's Wife," *Advocate Magazine*, January 31, 1989, 34-35

[474] Mackenzie,V: 465

Chapter 9

Colonel Joseph Whipple
The Whipples From Providence and Newport

Children and Relatives

Colonel Joseph Whipple, the seventh son of Captain John Whipple, was born at Providence about 1662 and died there 28 April 1746. He married Alice Smith, daughter of Edward Smith and Amphillis Angell, 20 May 1684 who died 20 July 1739. They were the parents of 12 children.[475] Of their children, Joseph married, lived, and died in Newport, Rhode Island, and Amphillis in Warwick, Rhode Island. The other children lived out their lives in Providence.

> i. *John, (Captain), born 17 May 1685; died 18 May 1769; married A Brown*
> ii. *Jeremiah, born 3 Sep 1686: died as infant*
> iii. *Joseph, (Captain) born 30 Dec 1687; died between May and Jul 1750; married*
>   *(1) Anne Almy (2) Sarah Redwood*
> iv. *Amphillis, born 6 Oct 1689; died 17 Dec 1776; married Moses Lippitt* [476]
> v. *Sarah, born 29 Mar 1691; died in 1762; married William Crawford.*
> vi. *Susannah, born 14 Mar 1692/93; died 15 Dec 1776; married S. Dexter.*
> vii. *Freelove, born 18 Mar 1693/94; died before 1781; married (1) A.Young*
>   *(2) William Temple*
> viii. *Alice, born 6 Feb 1695/96; married Arthur Young*
> ix. *Amy, born 16 Jun 1699; died 23 Dec 1757; married John Crawford*
> x. *Christopher, born 14 Sep 1701; died as infant*
> xi. *Mary, born 9 Apr 1704; died 8 Dec 1733; married Charles Bardin*
> xii. *Christopher, born 6 Mar 1706/07;died as infant*

"I give unto my son Joseph, my dwelling house, and my three house-lots, and the garden next: also a six acre lot lying on the southern side of the neck whereupon the town of Providence standeth: also twenty acres near Thomas Clemons, his dwelling: also I give unto my son Joseph my share of meadow near Solitary Hill, and two six acre lots lying on each side of said Hill: also a six acre lot near William Wickenden formerly dwelt: also one division lying on the "seven mile line" which is already ordered by the town, and papers drawn for: also I give unto my son Joseph, all other divisions which shall hereafter belong unto two rights-throughout...also I do make my son Joseph my executor: also my will is that my son Joseph do see that I be decently buried." With the above legacy acquired by virtue of his father's Last Will and Testament in 1685, the newlyweds Joseph and Alice Whipple began the process of joining Providence's leading real estate owners of the early eighteenth century.

In his earliest years, Joseph, like his father, became a successful innkeeper and businessman. Through the profitable marriages of his children, shrewd business contacts, and hard work, he built up a sizeable financial fortune--- by far, the largest of any of Captain John's sons. As the town grew, so did Joseph's mercantile enterprises.[477]

Providence's rival, Newport, was the recognized seat of economic and political power from the 1660s to the end of the Revolutionary War. All the same, eventually Providence became a success among the secondary Rhode Island mercantile centers. The town meetings of The Reverend Roger Williams' old home place began to grant small lots--twenty to forty feet square--along its waterfront for wharves during the 1680s. Samuel Whipple, one of Joseph's older brothers, was the recipient of one such grant.[478] John Whipple Junior and Benjamin Whipple became owners of oceanfront property in the early 1680s. "Another of the earliest grantees was Gideon Crawford in 1687. He married Freelove Fenner, daughter of Captain Arthur Fenner who was as close to being a merchant as anyone in town. The Crawford-Fenner enterprise prospered for years. After Crawford's death, his widow carried on the business, rearing up her two sons to commerce. These sons, who died in their 20s, married daughters of another up-and-coming trader, Joseph Whipple."[479] The Crawford brothers may not have lived long enough to give continuity to an economic dynasty, but their widows and father-in-law, Joseph Whipple, decisively did.

Building on the political base constructed by his father in the 1660s and 1670s, and continued by his oldest brother John, Joseph was early on elected to the Providence town council, and beginning in 1698, served in the colony's General Assembly in Newport for almost three decades. Additionally, in 1719, he was commissioned a Colonel of the militia on the mainland.[480]

Joseph Whipple in Early Town Records

In addition to the numerous times Joseph was elected to political office,[481] he appeared in other Providence Township records over 200 times. The following is a summary of a chronological listing of a selected few of these as extracted from The *Early Records of the Town of Providence, 21 Volumes,* (Providence: Snow and Farnham 1892-1915). Individual entries are noted with the volume number and page. As much as possible, original wording, spelling, and punctuation are retained.

7 July 1680.
Joseph Whipple took up a stray mare, of a sorrel color, with a flaxen mane and tail. He said that anyone who could lay just claim to her could have her for a charge. (IX: 199)

Last Monday in May, 1682.
Joseph Whipple and Jonathan Whipple took engagement of Allegiance before Joseph Jencks, assistant. (IV :55)

20 May 1684.
Joseph Whipple and Alice Smith were joined together in marriage by Joseph Jenckes, assistant town clerk. Their banns had been legally published first. Their children are also listed. (V:280-81))

27 April 1686.

Granted to Joseph Whipple that he may have a forty foot square piece of land adjoining the north side of his house, upon the Common, a little above his dwelling house, leaving a highway between it and Shadrach Manton's house. (VIII:163)

16 June 1693

In a deede of property Joseph Whipple is called a "cooper." (XIV:230)

27 January 1695/96.

Joseph Whipple and six others made a request to the town council for a small spot of land to set a schoolhouse. The request was granted and a plot of land [owned by Joseph] about forty feet square was granted for a school, provided that they build the school and improve upon it. If they neglected to build it, the grant would be null and void. (XI:22)

27 January 1696/97.

Joseph Whipple asked the town council to grant him a small piece of land lying on the north of his lot where his dwelling was in Providence. His request was granted on condition that he and his heirs keep the highway called Town Street in good and sufficient repair so that it may be a sufficient and passable Cartway all along the street from the northwest corner of the granted piece of land southward to the southwest corner of his land, next to John Whipple's land. (XI:30)

1 February 1696/97.

A piece of land laid out to Joseph Whipple about a quarter of an acre lying on the north side of his land where he dwells (XI:31)

23 August 1697.

Joseph Whipple chosen for the Grand Jury to serve at the Court of Trials. (XI:35)

18 April 1698.

Joseph Whipple chosen to serve on a Court of Trials at Providence. (XI:44)

7 January 1700.

Rebecca Whipple, widow of John, presented a paper to Joseph Whipple which she said to be John Whipple's last will and testament (X:55-57)

8 March 1700/01.

Joseph Whipple chosen for petit jury. (XI:62)

27 April 1700.

Granted to Joseph Whipple that he change about 25 acres of land upon the Wanasquatucket River near Gotham Valley. (XI:55)

22 April 1701.

Joseph Whipple witnessed the estate of John Whipple. (IV :235-40)

13 December 1701.

Deed between Joseph Whipple and Elizabeth Prey, widow of Richard Prey and Benjamin Hearnden. Joseph Whipple paid 50 and five pounds for her dwelling house in Providence, together with her adjoining lands, estimated at ten acres, in the row of house lots or homeshares in Providence towne, at present enclosed with a fence. The house stands on the land bounded on the east with a highway, on the west with a highway which leads through the town, on the north with a highway commonly called Hearnden's Lane, and on the south with a houselot formerly belonging to Elizabeth's late husband, Benjamin Hearnden, but now owned by Gideon Cruffurd. The property includes an orchard and out houseing. (IV:219-22)

27 January 1703/04.

William Edmunds requested a piece of land forty feet square to set up a blacksmith's shop. One boundary of the land was the north side fence of Joseph Whipple's home lands and the Prison house. (XI:80)

22 March 1703/04

James Mathason and Joseph Whipple were responsible for taking the inventory of movable goods of Joseph's brother Benjamin. (VI:242-45)

16 April 1703.

Deed of sale between Joseph Whipple and Peter Place. Joseph paid four pounds and ten shillings silver to Peter Place for fifteen poles of ground, more of less, lying towards the southern end of town, it being a warehouse lott and wharf. (V:83-87)

5 February 1704/05.

Joseph Whipple requested that he have liberty to remove his little house which he called his old shop and set it on the west side of the highway (Towne Street), over against his dwelling house or a little more south of it, provided that he leaves the street wide enough for all manner of passage, both for carting, all loadings, and for people to pass by each other without interruption and whatever passings are needed. (XI:95)

11 February 1705/06

The Towne approved a request from Joseph Whipple to build a landing and road to his wharf on the western side of the Pautucket River. (XI:103-04)

2 February 1707/08

Granted to Joseph Whipple ye liberty of 20 foote wide ground adjoyneing the southerne side of his ware house. (XI:125)

22 April 1708

"In Providence; William Crawford and Sarah Whipple both of Providence, in ye colony of Rhode Island and Providence Plantations (daughter of me Joseph Whipple) came before me the 22 day of April Annoqe Domini 1708, and was lawfully joyned in marriage. Richard Waterman, Justice of the Peace. (V:259)

2 March 1709/10
It was granted by ye Towne to Joseph Whipple that he might have 60 acres of land which his ffather bought of Benedict Arnold changed...on the east side of Mashapauge Pond the bounds being lost and other people having taken up the land... (XI:142)

31 March 1709/10.
Coroner's jury impaneled upon the death of the young son of James and Halelujah Olney of Providence who died suddenly on 30 March 1709 in the night. The jury found that the child died a natural death. Joseph Whipple was a member of the jury. (V:254)

17 January 1710/11.
Joseph Whipple gave notice that he had taken up a stray mare. Her color was between a bay and a brown, and she was branded on the buttock. He also took up a mare colt, bay color, with a white spot on its head. (IX: 173)

20 March 1710/11.
The inventory of Samuel Whipple, taken on 16 March 1710/11, by Joseph Whipple and James Olney, examined by the Town Council and allowed. (Vll:21)

11 December 1710.
Granted to Joseph Whipple that he may retail strong drinks for one year's time, and that he should have a license for the same. He had to post bond to keep good order in his house. For the license he paid 20 shillings. That 20 shillings was taken off Anne Turpin's 40 shillings which she was to pay for a license for her public house of entertainment, so Turpin would only have to pay 20 shillings. (X:114))

9 August 1711.
Joseph Whipple witnesses an agreement between Anne Turpin and her son William Turpin. (Vll: 181)

12 November 1711.
Thomas Olney, town clerk, was ordered to give a bill to James Brown to Mr. Joseph Whipple for 20 shillings, which was due for license money for the year 1710, beginning 14 August 1710 and ending 14 August 1711. (X:118)

17 September 1713.
A stray mare, taken up by Joseph Field, was appraised by John Whipple, son of Joseph Whipple. (IX: 166)

8 April 1714.

Joseph Whipple held a mortgage of twenty seven pounds and seventeen shillings for John Mitchell, to be paid by Zechariah Field, to whom John Mitchell sold the property that was mortgaged. This money was to be paid at the dwelling house of Joseph Whipple. (IX:7-8)

27 June 1714

In his role of Assistant, Joseph Whipple approved the administration of an estate. (VI:176)

6 June 1715

Joseph Whipple chosen to serve on the town council. (IX:1715)

8 January 1716/17.

Joseph Whipple served on a coroner's jury of inquest concerning the death of a female child, born two days earlier under an apple tree a few rods from the mother's house. The jury found that the child died because the mother did not have suitable help. (IX:17-8)

26 February 1716/17.

Joseph, John, and Job Whipple served on a coroner's jury of inquest to inquire into the death of Samuel Wright who was found dead by the waterside near his house. They viewed his body and found that there was no harm due him. (IX:21)

31 August 1720

Joseph Whipple was given power to administer the estate of his son-in-law Major William Crawford. Sarah Crawford widow of William Crawford…at present troubled with insanity of mind… (XII:17-19)

7 October 1720.

Joseph Whipple took up a stray steer supposed to be two years old, red with a white face, with white under the belly, and with white feet. (IX: 155)

27 January 1723/24.

Col Joseph Whipple chosen Town Moderator. He was also appointed to a committee to oversee the work of Mr. Thomas Staples, who petitioned to dig clay at Weybosset Hill to make bricks. (IX:41)

27 October 1725.

Joseph Whipple was the foreman of the jury of an inquest into the death of a male child born of Elizabeth Steere, a single woman, on the 26th day of October. The jury examined the child and concluded that it was born dead, as the result of a fall from a horse that the woman had a few days earlier. (IX:43)

11 August 1731

     Joseph Whipple and his sister's son, William Hopkins, granted licenses to sell strong drinke...XII:92)

8 November 1737.

     Col. Joseph Whipple freely gave some land to the town for a new highway. (IX:73-74)

13 March 1738.

     A highway was laid out from Providence Towne Street along the west end of Colonel Joseph Whipple's Cooper shop over the mill river. (IX:81)

28 May 1738.

     A new highway being laid out was to be between the land of Nicholas Power and Colonel Joseph Whipple. (IX:76)

An Anglican Convert

     Joseph was the only Whipple brother known to have become a member of the Anglican Church. And although the wives of Joseph Junior and some of their children were members of the Society of Friends, it may be assumed that the remaining children and in-laws lived out their lives as Anglicans. It has been erroneously believed that Joseph Whipple bequeathed one of his real estate holdings, on the north end of Benefit Street, to construct one of Providence's earliest schoolhouses, called Whipple Hall.[482] [Actually, his grandson Joseph accomplished this in 1768.] Then, in 1722, St. John's church, originally King's Church, the first one of the Anglican persuasion in Providence, received £100 [the largest amount contributed] from the family toward its completion.[483] Information regarding the Whipple influence upon the construction of the church is seen in correspondence addressed to James Honeyman, a leading Anglican clergyman of the time. "Gabriel Bernon wrote to Mr. Honeyman, concerning the future prospects of building Kings Church. He mentioned as the 'three chief men' were Colonel Whipple, Joseph Jenckes, the Lieutenant Governor, and Judge Waterman, a man of very good parts."[484] Kings Church is now St. Johns Episcopal Church. In changing religious denominations, the Joseph Whipples were riding a crest of the wave of social aspirations among those who sought increased prestige by closer association with the Church of England. "The Anglican Church began with few avowed communicants but quickly attracted the newly rich and powerful.... The Anglican celebration of kingly power. .. the celebration of rank and hierarchy in this world and the next... .enhanced the satisfaction that grew from their new affiliation."[485] Colonel Joseph Whipple died 28 April 1746. His will was proved 19 May 1746.

Last Will and Testament

"To son Joseph, farm on Chapatset Hill, in Glocester; also 100 acres in Glocester, near Wolf Hill, &c. To grandson Joseph, son of John, land toward southern end of Providence, and dwelling house west side of Town Street, land on Weybosset Plains, &c.

To daughter Alice Young land. To son John, my homestead and all other farms in Providence, Smithfield and Glocester, undisposed of, reserving half acre at the burying place in my homestead 'for the generations that shall proceed from my line forever.' To daughter Sarah Crawford, 300 pounds, reserved by executors for her support, and at her death half of sum to her surviving children. To daughter Alice Young, Negro girl Sarah, a cow, and 30 pounds. To daughters Ann Lippitt, Susannah Dexter, and Amy Gibbs, 300 pounds each. To grandson Jonathan Bardin, son of daughter Mary, deceased, 300 pounds. To grandson Joseph Dexter, son of daughter Susannah, 100 pounds, at age. Inventory, 5,292 pounds. viz: books, sword, pistols, cutlass , canes, bonds 3,640 pounds, 5 feather beds, 5 flock beds, clock, 24 chairs, 10 cushions…6 negroes viz. Caesar, Aaron, Jeffrey, Betty, Jenny and Phebe." A summary of the will is found in Beaman. "Joseph Whipple, of Pr. merchant, now grown ancient and well stricken in years. Will dated 20 Jan 1743/4, proved 19 May 1746. pgs. 193-195. Mentioned: 2 sons, John Whipple and Joseph Whipple. Daughters Alice Young, Sarah Crawford is to be supported, Ann Lippitt, Susannah Dexter, Amey Gibbs, and Mary Borden dec. Grandson Joseph Dexter under 21, son of daughter Susannah Dexter. Brother John Whipple. Witn: Thomas Olney, Thomas Hardin, & Daniel Smith."[486]

The total of Joseph's movable estate was approximately £10,000, including seven slaves. This was, by far, the largest estate of any of Captain John's children. Joseph Junior received comparatively little in the will, but by this time was a successful entrepreneur and wealthy in his own right in the colony's capitol city of Newport, as well as having been elected deputy governor of the colony.

Death and Burial

In an article by Chase, the author may have been disingenuous, or at least inaccurate, in his assertion that Colonel Joseph's son graduated from Harvard College in 1720. However, as will be shown, Joseph Junior's son, William, did graduate first in his class from Harvard in 1749. Being placed first in his 1745 entering freshman class indicated just how powerful and socially prominent the Colonel Joseph Whipple family had become by just its second generation. The photo below is of the broken headstone of Joseph Whipple Senior.

Whether due to mere fortuity or preternatural insight, Captain John's choice of his 20-year-old seventh son to serve as executor of his estate and to see that "I be decently buried," proved wise. Because of his eventual social prominence and wealth, Joseph was allowed to purchase extensive space in the town's common cemetery. Sometime around the mid-1700s, he or his sons had his parents remains moved from their house lot to the cemetery. At that time, the Providence town council asked that the remains of the town's earliest citizens, buried in family home plots, be relocated to the North Burial Ground. Parenthetically, it has been suggested that perhaps only markers "in memory" of his parents were set up at Joseph's burial property location, and their remains left where they lay. [487] At any rate, the headstones of Colonel Joseph Whipple and wife; his son John and John's son, Joseph, and their children and their spouses; as well as other of Joseph's descendants, including those of Captain John and Sarah Whipple can yet be viewed on Dahlia Path in the North Burying Ground. [488]

Captain John Whipple the Younger

Colonel Joseph's oldest son, John Whipple, bonesetter (physician), military captain and Justice,[489] appears to have received the lion's share of property in his father's Last Will and Testament. Captain John Whipple the Younger was born 17 May 1685 and died 18 May 1769.[490] He was married to Alice Brown in 1724. They were parents to four children. The family is buried in the North Burial Ground.

   i. Abigail, born 23 Jan 1725; died 19 Apr 1751; married John Andrews
   ii. Freelove; born 24 Dec 1728; died 21 Aug 1751; married James Fenner
   iii. Jeremiah, born about 1729; died 2 Jan 1731.
   iv. Joseph, 1734; died 6 Jan 1816; married Sarah Mawney.

Alice Brown[491] was the great granddaughter of Chad Brown and the daughter of Lieutenant Joseph Brown. She was the niece of James and Obadiah Brown, thus a first cousin to the four famous Brown brothers of Providence, benefactors and contributors of the name of Brown University.

By the time of Colonel Joseph Whipple's death, John and his father had become widely recognized merchant land barons, both prominent in Providence and Newport politics.[492] This was brought about by a series of shrewd land purchases, as shown on the map below. In addition to inheriting three of his father's four original lots on Town Street, Joseph bought the lots of his brother, John Junior, from John III in 1705.[493] In 1726, Joseph traded with a son-in-law, Stephen Dexter, for an additional three lots, those of Thomas James, John Greene Senior, and John Smith, which lay immediately to the south of the John Whipple Junior lots.[494] Captain John Whipple, in 1738, bought from the heirs of Richard Arnold[495] the two house lots that had long been unoccupied on the north side of the original Whipple 1659/61 purchase, which had originally been laid out in 1638 to Thomas Painter and Edward Manton. With this last purchase, Colonel Joseph and his son became the owners of nine consecutive house lots along Town Street extending from about 100 feet of the top of Constitution Hill to within 150 feet of Roger Williams' fresh-water spring. In addition to these, in 1728, the Whipples bought three lots toward the southerly end of the street: those of William Mann, William Burrows, and William Wickenden. By the time of Joseph Whipple's death in 1746, between 70 and 80 downtown acres were in the possession of one man and his son. Each lot granted the owner an additional six acres of farmland; thus the Whipples owned over 150 acres of highly coveted property in the heart of the city. They also owned hundreds of other acres in the northern and central parts of the colony.

Joseph Whipple Headstone

209

When Henry E. Whipple wrote his 1873 history on Rhode Island Whipple families, he appended an article written by Henry R. Chace entitled "Part of the Whipples in Early City History." Among others, Chace shows that "When Col. Joseph Whipple died in 1746, he and his son, John, were probably the largest owners of valuable real estate in Providence, the accumulation of three generations. The Whipple family in the third generation numbered nearly 100 descendants, most of them living on farms that had been laid out by the proprietors to their grandfather, the first John.... The death of Col. Joseph Whipple removed the most active merchant in town and the recognized head of the large and wealthy family bearing this name.... The accumulation of land by the Whipples ceased about 1740, and for the next 50 years the home lots that had remained as originally laid out ... were cut up into small parcels and sold...."[496] At least one parcel of land given to the town of Providence to build a schoolhouse has figured prominently in Whipple family lore.[497] The below is a photo of the property given to St. John's church by John the Younger, also in 1767, for a cemetery.

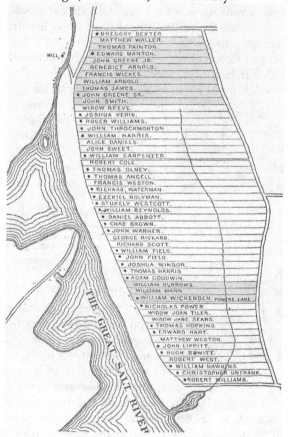

Joseph Whipple Property

Whipple Hall

The Whipple Hall schoolhouse was chartered in 1768 by 50 contributing subscribers, including George Whipple. George[5]Whipple (David[4], Jeremiah[3], David[2], John[1]) was born in Cumberland, RI in 1742, and moved to Providence about 1766. His son David came of school age just after the Hall was founded. He and his three children lived and died in Providence, and were buried in the North Burial Ground. Two other of the "subscriptions" or rights, went to Captain John Whipple and his son Joseph[4] Whipple (John[3], Joseph[2], John[1]) who donated the land. Each right carried the privilege of sending "one Scholar to the Master's Apartment and one to the Mistress's apartment and no more."[498]

In 1667, a town education committee agreed with Joseph Whipple to accept "for two Lotts for the small school Houses that is, one at the upper part of the Town, and one in the lower."[499] Whipple Hall was built on the corner of Benefit and Halsey Streets. The 1638 proprietor who originally owned this property was Edward Manton. As noted, John Whipple and his father, Colonel Joseph Whipple, bought the lots in 1738 from the heirs of Thomas Arnold, the father of Richard, the second husband of Sarah Smith, Colonel Whipple's sister. The Manton property was the next lot north of the 1659/61 purchase of Captain John Whipple, about three-quarters of the way up Constitution Hill.

The construction of Whipple Hall was completed in November of 1768, at a cost of £120 old tenor, to each proprietor. It was constructed of wood, one story in height, having a hipped roof, with a belfry. George Taylor was the first teacher in the upper grade, and was compensated by tuition fees of four shillings sixpence for each scholar; an additional charge of two shillings was charged to parents who were not subscribers. The curriculum was extremely rigid, particularly in matters of morality, politeness, and general good conduct.

The founding of Whipple Hall was the culmination of educational goals that had commenced a century earlier when, "Att a Towne Meeting May the 9th 1663 Thomas Olney Senior Moderator: It is ordered by this present Assembly, that 100 acrs of upland, and 6 acres of Meddow, or low land Shall be Laide out within the bounds of the Town of Providence; The which land, shall be reserved for the maintenance of A Scoole in this Towne."[500] It does not appear that progress was forthcoming for next two decades. Then in 1683, the first request to open a school in Providence was recorded: "My request is whereas there is an order formerly made, in this Towne, of a Grant of a purchase right of land to be layd out in the Town for ye use and Bennefitt of a Schoole; which hath nott bene yet done, my Humble request is that the same may be fullfiled or accomplished according to the tenor of the syd order, and in soe doing you will oblige your Servant to Command. Jon Whipple, Jun'r."[501] Subsequent to this petition to the town council, William Turpin, a brother-in-law of John Whipple III,[502] was contracted to teach individual students at his residence or at theirs.

The next recorded action regarding an educational institution occurred approximately ten years later: "Towne Meeting Jan. 27, 1695-6. Where as, there hath ben a Request made unto ye Town by Jon Dexter, William Hopkins, Enenetus Olney, William Turpin, Joseph Whipple, John Smith, Philip Tillinghast, and Joseph Smith, that the Towne would accommodate them with a Small spot of land to set a School House upon in some place in this Town about ye Highway called Dexter Lane or about ye Stampers hill, The Town has Considered of the mater and Do by these presents freely Grant unto ye aforesaid persons...a Spot of Land of Forty foot square...about the place where it may be most convenient."[503] It should be noted that, with the possible exception of Tillinghast, all the above petitioners were part of the extended Whipple family at that time.[504] It also must be noted that genealogical literature, following the lead of Austin,[505] has erroneously supposed that the creation of Whipple Hall was due to the above town council vote.

Rather as a consequence of the town's foresight, it appears that Turpin was finally given access to a schoolroom on Stampers Hill at a location a few yards north of

Olney Lane on Towne Street and across the street from the Olney Tavern, which was owned by Captain John Whipple's daughter and her husband. However, school teaching proved financially unprofitable, so he too soon opened a tavern in that same neighborhood. Turpin died in 1709 as a noted citizen and well respected tavern owner.

It was not until 1735 that town records next mention that a Mr. George Taylor, schoolmaster, was holding classes in a chamber room of the country courthouse, next to the Friends Meeting House. This was soon followed by the founding of a 1747 school opposite the courthouse on the west side of Main Street, and the appointment of a schoolmaster in 1752. An additional school was started on the west side of the town near Broad Street. These proved sufficient to the educational needs of the community until the mid-1760s, when a commission of interested townsmen proposed to build three new school buildings: two on north and south Benefit Street, the other "west of the Great Bridge." The town treasury was to be responsible for the expense of building and maintenance, and for furnishing free instruction to the children of every inhabitant of the town. The voters did not subsequently approve this proposal. As a compromise, the commission accepted the above offer of Joseph Whipple and contracted for two buildings only. A two-story building was constructed of bricks on Meeting Street. "This building has ever since been occupied by the town and city for educational purposes."[506] Whipple Hall, as described above, was the second school built at that time.

Shortly after its creation, the Hall was closed due to the Revolutionary War. From 1773 until 1781, a council of war, which included a store of explosives, instead occupied it. The town eventually provided the funds to repair the extensive damage done to the school during that time, placed at over 113 Spanish milled dollars. It was not until the year 1800 that the state of Rhode Island passed a free school act. At that time, a Providence committee of citizens recommended that four free schools be established-- one to be kept in Whipple Hall...and that it be repaired. "With the passage of the school act of 1800, 'Whipple Hall,' which stood on the site later occupied by Benefit Street

Cemetery property donated to St. John's Church by John Whipple in 1767

212

Grammar School, was bought by the freemen and some $500 expended on it for repairs."[507]

"The Rhode Island General Assembly...incorporated the Whipple Hall Society of Providence. This was an educational movement made by the proprietors of 'Whipple Hall' a building erected in the north part of Providence for a private school, which afterwards became the first district free public school, and continued for sixty years."[508] "Typical of the grammar schools was the Benefit Street School, erected on the site of Whipple Hall, a two-story brick building, 70 by 40 feet in area, enlarged in 1893 and still in use in 1950 at the corner of Benefit and Halsey Streets."[509] It is thus seen that although Colonel Whipple did not play a direct role in the founding of the Whipple Hall schoolhouse in 1695, his son and grandson, over 70 years later, decidedly did.

By the death of Captain John Whipple the Younger, in 1769, his only surviving son, Joseph of Smithfield, had moved to a large manorial estate in Smithfield Township, some three miles north of downtown Providence.[510] For the next several decades, he and his four sons slowly but inexorably sold off the lands that had taken their ancestors over a century to accumulate. Of these sons, three served in the Revolutionary War: Captain William Whipple, General John Whipple, and Captain Samuel Whipple.

By consensus, the most notable Rhode Island Whipple in the nineteenth century was John, son of Captain Samuel Whipple. John[6]Whipple (Samuel[5], Joseph[4], John[3], Joseph[2], John[1]) built an extant house, located at 52 College, in the 1850s. Henry E. Whipple, in his 1873 book, devotes pages 42 to 44 to his biography. "John Whipple was then [early to mid 1800s] leader of the bar in this state. He had gained the position in contest with such men as Nathaniel Searle, Tristam Burges, and Daniel Webster, both in the courts of this state and in the supreme court of the United States. By some he was pronounced the equal of Webster, where they appeared in contest, and Webster himself is reputed to have said that John Whipple and Jeremiah Mason were the two ablest opponents he had ever met at the bar....He was a student of history, a profound thinker on all social, moral and political questions. He belonged to the school of Hamilton, and had no confidence in that of Jefferson."[511] "The head of the profession was located in the old wooden building at College and South Main---the Whipple Building."[512]

The last few years of his life were spent at his country residence in Warwick. "His widow, with a son and a daughter by his first marriage, survived him. By his first wife he had seven children. Mr. Whipple will long be remembered as one of the most brilliant and successful lawyers of Rhode Island."[513] John Whipple, attorney, had two sons: John and William. John died in Newport, Rhode Island in 1902, his two sons having died in infancy. William, who also had two sons, died in1856 and was buried in Bureau County Illinois, to where he had removed at the age of 16 or 17, immediately following his father's second marriage. Moreover, because Joseph Whipple Junior's sons, as described below, did not marry, with William's move to Illinois, the Whipple male line of Colonel Joseph Whipple ended in Rhode Island.

213

Deputy Governor Joseph Whipple Junior
Wealthiest of the Merchant Princes

Captain Joseph Whipple Junior was born at Providence, 30 December 1687, and died between the months of May and July in 1750.[514] In his early 20s, he apparently took over the property that his father inherited, "all my property in the Narragansett" (which included Newport) from Captain John Whipple in 1685. He married first Anne Almy, in Newport, at about the age of 25, their four sons dying in infancy. The dates of their deaths were: Joseph, 23 September 1713; Christopher, 11 January 1716/17; Joseph, 28 September 1717; William, 16 December 1720. Anne died 12 days after the death of her last child, 28 December 1720. The children, and their mother, were buried in the Almy family burial plot of Newport's Common Burial Ground. Joseph married next Sarah Redwood, at a Friends meeting in Newport, 1 March 1721.[515] She and Joseph had nine children:[516]

i. Sarah, born 28 Jun 1723; died before 5 Nov 1761; married M. Borden
ii. Joseph, born 2 Jul 1725; died 1761.
iii. Benjamin, born 4 Sep 1727; died in infancy
iv. Abraham, born 13 May 1729; died in infancy.
v. William, born 24 Aug 1730; died 23 Jun 1750.
vi. Amey, born 18 Oct 1734; died after 28 Sep 1752; married Thomas Greene
vii. Alice, died 5 Dec 1795; married Benjamin Davis.
viii. Mehitable, died after 28 Sep 1752.
ix. Mary, died before 10 Jun 1754; married Joseph Sylvester

It could be said of Joseph Junior that, like most of his siblings, he married well. It has been contended that he would have had to be a member of the Society of Friends before his marriage to his first wife, as she was related to the Almys of Portsmouth and Newport, noted Quaker farmer merchants.[517] However, a "Joseph Whipple" was known

to have maintained a parishioner relationship to Trinity Anglican Church in Newport.[518] One of the Almy family, Christopher, served as a special representative for the colony to England in the year 1693.[519] Job Almy was the Whipple's next-door neighbor in Newport.[520]

Joseph and his second wife built the mansion opposite in 1745. It has 12 rooms and a large attic and basement--- the latter to house their many slaves. It is

Joseph Whipple Jr. Mansion

located at 299 W. Main Road, Middletown, and was recently purchased by a non-profit organization. It was recently moved from its original site about 50 yards to the west in order to save it from the wrecking ball. Sarah was the daughter of Abraham Redwood and Mehitable Langford. The Redwoods were recent (1712) arrivals from Antigua, West

214

Indies. Abraham was known to have been a business associate of Joseph Whipple before his marriage to their daughter. Ship owner, merchant, slave owner, plantation owner, and philanthropist, Abraham Redwood was one of the richest men in the colony; his fortune derived from plantation interests in Antigua. He was founder of the library (of which Joseph Whipple Junior was an original trustee)[521] that bears his name. In the later stages of life, he came into conflict with other members of the Quaker faith due to his use of human slaves. Redwood and his son Abraham Junior depended upon slaves to maintain the operation of their plantation. Nevertheless, in his will, he left £500 to establish a Friends' School and the same amount to be given to the founding of a college of Rhode Island, provided it would be built in Newport. [522] The college, now Brown University, was instead built in Providence.

It would have been to Joseph's economic advantage to convert to the Society of Friends, and certainly his Redwood marriage provided economic advancement. "By the 1680s, the Quakers had gained a virtual monopoly on Rhode Island's trade. From 1672 to 1677, the Friends controlled the government of the colony, and frequently thereafter one of their numbers occupied the office of governor [and deputy governor]. Close to one-half of the colony in 1690 belonged to the Society of Friends."[523] The Quakers were good at "keeping their trade within themselves and maintaining a strict correspondence and intelligence over all parts were they are." [524]

Sea Captain and Merchant

Joseph's success as a sea captain and merchant could have been a boon to Whipple relatives, who likely invested heavily in his mercantile shipping ventures. Northern Providence Township, where most of them resided, was a region of small farms but prolific families, mostly Baptists, Quakers, or irreligious. Lumber, farm produce, and rum from the enterprises of Joseph's many cousins, and their relatives and friends, would have made their way to his wharves. And as previously shown, in time several Whipple families became successful mill operators and lime manufacturers, and likely depended heavily on him to see to it that their products safely reached domestic and foreign markets. And like most of their fellow colonists, they probably cared not whether these trading ventures were sanctioned by London.

England was at war with Spain and France during these decades, and so had forbidden trade with the enemy, in particular with the enemy's colonies in the West Indies---where most of Rhode Island's trade was centered. Typically, Rhode Island merchant/ship owners simply ignored London's dictates, including Joseph Whipple. There was some risk in the enterprise: if caught by the British, the penalty suffered was loss of both cargo and ship. "In the illicit traffic with the French, the officers and crew were interested in the venture of the cargo. In 1747, the brigantine *Victory*, owned by Joseph Whipple, a merchant of Newport, was captured by his Majesty's sloop *Hind*. She was libeled as a lawful prize concerned in illicit trade with enemies of the crown. The libel was lost, but the case was appealed. Meanwhile Cooper, the master, shipped at 20 pounds per month, New England currency, Downer, the mate, at 14 pounds, Vickers, a mariner, at 12 pounds, Concklin, a mariner, at 10 pounds, all sued Whipple for their wages. Whipple answered that he had received nothing from the vessel, and that officers

215

and crew were concerned in the cargo, having "goods of great value on board.' Judge Strengthfield decided that, the vessel having been released on bond, the mariners could have their wages on giving bond to restore them if the vessel and cargo should be condemned finally. Whipple paid the amount of wages into court under this decree...this shows clearly that the commercial business went forward...always toward one end. That end was money and profit, parliamentary law and crown to the contrary notwithstanding."[525]

Rhode Island's notorious practice of trading directly with Britain's enemies was criticized by other colonies. Even legitimate complaints by its own ship owners sometimes were ignored. "On Tuesday, July 18th 1749, one John Clarke, one of Mr. Whipple's shipmasters, informed Deputy Governor Ellery that a French ship was seen going by Conanicut, through the west passage. Our old friend Whipple and his captains seem to have had sharp eyes for detecting illicit goods on an alien and competing vessel. Deputy Ellery was not over-hasty, nor did he give information to the customhouse officers. He sent for Governor Green, of Warwick, who went to Newport and called a council. The council, 'on mature deliberation, 'found they could not act in the affair....'"[526]

Captain Joseph Whipple Junior was known to have owned at least four other ships: the Brigantines *Providence* and P*elican,* and the Sloops *Wheel of Fortune* and the *Sarah.*[527] In 1730, one of Joseph's employees was caught in the act of taking 1000 "Hogshead Hoops" from a wharf. Subsequent trial testimony revealed that "John Mitchell of lawful age, that he being Mate on board the sloop *Sarah* of which Capt. Joseph Whipple was chief owner, was 'ordered by sd Whipple to take one thousand of Hoops from off Mr. Goulding's Wharfe and carry them on bord sd sloop which accordingly I did, and while I was taking off sd hoops there came a man and forwarned me taking anymore and also bid me land them I had gott, but sd owner told me to go off with them I had gott.' Verdict for the plaintiff 5 pounds, damages, and court costs."[528]

An instructive, ongoing history can be gleaned from these and others of Joseph's ventures and adventures as recorded in court files, such as the incident of the youthful run-away mariner: "A memorandum dated 29 September 1725, signed by Justices D. Updike and John Coddington stated that 'Caleb Kinion, Mustee...who had deserted his Master Mr. Joseph Whipple for Some Space' was brought before them. 'We find that he hath put his said Master to great Charge in apprehending him and therefore order that he serve his sd Master for the Space of One Year and Eight months' [from this date]."[529]

Among other cargo aboard Joseph's vessels was that of slaves. "Bill of sale shown, from Joseph Whipple of Newport, merchant, for 70 pounds to Samuel Dyre...sometime in September 1724, for a Negro man named Fortune...Jury verdict for the plaintiff.[530]

"Benjamin Norton was a Newporter, and apparently, a great-great-grandfather of Harvard University's Professor Charles Norton. In the fall of 1720, he and Joseph Whipple, merchant of Providence (and later Deputy Governor), had outfitted a brigantine to trade to the West Indies under Norton's command. In January 1721, she was attacked by pirates at St. Lucia and surrendered, apparently after very little resistance, to the most successful pirate of them all, an Englishman named Bartholomew Roberts. A few weeks later, Roberts captured a Dutch-built ship of 250 tons...and entrusted the ship to Norton...Norton sailed the ship north, brought her into Tarpaulin

Cove on Naushon, and got word to Captain Whipple of his arrival...Whipple, Christopher Almy (his father-in-law), and one Pease of Newport, as well as some others, came down to the Cove in sloops and took much of the cargo off and up to Providence before they were interrupted....[531]

Joseph's possible conversion to the Quaker faith or at least his marriage to the daughter of a prominent Quaker, and move to Newport were likewise necessary to a political career. In early to mid-eighteenth century Rhode Island, political power resided only in Newport. On only one occasion did a governor reside outside of the island itself. "Even then, it was promptly voted that it was 'highly necessary' for the governor of the colony to live in Newport. One hundred pounds was allowed from the treasury to allow Governor Jencks to defray the charges of removing his family to Newport."[532]

Whitehall

Beginning in 1728, the eminent Anglo-Irish philosopher and theologian George Berkeley lived for over two years in Newport. Landing in Virginia, Berkeley found passage to Newport, where he intended to purchase a farm. The farm was to supply provisions for a proposed college in Bermuda while awaiting final arrangements for a

subsidy from the royal treasury in London. To that end, "Berkeley purchased the ninety-six acre farm of Joseph Whipple and his wife, Sarah, the daughter of Samuel Redwood... in present day Middletown. Berkeley enlarged the dwelling house on it and named it 'Whitehall.' From early May 1728, Berkeley and his wife settled into their life, making plans for the future college and tending the property."[533] A copy of the "Deed of the Whipple Farm To George Berkley" hangs in the living room of the house (seen opposite), and reads in part:

Whitehall, 2004

To all Christian people whom these presents shall come, I, Joseph Whipple of Newport in the Colony of Rhode Island and Providence Plantations, Merchant, sendeth Greeting. Know ye that the said Joseph Whipple for an in consideration of the sum of 2500 pounds in current money of New England, to him in had well and truly paid by George Berkeley D.D., Dean of Derry in the Kingdom of Ireland at and before the sealing and delivery of these presents. The receipt whereof the said Joseph Whipple doth acknowledge and thereof doth acquit and discharge the said George Berkeley, his heirs, executors, and administrators, and every one of them...a certain tract of land to the same adjoining and belonging containing about 96 acres, or the same more or less, and consisting of one orchard, and the rest arable pasture, meadow, and woodland, situate, lying and being in Newport aforesaid....And Sarah the wife of the above Joseph Whipple doth by these presents freely and voluntarily resign quit claim and surrender

217

unto the said George Berkeley, his heirs and assigns, all her right of dower and power of and to all other demands which she hath or hereafter might have…In Witness whereof the said Joseph Whipple and Sarah his wife have hereunto set their hands and seals the eighteenth day of February in the second year of the reign of our Sovereign Lord George the Second, King Of Great Britain, etc, Annoque Domini 1728.[534]

It is likely that Joseph Whipple was a member of Berkeley's inner circle; certainly his father-in-law Samuel Redwood was.[535] Berkeley founded a society for the promotion of knowledge and virtue that "met in various choice homes, had sumptuous banquets,

Anne Whipple Headstone

and, over good wine, discussed the latest political and intellectual news from Europe.[536] Could this association have inspired Joseph to see to it that his son, William, born in 1730, was properly educated at Harvard University? "Less than three short years the dean remained in Rhode Island,---an interval which he improved by building a home (Whitehall) near the Hanging Rocks and the sea, and by composing his Plato-like 'Alciphon,' but the radiance with which his coming had been attended did not vanish away at his departure."[537] Among those[538] that Berkeley brought from Britain was the noted portrait painter, John Smibert, who inspired the local painter, Robert Feke, to paint many of the locals of the colony. It was Feke who painted the portrait of Joseph Whipple III seen below.

"Of the new or mercantile class, the class of genuine sea lords…ship building, privateering, and mercantile adventuring were interchangeable occupations. A later group of merchants (and upon the whole the group most characteristic of eighteenth century Rhode Island) embraced in large part men already known to us through their protest to the king against paper money. These men (Newporters all) were Abraham Redwood, William Ellery, Henry Collins….and Joseph Whipple. And not only were these men merchants, they in the main were merchants of magnanimous minds. They belonged to the class that in the Italy of the fifteenth century delighted to adorn the State with palaces, and to fill these palaces with beautiful and costly objects….[539]

On 27 July 1746, Joseph bought the birthplace home of his thirteen year old cousin, the soon to become Commodore Abraham Whipple, from his father Noah Whipple. Joseph Whipple III subsequently sold this property, 14 December 1750, to John Checkley, Rector of St. John's Church in Providence.[540]

Perhaps due to the economic power and the social influence of his extended family, Joseph served as Deputy Governor of the colony from 1743 to 1746.[541] At least four documents are known to exist that bear his name while in that office.[542] The documents' quaint phraseology, grammar, and spelling of the time are preserved. One letter was sent to Governor Shirley of Massachusetts, dated 29 August 1746:

218

"Gentn. Your Letter of the 25th instant came to Me in the Absence of Governour Green, and in Answer to which I am to inform You, That our Forces embarked the last week, and will be ready to join the Forces of the Neighbouring Governments If They undertake the Reduction of Crown Point. I should be glad to be inform'd Whether you carry all or what Part of the Provisions to Albany, which we designed for your Forces Provided They had gone up the River of St. Lawrence, and also what Quantity of Powder will be this Colony's Proportion. I am Gentn. Your most oded. Humble servt. Joseph Whipple. To his Excy. Shirley Esq. And the Honble P. Warren Esq, Boston."

Deputy Governor Whipple subsequently responded with a letter on 6 November 1746. "Your Excelcy. Favour of the 4th instant came Safe with the Agreeable News of the French Fleet leaving the Coast, and the Canadians raising the Siege of Annapolis, and in the Absence of Governour Green, It falls to my Province to let Your Excelcy know That agreeable to a Representation made by You and the Honble Admiral Warren for our Men to be sent to Annapolis, the General Assembly immediately ordered the Same to be done, and I can now inform You That on Tuesday last our Three Companies sailed in the Three Transports under Convoy of our Colony Sloop for Annapolis with all the Able and healthy Men belonging to said Companies (being somewhat reduced by Several that have dyed and others that are now Sick)and hope they may be Instrumental by assisting the other forces to perform the necessary Operations for distressing the Enemy, and prevent their making any further Attempts on the aforesaid Place, and for the Preservation of Nova Scotia. Your Excelcy will always find this Government ready and willing to exert Themselves to the Utmost for his majesty's Service and Interest. I am with due respect, Your Excelcy's most obedient humble Serv. Joseph Whipple. To his Excelcy Wm Shirley, Esq."

Deputy Governor Whipple received a letter [from Secretary Willard of Massachusetts] dated 1 September 1746, perhaps sent to him in that the governor's wife had just died. It addressed Rhode Island's participation in the war with France in the colony of New York. The letter ends with, "I am Your Honour's most Obedient humble Servant, Josiah Willard. To the Honble Joseph Whipple, Esq."

One other very lengthy letter was received from Richard Partridge, the colony's agent in London, and dated Xber 15 1744. It addressed several concerns including the colony's Charter, its boundaries with Connecticut and Massachusetts, and Partridge's need for more money. A postscript may be of general interest:

"The war continues and I think likely to, tho' some imagine we shall have a peace by the Spring: we have had a pretty deal of damage done to the Shipping lately by Stormy Weather. The King of Prussia who had broke out again against the Queen of Hungary has now quitted Prague and all Bohemia and gone home with the loss of about half of his army and a part of the Q of Hungary's forces has entered Siletia and probably will retake it. Capt. Jephson is here and I suppose intends home as soon as convenient he can, he has been taken by the ffrench and as he was coming for France in a St. Dominga Ship was taken in her by one of our Men of War. RP. To Joseph Whipple, Esqr. Deputy Governor of the Colony of Rhode Island and Providence Plantations."

There exists the possibility that Joseph Junior, though married into the Redwood family, was not himself a convert to the Society of Friends. As noted, records of Trinity

Church in Newport evidence that he purchased pews in that sanctuary in 1726, as did his son Joseph III in 1752. Likewise, a second son, William, was known to be Anglican. "In 1745, the Harvard Faculty was being adamant against admitting late applicants, but on August 14 it agreed to 'examine Whipple (son of Capt. Whipple late Deputy Governor of the Colony of Rhode Island) in order to his admission in to College as a Freshmen, although it be out of Time, and especially in regard to his living in another Government, and may be suppos'd not to be acquainted with the College rules and Customs in that Affair.' So William was admitted, and was placed at the head of the Class of 1749, not, as some have thought, because of the fact that the Whipples were Narragansett Episcopalians, but because of the Captain's civil office."[543] But tragically William died about one year after his graduation, on 23 June 1750. His college friends probably smiled sadly as they read his obituary: "His sacred Thirst of Knowledge discovered itself very early, and to cultivate so promising a Genius, his Father procured him the best Masters....As he was inferiour to none of his age, in useful Learning, Knowledge and Virtue, his Death is universally lamented."[544] For almost 150 years after its founding, the names of Harvard University students were arranged not alphabetically, but in an order established for each class during the freshman year according to social rank. In the freshman class of 1745, William Whipple, son of Deputy Governor Joseph Whipple, was ranked first in his class by the faculty and administration, indicating the social and political position of the family not just in his hometown or colony, but also in the whole of the New England Colonies.

Captain Joseph Whipple Junior died between the months of May and July of 1750---most likely in June. His will was written 28 May 1750, and proved 2 July 1750. The fragmented document mentioned that he died of a "short but severe illness." One wonders that he may have died from a broken heart caused by the unfathomable death of his beloved son that same month. It is evident that he had put all of his wealth, influence, and love into educating the boy and surely was looking toward his joyous future, and toward the continuance of the powerful Whipple family legacy. It must be lamentably recalled that six of William's brothers and half-brothers had preceded him in death. In his Last Will and Testament, Joseph named his widow Sarah, daughters Alice, Amey, Mehetable, and Sarah; sons Joseph and William; and grandchildren Christopher, Amey, and Joseph Sylvester, children of Amey.[545] It would have been instructive to know his net worth including movable estate, considering the size of his brother's estate and that of their father.

The Honorable Joseph Whipple Junior, Esq, Deputy Governor of the Colony of Rhode Island and the Providence Plantations, was buried in an unmarked grave beside his first wife, Anne, and their four infant sons.[546] It should be noted lamentably that even his two sons who did survive into young adulthood died without issue. It can be stated with regrettable assurance that with his passing, and that of the death of his father four years earlier, the Whipple financial empire reached its terminus. For within three years, his only remaining son would become financially insolvent and conclude a promising political career in disrepute.

Deputy Governor Joseph Whipple III
Last of the Whipple Merchant Princes

Joseph Whipple III was born 3 July 1725 in Newport,[547] and seems never to have married. He must have been a remarkable young man, in his own right, to have ascended to the office of deputy governor at the unprecedented age of 24. Admittedly, his father and others of his politically active and socially prominent family, likely made the way less tenuous. They, and their political allies, could have been grooming the young man for even higher political office.

Following the political campaign of 1749, should there have been the customary victory dinner-dance in the Whipple's substantial, yet not ostentatious, country home near the Newport line in Middletown[548] (seen above and described in Joseph's bankruptcy petition of 1753, as being quite large with an expensive gambrel roof) one could have witnessed a gathering of Rhode Island's most notable social, military, and political elites.

From among others of his own immediate family, come to share in his victory, likely was his brother William, the first descendant of Captain John Whipple to graduate from Harvard University. Then there could have been Captain John Whipple, his father's

brother, the well-known land baron and "Bonesetter." John's 15-year-old son, Joseph, likely was in attendance. His sons, Captain William Whipple, Captain Samuel Whipple, and General John Whipple, soon would assume leading roles in America's war for independence.[549] Joseph's great aunt Freelove Whipple and her husband, Major Arthur Young, could have been there. Other relatives from the military hierarchy to attend could have been Captain Job Whipple and Captain William Whipple, Junior from Smithfield, as well as Colonel Stephen Whipple from Cumberland. Then there could have been the 16-year-old Abraham Whipple, grandnephew to his father, soon to become Commodore of the Continental Navy.

Joseph Whipple III

The victory party likewise would have numbered many of the colony's mid-eighteenth century political sophisticates, including close members of Joseph's own inner circle. For example, Joseph Greene, husband of his aunt Amy Redwood Whipple, and nephew of Governor William Greene; and Phillip Wanton, from his aunt Sarah Redwood Whipple's side of the family, a cousin and nephew to four Rhode Island governors who bore that surname. Aunt Martha Coggeshall, his uncle Abraham Redwood's wife, a granddaughter of John Coggeshall of the early political dynasty of Portsmouth, Rhode Island, might have graced the party with her presence.[550] Also entering into the festivities could have been his aunt Ami Whipple and her husband Robert Gibbs, the son of Sir Henry Gibbs of Dorset, England. Then, an up-and-coming politician named Stephen Hopkins (Joseph's great grandfather Captain John Whipple's great grandson through his youngest daughter

Abigail), who would become the colony's governor within just six years and go on to sign the Declaration of Independence, conceivably joined the festivities that night to share in his cousin's triumph. And the list goes on.

Robert Feke, who flourished c 1741 to 1751, painted the portrait above of Deputy Governor Joseph Whipple III in 1750. Oil on Canvas, 47 by 37 inches, it was auctioned at Sotherby's (Lot 1302, Sale 5968) on 26 January 1990, and sold for $25,000. The auction catalog misattributed the painting as being that of Joseph Whipple Junior, who became Deputy Governor at the age of 56. It further states, "He and his wife were Quakers, despite the fact that most other members of his family were Anglicans. Whipple's Quaker beliefs possibly accounts for the absence of a sword within the portrait. Provenance: Descended in the family of the subject to the present owner." The identity of this Whipple descendant is unknown.

End of a Mercantile Empire

The end of the all-too-brief political achievements of the Newport Whipples was announced in a terse statement of a summary of the Minutes of the Rhode Island General Assembly: "Both houses resolved into a grand committee, on the second day of Nov., when the Hon. Joseph Whipple Esq., resigned the office of Deputy Governor, and therefore, the Hon. Jonathan Nichols, Esq., was chosen in his room, for the remaining part of the year, and engaged accordingly."[551] After five years in office, at the age of 28, Joseph had become financially insolvent. "He was concerned in the mercantile operation, and the ruinous system of paper money was working its ruinous results. He surrendered all his property to the use of his creditors and received the benefit of a "special act" (by the General Assembly).[552] Specifically, in May of 1753, he mortgaged the family's manorial estate that had been left to him in his father's will. Then, between the months of December 1753 and March 1754, over £25,000 was raised from its sale, and that from other properties, to cover accumulated debts.[553]

Prior to the advent of the modern banking system, colonists borrowed money directly from the government in the form of paper scripts (as it did not have enough silver or gold to loan), usually with property as collateral. Due to the vagaries of war, by the year 1750, the majority of debtors could not repay their debts. Rather than go into bankruptcy itself, the government called in all overdue notes at once. Concomitantly, paper script (which most possessed and conducted business with) was devalued to about half its original value. This meant that, for those not possessing silver or gold, twice as much paper was needed to repay their debts. Apparently, the Whipple family had borrowed heavily during the 1740s, gambling what venture capital was available to them, and, like so many other Newport ship owners, they lost all.[554]

"Rhode Island lost still more (than Massachusetts) in her commerce and business at home. Her bills depreciated about one half at once. This broke down her whole system of trade for the time. She lost a large portion of her active West India trade, and Joseph Whipple (III), one of her largest merchants at Newport, failed. She passed her first act in bankruptcy for his special relief, it being the first failure of consequence the colony had known....She had issued paper money more heavily than Massachusetts, she

222

had less property as a basis, and received a smaller relative proportion of specie (silver and gold) from England.... To have redeemed (all the paper money) outstanding, would have required a tax of nearly 14 pounds per head. This large sum could not have been collected."[555]

The collapse of a family fortune was not an uncommon occurrence in mid eighteenth century Rhode Island. The majority of those Newport merchants who filed for bankruptcy during this period were forced to do so primarily because of the trauma of war. The loss of just one of a family's ships due to piracy or war during the protracted British, Spanish, and French conflicts of the 1740s and 1750s brought financial ruin to many Rhode Island business men: "The war spawned privateering and similar seafaring as well as battles on land....Vast profits flowed into the coffers of some investors, while others, such as Henry Collins and Ebenezer Flagg (and Joseph Whipple) suffered disastrous losses. During 1758, almost a hundred vessels were captured; during the whole war, sixty-five from Providence....Many were killed, ships sank or fell prey to the enemy, some merchants were ruined....Several major mercantile firms sank hopelessly into debt as a result of losses at sea....Internal division, rivalry over increasingly constricted commerce, death and debt, such were the consequence of the outpouring of patriotic bellicosity of 1739 to 1763."[556]

Financial setback became immediately apparent after the untimely deaths of Joseph's father and brother in the summer of 1750. This had been preceded, just four years earlier, by the death of his grandfather, the family's patriarch and putative founder of the Whipple mercantile trading empire. It is conceivable that Joseph had not had enough time and opportunity, or perhaps lacked the innate inclination of his forbears, to develop those skills requisite to successful entrepreneurship. William, his Harvard University-educated brother and potential business partner, mentioned in their father's will of 1750, but described as "late" in Joseph's declaration of bankruptcy three years later, was also deceased.[557] Not even the possible business acumen and social influence of his mother and her Redwood kinsmen could be relied upon, as she had remarried in 1752 and moved to Boston.[558] Thus the under-girding of a decade's long foundation of unprecedented familial support was abruptly swept away well before Joseph's thirtieth birthday.

To his credit, it must be noted that Joseph had been elected by his peers to the second highest political office in the colony for five consecutive years. Apparently, he was a good politician! The only known extant document bearing his signature is a letter written to the colony's representative, Richard Partridge, in London, dated 18 June 1749. It relates his administration's concern with the amount of money needed to pursue the war with France and other matters: "Sir, Letters I have lately received from You with that directed to the Committee who disposed of the Sterling Money on your hands have been communicated to the general Assembly; who have ordered me to inform You that on examining the Accounts of your Agency, they find four hundred Pounds sterling charged November 21st 1744, as a reserve in your Hands for future Services, for which they judge You ought to have given Credit, inasmuch as all the Expenses from that Time to this which had been at on the Colony's Behalf are charged in your several Accounts, the Article of Eighty two pounds Sterling charged as a Loss on the Bills of Exchange you drew payable to Messrs Oliver and Phillips, the Assembly expect a further Explanation of the Equity and Reasonableness of before they can readily allow it, and as to the Article of Commissions for negotiating the Affair of the money advanced by this Government for the Canada Expedition, they have voted You two per Cent for receiving the same; as they have also an hundred Pounds Sterling as a Gratuity for your extraordinary Trouble respecting the Boundary line between the Providence of Massachusetts Bay and this Colony, the Remainder of your Account seems to meet with Approbation.

As to Mr. Lockman's Petition relating to the naval office We doubt not but that the two acts of Parliament made in King Charles 2nd and King William's Reigns relating to said Office will sufficiently vindicate the Colony's Conduct in rejecting his Patent, and as to his Aspersions so liberally cast on Us, was his character as well known in London as it is in Rhode-Island he would not have Access to any publick Board to spread his false Reports which it is obvious are only the Result of his Disappointment."[559]

The particulars of Joseph's life from his resignation in 1754 until 1761, the year of his death, are obscure. It was left to the local newspaper, the *Newport Mercury*, to describe the final malevolent scene of an all-too-brief and undeservedly anguished later life: "Joseph Whipple, formerly Dep. Govr. Facted, became intemperate, and was drowned from the Point Bridge, while returning from the theatre on the Point."[560] Records of his burial or possible wife and children have not been found.

It is interesting to speculate as to what might have happened to the Whipple fortune and political dynasty had not illaudable circumstances intruded. In reality, the dynasty likely would not have continued if Joseph had been, as thought, like his mother, a Quaker. For after the war, Rhode Island Quakers decided they should avoid public office. "Gone was the hope that Friends could serve themselves and their society by holding the reigns of government. Instead, there was a new belief that holding office was itself a corrupting form of worldliness...This change of heart signaled the end of Newport Quakerism....Between the expulsion of some who would not go along with this new spirit [would Joseph have been excommunicated?], and the departure of others for Philadelphia or New York, by the end of the century, few of the rich and powerful Friends remained."[561] Possibly, immediately following his mother's remarriage and move to Boston in 1752, he became a communicant in the church of his father and grandfather, for it is recorded that a "Joseph Whipple" paid for a row of pews at Trinity Church at that time.[562] At any rate, the Whipple surname does not appear in the Newport census records of 1774 and 1790.

The capricious vicissitudes of war, politics, banking, and untimely deaths dictated that the astonishing success story of the Whipples of Newport, Rhode Island ended in the mid eighteenth century. Consequently, the mantle of high political office in the colony was lost to the descendants of Colonel Joseph Whipple, but would then fall to those of his youngest sister, Abigail Whipple Hopkins. The life of Stephen Hopkins is discussed in the chapter on the daughters of Captain John Whipple.

224

End Notes

475 John O. Austin, *Genealogical Dictionary of Rhode Island* (Albany, NY: 1887: reprint edition, Baltimore: Genealogical Publishing Company, 1978) 223. James N. Arnold, *Vital Records of Rhode Island, 1636*-1850 (Providence: Narragansett Historical Publishing Company, 1892). *The Early Records of the Town of Providence*, 21 vols., collected and printed by the Record Commissioners (Providence: Snow & Farnham, city printers, 1892-1915) V:280-81 [hereinafter ERP]. Henry E. Whipple, *A Brief Genealogy of the Whipple Families who Settled in Rhode Island* (Providence: A. Crawford Greene, 1873). To see more recent corrections and additions consult www.whipple.org, Weldon Whipple, Webmaster.

476 Ancestress of Charles Lippitt, Rhode Island governor 1896, and Henry Lippitt, U.S. Senator from Rhode Island 1911. Also, John Chafee, Rhode Island governor 1962, and U.S. Senator from Rhode Island 1977-1999, and Lincoln Chafee, U.S. Senator from Rhode Island, 2000-2006.

477 Alice was obviously a constructive partner in her husband's business enterprises. Welcome Arnold Greene, *The Providence Plantations for Two Hundred and Fifty Years* (Providence: J.A. & R.A. Reid Publishers, 1886) 221. "In 1698 an industry, hitherto unpracticed in the United States, was started...It appears that in 1698, Col. Joseph Whipple kept a variety store on North Main Street, at the foot of Constitution Hill. His wife assisted him, and, having decided taste, she was in the habit of trimming for her customers the imported Dunstable Bonnets which she kept for sale. The locality of this store was the seat of female fashions in the old town of Providence. It abounded then, and for years afterwards, the milliners' shops..."

478 *ERP*, VIII:94

479 Sydney V. James, *Colonial Rhode Island, A History* (New York: Charles Scribner's Sons, 1976) 262. Gertrude S. Kimball, *Providence in Colonial Times* (Boston: Houghton Mifflin Company, 1912) 150-152. Capt. John Crawford and Major William Crawford lived...on the old John Whipple Inn lot on the North end of Towne Street at the corner of Mill Street. Their personal estates were "almost overwhelming in sumptuousness... His (Major William) sloop, Sarah Boate, evidently named for his wife, Sarah Whipple, was appraised at four hundred pounds." As shown herein, this boat became the property of Captain Joseph Whipple Junior. Colonel Joseph Whipple was given power of administration of his estate, "Sarah Crawford...at present troubled with insanity of mind." XII:17-19. "Crawford street bears the name of the distinguished merchant, William Crawford." Bicknell, 3:892. John Crawford and Amy Whipple were married for four years during which time they bought a homestead and built a house on Mill Street near to her father's tavern. "Their home might have been the most elaborately furnished in the town... The house in the course of time became the possession of their granddaughter, who married Benjamin Steele... It was here on the 22d day of July, 1801, that Nicholas Brown, the 'eminent merchant' the friend of the friendless (etc)...was married to Mary Bowen Steele..." Field, 3:634-638. A photograph of the Crawford/Whipple house is on page 635 of this book.

480 Austin, 223. Henry E. Whipple, 39

481 Austin, 223

482 Austin, 223. Benefit Street did not exist until around the year 1750.

483 Franklin R. Cushman, King's Church-St. John's Church, 1722-1929 (Providence: St. John Church, 1949) 1. "Colonel Joseph Whipple not only gave a generous subscription of one hundred pounds but also boarded the workmen who built the church."

484 Kimball, 180-81

485 James, 226

486 Allen G. Beaman and Nellie Beaman, Rhode Island Genealogical Register, Vol. 1-20, Volume 3 No. 3, Princeton, Mass., Abstracts of Providence Wills, 206. Austin, 223

487 Rosemarie Polce, Secretary, North Burying Ground, "Cemetery Records date from March 1848 and do not tell how or when Sarah and John got here. The stones suggest it is just in memory of them, not that the actual bodies are here." On-line at www.whipple.org/blaine/johnswife/html. John E. Sterling, *North Burial Ground, Providence, Rhode Island, Old Section 1700-1848* (Providence: Special Publication 5, Rhode Island Genealogical Society, 2000) 13. "Both of these gravestones (Capt. John and Sarah Whipple) are probably replacements for markers in the original family cemetery. They were carved by George Allen about 1740, possibly when the bodies were moved to North Burial Ground."

[488] Sterling, 12-13. The Joseph Whipple family burial site (Area AA) lists 27 burials. (1) In memory of Capt. John Whipple first son of Col Joseph Whipple who departed this life the 18th of May died 1769 aged 84 years 5 mos & 19 days (2) In memory of ye Hon Col Joseph Whipple who departed this life anno dom 1746 in ye 85th year of his age (3) In memory of Mrs Alice Whipple ye wife of Col Joseph Whipple Born in Providence and died July 20th anno dom 1739 aged 75 years (4) Jeremiah son of Capt John Whipple & Abigail his wife died Jan 2d 1731 aged 14 mos 23 days (5) In memory of Mary wife of Capt Charles Bardin youngest daughter of Col. Joseph Whipple died Dec 8 1733 aged 29 years & 8 mos (6) In memory of Capt John Whipple who was born in England & died in Providence Town 16th day of May anno dom 1685 about 68 years of age (7) In memory of Mrs Sarah Whipple wife of Capt John Whipple she was born in Dorchester in New England died in Providence anno dom 1666 aged about 42 years (8) In memory of Capt William Whipple a Revolutionary Purist who died on the 5th of July. Suppress not your tears. This is a soldiers grave (9) In memory of Mrs Abigail Whipple wife of William Whipple who died Nov 16 1818 age 64 years (10) Miss Sussanah Whipple daughter of Joseph & Sarah 27 May 1797 in 23 year of her age (11) Mrs Mary Olney wife of Capt Stephan Olney daughter of Josf Whipple died May 24 1798 age 27 years 4 mos (12) Miss Freelove Whipple daughter of Joseph died Dec 4 1798 age 30 years 5 days (13) Miss Mehitable daughter of Joseph Whipple died 3 Feb 1799 age 17 years 11 mos (14) Miss Elizabeth daughter of Joseph Whipple esq & sara his wife who expired Feb 27 1800 age 21 years 3 months 2 days (15) In memory of Amy Hurd wife of Ambrose Hurd & daughter of Joseph Whipple died 17 Jan 1803 42 years & 19 days (16) In memory of Miss Hatty Whipple Hurd adopted daughter of Gen John Whipple & Naomi his wife who died May 3 1827 in her 26th year (17) Joseph Whipple, veteran of Revolutionary War, died Jan 6 1816 age 82 (18) Sara Whipple wife of Joseph Whipple died Apr 20 1820 age 85 years (19) In memory of Mrs Abigail Jastram relic of Mr. John Jastram & daughter of late Joseph and Sara Whipple of Smithfield. She died June 31 1841 in her 83d year (20) In memory of Gen John Whipple, veteran of the Revolutionary War, 21, Dec 1811 (21) In memory of Mrs Naomi Whipple relict of Gen John Whipple who died Feb 18 1837 in the 83d year of her life. (22) In memory of Pardon Whipple, Lieut, son of William, USN veteran c1791-11 May 1827 (23) Hannah Whipple, wife of Samuel, c1819-27 Jan 1892 (24) Samuel Whipple, Veteran of Revolutionary War, c1758- 17 Oct 1809 (25) Deborah Whipple, wife of Samuel, c1757- 1 Nov 1831 (26) Joanna Whipple 2d daughter of Samuel c1781- 22 Oct 1784, (27) Joanna Whipple daughter of Samuel and Deborah c1796- 26 Aug 1832. Note: several of these headstones no longer can be read.
[489] ERP, IX:99. Dorothy S. Towle, ed., Records of the Vice-Admiralty Court of Rhode Island, 1716-1752 (Washington, D.C.: The American Historical Society, 1936) 382. "Sworn To in the Presents of Stephen Hopkins this forth Day of September AD 1746. Before Mee John Whipple Jus Peese." At this time, he was living in Newport. Barbara Mills, Providence, 1630-1800: Women are Part of Its History (Bowie, Md: Heritage Books, 2002) 362. "Other doctors who practiced in Rhode Island...were John Whipple, called a 'natural bone setter'...
[490] Information on his headstone indicates that he died at age 84 years, 5 months, and 19 days. He was born one day after the death of his grandfather Whipple.
[491] Died at age 32 and not buried in husband's cemetery plot. Her husband apparently never remarried.
[492] As Joseph was a member of the Providence town council and 20 year representative to Newport, so likewise John from 1741 to 1746. William R. Staples, Annals of the Town of Providence (Providence: Knowles and Vose, 1843) 657.
[493] ERP, II:171-72.
[494] Stephen Dexter was the son of John Dexter, the brother-in-law of Joseph's sister Abigail. His mother was Alice Smith, the daughter of Joseph's sister Sarah. Joseph's daughter, Susannah, married Stephen Dexter in 1709. He inherited the Smith, and other nearby properties, through the Smith line. This land is now occupied by St. John's Episcopal Church, given to the church by the Dexters and Whipples.
[495] Arnold was Joseph's sister Sarah's second husband.
[496] Floy S. Hyde, Captain John Whipple of Providence Rhode Island, 1616-1685, (Mountain View, NY: Privately Published, 1984) 10-11
[497] Also, "Back of these three house lots was an oblong piece of land one hundred seventy feet by one hundred sixty, which Mr. John Whipple deeded to King's Church in 1767 for a burying place." Cushman, 4. Photograph courtesy of Special Collections University of Rhode Island, 26 March 2007.

⁴⁹⁸ Edward Field, *State of Rhode Island and Providence Plantations at the End of the Century: A History* 3 Vols. (Boston: Mason Publishing Company, 1902) 2:257

⁴⁹⁹ Providence Town Papers, #402. William R. Staples, *Annals of The Town of Providence* (Providence: Knowles and Vose, 1843) 602.

⁵⁰⁰ *ERP*, III:35.

⁵⁰¹ Providence Town Papers, #418. *Welcome Arnold Greene, The Providence Plantations For Two Hundred and Fifty Years* (Providence: J.A. & R.A. Reid, Publishers, 1886) 52.

⁵⁰² James P. Root, *A Record of the Descendants of John Steere who Settled in Providence, Rhode Island About the year 1660* (Cambridge: Riverside Press, 1890) 191.

⁵⁰³ *ERP*, XX:22.

⁵⁰⁴ John Dexter was Abigail Whipple's first husband's brother, William Hopkins was Abigail Whipple's second husband, Epenetus Olney was Mary Whipple's husband, John and Joseph Smith were sons of Sarah Whipple Smith, and Turpin was the brother-in-law [their wives were sisters] of John Whipple III.

⁵⁰⁵ Austin, 223. Henry E. Whipple, 39.

⁵⁰⁶ Greene, 163.

⁵⁰⁷ Richard M. Bayles, ed., *History of Providence County, Rhode Island, 2 vols.* (New York: W.W. Preston and Company, 1891) 1:500.

⁵⁰⁸ Samuel G. Arnold, *History of the State of Rhode Island and Providence Plantations* 2 vols. (New York: D. Appleton & Company, 1860) 2:292

⁵⁰⁹ John H. Cady, *The Civic and Architectural Development of Providence, 1636-1950* (Providence: The Book Shop, 1957) 43 & 103.

⁵¹⁰ James N. Arnold, Vital Records of Rhode Island (Providence: Narragansett Publishing Company, 1892) XIV:411, XV: 572. "Joseph of Smithfield, within 22 months he has lost by death 5 daughters of mature age" *Providence Gazette*, 28 February 1799. "Robert, son of William, at the house of Joseph Whipple, at Smithfield, in his 25th year. Since May, 1797, there have been 13 deaths in this house, 11 from consumption." *Providence Gazette*, 8 January 1811. The above Robert was Joseph's grandson. There was unfathomable tragedy in Joseph's home, but at least four sons did not die during that epidemic. His entire family was buried in the North Burial Grounds next to Captain John and Sarah Whipple.

⁵¹¹ Bayles, 1:49.

⁵¹² Bayles, 1:36. He built a mansion that is still standing at 52 College Street, Providence.

⁵¹³ L.E. Rogers, ed., *Biographical Cyclopedia of Representative Men of Rhode Island* (Providence: National Biographical Publishing Company, 1881) 217.

⁵¹⁴ Genealogical research on colonial Newport is often hampered by the poor state of many surviving documents, which were damaged during the Revolution. In 1778, after nearly three years of British occupation, Walter Chaloner, the town's sheriff and a Tory, fled on a British ship with all the probate records, deeds, and vital records under his jurisdiction. His ship ran aground in New York harbor. Retrieved from the watery depths, the boxes were left in storage for some time. When they were finally unpacked, the extent of the damage was revealed. The remnants of the records are now preserved in bound volumes at the Newport Historical Society, but the contents of any given page may be from different documents, often of different dates. Furthermore, almost all are faded to differing degrees of indecipherability. Fully one-half or more of the documents were lost, so it is hard to draw unchallengeable conclusions in Newport. Vincent F. Luti, "Mallet & Chisel: Gravestone Carvers of Newport, Rhode Island, in the 18ᵗʰ century," 8. Had not this been the case, perhaps a clearer picture of Joseph Junior and Joseph III could be painted. Where were they buried? In unmarked graves? What happened to Joseph III between 1754 and 1761? Did he recover from the bankruptcy? Did he have a family? Etc.

⁵¹⁵ James N. Arnold, *Vital Records of Rhode Island, 1639-1850* (Providence: Narragansett Historical Publishing Company, 1892) 7:27

⁵¹⁶ James N. Arnold, Vital *Records of Rhode Island, 1636-1850* (Providence: Narragansett Historical Publishing Company, 1892). John O. Austin, *Genealogical Dictionary of Rhode Island* (Albany, NY: 1887: reprint edition, Baltimore: Genealogical Publishing Company, 1978). Vital statistics of the children and grandchildren of John and Sarah Whipple are taken from the above and numerous publications that quote from them. To view more recent information consult www.whipple.org, Weldon Whipple, Webmaster.

⁵¹⁷ Rufus Jones, *The Quakers in the American Colonies* (New York: W. W. Norton & Company, 1966) 547.

[518] John B. Hattendorf, SempreEdem: *A History of Trinity Church in Newport*, 1698-2000 (Newport: Trinity Church, 2001) 78. Nine parishioners, one a "Joseph Whipple," purchased pews in 1726.

[519] Bridenbaugh, 41, 90

[520] Jane Fletcher Fiske, transcriptionist, "Newport Court Book A" Rhode Island General Court of Trials, Boxford, Mass: privately published, 1998, 1720.

[521] George C. Mason, Annals *of the Redwood Library and Athenaeum* (Newport: Redwood Library, 1891) 34.

[522] Gladys E. Bolhouse, "Abraham Redwood: Reluctant Quaker, Philanthropist, Botanist," Redwood Papers: A Bicentennial Collection. Newport: The Redwood Library and Athenaeum, 1976. Extracted and liberally summarized.

[523] Bridenbaugh, 65

[524] George Keith, Protestant Episcopal Historical Society Collections, 1:xix-xx.

[525] William B. Weeden, *Economic and Social History of New England*, 2 vols (New York: Hillary House Publishers 1963) II:660

[526] Weeden, II:662

[527] Towel, 125, 418, 520 and 545.

[528] Fiske, 1720.

[529] Fiske, 1726

[530] Fiske, 1735. Jay Coughtry, *The Notorious Triangle: Rhode Island and the African Slave Trade 1700*-1807 (Philadelphia: Temple University Press, 1981) 245. Joseph Whipple is listed as a captain of a slaver ship. He is not listed as an owner of such ships but his father-in-law Abraham Redwood is.

[531] Alexander Hawes, *Off Soundings, Aspects of the Maritime History of Rhode Island* (Chevy Chase: Posterity Press, 1999) 55-56

[532] Gertrude Kimball, ed., *The Correspondence of the Colonial Governors of Rhode Island, 1723-1775*, 2 Vols (Freeport, NY: Books for Libraries Press, 1902-03) xxiv

[533] Hattendorf, 66. The author incorrectly states that Joseph's wife's name at that time was Anne. Her name was Sarah. Joseph's first wife, who died in 1720, was Anne Almy.

[534] On the glass covered copy of the deed was this notation: This Photostat (made from a negative Photostat, Aug. 1961) is of the original document owned by Yale University. The imperfect transcription by Norman Johnson, printed in Luce's Life of George Berkeley was made from the much damaged recording in the Newport Land Evidence Records, in the hand of W. Coddington, Town Clk, now in the Newport Historical Society...Notice by H. Jeffery, Aug. 3, 1963. On a private tour of Whitehall in June 2004, the author asked for and received a copy of the deed. He was taken to the basement area of the kitchen where it is believed that the only remains of the original Whipple property are extant. Whitehall is now a museum visited by and lived in (upstairs) by Berkeley philosophy students and scholars from around the world.

[535] William G.McLoughlin, *Rhode Island, A Bicentennial History* (New York: W. W. Norton, 1978) 72

[536] McLoughlin, 71

[537] Irving Richman, *Rhode Island, A Study in Separatism* (Boston: Houghton, Mifflin and Company, 1905) 134.

[538] McLoughlin, 70

[539] Richman, 119-120.

[540] In 1895, Albert Holbrook, Esq. of Providence, spent considerable time in searching early records for the history of this purchase and privately published the result as a broadside from which this summary was taken.

[541] John R. Bartlett, *Records of the Colony of Rhode Island and Providence Plantations In New England* (Providence: Knowles, Anthony, and Company, 1860) V:66

[542] Kimball, 2:8-9, 2:9, 2:33, & 1:291-95

[543] Clifford K. Shipton, *Biographical Sketches of Those Who Attended Harvard College in the Classes* 1746-1750 (Boston: Massachusetts Historical Society, 1962) XII:506 Other Whipple Harvard 18th century graduates were Oliver, 1766 and Bela 1774, sons of Jeremiah Whipple of Cumberland, RI, Enoch 1779 of Sherburne, Ma., and Joseph 1720 of New Hampshire. Andrea Goldstein, Harvard University Archivist, Personal Correspondence, 7 August 2003.

[544] Boston Evening Post, 2 July 1750, 2/1

[545] Council Records of Newport, RI, Newport Historical Society, 9:346,363. (Codicil 10:283)

[546] Alden G. Beaman, Ph.D., Rhode Island Vital Records: New Series, Volumes 1-13, Princeton, Massachusetts, 1976-87. Volume II, "Births From Newport Common Burial Ground, Inscriptions 1590-1930," 445. The present authors visited this cemetery and noted an empty space (no headstone) next to that of Joseph's first wife and infant sons. It is probable that he was buried there.

[547] Arnold, *VR*, 7:82

[548] James N. Arnold, 4:3 iii. When Middletown, RI was formed out of the town of Newport, in 1743, a creek separating the estates of Godfrey Malbone and Joseph Whipple was used as the dividing line between the two communities.

[549] Henry E. Whipple, 41. Henry E. Whipple also states (incorrectly) that Joseph was a graduate of Cambridge (Harvard) College. As previously shown, five Whipple men graduated from Harvard in the 1700s. Joseph Whipple, class of 1720, was a descendant of the Whipples of Ipswich, Massachusetts. The first individual from Rhode Island to graduate from Harvard was Samuel Niles in 1699. Joseph III's brother, William, did however graduate from Harvard in 1749. Personal correspondence 7 October 2003, Andrea Goldstein, Reference Archivist, Harvard University, quoting "Harvard University Quinquennial Catalog of Officers and Graduates, 1636-1930."

[550] Bertram Lippincott, *The Redwood Genealogy*. Unpublished Manuscript, 1986. 11-16

[551] John R. Bartlett, V:377

[552] Henry E. Whipple, 41

[553] Land Evidence, Middletown, RI, 1:175-180, and 1:181-195

[554] Thomas Bicknell, The History of Rhode Island and Providence Plantations, 3 vols (New York: The American Historical Society, 1920) 3:1071.

[555] Weeden, II:676-77

[556] James, 187-93

[557] Council Records, Newport, RI, Newport Historical Society, 9:346, 363. As previously noted, William died 23 June 1750.

[558] Rhode Island Friends Records, Marriage Book 825, and Witnesses Signatures. Her children witnessed the wedding: Joseph, Alice, Mehitable, and Amey. It is possible that the Whipple's had been an interfaith marriage. Mehitable had been a Quaker, though she was "read out of meeting for having forsaken Friends meetings and joined another society." Rhode Island Friends Records, Women's Monthly Meeting Minutes, Book 813, p. 132). As previously shown, Joseph Junior possibly remained an Anglican.

[559] Kimball, II:91-92

[560] Genealogy & Biography Card File, Newport Historical Society, 82 Touro Street, Newport, Rhode Island. Quoting from the Newport Mercury, 29 May 1915

[561] James, 224

[562] Hattendorf, 493. "Vestry room converted to pews, 1752, and sold to Joseph Whipple and John Bannister."

Chapter 10

Lieutenant Jonathan Whipple
The Whipples From Wanskuck

Lieutenant Jonathan Whipple, youngest child of Captain John, was born about 1664 at Providence Rhode Island, and died at Providence 8 September 1721. He was married to Margaret (Margery) Angell about the year 1690. She died after 1703. Margaret and Jonathan had seven children,[563] all born and married in Providence:

i. Jonathan, born 22 Feb 1691/92; died 6 Aug 1741; married Amy Thornton.
ii. Thomas, born 26 Feb 1693/94; died 13 Oct 1770, married Naomi Dexter.
iii. Sarah, born about 1696; died before 8 Sep 1721; married Samuel Irons
iv. Marjery, died after 31 Dec 1726; married Peter Barnes
v. Parratine, married Peter White
vi. Mary, died after 1725; married William Hamman
vii. Alice

The marriage of Jonathan and Margaret is the second occasion where two children of Captain John and Sarah Whipple married into the same family (Margaret Angell's older sister, Alice, married Eleazer Whipple, Jonathan's older brother.)[564] Jonathan's father-in-law, Thomas Angell, and mother-in-law, Alice Ashton, were born in Old England. Thomas Angell, a cousin of The Reverend Roger Williams, and his apprentice, came from London as a boy of 12 or 13, and moved to Providence with him some five years later. On 27 July 1640, he was one of thirty-nine signers of the agreement to found a government at Providence. Thomas held several town offices, despite being illiterate (or at least unable to write his name--one wonders why Williams did not teach him), including membership on the town council and commissioner. His name appeared on several documents along with the names of the Whipple brothers, including the 5 June 1676 Providence town meeting, where five men were chosen to settle the question of what to do with the surviving Indians subsequent to King Philip's War. As one of the five, Thomas Angell subscribed to the decision that they should be placed in servitude for a number of years, according to their present ages. Other colonies were not so generous, either killing their vanquished foes or selling them to slavery in distant lands.[565] It should also be noted that Jonathan's oldest brother John Junior's mother-in-law was Marie Ashton, Jonathan's mother-in-law's sister. See the chapter on Eleazer for more information on the Angell family.

The Venerable Jonathan Whipple House

Through his father's Last Will and Testament, Jonathan received "twenty-five acres on which he now dwelleth. Also, I give unto my son Jonathan, one division of land which is ordered by the town to be laid out between the 'seven mile line' and the 'four mile line' and papers already drawn for." In an addendum to the will, Jonathan also received "one of his rights of land and common, on the west side of the 'seven mile line,' to be unto him, his heirs and assigns forever; and that that was his mind when the said will was written. However, it was omitted in part by the scribe of the said will."

Jonathan sold this latter property to his brother, Joseph, about ten years later. He subsequently bought over 150 acres of land (in addition to a gift of "one division," usually 100 acres, of land between the four-mile line and the seven-mile line) nearer to his homestead, including 10 acres from his cousin, James Dexter, on 20 September 1701, "which is described in the deed as laying about one and a half miles Northerly from the salt water or town harbor, bounded on the south and west sides, by the river called the West river, and on the north by his own lands, which evidently was the land that was given to him by his father, by will, where he then lived."[566]

Jonathan built the house below, at 238 Lexington Avenue, about the year 1701.[567] The photograph was taken about the year 1925. This house and those of his brothers Samuel and Eleazer are the only known images of houses built or lived in by any of the first two generations [with the exception of a 1912 photograph of Captain John's house] of Rhode Island Whipples.

Having access to almost unlimited virgin stands of timber, and living so close to the town's salt-water harbor, Jonathan and three others applied for land to build a wharf. On 19 May 1707, the town council ruled that "they shall have the vse of a percell of land by the salt water side in the Towne, that is to say from the Towne street west ward to the sea Chaniell for the vse of laying Timber, Boards, or other matter for transportation... and of loadeing of Boates...." This enterprise was an obvious success, for as noted herein his descendants were for over a century actively involved in the "Jonathan Whipple Sawmill" on the West River.[568] There is no direct mention of the enterprise in his last will and testament. In that document, as throughout his lifetime he was consistently referred to as "yeoman" or "husbandman," nevertheless, the lumber business undoubtedly was a major source of income.

Jonathon Whipple House

The map below shows the approximate limits of the land of Jonathan and his sons. As was to be expected, later descendants of both Jonathan and Benjamin purchased nearby properties to add to the combined estates, and in time their properties stretched from Smithfield Township (now Lincoln) on the north to Providence on the south. The letter "A" indicates the approximate location of Jonathan Senior's house shown above, built around the year 1701. The letter "B" denotes a house built by Thomas, in 1719, as shown on a map drawn in the year 1835.[569] It may be assumed that Jonathan Junior inherited his father's old house. The southeast portion (lower right) of the "Whipple Estate" was sold to the Wanskuck Company as late as the 1880s and 1890s, thus ending approximately 220 years of Whipple ownership. The letter "C" indicates Whipple's Pond, the adjacent Whipple house, and the Jonathan Whipple 1772 (or earlier) Sawmill. The North Providence township line extended further to the south in the early years; thus, in Jonathan's day, the south portion of his property was not within the city limits of Providence as shown on the map below. The letter "D" shows the approximate location of Jonathan's brother Benjamin's house. This 300-acre property was approximately one mile southwest at Fruit Hill. This property, and that added by Benjamin's descendants, abutted the Woonasquatucket River on the west and was within a stone's throw of Jonathan and his descendant's property on the east, at the West River. Benjamin house, built in 1684 but no longer standing, was located just west of Fruit Hill Avenue near its intersection with the Providence line, about one block from the river. Its present day address would have been on Metcalf Street.[570] Richard Whipple (Daniel, Benjamin, Benjamin) sold what was left of the original property, 80 acres or so, soon after his father's death in 1792, and moved to Massachusetts.

"Wanskuck appears in Providence records as early as 1655. The name, also spelled

Jonathan Whipple Property

Wanscott, Wenscott, or Wenscutt in old documents and still pronounced with a final 't' by present-day residents, is an Indian word perhaps meaning 'low lands,' an apt designation for this territory bracketed by steep hillsides (see USGS map). The area was part of a section of the Providence 'north woods' set off as a separate town in 1765. Residents petitioned to have the new municipality called 'Wenscutt' but officials insisted that it be called North Providence (the Wanskuck vicinity was reannexed to Providence in 1874). In 1772 the North Providence town council authorized the layout of a road through Wanskuck '...leading by Jonathan Whipple's sawmill.' That highway, known for many years as Old Sawmill Road, is now Veazie Street, and the sawmill stood near the Veazie Street Bridge over the West River. Though the mill is gone, a gambrel roof, center-chimney dwelling still standing at 9 Houghton Street, behind the Steere Mill, may well be the old Whipple homestead.... With this road system in place, water privileges along this section of West River were opened to development. In March 1811 Providence merchants...purchased a tract of land with a mill privilege on West River, downstream from the Whipple land and sawmill. The company foundered, however, and in 1816 and 1817 various creditors brought suits against the partners for repayment of debts.... "The Wanskuck Company continued to prosper through the late nineteenth and early twentieth century. In 1882 it purchased the Whipple Estate further up West River, site of the old eighteenth-century sawmill and a late cotton mill established by 1835 and known as Thomas Whipple's

233

Factory. Two years later the Steere Worsted Mill was built on the Whipple property."[571] On the below map the letter "A" is Whipple's Pond. Letter "B" was the location of Jonathan Whipple's sawmill. Letter "C" represents the location of the former Whipple Cotton Factory. Letter "D" is the Thomas Whipple house at 9 Houghton Street. The National Register's description of this house is as follows: "Houghton Street 9 (late 18th or early 19th century): A one and one-half story, flank-gambrel-roof, shingled dwelling with a massive brick center chimney, a 4-bay façade, and front entrance in a small 1-story ell on the west side, and an entrance in the east side. The property from Whipple's Pond to Veazie Street, occupied in part by this house and the Steere Mill (see entry at 81 Wild Street), belonged to the Whipple family for more than a century prior to its acquisition by the Wanskuck Company in 1882. By 1772 Jonathan Whipple was operating a sawmill here on the West River near a newly established road which is the present Veazie Street. This house may date from that period or earlier, and was certainly standing by the time Thomas J. Whipple was operating a factory near the site of Steere Mill in the early 19th century."[572] It is likely that Jonathan III built the Houghton Street house as well as the

Wanskuck Industrial District

sawmill. The house on Houghton Street was no longer standing in March 2004, when the present authors tried to locate it. Also seen on the map is the Roger Williams Baptist Church, designated by the letter "E". The Whipples played a part in its founding and prosperity: "The entrance tower contains a belfry with pairs of louver-filled pointed arches on each side, and each end of the tower transept has a single, large pointed-arch window with 'Roger Williams Baptist Church' in bronze lettering applied in a line undulating over each window. The congregation's inception dates before 1865, with the organization of Sunday school that met first in a private home, then in a room at the Thomas Whipple Mill (formerly near the site of the Steere Mill, now demolished). In 1866 the Metcalf family donated the triangular plot at the corner of Veaszie Street and Woodward Road to the congregation...."[573] A portion of the Whipple estate located at 383 Woodward Road, north of Wanskuck Park in North Providence, reveals more of the extent of the original Whipple Estate. "This property was an empty lot through the 1890s, when ...purchased from devisees of the estates of Thomas and James M. Whipple...."[574] As discussed later, the Whipple property was sold off because no Whipples remained. After the death of Thomas J. Whipple in 1868, his brother James continued to maintain the estate. However, James, who died in 1885, never married, and the sons of Thomas had long since left the area.

Jonathan Whipple in Early Town Records

Lieutenant Jonathan Whipple appeared in township records on several other occasions. The following is a chronological summary of some of these taken from *The Early Records of the Town of Providence, 21 Volumes* (Providence: Snow & Farnham, 1892-1915). Individual entries are noted with the volume number and page.

16 August 1676

Wee whose names are hereunto Subscribed haveing Right with Some others to a percell of Indians which came in at two seaverall times, doe Committ them or sole many of them as shall be putton board to the Care of mr Auther ffenner william Hopkins, and John whipple Jvnr to make Sale and Delivery thereof, and to defray such Charges out of the product thereof, as shall Arise by the sayd Indians, and after reasonable Sattisfaction to the above named made, to make return of the remainder of the product of the sayd Indians to the Company Conserned. Signed by Roger Williams, Eleazer Whipple, Benjamin Whipple, Jonathan Whipple: Saml Whipple and eight others. ((XV:155-156)

7 December 1680

Knowe all men by these presents that I William Hernton of ye Towne of providence...haue sold unto Andrew Edmund: A Horse of a light Gray... witnessed by The Marke Jonathan X Whipple and John Whipple: Junr (XV:217)

28 May 1681

Memorand: That Jonathan whipple did Take vp into his Care & Custody a Certain Bay-colour, Saddle-gauld, haveing a white strake and Branded on ye neere shoulder...   (IX:200)

27 April 1682

To the Towne mett the 27th:of Aprill1682. Forasmuch as I understand that Mr. Dexter hath prefered a bill to the Towne concerning some Landes Lieing upon the west river which he maketh claime unto although some pvart of the said Land hath by the Towne sirveior benn Laid out unto me, I desire the Towne To Consider what land mr Dexter there hath, & how it is Bounded; that if the boundes by him cann be made apeare, & Layd out by the Towne Order; which if he cannot so doe, then I know no reason why I should be Molested upon that which by the Townes sirveior was Laid out unto me, And no other can shew boundes unto, to make claime by, but only theire bare word; neighbours I desire your consideration, upon the matter that so I may not be wrongfully put beside my right. Your neighbor, Jonathan Whipple (XVII:1)

Last munday in may: 1682

The names of such, as took theire Engagements of Eleageance ...before Joseph Jiencks: Asist. Jonathan Whipple and thirty-seven others. (IV:55)

29 October 1684

Rate levied upon ye inhabetants of ye Towne of Providence: Jonathan Whipple 00-01-00 (XVII:46)

24 June 1685
   To the Towne of prouidance met this 24th of ye 6th mounth 85 frieds my
Request is that you would let me take up 10: ackers of land I hauing land due to me
your fried: Jonathan Whipple. (XVII:61)

1 September 1687
   A List of Names of those Rated in Providence:
Jonathan Whipple 0-02-08 (XVII:100)

31 October 1687
   A Rate made & Proportioned against the inhabetants of ye towne of Providence
for ye payeing of Joseph woodward for takeing & bringing up ye Child of Thomas
Waters & to pay for ye pound & other things.Jonathan Whipple 0-01-00   (XVII:108)

August 1688
   A List of Names of those who were Rated in Providence:
Jonath: Whipple   0-2-0   (XVII:124)

27 January 1693/94
   Whereas Jonathan Whipple formerly gave in Bond to the Towne to secure the
Towne from what charge might accrue to ye Town by reason of his entertaining of one
Joshua Barsam. But forasmuch as the Towne is Certifued that the sayd Joshua Barsham
is no wayes at any time moew likely to be chargeable to ye towne the towne doe
therefore declare the sd Bond now to be anull & Voyd, & that the Clarke may at his
Convenient time deliver up the ye sd Bond unto Jonathan Whipple. (XI:8)

16 June 1693
   Know yee. That the said Jonathan Whipple for & in Consideration of a valuable
sum of money and other Currant pay of this Countrey in hand already well & truly payd
unto him by Joseph Whipple of the towne of Providence aforesaid (Coopper)...all that
his proper Right & Title which his ffather John Whipple (deceased) by his last Will and
Teastament gave unto him in all the lands within the Towneshipp of said Providence
which lye on the West side of the line Called & known by...the Name of the Seven Mile
line; That is to say one Right of land, as in his sayd ffather his last Will and Testament it
is exprest... (XIV:230-231)

10 June 1695
   Know ye that the sd Samuell Comstock for & in consideration of the Sum of
Twenty & five poundes of Currant Siver Money in hand already well and Truly payd
unto him by Jonathan Whipple...a parcel of land Containeing by Estemation Sixty acres
(be it more of less) with all ye Meaddow grounds also...(XIV:240-242

17 March 1696

Know ye that the sd James Browne for & in consideration of a valuable Sum of Currant & passable pay of this Coloney in hand already well and Truly payd unto him by Jonathan Whipple...a parcel of Meaddow land Containeing by Estemation about three acres...(XIV:252

8 April 1697

Whereas Jonathan Whipple hath desired of ye Towne to have ye Way Turned which was layd through his land which he bought of Sam: Comstock & hee to be all charge about it; & also to make ye way good over ye brooke & else where passable, the matter is left with ye surveior according as he approves it so it shall be allowed. (XI:32)

27 March 1699

I Daniell Browne for & in Consideration of the sum of Nine poundes & five shillings of Currant silver money of New England unto me in hand payd by Jonathan Whipple of Providence...a Certaine piece of land containeing by Estemation fforty six acres... (IV: 175-176)

20 September 1701

I the said James Dexter for & in consideration of the sum of Eight pounds silver money in hand already well & truely paid unto me by Jonathan Whipple...a percell of land Containeing by Estemation Tenn acres...(IV: 216-219)

17 February 1703/04

It is Granted unto Jonathan Whipple that he may Change about 3 acres or foure acres, or there abouts of his land, at the place, or land which hee bought of Samuell Comstock & to take it up in some other Place where it may be convenient (XI:82)

16 March 1703/4

Laid out unto Jonathan Whipple seven acres of land... (IV:57-88)

6 April 1704

I the said John Whipple for & in Consideration of the sum of three pounds in silver money, in hand already well & truely paid unto Me by Jonathan Whipple (Husbandman) inhabetant of the aforesd Towne of Providence...a small Grassey Island, Containeing by Estemation about halfe one acre, of Land (be it more or less) & is scituate...in the Northerne part of the salt water Harbour which lieth before said Providence Towne... (IV:58-60)

28 April 1705

Jonathan Whipple witnessed a deed of gift between John Angell and his son Daniel Angell (XIV:297)

4 October 1705: Rate levied by the Towne of Providence:
        Jonathan Whipple   00-12-06 (XVII:211)

27 January 1706
"I Jonathan Whipple in Consideration of ye Sum of Six Pounds and Six shillings in hand already Well and truly paid umnto me by David Angell...a percell of Meaddowland Countaineing by Estemation five acres..." (XX:240-246)

10 May 1706
The said Jonathan Whipple of the sd Towne of Providence (Husbandman) for and in Consideration of the Sum of Three pounds and Ten Shillings anleady well and Truly paid...by Josph Smith...a percell of Meaddowland Containeing by Estemetion about three acres... (XX:98-99)

19 May 1707
It is Granted unto tho: Oley junior, Joseph Smith, Willm Olney & Jonathan Whipple that they shall have the vse of a percell of land by the salt water side in the Towne, that is to say from the Towne streete west ward to the sea Chaniell for their vse of laying Timer, Boards, or other matter for transportation, & also liberty there to make some buttment for the Conveniency of loadeing of Boates...(XI:116)

27 October 1707
Whereas Daniel Angell hath desired to Exchange five acres of Meadow with ye Towne the which lieth upon ye Westerne side of that branch of Wanasquatuckett River which runneth downe by ye place called ye Keyes, & also lieth a little way downe ye streame from sd keys, the which meadow formerly belonged to Mr. Joseph Williams of sd Providence, & by sd Mr. Williams sold unto Jonathan Whipple, & by sd Jonathan Whipple sold unto sd David Angell; the exchange is by the Towne Granted; so that the said Meadow shall be & is now Common land upon sd Exchange & free for any of ye Purchassers or Proprietors of sd Providence to take up who have Meadow unto them due to take up. (XI:121)

11 January 1710/11
Phillipp Tillinghast...for and in Consideraiton of the Sum of five Pounnds Current Silver money in hand already well and truly paid unto Mr Jonathan Whipple...Tenn acres of land which is yet lieing in the Common. (XX:425-26

27 Jan 1710/11
Gentelmen wee the subscribers heare unto haueing under stood that there is a Bridg building or at least some progress made in order thereunto, ouer ye passege at wayBossett & Considering all ought to haue ye Benefitt thereof it may be thought most Best ye yourselues would take it into Consideration for ye most Best & most profittable way to performe ye same that it may be most best for all that are therein Concerned. Signed by Jonathan Whipple and seven others (XVII:277-8)

19 June 1710

Whereas there hath been a bill this day Exhibitted to ye Towne by Jonathan Whipple desireing of them that the High way which was laid out to goe over ye west River at ye place called Dexters new Meaddow & so through his land northward may be removed and laid out Eastward of his land...& the aforesd way laid formerly out through Jonathan Whipple's land shall Returne to him againe. (XI:148-9)

23 January 1713

This day Margery Burdin, Widdow of the deceased Joseph Burdin presented to the Counsell an Inventary of her said deceased husband Joseph Burdin his estate...William Olney & Jonathan Whipple junior who made the Inventary...the two bondsmen to be bound with herselfe for the true performance thereof are Jonathan Whipple Senr: & Mercy Burden: of them the Councell do accept (X:135)

29 September 1721

It is voated and ordered that Richard Waterman Clerke shall grant a Letter of Administration vnto Jonathan Whipple and Thomas Whipple vpon the mouvable Esstate of theire Honrd father Mr Jonathan Whipple, deceased, and to take there Bonds In behalf of the Councill. Vpon the Reading att the Councill Bord the Last will and Testament of Mr. Jonathan Whipple deceased: It was demanded of his widdow Mrs Ann Whipple if she had any thing to object against the pooueing the will: she Replyed no seence it was her husbands will shee did accept Prouided shee might have what shee brought with her Where upon the executors declared they were willing shee should. (XII:26)

Last Will and Testament

I Jonathan Whipple of the Towne of Providence in the Colony of Rhoad Jsland and Providence plantation in New England: yeoman: being sick and Weake of body but of sound and dissoposeing mind and member praise be given to God for the Same; Doe make this my Last Will and Testament: in manner and forme following: first and principally I Commit my spirit into the mercifull hands of Almighty God my creator and my body I commit to the Earth to be decently buried after the discression of my Exccutors hereinafter named and as to the outward and worldly Esstate the Lord hath Lent mee in this present world: I Give and bequeathe as followeth

Jmprimis: my will is that my son Thomas Whipple shall pay unto his Brother Jonathan Whipple the Sum of five pounds in Good and Lawfull Bills of publick, Creadit or Currant money of New England.

2nly my will is And I doe hereby Give and Bequeathe unto my two Sons Jonathan Whipple and Thomas Whipple: all my lands both divided and undevided which are scituate Lieing and being with the Towneship of Provident aforesaid that I heave not before disposed of by deedes of Gift: To be Equally devided betwixt them my aforesaid two sons Jonathan Whipple and Thomas Whipple and to be unto them theire Heirs Executors administrators and assigns To have and To hold with the previledges and appurtinanses theire unto belonging forever

Jtem I Give and bequeathe unto my son Jonathan Whipple my Cane

Jtem   I Give and bequeath unto my two sons Jonathan Whipple and Thomas Whipple: my wareing Apparrill to be Equally devided betwixt them

Jtem   I Give and bequeath unto my Loveing Wife Anna Whipple one third parte of all my housing: and one third parte of my homestead Lands orchard and appurtinanses theire unto belonging: and aloes one third part of all my moveable Goods and Esstate to be for her use during the term of her naturall Life providing shee Remaine a widow: Butt in Case shee marrey then for the sd moveable Esstate to goe to my Executors for them to dispose of amongst my Children as they shall see Cause.

Jtem   I Give and bequeathe unto my daughter Alice Whipple the sum of twenty pounds to be paid to her by my Executors in Goods merchandize or publick Bills of Creadite and to be Leavied out of my Esstate.

Jtem   I Give and bequeathe unto my daughter Parrataine White the Sum of five pounds to be paid to her by my Executors in Bills of Creadite or moveable goods as they may be Raise out of my Esstate

Jtem   I Give and bequeathe unto my daughter Mary Haman the Sum of ten pounds to be paid to her by my Executors Jn Bills of Creadite marchandize or moveable Goods as it Can be Raises out of my Estate

I Give and bequeath unto my Grandson Jonathan Haman my Gun And my Will is that what silver money I have shall be Equally devided amongst my wife and all my Children Each to have an Equal parte thereof And my will is further is and I doe here by order that my daughter Alice Whipple shall have the Liberty of dwell in my dwelling house during the term of her Naturall Life provided shee Remaine single and unmarried. And my will is that after all my debts Legaces funeral charges and other Expences are duely paid: then what after Remaines of my moveable Esstate Jf any there be shall be Equally divided and I doe freely Give it unto and amongst my five daughters namely Sarah Irons Marjary Barnes Parrataine White Mary Hamman and Alice Whipple to be Equally devided amongst them.

And I doe name Ordaine and Apoynt my two sons Jonathan Whipple and Thomas Whipple my sole Executors to this my Last Will and Testament to Receive and pay all my debts: and Execute this my Last Will and Testament according to the true Jntent and meaning therof: and also to take Care to provide things sensory for my Wife provided shee Remaine a widow after my decease Jf what I have Given her be not sufficient: Jn witness whereof I doe here unto sett my hand and seale this fifth day of september Jn the year of our Lord one thousand seaven hundred and twenty one. Jonathan Whipple, his mark.[575]

Enumerated as part of his inventory of movable goods was one Negro boy valued at 47 pounds, the most expensive item in the inventory of approximately 220 pounds. Jonathan, it would seem, was a slave owner. His second wife Anna, who died four years later, willed all of her possessions, valued at just over 105 pounds, to her stepdaughter Mary Hamman.[576]

"Jonathan Whipple at his decease gave his land or farm to two sons, viz: Jonathan and Thomas, to be equally divided between them. This farm or land is situated in what is now the town of North Providence, a little north of the Waunscot factory, and has been retained in the name ever since the first settlement of the country. At this place there has been four Thomas Whipples lived in succession, and it has always been understood by them that they were a distant connection to those Whipples who live at Fruit Hill."[577] The 300-acre property of Jonathan's brother Benjamin, located on the map above, was approximately one mile southwest at Fruit Hill. This property, and that added by Benjamin's descendants, abutted the Woonasquatucket River on the west and was within a stone's throw of Jonathan and his descendant's property on the east, at the West River. Benjamin Senior's house, built in 1684 but no longer standing, was located just west of Fruit Hill Avenue near its intersection with the Providence line, about one block from the river. Its present day address would have been on Metcalf Street.[578] Richard[4] Whipple (Daniel[3], Benjamin[2], Benjamin[1]) sold what was left of the original property, 80 acres or so, soon after his father's death in 1792, and moved to Massachusetts.

Jonathan Whipple Junior, Lumberman

It is assumed that Jonathan Whipple Junior was, like his father, a lumberman and farmer. He was born in 1691/92 and died at the age of 49 or 50, on 6 August 1741. He married Amy Thornton 24 October 1717 in Providence. Three children were born to them: Mary, Amy, and Jonathan III.

Jonathan Whipple III, born 8 December 1723, was forced to take over the family businesses at the age of 17. Anne Smith, his wife, was born in 1719 and died 29 October 1810. She was the daughter of Edward Smith and Mercy Mowrey. Her paternal great grandfather was Thomas Angell, and her maternal great grandfather was Roger Mowrey. Both were prominent men in early-day Providence history. Their descendants married into the extended Whipple family on several occasions.

As shown previously, Jonathan III was the owner of a sawmill (founded by his grandfather in the late 1690s) by 1772, which apparently had existed for several years. It is not known how prosperous his business enterprises were, but according to the number of recorded real estate transactions, he and his family owned large sections of timberland as far north as Smithfield Township. Jonathan Whipple III died 5 November 1805. In his last will and testament, he bequeathed to his wife Anne "the use and improvements, rent and profits of all my estate, real and personal, for and during the term of her natural life." To his daughter Vashti, he gave "money and furniture." His son Eleazer received "one dollar, he having received by deed a full portion and share" of the extensive estate. His grandson, Jonathan Randall, son of William Randall, was given the homestead farm of 60 acres in North Providence and Smithfield, and cattle, horses, sheep, one feather bed, silver spoons, brass kettle, etc. The will was not to be in force until the decease of my wife."[579]

In the deed for a full share above, Jonathan bequeathed to "my son, Eleazer Whipple yeoman, about 90 acres with the Dwelling house, barn, corn crib, and other buildings—sixteen rods of land Viz, four rods square at the Burying Place within the afore described premises which I reserve for Burying Ground." The boundaries for the property were "ajoining the Joseph Whipple house, Joseph Whipple home farm, my other lands."[580] The deed was attested to by Oliver Angell and Christopher Brown.

As noted, Vashti Whipple married William Randall and bore him seven children.[581] They lived on a farm near her father. She and her entire family were buried in the North Burial Ground in Providence.

Eleazer Whipple, the son of Jonathan III, was born about 1750 and died 3 August 1825. It is supposed that he worked with his father and eventually took over the ownership of the sawmill and farms. He married Deborah Cushing 19 December 1781.[582] Deborah was born about 1745, died 2 February 1827, and was buried beside her husband. She was the daughter of Elijah Cushing, a descendant of William Cushing, who came to "Hingham in New England" in 1638 at the age of 50. He was "progenitor of many eminent descendants," dying in 1660.[583] The 1805 will, drawn when Eleazer was 55

241

years old, makes no mention of children. That Eleazer and Deborah apparently were childless may be the reason that Henry Whipple, in his 1873 book, knew nothing of Jonathan Junior descendants.

The burial sites of Lieutenant Jonathan Whipple and his oldest son are unknown, but ostensibly buried in their house lot. Jonathan Whipple III was buried in the Admiral Esek Hopkins Cemetery, as was his son Eleazer. On 7 July 1891, the Providence City Council voted to move the Hopkins Cemetery to make way for Admiral Esek Hopkins Square. Therefore, in August 1900, 102 graves (23 marked) were moved from the Hopkins Cemetery to the North Burial Ground in Providence. It took nine years after the vote to actually move them.[584]

Thomas Whipple, Mill Owner

The four consecutive Thomas Whipples referred to earlier, who lived on the property for approximately 175 continuous years, began with the second son of Lieutenant Jonathan Whipple, Thomas Senior, who was born 26 February 1693/94 and died 13 October 1770, intestate. He was buried in the Thomas Whipple lot, Wanskuck Section, Providence. On 5 January 1767, Thomas was adjudicated to be mentally incompetent: "Thomas Whipple of No Prov is deemed non corpus mentis and not of sufficient discretion to manage his estate and transact his secular affairs."[585] The Town Council appointed John Comstock of North Providence, Esq., as guardian. Thomas married Naomi Dexter 18 April 1720. Naomi Dexter (1698-1777) was the granddaughter of Stephen Dexter and Abigail Whipple Dexter Hopkins, the youngest daughter of Captain John Whipple. On her mother's side of the family, she was the great granddaughter of Thomas Harris, who accompanied The Reverend Roger Williams to America in 1631. Thomas and Naomi were parents of nine children, including one son, Thomas Junior.

Thomas Junior was born 8 July 1725 and died 30 December 1777. He was, like his parents, buried in the Whipple Lot. He was married to Anne Harris, who died after 21 July 1789. They had ten children:

> i. *Nicholas, born 25 March 1751; died 25 May 1828; married Prudence Olney*
> ii. *Levi or Henry, born about 1752; married Sarah Smith*
> iii. *Christopher, born about 1754; married Sally Cushing*
> iv. *George, born about 1756; married Dorcus Brown.*
> v. *Amy, born about 1763; died 28 Dec 1833; married Stephen Brown*
> vi. *Thomas, born 17 Sep 1766; died 7 Sep 1843; married Lydia Humphrey*
> vii. *Sarah, born about 1768; died before 5 Jul 1843: married Converse (_)*
> viii. *Abigail, married Smith*
> ix. *Anne*
> x. *Dorcus*

Thomas' will was dated 4 December 1777. It included the following among the many bequests to his wife Anne, his sons Christopher, Nicholas, Thomas, Henry, and George, and his daughters Abigail Smith, Anne, Sarah, Dorcas, and Amey Whipple: "To my Son Christopher Whipple, all that part of my Homestead Farm that I purchased of Jabez Whipple...dwelling house, corn crib, old grist mill, one half of 20 acre wood lot lying in Smithfield...and one desk that was my father Thomas Whipple's, and one gun called the old gun...Unto my son George Whipple the lower part of my meadow nigh the place called the old saw mill...Unto my two younger sons Thomas Whipple and Henry Whipple all the remainder part of my farm what I have not disposed of in this will, Together with the dwelling house, Barn Crib, Cider House, and all other building thereon standing and to be equally divided between them...."[586] Ann Whipple, "relick and widow" of Thomas Whipple, on 21 June 1779, refused to accept the terms of the last will and testament of her late husband.[587]

Nicholas was born 25 March 1751 and died 25 May 1828. He married Prudence Olney 31 July 1774. In 1775, Nicholas and Prudence moved to Pomfret, Connecticut,

Thomas J. Whipple

where they lived out the rest of their lives. Nicholas Whipple Junior was born 7 September 1776 and died 20 April 1855. He was buried at Rensselaer County, New York. He was listed in the 1825 New York census as a resident of Fairfield, Herkimer County. He was employed as overseer of highways for that county in 1845. The son of Nicholas Junior was Willoughby[7] Whipple (Nicholas[6], Nicholas[5], Thomas[4], Thomas[3], Jonathan[2], John[1]), who was born in Fairfield, New York in February of 1833, and is listed as a student in School District 7 of Herkimer County in 1848. He was living in Salisbury, Herkimer County in 1858. His son was Clayton Whipple, who died at the age of 25 in 1895. Willoughby Whipple died 25 March 1902.[588]

Christopher had one child, Abigail, and lived on a part of the homestead farm east from where his father lived. George settled in the Township of Burrillville, Rhode Island, married Dorcas Brown; they had one son, John, who was born in 1828 and died 14 October 1917. He was buried in the Harrisville Cemetery, Hill Road, Burrillville.

Thomas III was born 17 September 1766, died 7 September 1843, and was buried beside his father and mother. He was 11 years old when his father died. Thomas lived and died on the homestead farm that his father and grandfather had developed. He married Lydia Humphrey, 7 June 1790, and they became parents to seven children, including James, born 1809, who never married, and Thomas J. Whipple. Thomas III was the founder and owner of a cotton mill located on the West River. In his Last Will and Testament he left to his son Thomas "certain part of my homestead farm in No Prov, Cotton Mill, water privilege, privilege of flywings, machinery, tools, other articles in Cotton Mill." To his son James, he bequeathed "all the remaining part of my farm, woodlot in Smithfield, stock of cattle, horses, etc." He left various articles to his daughters Martha Whipple, Ann Whipple, Amey Arnold, Sarah Loring, and Julia Barney.[589]

Thomas Jefferson Whipple was born 30 November 1801, died 14 May 1868, and is buried in the North Burial Ground in Providence.[590] According to Henry E. Whipple,

243

he lived about half a mile west of the Wainscott Woolen Mill in North Providence and owned a cotton or woolen mill west of his house. His wife was Susan Cowing. Thomas and Susan had seven children, including five sons, two of whom (George and Henry) had sons. George W. Whipple moved to Chicago, Illinois and is known to have had one son (Frederick George Whipple); John C. Whipple was unmarried; Charles Mortimer Whipple, the father of Lois, died in 1907; Albert Whipple died as a child; and Henry Franklin Whipple, born 18 November 1849, died 23 January 1936, and was buried in the Harmony Cemetery, Glocester, Rhode Island. He married Adelaide Carter and had two children, Sylvia and Elliott[8] Whipple (Henry[7], Thomas[6], Thomas[5], Thomas[4], Thomas[3], Jonathan[2], John[1]). Elliott Whipple married Nettie Horton 5 June 1907 in Rhode Island. Their children, Russell and Virginia, both died in Yakima, Washington in the late 20th century.[591]

All four Thomas Whipples were buried in the Thomas Whipple Lot in the Wanskuck Section of North Providence. This cemetery could not be found when the Rhode Island Historical Cemeteries Project searched for it. An article concerning its desecration appears in the 6 March 1910 edition of the *Providence Journal*. Thomas J. Whipple and immediate family were subsequently reinterred in the North Burial Ground.

In the end, the descendants of Captain John Whipple, who bequeathed his 1665 proprietor right of land, located "one and one-half miles northwest of the Great Salt Cove" to his youngest son, sold the remains of their ancestral estate on the West River between the years 1882 and the 1890s. Thus was terminated the over-230-year presence of the Jonathan Whipple family in the Wanskuck. The great-great great grandchildren of Lieutenant Jonathan Whipple would begin their own twentieth century odysseys in other parts of the state and nation.

244

End Notes

563 John O. Austin, *Genealogical Dictionary of Rhode Island* (Albany, NY: 1887: reprint edition. Baltimore: Genealogical Publishing Company, 1978) 223. James N. Arnold, *Vital Statistics of Rhode Island, 1636*-1850 (Narragansett Historical Publishing Company, 1892). Henry E. Whipple, *A Brief Genealogy of the Whipple Families who Settled in Rhode Island* (Providence: A. Crawford Green, 1873). *The Early Records* of the Town of Providence, 21 vols, collected and printed by the Records Commissioners (Providence: Snow & Farnham, city printers, 1892-1915). [hereinafter ERP].Vital statistics of the children and grandchildren of Captain John and Sarah Whipple are taken from the above and numerous publications that quote from them. To see more recent corrections, consult www.whipple.org Weldon Whipple, Webmaster.
564 Austin, 221-223. Also, on line at www.whipple.org/charles/louquisset/index.html.
565 James Savage, *Genealogical Dictionary of the First Settlers of New England* (Baltimore: Genealogical Publishing Company, 1990) I:57. Dean Crawford Smith, *The Ancestry of Emily Jane Angell 1844-1910*, NEHGS, Register (Boston: New England Historic Genealogical Society, 1992) 107, 121-125.
566 Henry E. Whipple, 45.
567 Thomas E. and Barbara Greene, *Images of America, North Providence* (Hanover NH: Arcadia Publishing, 1996) 111. The photo was taken around the year 1925. The house was torn down in the year 2003. There are now four new houses on the land. Citation for the 238 address: Benjamin family entry, Joseph H. Armstrong compiler, *North Providence, Johnston, and Smithfield Street Directory*, (Joseph H. Armstrong, Cranston, Rhode Island, 1941) 80. Likewise, Benjamin Whipple's house on Metcalf Street has only recently disappeared.
568 *ERP* XI:116. Jonathan had previously bought a small grassy island of about one-half acre, probably also for the export of lumber, in Providence Harbor from his nephew John Whipple III, *ERP*, IV:58-60. Henry R. Chace, *Owner and Occupants of the lots, Houses and Shops in the Town of Providence Rhode Island in 1798* (Providence: Livermore and Knight, 1914), plates 10 & 11. In 1798, this island was still called "Whipples Island" and was on the north side of the cove near the entrance to the Moshassuch River. Throughout the 1700s and 1800s, lumber was one of Rhode Island's major exports.
569 Thomas E. and Barbara Greene, 110.
570 Thomas E. and Barbara Greene, 83. "The area known as Lymansville was first settled by Benjamin Whipple, who built a house c1684 on what is now Metcalf Avenue. The farm that the Whipple family owned extended from the Woonasquatucket River to the site of the St. James Episcopal Church on Fruit Hill Avenue. [A distance of about 1½ miles]. On November 9, 1807, Daniel Lyman of Newport purchased an 80-acre farm off Fruit Hill Avenue from William F. Megee, who had purchased the property from Richard Whipple, great grandson of Benjamin Whipple."
571 Robert O. Jones, Senior Historic Preservation Planner. *National Register of Historic Places Inventory Nomination Form*, 1983 (Washington D.C., US Department of the Interior, National Parks Services) 1,2 & 6.
572 Jones, 12
573 Jones, 26
574 Jones, 27
575 *ERP*, XVI:185-194
576 *ERP*, XVI:367-372
577 Henry E. Whipple, 45
578 Thomas E. and Barbara Greene, 83. "The area known as Lymansville was first settled by Benjamin Whipple, who built a house c1684 on what is now Metcalf Avenue. The farm that the Whipple family owned extended from the Woonasquatucket River to the site of the St. James Episcopal Church on Fruit Hill Avenue. [A distance of about 1½ miles]. On November 9, 1807, Daniel Lyman of Newport purchased an 80-acre farm off Fruit Hill Avenue from William F. Megee, who had purchased the property from Richard Whipple, great grandson of Benjamin Whipple."
579 Will of Jonathan Whipple, Probate Book #1, North Providence, A-4:220-224, Pawtucket City Hall, Pawtucket, Rhode Island.

[580] Deed of gift 20 March 1783. Jonathan Whipple Deed, Records of Deeds and Mortgages, No. 2, Part 1, p. 146. North Providence, Pawtucket City Hall, Pawtucket, Rhode Island.

[581] Representative Men and Old Families of Rhode Island, 3 vols (Chicago: J.H. Beers and Company, 1908) III:1639. "Most of their old farm is now the possession of the North Burial Ground."

[582] James N. Arnold, Vital Records, Vol. 2, Part IV, 19 December 1781. "Eleazer, of Jonathan, of North Providence, and Deborah Cushing, of Elijah, dec., of Pembroke Me., married at Smithfield, by Elder Ezekiel Angell." 43.

[583] James S. Cushing, The Genealogy of the Cushing Family, An Account of the Ancestry and Descendants of Mathew Cushing Who Came to America in 1638 (Montreal: Perrault Printing Company, 1905) 189. It was stated that Elijah Whipple was from Pembroke Maine, and was deceased by the time of his daughter's wedding to Eleazer Whipple. However, this town, on the Canadian border, was not settled until after the Revolutionary War. More likely he was from Pembroke, Massachusetts where several Cushings were known to reside in the 1700s.

[584] John Sterling, designer. Rhode Island Cemetery Database, Providence, Browse Cemetery Data, Cemetery PVO23, Admiral Esek Hopkins, Rhode Island Cemetery Transcription Project, 1990-2001. On computer at the Rhode Island Historical Society Library, 121 Hope Street, Providence, RI, 02906.

[585] Thomas Whipple Guardianship, Council and Probate Book A, North Providence, A1:44, Pawtucket City Hall, Pawtucket, Rhode Island.

[586] Thomas Whipple Will, Council and Probate Book A, North Providence A1:154-157, Pawtucket City Hall, Pawtucket, Rhode Island.

[587] Council and Probate Book A, North Providence A:194, Pawtucket City Hall, Pawtucket, Rhode Island.

[588] Letter to Blaine Whipple 14 January 1992, transferred to the authors, sent by Glenn Woodward of North Pole, Alaska, which traced his ancestry from Captain John Whipple.

[589] Thomas Whipple Will, Council and Probate Book #5, North Providence A-8:227-31, 5 July 1843, Pawtucket City Hall, Pawtucket, Rhode island. Part of the bequeath to his daughter Martha was located on "Constitution Hill." Their ancestor, Captain John Whipple, had property on this same hill in 1661.

[590] Four generations of Thomas Whipples, and other family members, were buried in a family burial plot called the Thomas Whipple Burial Lot, Wanskuck Section, North Providence. This cemetery could not be located when the Rhode Island Cemeteries Project tried to find it. An article on its desecration can be viewed in the 6 March 1910 issue of the Providence Journal. The remains of Thomas J. Whipple, and immediate family, were moved to the North Burial Ground around the year 1900.

[591] Henry E. Whipple, 45-47

Chapter 11

Sarah, Mary, and Abigail
Daughters of Captain John and Sarah Whipple

Sarah Whipple Smith Arnold

Sarah Whipple,[592] oldest of the Whipple daughters, like most of her siblings, married into one of the founding families of Providence. Immediately upon immigrating to Providence with her family in 1658/59, she married John Smith Junior, son of her father's former neighbor in Dorchester, Massachusetts. The births of their 10 children, all born and married in Providence, are approximate:

> *i. John, born 1661; died 20 April 1737.*
> *ii. Sarah, born 1663; died 14 Oct 1725; married Richard Clemence.*
> *iii. Alice, born 1665; died 19 Feb 1735/36; married John Dexter*
> *iv. Mary, born 1667; died 13 Dec 1737; married Arthur Fenner*
> *v. Joseph, born 1679; died 13 Jan 1749/50; married Lydia Gardner*
> *vi. Benjamin, born 1672, died 23 Apr 1751; married Mercy Angell*
> *vii. Israel, born 1674; died 1683.*
> *viii. Daniel; born 1676; died 1683.*
> *ix. Elisha, born 14 Apt 1680; died aft 25 Nov 1766; married E. Mowry*
> *x. William, born 1682; died 11 Dec 1753; married Mary Sayles*

"You may note that the Smiths named a daughter after her mother just as they named the son after the father. This common practice suggests that these early colonial women felt as strongly as the men about perpetuating their names, hence their identity. Though not legally allowed to keep their last names, at least this way they could pass on their first, but, regrettably, the women did not also suffix the 1st, 2nd, 3rd, etc. as usually happened with the sons. From the historians' and genealogists' point of view, this repeated use of the same first names with and between families, along with so many intermarriages amongst these early families, compounds the difficulty of tracing family members through the generations---and of ascertaining relationships."[593]

John Smith Senior's home in Massachusetts was at Ponkapog, in the southern foothills of the Blue Mountains. His name appears on the records of Dorchester in connection with a tract of land "about the mill."[594] Captain John Whipple lived near this same mill, and is thought to have played a role, as an indentured servant, in its construction for Israel Stoughton in 1634.[595]

Smith was exiled after the Massachusetts General Court ordered that "John Smyth salbe sent within theis 6 weekes out of this jurisdiccion for dyvers dangerous opinions, wch hee holdeth, & hath divulged, if in the meane tyme he removes not himselfe out of this plantation." He immediately joined Roger Williams, William Harris, Joshua Verin, Thomas Angell, and Francis Wickes as they fled through the wilderness to the mouth of the Moshassuck River. Williams stated on 17 November 1677, "I consented to John Smith, Miller, at Dorchester (banished also) to go with me."[596] Smith

247

was given the exclusive right to operate a gristmill on Mill Street as long as he provided satisfactory service in grinding corn for the townsmen. He served as Town Clerk in 1641 and died between 1647 and 1649. Below is a photo of the commemorative plaque that marks the location of the Smith gristmill. It is located approximately 100 yards northwest of where Mill [now Charles] Street crosses the Moshassuck River, and on the south side of the present Girl Scouts of Rhode Island Building.

"Smith, the miller (so-called to distinguish him from the other Smiths) was married to Alice (maiden name not found) who bore two children: John, Jr. and Elizabeth, who married Shadrach Manton, a cooper [Manton signed the Last Will and Testament of Captain John Whipple]. They found Shadrach dead on the road in 1714, but the town declared it of natural causes. Thirteen grandchildren and sixty-five great-grandchildren descended from Alice and John's two children. In his will John Smith left his mill to his son John, but it was his widow, Alice, who, after husband death in 1648, made an agreement with the town to continue the business, becoming, perhaps, the Colony's first businesswoman.... It was only after Alice had been operating it for two years that her son, John, Jr., took over...adding a sawmill. He operated both for the next thirty-five years.[597]

"Long before jail or meeting-house, the Town mill was the earliest institution of the Plantations. It received much careful oversight from the Town meeting...The mill fixed the centre of the town at the North end, and long kept it there. Around and near it, those who were able, set their houses, and it became not merely the nucleus of population, but the place of public rendezvous and exchange. It served the same purpose as the meeting-house in early Massachusetts, or as the newspaper and insurance offices of later days...it took part in many a sturdy encounter of the Baptist, the Gortonian, and the Quaker...During one hundred and eighty years the Town Mill fulfilled its office, and was one of the last memorials of primitive times. It was destroyed at last, by the Blackstone canal...."[598]

Site of Sarah Whipple-Smith Mill

"The earliest 'civic center' grew up in the vicinity of the falls of the Moshassuck, a short distance north of the present Mill Street bridge, where the town grist mill was established in 1646. John Smith, one of the original settlers, was a miller by trade. He was granted a home lot and erected a house on the Towne street but soon sold that property and removed to the Moshassuck valley. In 1646 the town granted him 'the valley wherein his house stands in case he set up a mill.' Upon its erection the mill became the center of the town's activities. On every second and third day of the week it was used 'for grinding of the Corne of the Town.' On other days it served as a place for informal gatherings by the townspeople and for occasional town meetings and religious services. The miller died about 1649 and was succeeded by his son, John Smith, Jr. The civic center was further developed in 1655 by the establishment of a tannery, operated by Thomas Olney, Jr., a short distance east of the mill at the foot of the 'Stampers', a hill formerly so-called rising east of Moshassuck river. A highway leading to the mill and tannery was laid out at that time...."[599]

Sarah Whipple and John Smith Junior inherited the Smith mill property, started a nearby sawmill on their own, and along with their 10 children, carried on the family business. Sarah and her family also played an important role in the Indian war. "On March 30, 1676, Providence was attacked by the Indians. Previously a large proportion of the citizens had removed to Newport with their families and effects, leaving only 27 men to defend the town...the Indians burned most of the houses on Town street as well as the mill, the tannery, and the miller's house on Moshassuck river. John Smith Jr., the miller, was then town clerk and the records were in his possession. They were thrown from his burning house into the millpond to preserve them from the flames, and to the present day they bear plenary evidence of the two-fold dangers they escaped, the two-fold injury they suffered."[600] One wonders what part Sarah could have played in saving the records.

In addition to the paid position of clerk to the town council during the mid 1670s, other responsible civic positions John Smith Junior held, as listed in *The Early Records of the Town of Providence* (Providence: Snow & Farnham, 1892-1915), were town sergeant and constable. The council also appointed him to serve as a representative to the general assembly in Newport (XI:157). Like her younger sisters, Sarah endured the loss of her first husband through death. He died sometime between 22 Ffebruary 1681/82 when he drew up his will (VI:60-62) and 10 April 1682 (VI:37) when "Sarah Smith (widow) hath this day preferred unto ye council a written paper for ye council to vew and approve for her deceased husbands will. And also a paper as an inventory of his estate..." On 2 June 1682, she and her son, John III, signed as administrators of his estate. And also like her sisters, Sarah signed her name with an "x" (XVII:2).

John Smith's Last Will and Testament reads in part: "I bequeath to Sarah my wife halfe the mill with ye halfe of ye land neare it, viz ten acres upon ye hill and ye valley whereupon ye house standeth...and ye halfe of all the lande and meadow at ye west river...halfe of ye sawmill..." Her brother John Junior and brother-in-law William Hopkins inventoried his movable estate at a little over £90. "Smith Street bears the name of John Smith, father and son, the first millers of Providence."[601] This major thoroughfare is one of the inner city's busiest, running east and west on the north side of the state capitol building. It dead ends at North Main Street about one block south of where Captain John Whipple's land was located.

Approximately six years later, on 21 May 1688, "Richard Arnold and Sarah Smith are this day Openly Published in way of Marriage in ye Open town meeting no person objecting" (VIII:175). Richard Arnold was a 46-year-old Quaker widower with four children, two young enough still to be under his care. His first wife was Mary Angell, sister of the wives of two of Sarah's brothers.[602] Sarah was also 46 years of age, with at least three children possibly still at home. They were married for 22 years, living on his estate about three miles west of Providence near her sister Abigail: "At a Town meeteing August ye 16th: 1704 held at ye house of Captain Richard Arnold at Wanasquatuckett" (XI:92).

Captain Richard Arnold, Esq., was a wealthy farmer/industrialist who had been prominent in town politics for years.[603] He took an oath of allegiance to King Charles the

249

Second 30 May 1667, the same day as Sarah's first husband (III:102). He was made a full purchaser (III:84). He began his lengthy tenure as a member of the town council in 1670, serving as its moderator on several occasions (VIII:110). He was frequently a deputy to the general assembly in Newport (VIII:47, VIII:92, X:54, XI:70) Among many civic activities, he served on a committee with John Whipple Junior to run "our western Line north from south which is the western bound of our plantation" (IV:43) And he was a member of the committee that met with Connecticut and Massachusetts to set the northern boundary of the colony (XVIII:153).

Richard Arnold died 22 April 1710. "First I give Sarah my wife for the time of her natural life my two lotts in the Towne with the orchard and house upon them and also my meadow at the west river...also two cowes, and one third part of my household goods...and all the Estate that was hers before I married with her...." (VII:1-9). "The Towne council tenders the Administration of the sd estate unto Sarah Arnold, widow of the sd Capt. Richard Arnold, but she refused it, whereupon the councill granted it to his sons...." On 12 May 1710 she "Quitclaimed" the two lots and meadow property in the will to her stepsons, Richard, John, and Thomas: "because of her age could not manage it." In return she was to receive eight pounds annually for life (XX:380-81).

Captain Arnold appears to have been good to his stepchildren, even assisting them to improve and enlarge their holdings. For instance, he and John Smith III built a second saw mill "downe streame from the dam of sd John Smith for setting up a saw mill" (XI:102-03). The mills stayed in possession of the Smith family for several generations.[604] The entire Sarah Whipple-Smith-Arnold family is thought to have been members of the Society of Friends.[605] And as noted, Sarah's granddaughter, Anne Smith, married her sister Abigail's grandson, Stephen Hopkins, in 1755, a few months before he became governor of Rhode Island at a Friend's Meetinghouse in Smithfield.[606]

Mary Whipple Olney

The John Whipple and Thomas Olney families witnessed marriages between four of their children: John Junior and Mary Olney and Mary Whipple and Epenetus Olney. Mary Whipple[607] and Epenetus Olney, who were married 9 March 1665/66, lived in their tavern house in Providence until their deaths in 1698.[608] Their children were born, married, and died in Providence:

> i. Mary, born 13 Jan 1668; died Bef 19 Jun 1725; married Nat Waterman
> ii. James, born 9 Nov 1670; died 6 Oct 1744; married Hallelujah Brown
> iii. Sarah; born 10 Sep 1672; married Nathan Waterman.
> iv. Epenetus; born 18 Jan 1674; died 18 Sep 1740; married Mary Williams.
> v. John, born 24 Oct 1678; died 9 Nov 1754; married Rachel Coggeshall.
> vi. Mercy, born 1684
> vii. Thomas, born 18 May 1686; died 28 Jul 1752; married Lydia Barnes.
> viii. Lydia, born 20 Jan 1688/89; died 1728; married Henry Harris.

The Olney family, of which Mary became an early member, was much revered from the earliest days of the colony. "Thomas Olney, the founder of this large and distinguished family, was among the first to take a title to 'Outlands' on the lower reaches of the Moshassuck and Woonasquatucket rivers. He was one of the original members of the First Baptist Church, Providence, of which his son Thomas was minister in 1668. Father and son held town offices from town clerk to assistant to the Governor for one hundred and fourteen years. The family estates extended from 'Observation Hill' on the east to 'Round Hill,' beyond the 'Seven Mile Line', on the west, and included the section named Olneyville. The Olney name found its way into Smithfield and Glocester, with intermarriages with the Whipples, Sayles, Waterman and Williams's families. In the fourth generation of this family, there were sixty of the name and blood."[609]

"The Olneys were another of Providence's early families. In 1635, Marie Ashton and Thomas Olney, Sr., originally from Hertfordshire, England, came on the ship Planter to Boston, Massachusetts. They had with them two young children: Thomas, Jr., three, and Epenetus....Their daughters were Mary, who married John Whipple, Jr., son of Capt. John Whipple; and Lydia, who married Joseph Williams, son of Roger and Mary Williams.... In 1659, Thomas established his son, Epenetus and his daughter-in-law, Mary Whipple, the daughter of an innkeeper, in a house adjoining his and next door to that of Gregory Dexter, Pastor of the Baptist Society of Providence. There they established the Olney Tavern that would soon become intertwined with Providence's history; a place where religious and political influences would happily converge. The tavern's traditions were continued by their son, James, and his wife Hallelujah Brown, and then by their son Joseph under whom it became the site of the many festivities that made it famous."[610]

"Toward the end of the century public houses were becoming more numerous and more commodious. One of these was built by Epenetus Olney, replacing his former tavern, which had been destroyed by the Indians. It stood for many years and was the rendezvous for travelers over the Common Road to Pawtucket. The town stocks were erected on Dexter's lane, adjoining the tavern, and close by a blacksmith shop was established by John Olney in 1699."[611]

"Olney's Tavern, which shared with Whipple's and Turpin's a celebrity that endured well into the last century...enjoyed a longer life and greater celebrity than either of the other two...The property passed to the descendants of Epenetus Olney through several generations, and saw its rivals die while it continued its successful career as a hostelry well into the last years of the last century...when Joseph Olney dedicated his big elm on the green in front of it as a 'liberty tree.' But in 1803, when the city was drifting away from it and it had seen its best days, Colonel Jere Olney built a house on the green before it, and it was a matter of a few years only before it passed away."[612]

As noted in the John Whipple Junior chapter, Mary and her husband owned competing taverns with her oldest brother and their father. The Olney tavern was just around the corner and up the hill from the two John Whipple taverns at the northeast corner of Town Street and Olney Lane. Hotel-taverns were places of great importance "before the building of the county court house in 1729. Those of Whipple and Epenetus Olney were famous...."[613] In 1682, a "competitor entered the field, and a rival hostelry now offered the town-meeting not house-room only, but 'fire roome and fireing and Candle at all their Towne Meeteings and Council meeteings', nor does it admit of doubt that the inner man might also be warmed and comforted should the necessity arise. This enterprising competitor was no other than John Whipple Junior. John Junior kept a tavern for many years on Mill Street and a brother, Joseph, was also at one time a licensed innkeeper with the town of Providence.[614] In the late 1690s, the Olney Tavern was the site of the Providence annual fair. Mary's brother-in-law, William Hopkins, was "clarke of the market."[615]

In addition to serving in the typical civic positions of a man active in town life, such as juryman, constable, fences viewer, etc., as well as buying and selling hundreds of acres of land, Epenetus Olney appears in *The Early Records of the Town of Providence* (Snow & Farnham, 1892-1915) as a moderator of the town council, and a deputy to the general assembly at Newport (VIII:14 & III:122). He took the Oath of Allegiance the same time as Captain John Whipple (III:101). He was called a "shoemaker" in a land deal of 8 March 1669/70 (IV:254). He took the side of his relatives (John Whipple Junior, William Harris, etc.) in the controversy over Indian lands (VIII:61). He was granted land for a wharf and warehouse (VIII:17-18). On 27 January 1695/96, he joined his in-laws Joseph Whipple, William Hopkins, John Smith Junior, John Dexter, and others in an appeal to build a school house on Whipple property (XI:22). Epenetus Olney died 3 June 1698. His son, James, wrote "Whereas Epenetus Olney...died intestate...if he had, had the opportunitye to have a written will, he would have disposed of his landes amongst his sons...I make over into my said two brothers John and Thomas Olney all of that land...being at the place called caucaunjawalchchuck...140 acres...." Mary Whipple-Olney, relict and widow, was made adminitrix of the estate ((II:216). She died 12 July 1698, five weeks subsequent to her husband.

Subsequent to the deaths of his parents, James inherited the tavern, and maintained the business until his death in 1744.[616] He passed it on to his son Joseph. At his death in 1777, Joseph Junior inherited the business, but closed it down and moved to the state of New York. During the time it was owned by Joseph Senior, the tavern began to be used as a stagecoach depot: "The first stage coach route, maintaining a regular schedule, was instituted... in 1767. It carried passengers every Tuesday morning from Olney's Tavern (North Main and Olney Streets) to Boston and made the return trip on Thursdays."[617]

Several historians recount the engaging story of Joseph Olney Junior's sister Polly's romance with a Bostonian named William Palfrey. "It was a time (just before the Revolutionary War) when tavern-keepers were typically showmen, and their taverns places where young and old gathered to 'dance the old square dances and minuets'...The Olney inn was no exception.... It was at one of these assemblies at the Olney Inn that William Palfrey from Boston first met Polly Olney, and managed to engage Moses Brown as a go-between in Palfrey's pursuit of her." [Moses Brown was the youngest of the four merchant princes of Providence]. Polly was the 'charming and strangely facetious daughter of Joseph Olney,' who carried on the favorite Olney Tavern of his parents." Joseph Junior arranged for his sister to meet Palfrey in secret on more than one occasion. A series of letters between Palfrey and Polly through Moses Brown, however, did not result in marriage. Instead, she married another Bostonian named Thomas Greene in 1764 and moved to that city. Moses Brown subsequently married Mary Olney, Polly's cousin. "Mary and Polly... were approximately the same age, their fathers both descendants of the pioneer settler, Thomas Olney, Sr., and both their fathers owned taverns in Providence."[618]

Joseph Senior's brother, Captain Jonathan Olney, was founder of the town of Olneyville, Rhode Island.[619] Epenetus Junior and family lived in North Providence on Fruit Hill near the farm of Benjamin Whipple, his mother's brother, and was a founder of the town of Centerdale, Rhode Island.[620] Mary Whipple-Olney's descendants became some of Rhode Island's and New England's most respected military men, professionals, and statesmen.[621] The oldest house in Centerdale, Rhode Island, built in 1701, was that of Epenetus Olney Junior.[622] The destinies of the Whipple and Olney families were intertwined for many years.

Abigail Whipple Dexter Hopkins

Abigail Whipple Dexter Hopkins, youngest daughter of Captain John, died in Providence 19 August 1725. The date and place of her birth are unknown. It has historically been placed at Providence about 1660. This arbitrary nativity assignment assumes that since records of her christening in Dorchester have not been found, she must have been born after the family's move to Providence. This places her birth four years subsequent to her brother David's christening in 1656, which is inconsistent with the ordinal positioning of her siblings.[623] It may be that her parents had been adjudicated anathema in Massachusetts society by the time of her probable birth in 1657/58, thus obviating her baptism/christening. It is known that the Whipples sold their property in Dorchester less than one month after Massachusetts passed a law, 19 October 1658, which required Quakers to absent the colony on pain of death.[624] Abigail is thought to have married Stephen Dexter in 1672, also highly unlikely had she been born in 1660. Her husband was born 1 November 1647 and died in 1679. They were the parents of two children, who were born, married, and died in Providence:

   i. *John Dexter, born 1673; died 22 Apr 1734; married Mary Field.*
   ii. *Abigail Dexter, born 1675; died Aft 19 Aug 1725; married T. Field.*

On 5 February 1671/72, The Reverend Gregory Dexter, former governor of the colony,[625] deeded to his twenty-five year old son, Stephen, several plots of land, including an eighty acre farm in the Louquisset about eight miles north of the settlement: "I acknoledg I do giue vnto my Eldest son Stephen Dexter...only Excepting which I do Relly Except this priueledge for the Inhabitance of the town of prouidence to fetch for their vse as much lime Rock from the rock Cled Hackeltons Rock as they please provided Also That Equall Allowance be alowed for a way to the said rock Through the said 80 acres be giuen to my said son...."[626] "Stephen Dexter, eldest son of Gregory Dexter, began making lime at Dexter Ledge before King Philips War.[627] Shortly thereafter, Stephen married fourteen or fifteen year old Abigail Whipple.

The Dexter family began to "burn lime" in the mid 1660s on this property, which was immediately west of the farms of Abigail's brothers William and Eleazer, and her sister-in-law Mary Harris Whipple's father's family, at what became known as the "Lime Rock settlement." As previously noted, these families eventually went into the lime-manufacturing business together. Gregory Dexter was mentioned in a letter from The Reverend Roger Williams to John Winthrop Junior, Governor of Connecticut, 19 August 1669. Part of the letter reads, "Sir I have incouraged Mr. (Gregory) Dexter to send you a Limestone and to salute You with this inclosed. He is an intelligent man, a Master Printer of London, and Conscionable (though a Baptist)....Sir if there be any occasion of Your Selfe (or others) to use any of this stone, Mr. Dexter hath a lusty Teame and lustie Sons and a very willing heart being a Sangwine Cheerfull Man to doe Your Selfe or any service upon very honest and cheap Considerations...."[628] "This limestone had been dug up at "Dexter's Lime Rocks" on Hackleton's Rock between the Moshassuck and Blackstone rivers in present Lincoln... Just how soon the Dexter limestone began to be hauled in carts to Boston is now uncertain, but by the early eighteenth century it was a common occurrence on the Post Road."[629]

In explaining why the village of Lime Rock was placed on the National Register of Historic Places, the Rhode Island Historical Preservation Commission stated, "The monopoly which the Dexters, Whipples, Harrises, Jenckesses and Mowreys held for so long over the industry...kept Limerock a close community; the interconnections among these families were labyrinthine and contributed to the social and physical stability of the village."[630] Gregory Dexter died in the year 1700, and Stephen in 1679;[631] however, his son John and several more generations kept the Dexter family in the lime manufacturing business for another century and a half.[632]

Abigail Dexter received approval, on 5 January 1679/80 from the town council to administer her deceased husband's estate.[633] The young couple's inventory of movable goods of only 10 items amounted to £23. Abigail's brother-in-law, Epenetus Olney, took the inventory on 22 December 1679.[634]

After the death of her husband, Abigail married Captain William Hopkins in 1682, their son being Major William Junior. William Junior's son was Governor Stephen Hopkins.

   i. William, born 1683; died Aft 1740; married Ruth Wilkinson.

William Hopkins Senior's father, Thomas, came to New England with his sister Frances Man and their uncle William Arnold in 1635. He followed The Reverend Roger Williams in 1636 from Plymouth to Providence. At first, he was assigned to a home share of land situated near the south end of the town, the fourth lot south of what is now Powers Street. He later moved to a location west of the Pawtucket River, about ten miles north of his first assigned home lot. "Another of those who early-on obtained wharves was Thomas Hopkins Sr. We must assume he is the same Thomas Hopkins who was the oldest of the three children of William Arnold's sister, Joanne, who came to this country with the Arnold family group in 1635....Thomas was allotted home shares at the south end of town...and additional land ten miles further out in what is now Lincoln.   He made this his home until he fled to Long Island [a Quaker colony] during the King Philips' War, never returning. By the time of his death, the elder Thomas had over 1,000 acres of land..."[635]

At his death in 1684, his son Captain William inherited the Pawtucket property and subsequently passed it on, in 1723, to his son Major William. Major William

Hopkins, in turn, sold a portion of it to Colonel Joseph Whipple on 22 August 1724, a plot of land estimated to contain 80 acres. On 19 October 1728, he mortgaged "his dwelling house" to Colonel Whipple and soon removed to Scituate, as he was a resident there by 10 April 1733. In these deeds he was called a carpenter.[636] Joseph Whipple was Abigail's younger brother. The young Dexter widow apparently met William Hopkins Senior while he lived on the Pawtucket farm of his parents, since her first husband's property was also located in the Pawtucket (Louquisset, Lincoln) area.

According to *The Early Records of the town of Providence* (Providence: Snow & Farnham, 1892-1915), the Hopkins family had been politically prominent in Providence affairs from the beginning. Early on, Captain William served on the town council, was an assistant, and was its moderator on numerous occasions (IV:70, III:223,VIII:59). He was a representative from Providence to the Rhode Island General Assembly for many years (XVII:144). Along with his eventual father-in-law Captain John Whipple, he was one of those who "staid and went not away" when the Indians attacked (VIII:12), and as such was later appointed to a committee to sell captives as was his eventual brother-in-law John Whipple Junior (VIII:15). "...William was a deputy from Providence for fifteen years between 1674 and 1715, acted in the town council of Providence for over twenty years, was town treasurer, major of the militia for the mainland of the Colony, and assistant or senator for seven years and speaker of the House of Deputies, one year. William's son, William, resided in Providence where his son, Stephen, was born. In Stephen's veins flowed good ancestral blood from the vigorous Hopkins line, crossed with that of the Whipples, Wickendens, and Wilkensons, all of whom showed special capacity for patriotic public service."[637]

Abigail and William gave the Pawtucket farm to their son and moved to Masipague, about three miles west of Providence, where they lived out the rest of their married life. William died 8 July 1723, and Abigail was bonded to administer the estate (XII:70). In his last will and testament, the farm was given to their oldest grandson, William, providing that "he shall allow his Grandmother my Wife Abigaill Hopkins one Convenient Roome in my dwelling house...provide for her a sufficient maintenance bothe in sickness and in helth during the term of her natural life...." He also bequeathed to "my Grandson Rufus Hopkins my house Lott of Land which was Layd out upon my own Right upon the Hill Called the Stompers Hill in said Providence... in the last division of House Lotts..." Finally, "I Give and bequeathe unto my son William Hopkins all the Farme of Land and meadows: whereon he now dwells belonging to him to Give to & amongst his children..." The document was dated 1 July 1723.[638]

Abigail Whipple Dexter Hopkins died 19 August 1725. In her Last Will and Testament, dated 16 August 1725, she stated that "I Give & bequeathe unto my three Children John Dexter William Hopkins[639] and Abigail Ffield forty shillings a piece to be taken out of that mony that is due to mee from the proprietors of Providence for servis don by my husband...." Kitchen appliances, bedding, and household goods were given to grandchildren Abigail Dexter, Stephen Dexter, Hope Hopkins, and Abigail Hopkins. "I give to my grand son William Hopkins my husband and his Grandfathers silver buttins for a shirt." The last named was made executor of the estate, which amounted to just over £98.[640] It is of interest that in neither will was their grandson Stephen Hopkins mentioned, although he was in his teens by then.[641]

Stephen Hopkins
Rhode Island Governor
Signer of the Declaration of Independence
Great Grandson of Captain John Whipple

The portrait of Stephen Hopkins below hangs elevated above the fireplace in the Corporation Room in University Hall [the building in the portrait] at Brown University. The caption reads "Stephen Hopkins, First Chancellor of Brown University, 1764-1783."

"He was the first Chancellor of Brown, a chief justice and four-time [sic] governor of the state. He even signed the Declaration of Independence, but after Stephen Hopkins died in 1785 no one was too sure what the ol'guy looked like. In fact, for nearly two centuries he was mistaken as someone else, a mistake that was only corrected about 20 years ago when a new painting of the colonial statesmen was hung in the State House....The mix-up began when 'Signers of the Declaration of Independence,' the famous painting by 18th-century artist John Trumbull showing all of the signers of the historic document, mistakenly identified Hopkins as John Dickinson, the representative from Pennsylvania. Trumbull painted the work between 1788 and 1795...When Trumbull was ready for Hopkins, the Rhode Islander was dead. It is believed that a relative of Hopkins became the stand-in for Trumbull's original painting....In 1819, Congress approved funding for a large engraving of the painting for the Capitol Rotunda. At that time, Trumbull mistakenly concluded that Dickinson- a Quaker pictured wearing a Quaker's hat – was Hopkins, who also was a Quaker. It was a mistake easily made, since the painting contained 47 individuals.... Trumbull's sketch of Hopkins' relative remained undiscovered for nearly 200 years, when an art historian spotted the discrepancy in the 1970s. John Hagen, the artist responsible for correcting the 200 year old faux pas and revealing Hopkins' true likeness, has put the finishing touches on a second Hopkins portrait that will hang in the Corporation Room of the University Hall...." [642]

"Knowing nothing of armed ships, he [Adams] made himself expert, and would call his work on the naval committee the pleasantest part of his labors, in part because it brought him in contact with one of the singular figures in Congress, Stephen Hopkins of Rhode Island, who was nearly as old as Franklin and always wore his broad-brimmed Quaker hat in chamber. Adams found most Quakers to be 'dull as beetles,' but Hopkins was an exception. A lively, learned man...he suffered the loss of three sons at sea, and served in one public office or other continuously from the time he was twenty-five. The old gentlemen loved to drink rum and expound on his favorite writers. The experience and judgment he brought to the business of Congress were of great use, as Adams wrote, but it was in the after-hours that he 'kept us alive.' His custom was to drink nothing all day, nor 'til eight o'clock in the evening, and his beverage was Jamaica spirits and water...Hopkins never drank to excess, according to Adams, but all he drank was promptly converted into wit, sense, knowledge, and good humor." [643]

"Hopkins was a grand figure who had seen a lot in life. You can't miss him in the painting. He's at the back with his broad-brimmed Quaker hat on. [This is an error in McCollough's book]. In after hours he loved to drink rum and expound his favorite writers. 'He read Greek, Roman, and British history, and was familiar with British poetry,' wrote John Adams, 'and the flow of his soul made his reading our own and brought recollection in all we had read...'"[644]

Hopkins reputation among his colleagues in the Continental Congress as an extraordinarily intelligent and well-read person has been traced to his roots in the home of his childhood." His father, Major William Hopkins Junior, the only child of Captain William and Abigail Whipple Hopkins, lived in Cranston, a suburb of Providence, where Stephen was born in 1707. His mother was Ruth Wilkinson daughter of Samuel Wilkinson and Plain Wickenden."[645] The Wilkinson farm in Smithfield was near the farms of Abigail's brothers Eleazer, William, and David, and that of her deceased first husband, Stephen Dexter. Abigail's brother Eleazer's oldest daughter, Deborah, also married into the Wilkinson family. "His grandmother, Abigail, was a daughter of Captain John Whipple, very prominent in plantation life about 1660-1685. The best instruction of all came from his mother, and it was thorough and comprehensive. His grandfather, William, taught him mathematics and surveying. [Actually, all four grandparents lived into the 1720s, thus conceivable made a direct contribution to Stephen's personality and intellectual development.] Although his formal early education was limited, yet he excelled in the practical branches of mathematics, particularly surveying."[646] It would appear that his grandmother Abigail Whipple was quite assertive, opinionated, and outspoken when compared to typical women of that time. She objected to the town council that she was forbidden to vote, and almost single-handedly caused the Providence town council to change its policy of taxing "poore widows of low condition."[647]

Stephen Hopkins

In 1731, Hopkins early began making trips to Newport to participate in the philosophical society as one of its youngest members; the Anglo/Irish philosopher and theologian George Berkeley had founded the society. His cousin, Captain Joseph Whipple Junior, his grandmother Abigail's brother's son, was a fellow member of the society, and served as deputy governor of Rhode Island from 1743 to 1746, as did his son Joseph III, from 1749 until 1754.[648] Hopkins helped found the first library in Providence in 1750; he himself cataloged its first collection. He also helped found Providence's first newspaper in 1762. Indeed, the intellectual vigor of his mental powers enabled him to eventually surmount the lack of formal educational opportunities, and his

257

ardent pursuit of knowledge, at length, placed him among the distinguished men of his day.

As noted, after mortgaging their farm to his uncle Joseph Whipple, his parents moved to Scituate a few miles west of Providence, when Stephen was a young man, where his father earned his living as a farmer. For several years, Stephen followed the same trade. It was while living there that he was chosen town clerk, and afterward elected a representative from that village to the general assembly at Newport, where he became speaker in 1741. He became a justice of the peace, and subsequently a justice of one of the courts of common pleas. Then, in 1733, at the age of 27, he became chief justice of the court in that district.

Hopkins Memorial

He moved to back Providence in 1742, where he erected a house in which he continued to reside for the rest of his life. The house is still standing at the corner of Benefit and Hopkins Street and is on the National Register of Historic Places. At Providence, he immediately entered the mercantile trading and ship building businesses, as well as engaging in what the British considered to be illegal smuggling. He was a partner with the Brown brothers (for whom Brown University is named) co-owning an iron foundry with them. Hopkins served as the first Chancellor of that same school in 1764. The Brown brothers-- Nicholas, Joseph, John, and Moses-- exchanged the profits from these iron products in their slave trading business. At about the time of the Revolutionary War, they employed about 75 men. Then, during the war, the foundry produced guns and ammunition.

Subsequent to his move to Providence, Hopkins was often moderator of the town council and represented the town almost constantly in the general assembly at Newport, serving as its speaker in 1744 and 1749. He became Chief Justice of the Superior Court in 1751, and in 1754 was a delegate to the Albany convention in New York, where he voted for Benjamin Franklin's plan for the union of the colonies.

Ten years later, as governor of the colony, Hopkins wrote a pamphlet in defiance of England's intent to impose a tax on sugar. Called "The Rights of Colonies Examined," it was one of the first assertions of colonial rights. He asked, "Can it possibly be shown that the people in Britain have a sovereign authority over their fellow subjects in America? All laws and all taxation that bind the whole must be made by the whole. Thus early in the quarrel with the mother country, Rhode Island raised the cry no taxation with out representation."[649] This pamphlet was widely distributed in America, bringing Hopkins instant fame through out the colonies.

In summary of his Rhode Island political career, Hopkins served in the general assembly from 1732 until 1752 and 1770 to 1775, and was its speaker in 1738 to 1744 and in 1749. He was elected governor ten times 1755-56, 1758-61, 1763-64, and 1767, and appointed chief justice of the superior court in 1751.

While attending the Continental Congress, where he served from 1774 until 1776, Hopkins helped to draft the Articles of Incorporation and served on the committee responsible for the development of the Continental Navy. He persuaded the Congress, in 1775, to outfit 13-armed vessels and to commission them as the Navy of the United Colonies. He saw to it that Rhode Island received a contract to out fit two of these. He was able to get his brother, Esek, commissioned as Commander-in-Chief. His niece's husband, Abraham Whipple, the great grandson of his grandmother Abigail's brother Samuel, was then appointed Commodore of the Navy. Abraham and Esek had received their maritime training on slave ships owned by the Brown family.

Admirably, Hopkins, along with Moses Brown, was primarily responsible for securing action against slavery. In 1774, the Rhode Island general assembly passed an act prohibiting the importation of slaves. He also led the fight in the Continental Congress to ban slavery. At the time he signed the Declaration of Independence, Hopkins was almost 70 years old and of poor health, due probably to a paralytic stroke. He had to guide his writing hand with his other hand, stating "My hand trembles, but my heart does not." Due to his deteriorating medical condition, he resigned in September of 1776. However, he continued to serve his state during the years that followed and even attended several New England political conventions. Then, in 1780, he left politics all together.

Stephen Hopkins, Esq., Governor of Rhode Island and Providence Plantations, died 13 July 1785. The state of Rhode Island erected a monument to him in the North Burial Ground on which, with other commendations, is inscribed these words "His name is engraved on this immortal record of the Revolution, and can never die." [650]

End Notes

[592] Sarah Whipple was christened in Dorchester, Massachusetts 6 February 1641/42. *Records of the First Church at Dorchester in New England 1636-1734* (Boston: George H. Ellis, 1891) 267 and 173. She died after 12 April 1710. *Early Records of the Town of Providence, 21 vols,* collected and printed by the Records Commissioners (Providence: Snow and Farnham, 1892-1915) XX:380-81 [hereinafter ERP].

[593] Barbara Mills, *Providence: 1630-1800, Women Are Part of Its History* (Bowie, Md: Heritage Books, 2002) 62.

[594] http://www.fortunecity.com/marina/mudhouse/2435/id74htm

[595] If Smith had worked at the Stoughton Mill, this would have likely been the first time that John would have seen the consequences of religious bigotry in his new home.

[596] Charles W. Hopkins, *The Home Lots of the Early Settlers of the Providence Plantations* (Providence: Providence Press Company, 1886) 26. In deference to Smith, Roger Williams allowed a destitute boy named Frances Wickes to escape with them. John Whipple bought the property of Wickes in Providence. Perhaps Wickes had been a fellow apprentice in Dorchester.

[597] Mills, 61.

[598] Henry C. Dorr, *The Planting and Growth of Providence. Rider's Tract #15* (Providence: Sidney S. Rider, 1882) 48-50

[599] John H. Cady, *The Civic and Architectural Development of Providence, 1636-1950* (Providence: The Book Shop, 1957) 7. Welcome Arnold Greene, *The Providence Plantations for Two Hundred and Fifty Years* (Providence: J.A. and R.A. Reid, 1886) 36. "In the year 1646 the first public improvement in the town was commenced in the establishment of a grist mill under the town direction, by 'John Smith, the miller,' at the lower falls of the Moshassuck. The town granted him the land and water-power. He was to erect and repair the mill at his own cost; the town promising not to erect or permit another mill. The town directed that the second and fifth days of the week should be for grinding the corn of the town, the other days to be the miller's own. The one-sixteenth part of every bushel was to be the toll for grinding. The mill...pounded the grain into meal."

[600] Cady, 12.

[601] Thomas Bicknell, *The History of Rhode Island and Providence Plantations, 3 vols.* (New York: The American Historical Society, 1920) 3:893.

[602] Mills, 327. Apparently, their first child was born out of wedlock.

[603] Greene, 393. "...the village of Woonsocket has long been known by this name, and was first settled by Richard Arnold and Samuel Comstock. The Arnold family became owners of a large portion of the land in the vicinity of the falls...The first sawmill on the river was built by Richard Arnold...About 1712 a corn and fulling mill was erected upon what is called the island by John Arnold..."

[604] Charles W. Farnham, *John Smith The Miller, of Providence Rhode Island: Some of His Descendants,* (Baltimore: Genealogies of Rhode Island Families from Rhode Island Periodicals, 1983) 2:6. Also, on line at http://www.fortunecity.com/marina/mudhouse/2435/id74htm. Extracted from these sources and liberally summarized.

[605] Richard was the son of Thomas Arnold "a well known Quaker coadjutor of Roger Williams. The first Quaker meeting house in Providence was built on Richard's property on Stampers Hill." Field, 2:112.

[606] *The Pioneer Mothers or America: A Record of the More Notable Women of the Early Days of the Country, and Particularly of the Colonial and Revolutionary Periods* (New York: G.P. Putnam's Sons, 1912) 3:88-89

[607] Mary Whipple was christened in Dorchester, Massachusetts, 9 April 1648, *Records of the First Church at Dorchester,* 272 and 177.

[608] *ERP,* VI:216 & X:45.

[609] Bicknell, 3:921. Thomas Olney was one of the most powerful men in Providence. The Whipple family would have had to be highly respected and important itself to have been allowed to participate in these marriages. The Olneys left the First Baptist Church in 1652 to establish their own predestination church. Mary and her husband likely were members of this splinter group.

[610] Mills, 72-73

[611] Cady, 16.

[612] Richard M. Bayles, ed., The *History of Providence County, Rhode Island*, 2 vols. (New York: W.W. Preston and Company, 1891) 1:306.

[613] William B. Weeden, *Early Rhode Island, A Social History of the People, 1636-1790* (New York: The Grafton Press, reprint, Bowie Maryland, Heritage Books, Inc.) 220.

[614] Gertrude Kimball, *Providence in Colonial Times* (Boston: Houghton Mifflin Company, 1912) 126.

[615] Dorr, 190-91.

[616] *ERP*, VIII:9

[617] Edward Field, *State of Rhode Island and Providence Plantations at the End of the Century: A History*. 3 Vols. (Boston: Mason Publishing Company, 1902) II:544.

[618] Mills, 223. The account summarized from pages 213 through 218.

[619] "*Olney Family*" in the state of Rhode Island and Providence Plantations (New York: American Historical Society, 1920) 408-09.

[620] Preliminary Survey Report, Town of North Providence, Rhode Island Historical Preservation Commission, April 1978, 3

[621] Olney Family, 408-09.

[622] Frank C. Angell, *Annals of Centerdale* (Central Falls, RI: E.L. Freeman, 1909) 24. The house was located on Falco Street. It remained standing until 1898 when it was demolished.

[623] Henry E. Whipple does not give the date 1660, nor does Austin, 223. Anderson, 1973, gives the date of 1658.

[624] Suffolk Land Records, Deeds, 14 Volumes (Boston: 1630-1906) 3:204-05. Rufus M. Jones, *The Quakers in the American Colonies* (New York: W.W. Norton & Company, 1966) 76. William G. Mcloughlin, *Rhode Island* (New York: W.W. Norton, 1978) 36. "Beginning in October 1656, Massachusetts passed the first of a series of laws inflicting harsh penalties on Quaker and Quaker sympathizers. Starting with imprisonment, fines, and banishment, these laws subsequently included whipping, branding, ear cropping, and tongue boring. The final step, in 1658, was a law ordering death by hanging."

[625] Both of Abigail's husbands were from politically prominent families.

[626] *ERP*, III:228-29.

[627] Bicknell, 3:1185.

[628] Glenn W. LaFantasie, *The Correspondence of Roger Williams* (Providence; Brown University Press/ University Press of New England, 1988) II:591

[629] Carl Bridenbaugh, Fat *Mutton and Liberty of Conscience: Society in Rhode Island, 1636-1690* (Providence: Brown University, 1974) 87

[630] *Lincoln Rhode Island, Statewide Historical Preservation Report*, P-L-I. RI Historical Preservation Commission, January 1982:15. See also, on line at http://www.whipple.org/charles/louquissest/index.html

[631] Dorr, 30

[632] S.C. Newman, *Dexter Genealogy: Being a Record of the Families Descended from Rev. Gregory Dexter* (Providence: A. Crawford Greene, 1859) 14. Bradford Swan, *Gregory Dexter of London and New England* (Rochester, N.Y.: 1949). Gregory was at one time town clerk of Providence, and served as president of the colony 1653/54. Dexter, also a printer, printed Roger Williams' famous book *Key to the Language of America*. It is thus seen that both of Abigail's marriages were to men from politically prominent families.

[633] *ERP*, VI:4-5. She signed her name with an "X".

[634] *ERP*, VI:6-7. In the inventory of her worldly possessions she expressed her sense of the degeneracy of the times, or perhaps a lofty contempt of the vanity of the world by an entry of "a frying pan, a skillet, and other trumpery."

[635] Mills, 169-70.

[636] The Pane-Joyce Genealogy in http://babbage.clarku.edu//djoyce/gen/report/rr08/rr08_490html. 4-9-04.

[637] Bicknell, 3:1078. The Wickendens and Wilkinson's were also Quakers.

[638] *ERP*, XVI:229-35. In genealogical literature William Senior has typically been referred to as "Captain" to distinguish him from his son. However, by the time of his death he was also called "Major."

[639] It should be noted that William Hopkins military rank was not honorary as was the case in many instances. "In 1739 England declared war against Spain, and during the following year Providence raised a

company of 100 men under Capt. William Hopkins, to take part in the disastrous expedition against Carthagena." Welcome Arnold Greene, 53.

[640] *ERP*, XVI:408-13.

[641] Stephen Hopkins would have been bequeathed from his father's property in Pawtucket, and elsewhere, at the father's death in c1740, rather than his grandparent's deaths in the 1720s.

[642] Glenn Hare, "Can't Remember the face, But The Name is Familiar," *George Street Journal* of Brown University, 26 February 1999, Vol. 23:191

[643] David McCullough, *John Adams*, (New York: Simon & Schuster, 2001) 100

[644] David McCullough, 32nd Annual Jefferson Lecture in the Humanities, Ronald Reagan International Trade Center, Washington, D.C., 5 May 2003. From personal notes of the author taken at the lecture.

[645] Israel Wilkinson, *Memoirs of the Wilkinson Family in America* (Jacksonville, Illinois: Davis and Penniman, 1869) 48. The Wilkinson and Wickenden families were well known Quakers.

[646] Weeden, 229

[647] *ERP*, XV:230-31. Due to its social significance to Providence history, it is presented herein. "To ye Towne mett June ye:6th:i681: Honrd Gentelmen, if ye poore and low Condition, of a poore Widdow haue noe Jnflveance upon ye harts of yor rate makers, but to rate me where there is no justice for it before God nor man, that they should rate me to serjants wages, and House rent, I cannot see just Cause, for these reasons, first ye serjant haath neigher power, nor ocation to warne me to yor mettings, knowing I am not allowed any voate there, Seccondly all my lands meadows and orchard lys Comon to yor Benniffitt, and not to mine nor ye orphans of my Deceased Husbands. Thirdly if I should have Came to have Voated to day in yor Election, perhaps it would have benn sayd what had I to doe there: and Jf I have not to doe to Voate and make use of ye house you rate me for ye use there of, I leave to yor wisdoms to Judge of: praying your Consideration of it, and yor Determynation of the same, Yor poore Widow and ffriend, Abbigarll Dexter"

[648] On line at: www.whipple.org/charles/yeomenandprinces/index.html

[649] Sydney V. James, *Colonial Rhode Island, A History* (New York: Charles Scribner's Sons, 1976) 323

[650] In addition to the above references, the biography of Stephen Hopkins was extracted and summarized from several standard texts and journal articles.

264

267

271

272

273

274

277

278

279

281

Printed in the United States
By Bookmasters